LOVE OF SELF AND LOVE OF GOD

LOVE OF SELF
AND
LOVE OF GOD

in Thirteenth-Century Ethics

THOMAS M. OSBORNE, JR.

UNIVERSITY OF NOTRE DAME PRESS

Notre Dame, Indiana

Published in the United States of America

Library of Congress Cataloging-in-Publication Data

Osborne, Thomas M. (Thomas Michael), 1972–
    Love of self and love of God in thirteenth-century ethics /
Thomas M. Osborne, Jr.
        p.   cm.
    Includes bibliographical references and index.
    ISBN 0-268-03723-x (hardcover : alk. paper)
    ISBN 0-268-03722-1 (pbk. : alk. paper)
    1. Christian ethics—History—Middle Ages, 600–1500.
2. Ethics, Medieval.   3. God—Worship and love.
4. Psychology, Religious.   5. Aristotle. Nicomachean ethics.   I. Title.
    BJ1217.O83   2005
    241'.042'09022—dc22
                                                            2005012538

∞ *The paper in this book meets the guidelines for permanence and durability*
of the Committee on Production Guidelines for Book Longevity of the
Council on Library Resources.

I dedicate this book to my parents

Contents

Acknowledgments

This book has its origin in my dissertation at Duke University. Most of all, I am indebted to Edward P. Mahoney, who guided the dissertation, and made sure that its coverage of the issue and scholarly literature was complete. He has also been a regular source of encouragement and advice. I also am grateful to the other members of my dissertation committee: David Steinmetz, Michael Ferejohn, and Tad Schmaltz. David Steinmetz first alerted me to the importance of the natural love of God for the Reformation and later Middle Ages. Michael Ferejohn and Tad Schmaltz gave helpful advice during the long process of revision. Alasdair MacIntyre made some thoughtful remarks during the early stages of the dissertation.

Lucia Stadter read the manuscript carefully and helped me to make more readable and accurate translations. Any remaining infelicities are my own. Paul Schollmeier, Gordon Wilson, and Brian J. O'Donnell all read and criticized parts of the manuscript. Jeffrey Gainey at the University of Notre Dame Press encouraged me greatly and gave excellent advice for the revision. The anonymous readers were enormously generous with their comments. Margaret Hyre, the press editor, made valuable improvements.

Many of the revisions were made while I held a Gilson Fellowship at the Pontifical Institute of Mediaeval Studies. It was an honor to work alongside the fellows and post-doctoral colleagues. It was also humbling to work in the same building as many of the greatest twentieth-century historians of mediaeval philosophy. My colleagues at the University of Nevada Las Vegas provided a wonderful environment in which to finish (mostly) the revisions. I owe a great debt to the Inter-Library Loan Staff at Duke University, St. Michael's College (Toronto), and UNLV. Still more revisions were made at the Center for Thomistic Studies at the University of St. Thomas. My colleague Christopher Martin gave much literary advice.

The Augustinian Fathers gave me permission to work into this book my article, "James of Viterbo's Rejection of Giles of Rome's Arguments for the Natural Love of God over Self," *Augustinia* 49 (1999): 235–249.

Introduction

This book treats the thirteenth-century debate concerning the natural love of God over self with an eye to how the thinkers of this period saw the connection between one's own good and the aims of virtuous action. Medieval thinkers had concerns which were distinct from both those of the ancients and those of modern moral philosophers. Their understanding of loving God allowed them to develop a more careful understanding of eudaimonism than the ancients did. Thirteenth-century philosophers and theologians introduced a high level of sophistication to the study of how one's own good is achieved through virtuous action. They were forced to address the issue at great length because of their attempt to adopt some of Aristotle's philosophical insights into a Christian framework. For Christians, the central ethical duty is to love God more than anything else, including even oneself; but at the same time, most ancient and medieval Christians were committed to an ethical view which was at least broadly eudaimonistic. In general, they held that one's good is always maximized through virtuous action. The tension between these two aspects of Christian ethics reaches its highest point in texts about whether God can be naturally loved more than oneself. This book is a history of the development of this debate during the thirteenth century. It seeks to illustrate which concepts are most important for understanding eudaimonism and to show that the central difference between the ethical theories of such great ethical thinkers as Thomas Aquinas and John Duns Scotus is not about morality and self-interest. Instead, the difference is between Thomas's belief that morality is based on a natural inclination for the common good of the universe and Scotus's position that nature is self-directed. Consequently, although Scotus agrees with Thomas that there could be a natural love of God over self, Scotus thinks that this natural love is made possible by the fact that the will is not limited by a self-directed natural inclination in the way that non-rational creatures are. The importance of this difference can be shown through a comparison of their discussions of natural love with those of their most important contemporaries and predecessors.

I am primarily concerned with this contrast between Thomas Aquinas and John Duns Scotus. Their different positions on naturally loving God are rooted in different understandings of how ethics relates to human nature and the common good. Consequently, I do not provide a complete account of the thirteenth-century debate.[1] My emphasis is on the more significant thinkers who spent at least some of their careers at the University of Paris. I also restrict my discussion to those aspects of the debate which are most relevant to ethics and moral psychology. The goal is to tell a coherent story of how the debate over naturally loving God illustrates some of the most original and important aspects of Thomas's philosophy, and how Scotus's own position is better understood by looking at his reaction to the broadly Thomistic one. Furthermore, the debate over naturally loving God is rarely only about loving God. This issue is key for understanding a thinker's wider ethical theory. I will not only place each individual's thought in its historical context, but will also place his position on loving God in the context of his own thought.

Two difficulties threaten a project of this sort. First, there is a danger that contemporary debates and assumptions might not only color but also distort the presentation of medieval thinkers. Second, these thinkers often employ concepts which either are unfamiliar to contemporary thinkers or, what is worse, appear to be familiar when they are not. Therefore let me state here some of the relevant similarities and differences between premodern and contemporary understandings of morality and one's own good, and briefly explain the medieval understanding of natural love and how it relates to the will.

It is difficult to make generalizations about philosophy in different historical periods, but it is safe to note some general contrasts. Ancient philosophers did not simply assume that behavior commonly recognized as good is in the agent's own interest. A major part of Plato's *Republic* is based on the problem of why the just should be chosen for its own sake. Nevertheless, most ancient philosophers do argue that a good action is also good for the agent. In contrast, contemporary ethical theories tend to separate morality from self-interest. Kantianism and utilitarianism both evaluate actions by using impartial standards. They find no intrinsic connection between acting in accordance with these standards and acting in one's own interest. Among other problems, these positions can create a split between motivation and rationality.[2] For those who think that acting morally is identical to acting rationally, there is a problem of motivation. Why should the agent choose to act rationally? An alternative is to identify acting rationally with acting for one's own good, but this risks creating a rift between rational action and good action. In this view, moral behavior can be irrational, a standpoint foreign to ancient philosophers, who saw rationality closely connected as with the agent's own good.

What ensures a harmony between morality and self-interest? J. B. Schneewind argues that most pre-Enlightenment Christian theories depend on an assumption that the world is something like a corporation perfectly ordered by God, the supreme supervisor: "[God] . . . must give all the agents adequate instructions about their tasks; he must assign to them jobs within their powers; and he must reward them on the basis of their merits."[3] This description may apply to many early modern moral theories. The significant point is that on this description morality and self-interest are held together by an external orderer. They could come apart, but God prevents them from doing so. Many medieval philosophers invoke God to explain how the moral order is eventually just: he rewards the good and punishes the bad. Nonetheless, most medieval thinkers also agree with ancient philosophers that there is an internal connection between an ethical action and the agent's own good. This connection is usually based on some sort of teleology, even if it is not an Aristotelian teleology. In general, they think that humans have an end which they do not set themselves. This end provides a criterion for evaluating both the agent's action and his flourishing. A dogma of most modern and contemporary philosophers is that human nature is not teleological. Accordingly, philosophers have needed something like God to hold together morality and self-interest. But they are understandably reluctant to use God as a gap-filler for moral theory.

A complicating feature of medieval moral thought is that the figures of our period believe that an agent not only should but must prefer his own good to that of other human persons.[4] This position is a corollary of the belief that ethics is connected to the agent's end. The only way to prefer another's good to one's own would be by falling or turning away from one's own end so that someone else might better achieve their own. An example of such an act would be sinning in order to make it possible for someone else to avoid sin or to act virtuously. Medievals themselves do not give many examples of such an action. In contrast to most utilitarians, the medievals of our period do not even think it is possible to will the aggregate good of many other individuals more than one's own. Many think that the common good can be preferred to one's own good, but they also hold that each individual's good is ordered to and part of the common good. A preference for the common good would not involve the sacrifice of the agent's own good. For these medieval thinkers, the difference between a common and a private good is that a common good includes and is greater than the private. Similarly, all medieval thinkers, whether for religious or philosophical reasons, think that a virtuous agent should prefer God's good to his own. But this love does not require the sacrifice of one's own good. From the medieval point of view, it is impossible to act rightly by preferring another human's good to one's own. A good action is the type of action by which the agent approaches or achieves the end of his human nature.

The reader may be surprised to find no counterpart to the contemporary libertarian notion of freedom in thirteenth-century thought. The debate is not mostly about whether God should be loved more than oneself, but rather whether he can be so loved. The philosophers and theologians of our period all believe that humans are free at least in the sense that they can make choices between alternative real or apparent goods in this life. But none believe that humans are free in the sense that they can choose any action at all, or love just any good more than themselves. The contemporary libertarian view is a creation of late medieval and early modern thought, and the basis for this development was the shift away from a teleological view of human nature.

Though contemporary philosophers have varying notions of human freedom, they are generally agreed that human nature does not have a set end. The modern debate over freedom is not the medieval debate over how this end is chosen, but rather concerns whether actions are predetermined or not. The thinkers discussed in this book believe that humans can choose certain good actions because they have certain ends. The agent has an order to the good even if he does not act in accordance with the order. He may forsake his natural end to pursue some other good such as pleasure, but he still retains an order to the good. Consequently, the good is one kind of motive for action. In contrast, contemporary moral philosophers often adopt a neo-Humean theory of motivation which is based on a split between beliefs and desires.[5] Desires motivate whereas beliefs do not. Consequently, someone may recognize that an action is good even though he has no motive to perform the action. In general, the split between self-interest and morality has made it difficult to understand how humans with self-interested desires can choose moral actions which are not in their self-interest. Contemporary discussions over egoism and altruism are usually not about eudaimonism but about whether any of an agent's motives can be disinterested.[6] The medievals assume that the good can motivate a normal agent, and agree that an agent's good is maximized by his acting well. The problem is not so much whether the agent can will the good disinterestedly, but whether he can prefer God's good to his own. The medieval dispute is over the intention of the agent. The question is whether on a natural level the agent intends his own good most of all.

The teleological understanding of human nature is important for understanding what is meant by "the agent's good." For the eudaimonists discussed in this book, someone never sacrifices his own intrinsic good by acting virtuously. A great problem for understanding premodern eudaimonism is confusion over the good life. What would it mean for virtue to further someone's good? Generally, *eudaimonia* is translated as "happiness," but this translation is commonly regarded as insufficient. Some authors use the term "flourishing," which may be less misleading but certainly is not much more informative. What are these terms supposed to signify? Augustine thinks that there are limits to whatever happiness is available in this life. Indeed, the Christian tradition emphasizes that the saints have their own especially dark nights, yet Christian eudaimonists regard them as happiest. That many premodern theories connect happiness so closely to virtue can in great part be explained by the fact that this happiness is an objectively good state. This goodness is understood as the end of humans as such. A good thief steals well; a good human acts virtuously.

The contrast between ancient and modern ethical theories draws attention to the difficulty of using historically distant philosophers to answer contemporary problems. For example, ancient and medieval philosophers cannot be used to address directly the possibility of altruism because they are not concerned with egoism and altruism.[7] They do not share an understanding of morality and motivation with those who developed the problem. When discussing their thought, the use of terms such as "egoism" and "altruism" distorts the original ideas. Nevertheless, not every contemporary use of previous philosophers is misleading. Later philosophers ask questions which earlier thinkers considered implicitly or even not at all.[8] Answers to these questions may be related to principles which are stated by the earlier philosophers. In this book I shall attempt to show that this is how the better medieval thinkers used Aristotle's *Nicomachean Ethics* to address the question of the natural love of God over self.

Why is the debate over naturally loving God a debate over the theoretical basis of eudaimonism? To many contemporaries, loving God appears at first glance to belong to religion rather than philosophy, and love itself is understood as an emotion rather than a moral action. But thirteenth-century thinkers saw Aristotle's eudaimonism as relevant. To understand why the two issues connect, we need to understand what the medievals mean by "natural love." To introduce these issues, I shall neither assume the position of any particular thinker nor use an entirely scholastic vocabulary.

"Naturalism" is often used now to describe theories in which there is no room for beings which cannot be studied by contemporary physics. The "supernatural" includes God and the immaterial soul, whereas the "natural" includes everything else, namely those things that really exist. For example, "naturalism" in contemporary philosophy of mind involves the attempt to explain consciousness without having recourse to an immaterial mind or soul. The medievals did not use the word "natural" in this sense, although they used it in several different ways. For our purposes, the most important are (1) as distinguished from the rational and (2) as distinguished from the gratuitous or supernatural. The first meaning of the word is rooted in the philosophical understanding of "nature" as describing what something is or its principle of movement.[9] Stones naturally fall, flowers naturally blossom, and trees naturally spread their branches. These activities result from the nature of the substances. Many medievals contrasted the rational with the natural in this sense. Trees naturally grow, but humans think about and select among the various possibilities open to them. Consequently, the rational is connected to freedom. Natural creatures act in a predetermined way, whereas rational creatures can act freely.

The Christian tradition also uses the word "natural" to describe what humans do out of their own efforts without God's special help, which is called "grace." The natural in this sense describes what comes from human nature alone. For example, by thinking about creatures humans should acquire a natural knowledge of God. But through the free gift of faith, which is made available through the sacraments, the Bible, and preaching, Christians have a supernatural belief in the Trinity and the Incarnation. Similarly, by acting naturally any human can look after his family or build his house. But it is only through God's special help that someone can make such an action meritorious, which means that it would be accepted by God as worthy of reward in eternal life. In this sense of the word, the natural is what belongs to humans through their creation, whereas the gratuitous or supernatural is an unmerited gift of God. Some thirteenth-century scholastics make a further distinction between integral human nature and fallen human nature. This distinction is known through faith. In this view, the "natural" as we know it is not the "natural" which God first created. Humans were created with an integral nature by which they could act in a way which is now impossible. Human nature has been wounded by the first sin of Adam. Consequently, fallen human beings have corrupted natural abilities.

These various meanings of the term "natural" bear importantly on medieval debates over the natural love of God. Sometimes, "natural love" can refer to a pre-elective tendency or inclination of the will. What is the will? Unlike some late medieval and modern thinkers, the medievals thinkers of our period do not think of the human will as a radically undetermined source of freedom. Instead, it is a human tendency or inclination to act for the sake of the good. The will is often described as a "rational appetite." Just as animals and trees have non-rational appetites to act in a way which achieves what is good for them, so do humans have a rational appetite to act knowingly for the sake of the good. The will is "rational" as opposed to "natural" because the natural is not elective. Nevertheless, even the will has a pre-elective order to the good. Working from a teleological belief that humans have an order to an end which is not the result of their choice, most medievals, and especially those who lived before the fourteenth century, think that it is impossible to will what is bad. More often, "natural love" refers to an explicit act of the will which is performed without God's special help. Some thinkers, such as Thomas Aquinas, distinguish between that natural love which is possible for integral human nature and that which is possible for fallen human nature. In an integral state, humans could choose God's good over their own without grace. But for fallen humans, such love is impossible. The will is incapable of performing such an act unless it is healed.

Although medieval thinkers sometimes used the word "love" for a passion, it more importantly signifies an act or tendency of the will. Human actions are for some apparent or real good. Any act for the sake of a good thing is an act of love for that good. Consequently, love is central for understanding ethical action. Humans have a pre-elective order to the good; many philosophers identify this good with God. Consequently, there is a natural love of God or the good which is common to all humans and precedes deliberation. The natural elective love of God is based on this pre-rational order. Although medieval thinkers differ about how to describe this phenomenon, they all agree that humans have some sort of general desire for their end. Many think that there is a natural knowledge of God which is common to everyone. But they are also concerned with a love and knowledge which are natural only in the sense that they are not the result of God's grace or revelation. For example, the natural knowledge of God through creatures can lead to a natural love for him. This kind of natural love is contrasted with charity, which is that love for God which is a special gift of God to Christians.

The love that is natural in this last sense is the more important for understanding the medieval approach to eudaimonism. Such love is an act of the will and yet it does not presuppose grace or special revelation. It might seem that the obligation to so love God more than oneself should be available to those who know him without this revelation. Many medieval thinkers hold that if the agent knows that he should so love God, then he has an ability do so. Some distinguish between integral nature and fallen nature in this context. Although it is possible for humans in both states to know of the obligation, a natural love of God over self would only be possible for integral nature. This distinction between integral and fallen human nature becomes especially problematic for understanding the ethical theories of the pagan philosophers. Their human nature was fallen. Did they know that there is an obligation to love God more than oneself? Does their moral psychology allow for such a love?

The thirteenth-century introduction of Aristotle's *Nicomachean Ethics* into the philosophical curriculum presented particular problems for the question of the natural love of God over self. Aristotle himself does not discuss whether a virtuous agent primarily intends his own good, but his treatment of friendship can be read as implying that all love is primarily self-love. For example, the thirteenth-century thinkers often quote in some form Aristotle's statement, "Amicabilia quae sunt ad alterum venerunt ex amicabilibus quae sunt ad seipsum."[10] (The notes of friendship which are for another come from those notes which one has for oneself.) By distinguishing virtuous from vicious self-love, Aristotle wishes to refute the belief that all self-love is vicious. He argues that those who desire for themselves such goods as money, honors, and bodily pleasure practice a vicious self-love. But the virtuous person loves his reason, and he manifests this love through fine actions. Since this self-love is based on a knowledge of what is truly beneficial for the agent, the virtuous agent loves himself more than others do. A vicious person neglects his own good of virtue. This description of self-love might seem incompatible with the Christian belief that one should love God more than himself.

Perhaps even more problematic is Aristotle's description of the virtuous citizen who dies for the sake of his political community. Aristotle writes:

> Besides, it is true that, as they say, the excellent person labours for his friends and for his native country, and will die for them if he must; he will sacrifice money, honours and contested goods in general, in achieving what is fine for himself. For he will choose intense pleasure for a short time over mild pleasure for a long time; a year of living finely over many years of undistinguished life; and a single fine and great action over many small actions. This is presumably true of one who dies for others; he does indeed choose something great and fine for himself.[11]

On one reading of this passage, someone who dies for the political community intends his own good more than that of the political community. Some contemporary scholars think that these passages imply a psychological or ethical egoism in which the virtuous person primarily intends his own good of virtue.[12] Thirteenth-century thinkers often discussed these passages in the context of whether it is possible to love God more than oneself. Just as contemporary scholars disagree about the significance of Aristotle's eudaimonism for debates over egoism and altruism, so do thirteenth-century thinkers disagree about its significance for the debate over the natural love of God over self. Some interpret Aristotle in way which makes his theory compatible with Christian ethics, whereas others do not. Some think that Aristotle is almost entirely correct, whereas others think that he is correct only with respect to natural reason, and still others think that his ethical theory could be seriously flawed. There is some reason for thinking that contemporary philosophers are anachronistic to use Aristotle to discuss egoism. Is it similarly anachronistic for medievals to use him in debates over loving God?

The answer to this question depends in large part on one's understanding of developments in the history of philosophy and whether the great medieval thinkers primarily absorb or distort Aristotle's philosophy. It is not obvious that Aristotle's discussion of friendship and the good citizen is about the agent's intention. His discussion occurs only in the context of distinguishing between a good and bad self-love, and he does not directly ask the question of what is primarily intended. The debate over loving God forced the medievals to ask a question which had not previously been treated with any great sophistication, namely, whether in a eudaimonistic theory the agent intends primarily his own good or that of God and perhaps the political community. They all firmly accepted a generally eudaimonistic framework. Although they interpret Aristotle differently, the figures discussed in this book accept his view that the good which is possible for an agent in a particular situation is maximized through virtuous action.

Whereas some contemporary scholars who read Aristotle through the lens of contemporary and modern ethics are concerned with whether Aristotle is an egoist or not, medievals are concerned about the agent's intention. This concern does not imply that medieval thinkers distort Aristotle's ethics. The Christian tradition makes it possible to develop Aristotle's philosophy in directions which were not available to Aristotle himself. The debate over naturally loving God is a prime example of this development. First, it allows for a discussion of eudaimonism and the agent's own good which is quite possibly superior to contemporary treatments. Second, these debates over eudaimonism shed light on the theoretical framework which supports the ethical theory. The dispute over naturally loving God becomes a dispute over the connections between obligation, the will, and human nature.

The organization of the book is primarily historical. The first chapter provides the background to the debate and shows how the question about naturally loving God more than self was first formulated in the Middle Ages. The "Fathers" are those early Christian writers whose beliefs are considered to be normative by the Christian tradition. Augustine of Hippo is by far the most significant Father for the Western Church. Augustine sees the Christian emphasis on loving God as an answer to philosophical questions about the happy life. In this respect he does not differ greatly from many other Fathers. But on account of his later influence, his own discussion of the issue has the greatest weight with the scholastics. After discussing Augustine himself, I describe how his thought is developed and retained during the theological renaissance of the twelfth century. Every theologian adopts Augustine's belief that one loves oneself more by loving God even more than oneself. Nevertheless, they have varying approaches on whether to emphasize the disinterested aspect of loving God. The position that nature is primarily self-oriented is often later attributed to Bernard of Clairvaux, who is one of the great mystics of this period. The issue of whether it is possible to naturally love God more than oneself is first formulated by the scholastics of the early thirteenth century. They initially address this question in the context of whether the angels were able to love God more than themselves before they were given grace. This discussion of the angels leads to a discussion of human love and how it can be seen both in the natural tendency of the human will to happiness and in the possibility of freely choosing God's good more than one's own.

The second chapter focuses mostly on moral psychology and problems in adopting pagan philosophy. Franciscan theologians developed a theory of loving God which in large part depends on a natural order of the will to God. The Franciscan Bonaventure emphasizes that humans in their first state must have been able to naturally love God, since God created them so. The Dominican Albert combines the attention to willing with a concern for pagan ethics, especially the philosophy of Aristotle. On Albert's view, ancient philosophers knew that the common good should be loved more than themselves. Many pagans acted on this belief. Assuming that the pagans did not have grace, they were able naturally to love the political common good more than themselves. Should it not be easier to have such a love for God? But if such a love is possible, is grace then superfluous?

The third chapter describes Thomas's original approach to the issue. Thomas argues that every creature has a natural inclination not only to its own good, but even more to the good of the whole. This whole can be the species, the political community, or even God. He argues that the human will does not differ greatly from non-rational creatures in this respect. He thinks that human beings act rightly when they make a deliberate act of the will in accordance with the natural inclination for the whole. Consequently, humans should act on this natural inclination to love God and the political community more than themselves. This theory is at least partially based on aspects of Aristotle's thought, namely the belief in both natural teleology and a Prime Mover who is the separate good of the whole universe. Thomas understandably identifies the Prime Mover with God. Every creature in its own way is directed to God's good more than to its original good. To take into account the effects of original sin, he emphasizes that the natural love of God over self is impossible only because of the effects of original sin on human nature. If human nature were integral, this natural love would be possible.

The fourth chapter shows how the dispute over naturally loving God becomes an explicit dispute over Aristotelian eudaimonism. Members of the Arts Faculty at Paris understood Aristotle to hold that the virtuous individual loves primarily his own good of virtue. Henry of Ghent responds to the Arts Faculty in part by criticizing Aristotle. His approach resembles that of earlier scholastics. In contrast, both Giles of Rome and Godfrey of Fontaines defend the basically Thomistic position on natural inclination. Non-rational creatures have an inclination not only to their own perfection, but even more to the perfection of the whole. Similarly, for Aristotle the virtuous agent is concerned not only for his own perfection, but also for the perfection of the whole. Godfrey thinks that Aristotelian ethics is in fundamental agreement with Christianity. James of Viterbo takes the opposite view. He accepts the Arts Faculty's interpretation of Aristotle's ethics. Consequently, he argues that the orders of nature and grace are inverse. By nature someone loves himself most of all; by grace someone loves God more than himself.

John Duns Scotus reiterates this self-oriented understanding of nature. He thinks that each non-rational creature has an inclination only to its own perfection. It is God who ensures that all these creatures are ordered to the good of the whole. Unlike James, Scotus sharply contrasts the will with self-oriented nature. Humans have a will which is capable of willing the just for its own sake. This aspect of the will is distinct from its natural tendency towards its own good. The natural love of God is possible only because humans differ from non-rational creatures on account of their will. Nevertheless, although Scotus thinks that humans can will the good for its own sake, he falls squarely in line with seeing the ability to will God's good as expressive of a built-in ordering of the human to God. It would be impossible for humans to achieve their good in any other way than by loving God more than their own good.

This last chapter provides the remaining evidence for my basic thesis that the main difference between the ethical theories of Thomas and Scotus is not so much in their understanding of eudaimonism as it is in their conception of the relationship between ethics and natural inclination. The history of the debate over naturally loving God shows what the difficulty was in basing ethics on human nature.

CHAPTER I

The Augustinian Tradition and the Early Scholastic Background

Although the possibility of naturally loving God over oneself was first raised explicitly in the early thirteenth century, its formulation occurred in the context of the Augustinian tradition's long-standing focus on loving God. This love holds the central place in Augustine's ethical theory, which draws not only upon biblical sources, but also upon the richest elements of the ancient philosophical tradition.[1] Augustine identified the philosopher's search for the happy life with the Christian emphasis on loving God. Neoplatonic metaphysics provided a basis for this ethical theory, which in outline remained largely intact throughout the medieval period. Nevertheless, in the eleventh and twelfth centuries theologians began to raise questions within this tradition. Perhaps their most significant ethical questions concerned the connection between loving God and self-love. These debates provided the background to a key question raised by the early scholastics, which was whether without grace God can be loved more than oneself.

I. AUGUSTINE OF HIPPO

In the middle of the twentieth century, Anders Nygren criticized Augustine's attempt to harmonize a pagan philosophical view of love with Christian ethics.[2] Focusing on two different Greek words for "love," Nygren argued that Augustine and the Christian tradition are guilty of substituting a self-seeking philosophical love, *eros,* for self-giving Christian love, *agape.* Whereas the Bible teaches an ethics based on self-denial, the philosophers teach a eudaimonistic ethics based on the happiness of the individual. Nygren saw Augustine's ethics as a self-oriented betrayal of the Christian understanding of love. Despite the importance of *agape* for the Christian understanding of love, Nygren was wrong to think that such love has an altogether unique meaning in the New Testament and that the Christian tradition has betrayed this meaning. This controversy is important because Jesus Christ makes love the foundation of his ethical teaching.[3] When a teacher of the Mosaic Law asks him to name the greatest commandment, Jesus answers:

> You shall love your Lord God from your whole heart and with all your soul, and with all your mind. This is the first and greatest commandment. And a second is like it, You shall love your neighbor as yourself. On these two commandments depend all the law and the prophets.[4]

Love for God is the highest commandment, and love of self is tied to the love of neighbor. The Christian tradition will understand loving one's neighbor as being ultimately about loving God. In the above passage, Matthew uses the Greek verb which corresponds to the noun *agape*. Does he employ it in a unique biblical sense? The use of this word may reflect its presence in the Septuagint, but its sense is not at odds with the classical understanding of love.[5] In John's Gospel, for example, Jesus says, "Greater love (*agape*) has no man than this, that a man lay down his life for his friends."[6] This idea of choosing death for a friend is a staple of classical discussions about friendship. Moreover, some scholars argue that it can be interchangeable with *philia*, another Greek word for love.[7]

Although the earliest Christians preferred the term *agape*, the rehabilitation of the word *eros* by the Neoplatonists had an impact on Christian intellectuals.[8] Origen and Gregory of Nyssa used it more or less interchangeably with *agape*.[9] According to Nygren, the two words express a theoretical divide between the giving love of the New Testament, which rejects self-interest, and that of pagan philosophers, which emphasizes possession and desire. He thinks that many Fathers, including Augustine, replace Christian love with pagan love. Nygren's position has come under severe criticism both for failing to show that there is any clear difference between the words and for misunderstanding the way in which Greek Fathers such as Gregory of Nyssa and Pseudo-Dionysius use *eros* to signify not only a love for God but also God's generous love for creatures.[10] In this context, *eros* is not selfish. The Greek Fathers used the word "*eros*" because they were writing in an intellectual context that included a Neoplatonic vocabulary, whereas *eros* in the Neoplatonic sense was not even present in the vocabulary of the New Testament writers. The linguistic distinction between *eros* and *agape* points not to a divide between Christian thought and philosophy, but rather to different intellectual and historical contexts. Although the early Christians recognized the distinctiveness of their own tradition, many also welcomed what truth they could find in the philosophers.

Augustine associates the Neoplatonic understanding of love as *eros* with Christian love, just as the Greek Fathers did. He states that loving God is required not only for a Christian's happiness, but for any sort of happy life. The philosophical question about the happy life (*beata vita*) and the highest good (*summum bonum*) is answered by Christianity. Consequently, when explaining the importance of the love of God, Augustine relies upon both human reason and Christian revelation. In his view, the pagan philosophers who discussed the *summum bonum* were attempting to arrive at a truth that can only be reached through this revelation.[11] In a brief discussion in one of his earliest works, *De moribus ecclesiae catholicae,* Augustine claims that it is certain that everyone wishes to live happily (*beate*). In order to have happiness, we must love that which is best for man (*hominis optimum*).[12] The happy life, then, is the state in which we enjoy (*frui*) that which we love (*diligere*), the good for man, which is greater than all other goods. Later in the work Augustine shows that God is this good: the happy life is the love and enjoyment of God.[13]

This basic argumentation of the *De moribus* is reproduced in Augustine's writings.[14] At the beginning of Book X of the *De civitate dei,* Augustine praises the Neoplatonists for coming close to the truth that the happy life is the love for God, who is the best good. He writes:

> For we chose the Platonists from all philosophers as most noble in merit, because they were able to understand that the human soul, even though it is immortal and rational or intellectual, is not able to be happy unless by participation in the light of that God who made both it and the world; thus that which everyone desires, that is the happy life, they refuse attainment of it, except to him who will adhere by the purity of chaste love (*puritate casti amoris*) to the one best thing (*uni optimo*), which is the unchangeable God.[15]

Throughout the remainder of Book X Augustine will be critical of Neoplatonic theology, but he thinks that the Neoplatonists grasp an important truth. The Neoplatonists had removed the morally dubious connotations from the word *eros,* which was translated by the Latins as *amor.* In this passage, Augustine takes pains to show that the Neoplatonists refer to a pure and chaste love of the highest good, which in fact is God.

Throughout the *De civitate dei* Augustine emphasizes that Christians possess those truths which the Neoplatonists only feebly expressed. The Gospel command to love God and neighbor is a description of the happy life which the philosophers sought. The *bonum nostrum* of the philosophers is the God whom Christians are commanded to love.[16] Since the adherence to God as the final good is the *beata vita,* the only man who loves himself is the one who loves God. Plotinus was even right to say that the happy life involves the vision of God, which Christians know to be the life which is the vision of God's beauty in eternity.[17]

What does it mean for God to be the highest good? Plotinus thinks that happiness is an intellectual illumination which occurs through participation in a light which Augustine identifies with God. Augustine argues for a similarity between the description of God in the beginning of the Gospel of John and Plotinus's notion of happiness as participation in the light. Nevertheless, John the Baptist realized that he only bore witness to the light and was not the light himself.[18] Augustine departs from the philosophical tradition in emphasizing that to reach the highest good the Christian must depend on God rather than on himself.

In Book VIII of the *De trinitate,* Augustine discusses God as the *summum bonum* before he explains that God is the absolute good (*bonum absolutum*), whereas every other good is good by participation in him. The discussion of God as the *summum bonum* resembles the discussion in the *De moribus* inasmuch as Augustine claims that only the good is loved. When someone loves mountains, fields, a well-proportioned house, health, or any other object, the real object of the love is the good, which is always loved. Here Augustine introduces a philosophical argument to buttress the claims that he made in the *De moribus.* Love is necessarily directed towards the good. When we love any of the objects listed above, we love *this* good and *that* good (*bonum hoc et bonum illud*). What happens if you take away the "this" and the "that"? You will see God, who is not some good, but good itself (*bonum ipsum*) and the good of every good (*bonum omnis boni*).[19]

What is the relationship between God and other goods? Augustine writes:

> Therefore there would be no changeable goods, unless there were an unchangeable good. When you hear "this" called good and "that" called good, even those things which can otherwise be called non-goods, if you will be able to see (*perspicere*) the good itself (*bonum ipsum*) of whom by participation (*participatio*) goods are, without those goods which are good by participation; and likewise truly you understand it [*bonum ipsum*], when you hear about this or that good; if therefore you are with those goods taken away able to see (*perspicere*) through itself (*per se*) the good, you will see God. And if you adhere [to him] in love (*amore inhaeseris*), you will be happy immediately.[20]

Augustine's argument that God is to be loved above all things rests on two premisses. The first premiss is that all love is a love of the good. The second premiss is that God alone is the good itself, and therefore all other goods are good merely by participation. From these two premisses we can conclude that whatever good is loveable in a creature exists only because of its participation in the more loveable good which is in God. God is the *summum bonum,* and the enjoyment of the Holy Trinity is the happy life (*beata vita*).[21] Consequently, it would be folly to prefer a changeable good to the changeless good from whom it receives all the goodness that it has. Augustine's emphasis on participation as a reason to love God above all other goods is repeated in thirteenth-century discussions of loving God.

Augustine's belief that all love is a love for some good, and that all good is good by participation in God, shows that there is in the human soul a natural tendency to love God. This tendency is especially described in the first and the last chapters of the *Confessiones*. In the very first chapter of the first book, Augustine writes, "you have made us for yourself and our heart is restless (*inquietum*), until it rests in you."[22] The final explanation of this statement occurs only in the last book, in which Augustine explains how God is the highest good and the rest for the human heart. In this book, Augustine describes love as a weight: *Pondus meum amor meus*.[23] Just as weight is the rock's tendency to fall to the earth, so is love the soul's tendency to be moved towards God. The human heart has a natural desire for God.[24] Augustine's distinction between a fruit (*fructum*) and a gift (*datum*) sheds light on how created goods differ from God. Every created good is God's gift, which he intends only for our use (*usus*), since he himself is our enjoyment (*fructus*).[25]

Augustine's most extensive treatment of this distinction between gifts, which we should use (*uti*), and the Creator, whom we should enjoy (*frui*), is in Book I of the *De doctrina christiana*. We have already seen that in the *De trinitate* and the *De civitate dei*, Augustine describes God as the *summum bonum*. In the *De doctrina christiana*, he discusses God as the *summum bonum* only after he has already discussed the different ways in which goods are to be loved. At the beginning of Book I of the *De doctrina*, Augustine states that there are some things (*res*) which are to be used (*utendum*) and others which are to be enjoyed (*fruendum*). Happiness is concerned with enjoying (*frui*) those things which make us happy. In contrast, those things which are merely aids to happiness should be objects of use (*uti*), since they are not constitutive parts of happiness. These objects should be used but not enjoyed.[26]

> For to enjoy (*frui*) is to cling to something by love for its own sake (*propter se ipsam*). To use (*uti*), on the other hand, is to bring back (*obtinendum*

referre) what comes into use to that which you love, if, however, it [is something that] should be loved. For illicit use (*usus inlicitus*) should more exactly be called a misuse (*abusus*) or a catachresis (*abusio*).[27]

The use of the word *propter* occurs throughout Augustine's writings and in the medieval tradition. Only God is to be loved on account of (*propter*) himself. All other goods are to be loved on account of (*propter*) God.

To explain why God should be the sole object of *frui*, Augustine compares the Christian to a traveler.[28] If someone is travelling to a destination and is distracted by objects along the way, he will not arrive at his destination. Such a traveller is misusing the objects along the way when he should merely be using them as a means to attain his destination. Similarly, the Christian, who is a wayfarer in this life, should use and not enjoy the goods of this world, so that at last he may arrive at the enjoyment of God in heaven, which is the final destination of his life. Augustine's view that God, the *summum bonum,* should be the sole object of *frui* underlies his conception of the proper ordering of love.[29] This doctrine of the ordering of love serves as the foundation for later Christian ethics. Clearly, it explains why God should be loved more than oneself. But should someone love himself and his neighbor with *uti* or *frui?* Not surprisingly, Augustine argues that someone should love himself or his neighbor only on account (*propter*) of God, since only God is the proper object of *frui;* a man's love for his own self or neighbor must be a form of *uti* and not *frui*. It is important to remember that Augustine is not using *uti* in a derogatory sense, but rather as a way of indicating how an object is loved for the sake of something else (*propter aliud*).[30] Nevertheless, there is a subordination. Someone should love himself for God's sake.

What does it mean to love oneself for God's sake? Augustine, like Aristotle, distinguishes between a culpable self-love and the self-love of a virtuous person. According to Augustine, some individuals love themselves in such a way that they want to dominate (*dominari*) other individuals. Augustine argues that this self-love is incompatible with loving God, since such a person is really trying to acquire for himself what is due to God. But it is impossible for someone to be happy without loving God; this dominating self-love is really a form of self-hatred. To support his point, Augustine quotes Psalm 10: "He who loves iniquity, hates his soul." The Psalm does not say that the person hates his own body, for by nature all men love their bodies. But the vicious person hates his soul because the health of the soul involves not domination over fellow human beings, but an attachment to God through love.[31]

It is in the context of this discussion that Augustine discusses the Gospel's two precepts of love. The first precept commands a love for God above everything. The second commands a love for neighbor as oneself. The second is included in the first, because we love our neighbor on account of God.[32] What about virtuous self-love? Augustine argues that since we must love our neighbor *as ourself,* the love for self is included in this second precept. At this point Augustine sets forth his influential doctrine of ordered love:

> And if God is to be loved more than any man, each one must love him more than his own self. Likewise, another man is to be loved more than our body, since on account of God (*propter Deum*) all things are supposed to be loved, and it is possible for another man to enjoy (*perfrui*) God with us, which the body is not able to do; since the body lives through the soul by which we enjoy God.[33]

There is a clear order of love here: first, God; second, one's own soul and one's neighbor; and third, one's own body. Love for neighbor is a desire that the neighbor be able to enjoy God with us. The neighbor, like all other objects, is to be loved on account of (*propter*) God.

Augustine's use of the word *uti* to describe the love for neighbor has been much controverted. Some have criticized him for an inadequate treatment of neighborly love. Augustine's defenders point out that in his later writings Augustine does use *frui* to describe love for one's neighbor. Some have suggested that Augustine could no longer accept a merely instrumental love of neighbor. It seems plausible that Augustine may have wished to modify his use of the term. The secondary literature is almost silent on the underlying metaphysical issues,[34] but a consideration of *frui* and *uti* as they appear in the *De trinitate* and the *De civitate dei* will show how important it is to Augustine's metaphysics and ethics that God alone should be the object of *frui*.

We have seen that Augustine's position that only God should be the object of *frui* is based on philosophical argument. God is the *summum bonum,* and all other good things, including our neighbor, are good because of their participation in him. It follows from this that we should love all these other good things, including ourselves and our neighbor, on account of God. Such love, since it is *propter aliud,* is *uti*. It is true that in some contexts Augustine does use *frui* with reference to love for neighbor. But it should be noted that even when Augustine uses *frui* or *perfrui* to describe love for those neighbors who also enjoy (God) along with the one who loves, Augustine is careful to modify it with an *in deo, in domino* or *propter deum*.[35] If we accept Augustine's description of *uti* as being a love for another on account of (*propter*) something else, then it seems clear that when Augustine uses *frui* to describe love for neighbor, he is not using the term in the technical sense in which such love of an object for the object's own sake is due to God alone. If critics of the *De doctrina* wish to hold another description for love of neighbor in which the neighbor is in a pure sense the object of *frui*, then they would have to present an understanding of the relationship between human love, created goods, and God, which differs entirely from that which is found in Augustine.

In the *De trinitate*, Augustine distinguishes between *uti* and *frui* with respect to the final end which is loved. In Book X, Augustine writes, "For we enjoy (*fruimur*) the things that we know, in which the delighted will rests on account of itself; but we use (*utimur*) those things which we refer back to something else to be enjoyed."[36] The assumption here seems to be that everything that is not the final good, namely God, should be the object of *uti*. Earlier in Book X, Augustine condemned the enjoyment (*frui*) of created beauty, when all created beauty is from God.[37] Here again Neoplatonic metaphysics underlies the *uti/frui* distinction. Elsewhere in Book X, Augustine distinguishes between goods that are only used and those which are used and enjoyed. Nevertheless, Augustine also states that everything is the object of *uti* which is loved on account of another (*propter aliud*).[38] Since even neighbors who are fellow lovers of God are to be loved on account of God, it seems that any enjoyment of them must involve *uti* as well as *frui*.

Augustine's application of the *uti/frui* distinction to the love of self, neighbor, and God is nicely summarized in *De trinitate*, Book XIV, chapter 14. When the soul loves God, it loves itself and its neighbor because they are images of God by participation. The soul who loves God rejoices in his light. When a soul loves a lower good more than God then its love is disordered.[39] This discussion of love again presupposes that God is the highest good, and that other creatures are only to be loved because they are good insofar as they participate in him.

Perhaps some of the confusion about the meanings of *frui* and *uti* can be explained by Augustine's remarks in Book XI of the *De civitate dei*, where he remarks that the two words can be used either loosely or in a technical sense. In the technical sense, ". . . we are said to enjoy (*frui*) that thing, which delights through itself, and does not bring us back to another; but to use (*uti*) that thing, which we seek on account of another (*propter aliud*) . . ."[40] Immediately after this passage Augustine admits that in a loose sense of the terms we can use that which we enjoy, and enjoy that which we use. The stricter, technical sense of *uti*, which is to love something on account of another (*propter aliud*), has the greater influence on medieval discussions of loving self and neighbor.

How is Augustine's understanding of *frui* related to philosophical eudaimonism? As he grew older Augustine became pessimistic about the possibility of happiness in the present life.[41] His later concern is more with heaven than with the present life. In what sense does his theory and the subsequent tradition remain eudaimonistic? Augustine and others do not use the word "eudaimonistic" to describe their own theories, and so we cannot look directly to Augustine for an answer to this question. Nevertheless, if "eudaimonism" is understood in a broad sense to refer to theories in which the virtuous agent's good is maximized, then Augustine's outlook is eudaimonistic. Virtuous individuals may not be completely happy in this life, but the wicked harm themselves. One loves oneself most by loving God more than anything else.

It cannot be overemphasized that this doctrine of ordered love is the driving force behind medieval ethical theories. Even the virtues are subordinated to love. In the *De civitate dei,* Augustine restates his position that true virtue is a rightly ordered love in which God is loved above all things. The cardinal virtues are not of themselves sufficient for a happy life, because they involve an element of struggle or imperfection. This incompleteness is most apparent in the virtue of temperance, which is a struggle against the inordinate desires of the flesh.[42] According to Augustine, every created thing can be loved impurely. The only love that by its very nature cannot be disordered is the love for God. Augustine writes:

> For even love itself should be loved in right order (*ordinate*). By which we might love well that which should be loved, so that there might be in us the virtue by which one lives well. Whence it seems to me, that the short and true definition of virtue is the order of love (*ordo amoris*).[43]

The Platonists also recognized that God is the highest good (*summum bonum*). Augustine thinks that the Platonists were able to grasp this truth at least to some extent. The theory of ordered loves helps to reconcile the New Testament view of ethics as loving God and neighbor with philosophical views. But there remains a more serious problem with purely philosophical ethics. Augustine's anti-Pelagian writings show that he is skeptical not only about whether the commandment to love God can be fulfilled in this life, but whether it could be fulfilled at all without grace.[44]

In the *De perfectione iustitiae hominis liber,* Augustine argues that the commandment to love God more than self is impossible in the present life. Augustine notes that charity is unlike faith and hope in that these other two virtues will not be possessed in heaven, whereas the virtue of charity will be augmented and fulfilled. But in this life the soul always has carnal desires:

For the flesh does not lust without the soul, although the flesh might be
said to lust, since the soul lusts carnally. The just one [in heaven] will be
without any sin at all, for there will be no law in his members repugnant
to the law of his mind, but absolutely from the whole heart, the whole
soul, the whole mind, he will love God, which is the first and highest
precept.[45]

Does Augustine mean that someone who loves God will always have lusts
which are not culpable, although these desires prevent him from loving God
with his own soul?[46] Later theologians will recognize that Christians in this
life have at best an imperfect love of God. But they will also emphasize that
Christians here can still love God more than themselves, albeit imperfectly.

Augustine's reaction to Pelagianism caused him to emphasize the insufficiency of human nature. Pelagius seems to have thought that Christians
could live well without the special help of God—if they tried hard enough.
In the *De gratia et libero arbitrio liber unus,* Augustine raises the question of
whether the command to love God can be fulfilled at all without the grace of
God. The command would be useless if humans were unable to use their will
to fulfill it. But how are men able to choose to love God? Augustine writes:
". . . whence is this love of God and neighbor in men, unless from God himself? For if not from God, but from men, the Pelagians prevail; if however
from God, we prevail over the Pelagians."[47] The command to love God can
only be fulfilled through a special gift of grace.

Augustine's battle with the Pelagians will inform the rest of this book.
Augustine thinks that through philosophy we can know that God is the *summum bonum,* but that only through grace can we fulfill the command to love
him. It is uncertain how much the medievals understood about the Pelagian
controversy. They did not have access to the canons of the Second Council
of Orange and they attributed Augustine's authorship to books heavily influenced by Pelagius. Indeed, some of Pelagius's books were attributed to St.
Jerome.[48] Consequently, while medieval thinkers do not have a clear consen-
sus about the relevance of the Pelagian controversy to the issue of whether
God can be loved more than self, they nevertheless do bring the Pelagian
controversy to bear on the question, both directly and indirectly.

If Augustine's anti-Pelagianism has a somewhat limited influence on the
later theories of loving God, the rest of his theory provides a framework in
which new questions will be raised. The Christian understanding of loving
God more than self has been explicitly united with that part of the ancient
ethical tradition which identifies ethics with living the happy life. Even though
he criticizes this tradition for its focus on this life and its ignorance of grace,

Augustine's ethics can be described as broadly eudaimonistic. The one who most loves himself is he who loves God more than himself. But although Augustine states that happiness is found in loving God more than oneself, he does not specify the relationship comprehensively. Can God be loved at least partially for the sake of one's own happiness? Would such a love be vicious? Furthermore, how is self-love connected with the way in which one's own goodness participates in that of God? Might God be loved for his own sake only because he is the source of one's own good? Moreover, although Augustine distinguishes between loving God and loving creatures, there seems to be a difference between rightly loving an inanimate creature and rightly loving oneself or another human being. How can this difference be explained if it is not the case that other humans should be loved for their own sake?

II. The Eleventh and Twelfth Centuries

In the eleventh and twelfth centuries, the Augustinian tradition had a rebirth which was centered around monasteries and cathedral schools. The monasteries had long been the conservators of patristic thought, but in this period there was progress in reflecting on this tradition and even renewed study of the classical authors. In addition, there was an economic and political shift away from the feudalism of the countryside and towards towns. Schools connected to cathedrals grew in cities and attracted students from many parts of Europe. Some of these schools eventually became the great thirteenth-century universities. But the revival of learning began in monasteries such as those in which the Benedictine Anselm of Canterbury studied, wrote, and eventually governed. A new kind of thought was developed which was both classical and patristic. Although there was a revival in pagan literature, the discussions of loving God were almost entirely Augustinian and biblical in character. The Augustinian tradition takes various forms during this period. Anselm's ethics involve a moral psychology based in large part on a distinction between the advantageous and the just. Consequently, his thought emphasized the distinction between happiness and obligation. Peter Abelard and his followers also emphasized the disinterestedness of the love of God, while Hugh of St. Victor developed Augustine's theory in a way that emphasized the connection between loving God and loving one's own good. Peter Lombard, who created what was to become the most influential theology textbook of the following century, presented Augustine's understanding of love in a context which was clearly influenced by Hugh. Consequently, this emphasis on the agent's own good would influence thirteenth-century thinkers.

Finally, during this same period mystics such as Bernard of Clairvaux developed theories of loving God which emphasized that God must be loved entirely for his own sake. In this section, I shall show that although these various theories give different weights to loving God and self-love, ultimately they are probably compatible with each other. Although it is often difficult to compare the doctrines, since these authors did not write with scholastic precision, these different approaches prefigure important thirteenth-century interpretations of the command to love God.

Anselm of Canterbury was among the first to revive Western theology after the relative insignificance of the early medieval period. Although medieval theologians in general treated Augustine with reverence, Anselm's reliance on Augustine is especially pronounced.[49] It is therefore not surprising that he emphasizes the patristic and Augustinian position that happiness is attained only through loving God, but in addition he developed an ethical theory in connection with his new understanding of the will.[50] According to Anselm, freedom should be understood in the context of two conflicting tendencies or aptitudes of the will, one for the advantageous (*commodum*) and another for the just (*iustitia*). Humans and angels have an aptitude to will both what is advantageous for themselves and what is just for its own sake. Anselm sharply contrasts self-oriented willing with willing the just, and implies in his moral psychology that freedom is bound up with the choice between the two. Whereas Augustine thinks that someone ultimately wills most either himself or God, Anselm makes a related distinction between two possible motives, namely one's own happiness or justice. An unjust person is ultimately someone who primarily intends what is advantageous for himself rather than what is just.

Some scholars have contrasted this emphasis on rectitude with eudaimonism, and conclude that Anselm rejects the ethical importance which pagans assign to happiness (*beatitudo*).[51] This view rests on the role of justice in Anselm's moral psychology and his related emphasis on rectitude (*rectitudo*) in his moral theory.[52] Although he emphasizes rectitude over happiness, the non-eudaimonistic interpretation of his thought conflates Anselm's understanding of rectitude with a modern understanding of morality as something separate from happiness. Anselm does not separate the two, even though he subordinates human happiness to an order in which everything is directed to the highest good, which is God. In doing so he falls squarely in the Augustinian tradition. With Augustine, he emphasizes both that God is the highest good and that humans are created to enjoy God.[53] Anselm's morality draws on what seem to be the remnants of Neoplatonic participation. Creatures may be just through another (*per aliud*), namely God, whereas only God is justice.[54] Consequently, with the assistance of God's grace the virtuous individual is able to conform his love and his acts to the order in which justice itself is loved above all. Moral error in preferring one's own happiness to God is an error about what happiness is. Nevertheless, Anselm does state that the angels who loved God freely did so only because they did not know that their happiness was in God.[55] This statement suggests a rift between self-love and loving God which is not clearly present in Augustine, since Anselm implies that if the angels knew that their happiness was in God, they would not have an opportunity to choose the just rather than the advantageous. But in no place does Anselm even suggest that it could be possible for an individual not to find his happiness in God.[56] Anselm's views of happiness and moral rectitude do not depart significantly from an Augustinian eudaimonism.

Although various twelfth-century figures give different weight to self-love in their treatments of loving God, they all adhere to a basically Augustinian eudaimonistic framework. They were more concerned with practical and ascetical problems than about a more sophisticated scholastic understanding of ethics. Their different emphases should be treated with caution. Indeed, these different emphases can sometimes be found in the same writer. Some scholars argue that the relationship between loving God and self-interest was a central tension for twelfth-century theories of love. In his justly famous work, *Pour l'histoire du problème de l'amour au môyen age,* Pierre Rousselot argues that Hugh of St. Victor, along with St. Bernard of Clairvaux, was one of the predecessors for St. Thomas's "physical" theory of love. According to Rousselot, before Thomas Aquinas there was a rift between the "physical" theory of love and the "ecstatic" theory of love. The main feature of the "ecstatic" theory of love, which was held by Abelard and his school, mystics, and some Franciscans, is the description of love as "violent" and "free." Such love by its very nature would be altruistic. In contrast, Thomas Aquinas followed more closely those who held to the physical theory of love, which is based on Greek thought and understands love in terms of unity between the lover and the object loved. This love of God is disinterested, but it is based on the natural inclination of the lover. According to Rousselot, Hugh of St. Victor had a "physical" theory of love that was egoistical and did not move beyond self-love.[57]

Hugh's theory of love, along with that of Peter Lombard, may have been developed partially as a criticism of Abelard's understanding of love.[58] Rousselot describes Abelard as a proponent of the "ecstatic" theory.[59] This description is accurate insofar as Abelard stresses the widely held position that God should be loved for his own sake. In his *Commentaria in epistolam Pauli ad romanos,* Abelard distinguishes between loving freely (*gratis*) and loving for the sake of a reward.[60] For example, if someone's wife loves him when he is rich but then commits adultery when he loses his money, it is clear that his wife loved her husband not for his own sake, but for the sake of his money. Similarly, Abelard argues that if we love God for the sake of any reward, then we do not love God for his own sake but for the sake of the reward.

Abelard's example is interesting, but like his contemporaries he does not present a fully developed theory of love. He explicitly states that he is repeating Augustine's position that God must be loved for his own sake.[61] Hugh of St. Victor, Peter Lombard, and St. Bernard of Clairvaux would all agree with Abelard that God should be so loved, but these authors differ from Abelard in that they do not stress the disinterested element in love.[62] As we shall see, Hugh emphasizes that aspect of Augustine's thought which sees God as the lover's own good. Nevertheless, the fact that authors such as Hugh differ from Abelard on this emphasis does not entail the conclusion of Rousselot that Abelard has an "ecstatic" theory of love which can be neatly contrasted with the egoistic theory of his contemporaries.

Rousselot not only overemphasizes the disinterested aspect of Abelard's approach, but he also misconstrues Hugh's theory as "egocentric."[63] The attribution of egoism to Hugh does not have any clear basis in the text. In his understanding of love for God, Hugh is merely repeating Augustine's belief that God is to be loved on account of himself and that everything else is to be loved on account of God. Hugh may at times emphasize some aspects of Augustine's position out of proportion, but he leans heavily on Augustine and does not advocate a novel "physical" theory of love.

Hugh's definition of charity is important because it reflects the traditional definitions of charity of his time and it influences the scholastics by being appropriated almost verbatim by Peter Lombard.[64] In the *De sacramentis christianae fidei* Hugh writes:

> Sacred Scripture commends to us a twofold charity; namely of God and of neighbor: the first to love God so that we rejoice in him; the second to love our neighbor so that we rejoice not in him, but in God with him. That is, that we love God on account of himself (*propter se ipsum*), the neighbor on account of God.[65]

Hugh explains that we love God because he is to be loved for his own sake, since he is our good (*bonum nostrum*). We love our neighbor because we share our good, who is God, with him. The accomplished scholar Artur Michael Landgraf claims that this Augustinian definition of charity is held by many twelfth-century writers, and could only be confirmed by the later reception of Aristotle's dictum that love for our neighbor comes from self-love. Both Rousselot and Landgraf think that since on Hugh's view we love God as our good, such love is to some extent egoistic.[66]

It should be remembered that none of the twelfth-century authors had any direct acquaintance with Aristotelian eudaimonism. Consequently, it is unlikely that some of them are returning to a Greek theory of love. Moreover, they do not identify the love for God merely with self-love. Hugh's description of God as *bonum nostrum* has its roots entirely in the teaching of Augustinian belief that every human is made to love God alone and has his good in the enjoyment of God. Consequently, only God is to be the object of his *frui*. Hugh's definition of charity clearly rests on Augustine's description of God as the *summum bonum,* which is to be loved for its own sake and on account of which everything else is to be loved.

Hugh agrees with Augustine's position that the commandment to love one's neighbor is included in the commandment to love God. Since God is present in everyone, someone who loves God must also love his neighbor.[67] There is no conflict between the love of God and the love of neighbor; created goods are to be loved because God can be loved by loving them. Hugh explains the relationship between love of neighbor and love of God by comparing God to honey and one's neighbor to the honeycomb. Honey is loved on account of itself. In contrast, the honeycomb should be loved because it is a receptacle for honey. If the honeycomb were dry, then it would not be loved. The receptacle is loved on account of that which is received. Similarly, one's neighbor is a receptacle of sweetness, goodness, and truth. But all these goods come from God. If one's neighbor were, like the dry honeycomb, stripped of his lovable qualities, then one's neighbor would not be loved. Like Augustine, Hugh bases his theory of love on the fact that every good ultimately depends on God's goodness. Although he does not approach the question of love for God and neighbor by explicitly using the metaphysical principles of the Neoplatonists, Hugh's example drives at the same point.

In his description of self-love Hugh quotes two biblical passages which are used by Augustine. Like Augustine, Hugh asks why there is no commandment to love oneself, and he similarly replies to the question by quoting St. Paul: "No one hates his own flesh."[68] Hugh further follows Augustine by making it clear that the man who loves God loves himself, whereas the man who hates God hates himself, since God is the good and the health of the soul. Just as Augustine did in the same context, Hugh quotes Psalm 10: "He who loves iniquity, hates his soul."

Unlike Augustine, Hugh does address the problem of whether there can be a disinterested love for God. On this point Hugh's approach contrasts with that of Abelard.[69] Hugh considers an objection which resembles Abelard's argument for purely disinterested love: if God is the good of the soul, then such love appears to be mercenary (*mercenarius*). Hugh responds that the one who makes such an objection does not know the meaning of love. What would it be to love someone if there were no wish to possess the person in some way? He does not reject Abelard's position that God should not be loved for the sake of a reward, but he does think that the dichotomy between loving God and the reward is false. Following Augustine, Hugh states that the soul acquires its own good by loving God above all things. Moreover, in loving God it loves its own self.

Hugh's greater emphasis on God as the agent's good may have had the most impact on later theologians because of its influence on Peter Lombard's *Sententiae in IV libris distinctae*. This work was the standard textbook of theology for the thirteenth-century scholastics. In his discussion of love, Lombard for the most part presents texts from Augustine which are explained and tied together with comments representing or following Hugh's writings. Yet Lombard presents the position in his own way.[70]

First, he twice separates the *uti/frui* distinction from his discussion of charity. In I d. 1, he assembles remarks about *uti* and *frui* from Augustine's *De trinitate* and from the *De doctrina christiana*.[71] He accurately presents Augustine's position that God alone should be the object of *frui,* but he does not consider Augustine's explanation for this position, which is based on the participation of created goods in God. Peter Lombard seems comfortable simply to assume that God is to be loved for his own sake (*propter seipsum*), whereas Augustine used philosophical argument to establish this thesis. It is perhaps more odd that he does not use the *uti/frui* distinction in his discussion of charity, which is in III d. 27.[72] Although he does not mention the distinction, he does assume that the love of God has the unique characteristic which is based on this distinction, namely that it alone should be for the beloved's own sake.

Lombard's discussion of charity, like the discussion of the *uti/frui* distinction, consists largely of quotations from Augustine's *De trinitate* and *De doctrina christiana*. For example, he gives the following definition of charity: "Charity is the love (*dilectio*), by which God is loved on account of himself (*propter se*), and the neighbor on account of God or in God."[73] Hugh's influence can be seen in the choice and wording of this definition. Indeed, the passages of Augustine which Hugh and Lombard quote are so similar that probably either Hugh influenced Lombard or both are drawing on an unknown common source. At any rate, Lombard hands down to later generations a theory of love which retains Hugh's balance between loving oneself and everything else for the sake of God. There is no tension between loving God and other loves because one rightly loves oneself and one's neighbor for God's own sake. Lombard's arrangement of texts may also be important because of the way he separates Augustine's doctrine on charity from its theological and philosophical background. Subsequent thinkers are all concerned with how to love God on account of himself and one's neighbor on account of God, but they will feel free to graft these conclusions onto their own metaphysical systems. One might speculate that Lombard prepared for these developments through his separation of Augustine's vocabulary from the metaphysical basis for the vocabulary. It may be that through him Augustine's religious doctrines and vocabulary become less firmly tied to Augustine's own philosophy.

Although Peter Lombard wrote the most influential medieval textbook on theology, he was by no means the only twelfth-century influence on later thought. The mystical writings of this period also had a profound influence. Perhaps the most significant writer for our discussion is St. Bernard of Clairvaux, whose doctrine of the *natura curva* was sometimes understood as implying that nature is self-interested. He emphasized that only through God's help can the Christian escape from self-love.[74] Bernard's great authority for thirteenth-century scholastics ensured that this understanding of nature would be assimilated into many later theories of love.

Both Landgraf and Rousselot pair St. Bernard with Hugh of St. Victor as major proponents of the "physical" theory of love. According to them, Bernard's conception of love has difficulty rising above the understanding of love as self-interest. Although, Bernard is not consistent on this issue, some aspects of his thought lead to the conclusion that all love has its roots in self-love. Support for their interpretation is provided by a statement that is often attributed to St. Bernard: *natura semper in se curva est, et ad se reflectitur* (nature in itself is always curved, and reflected to itself). However, this statement does not entail that in Bernard's view the love for God is basically self-oriented.[75] First, the statement as it is normally quoted is not in the writings of Bernard. In his sermons, and especially his *Sermo 24 super cantica canticorum*, Bernard does discuss an *anima curva*, which has its eyes focused on things below. Since it belongs to the world, it is incapable of loving the Spouse, which is God.[76] Bernard also often uses the adjective *curva* to describe the sinful soul and the verb *curvare* to describe its turning away from God. However, the use of these words is not peculiar to him, but has its roots in the Vulgate translation of the Psalms.[77]

Bernard's use of the word does not imply that he is developing a new theory of love. St. Augustine frequently used the verb *curvare* to describe the activity of a soul which is turned away from God. In Sermon 11, Augustine writes: "Do not, having left behind the superior God, curve yourself towards the inferior good . . . Be a good user of inferior things, and you will be a correct enjoyer of the superior good."[78] For Augustine, the soul curves down when it tries to enjoy goods which are inferior to God. *Curvare* describes what happens to the soul when it tries to make those things which should be objects of *uti* into objects of *frui*. Bernard himself does not describe the notion of the *anima curva* in terms of an explicit *uti/frui* distinction. His use of the term *anima curva* does not reflect a philosophical doctrine about nature and self-interest, but rather has its roots in a biblical and Augustinian description of the disordered soul.

A second and more serious problem with the interpretation of Bernard as holding the self-oriented theory is that it does not adequately take into account his widely influential four degrees of love, which are presented in the *De diligendo Deo*. Bernard understands the first two degrees of love to be self-interested. According to the first degree of love, which is carnal, every man loves himself on account of himself (*seipsum propter seipsum*). St. Bernard describes this desire as an animal desire which must precede the other grades of love, to which the soul is led by grace. He also quotes the now familiar passage from St. Paul which states that no one hates his own flesh. According to this first level, a man loves his neighbor not because of God, but rather because of the common nature that he shares with him.[79] It seems that in Bernard's mind the carnal desire present in this first level is always self-interested. In such a case the neighbor is not loved properly, because the neighbor ought to be loved in God (*in Deo*).[80]

According to the second grade of love, a man still loves God on account of himself (*propter se*) and not yet on account of God (*non propter ipsum*).[81] At this stage, he has begun to seek God through faith and to love him, but he has not yet gone beyond self-love. Consequently, the first two grades of love ultimately are rooted in self-love. According to the third grade, God is loved for his own sake (*propter seipsum*).[82] And according to the fourth grade of love, a man loves even himself on account of God. He has such union with God that the self disappears.[83] Bernard thinks that this fourth degree of love is the perfect implementation of the Gospel mandate to love God with your whole heart.[84] Bernard's belief that this love for God involves only an indirect self-love does not have a clear counterpart in Augustine's teaching.

How do these four grades of love inform Bernard's general theory of loving God and self-love? Although some authors will use it in the discussion of the relationship between nature and grace, Bernard did not address issues in these terms. As Landgraf explains, the distinction between nature and grace becomes much more precise with the scholastics of the thirteenth century.[85] Some authors have argued that Bernard's discussion about nature is really a discussion about fallen nature, and not the human nature that God created at the beginning.[86] Moreover, there are controversies about where in Bernard's fourfold schema grace begins to work.[87] The first grade of love seems to make it clear that natural love is self-interested, but it is not clear that this is the only kind of natural love. According to Bernard, love that is not self-interested is possible in the third and fourth grades. Bernard's lack of precision will enable subsequent authors to respect his authority while at the same time interpreting him in an expedient fashion.

Although at the end of the pre-scholastic discussions different theories have different emphases, none of these is stated with precision. Only in the following century, beginning with Philip the Chancellor and William of Auxerre, do theologians develop the ability to distinguish precisely between nature and grace. These later writers are the first to address the question of whether God can be naturally loved more than self, but they do so having inherited from their predecessors both a vocabulary to describe the love of God and a concern about the metaphysical and psychological foundations of such love.

Perhaps the greatest difference of emphasis in the pre-scholastic, Augustinian tradition concerns the relationship between loving God and reward. Nevertheless, these differences of emphasis do not entail strong doctrinal differences. The various thinkers all subscribe to the same general view of God's role in ethics, not just a lawgiver but more importantly as the *summum bonum*. The moral life consists in ordering one's actions towards this good, and the agent maximizes her own good if she loves the highest good most of all. Someone who sins either does not recognize or does not take into account his own true good. This ethical framework can be regarded as eudaimonistic, even though it clearly subordinates the agent's good to the highest good and requires that the agent incorporate this order into his own actions. This ordering to God is seen as an answer to the question of how to be happy.

The pre-scholastic lack of precision would prove to be of historical value. When confronted with the new texts of Aristotle in the mid-thirteenth century, the scholastics were able to draw upon the tradition without being bound by any fixed formulation. This freedom would allow them scope for creativity in their incorporation of Aristotle into a basically Augustinian and Christian view of ordered love.

III. THE FIRST FORMULATION: WILLIAM OF AUXERRE AND PHILIP THE CHANCELLOR

Only in the early thirteenth century did theologians clearly formulate the issue of whether God can be loved more than one's own self out of one's own natural powers. This development occured in the context of new distinctions about nature, love, and the theological virtue of charity. The two most significant figures for our purposes are Philip the Chancellor, a master of theology and chancellor of the cathedral of Notre-Dame in Paris, and William of Auxerre, also a master of theology at Paris and one of the first to write a scholastic *summa*. They are among the first to distinguish between two meanings of "natural," one which is in opposition to the rational, and the other which is in opposition to the gratuitous (supernatural). This distinction first occurred in the context of a question about whether the angels loved God more than themselves in their first natural state. This problem presupposes that the angels may have been created without that grace which was later given to them. The word "man" (*homo*) is frequently used in these discussions, and the authors themselves sometimes explicitly discuss the impact of the Fall on human love. Consequently, the discussion of angels' natural powers leads to a discussion of humans' natural powers, although it is not until the time of Thomas Aquinas that the debate begins to focus almost exclusively on humans. Speculation about angels made it possible to consider human powers apart from the influence of grace.[88] These discussions of love invoked new distinctions about the different kinds of love and their relationship to the will. Whereas Augustine distinguished only between *uti* and *frui,* the scholastics also distinguish between concupiscence, which is something like an interested love, and friendship, which is something like willing someone's good for his own sake. The belief that God's good might be willed for his own sake out of natural powers is in tension with Augustine's emphasis on the necessity of grace for charity. Consequently, it becomes important to explain how natural love differs from the virtue of charity.

William of Auxerre and Philip the Chancellor are the early thirteenth-century theologians most important for the development of these themes. William helped to standardize the vocabulary and arguments of the earlier discussion, restating that everything should be loved for God's sake, but he distinguishes between concupiscence, which is a love for an inanimate object such as wine, and friendship, which is a love for a person. Moreover, William distinguishes between that love which is an ordering of the will to the good apart from deliberation and that love which is a deliberate choice of the good. According to William, by natural love a man loves God either equally with himself or less than himself. Later discussions were perhaps more influenced by William's vocabulary than by his solution to the question. Philip the Chancellor uses William's own vocabulary to argue for the position that God can be naturally loved more than self. In doing so he focuses more carefully on the relationship between nature and grace, and he also presents an alternative understanding of the difference between concupiscence and friendship.

In William of Auxerre's *Summa Aurea,* Liber II, Tractatus II, five chapters are devoted to the angels' love of God. In the fourth chapter it is finally asked, "Whether an angel in the first state loved God?"[89] William's discussion of this issue is preceded by a lengthy discussion of whether in the first state (without grace) the angels even had an obligation to love God more than themselves. William's concern is prompted by the Augustinian tension between the belief that the obligation to love God more than self can be known through natural reason and the belief that this obligation cannot be fulfilled without the assistance of grace. As objections to his final position about natural obligation, William gives two arguments which both more or less reduce to the following:

(1) In the first state without grace, an angel would be obligated to love God more than itself.

(2) The love of God more than self requires grace.

(3) If such a state existed, then the angel was obliged to perform an action that it could not perform because it lacked the grace.

(4) There cannot be an obligation to perform an action which is beyond one's power.

(5) Consequently, such a state could not have existed.

William responds by rejecting (1). He does not attack that aspect of the objections which states that loving God more than self requires grace; instead he attacks the assumption that an angel in a purely natural state would be obligated to have such a perfect love for God. To explain William's position, it is helpful to look at the objections individually.[90]

One objection asks whether an angel in the first state loved God as much as he should. William states: "If yes, therefore from charity he loved him, since by charity alone is God thus loved. If not, therefore he omitted this precept that was written in his mind: You shall love the Lord your God, etc."[91] This objection shows the difficulty that early scholastics had in formulating a notion of purely natural love (*dilectio naturalis*) for God that differs from charity (*caritas*). William replies to the objection by stating that an angel in the first state loved God as much as he should from natural powers, but not according to the law which is written in his mind, since this precept can only be fulfilled once grace has been accepted.[92]

The other objection also sheds light on the relation between nature and grace. This objection brings up the question of whether it is a mortal sin to love oneself on account of one's own self (*propter se*). The objection runs:

> Again in the first state an angel either loved God on account of himself and above everything, or not. If so, therefore by charity, because God cannot be loved in a better way. If not, he did not love God on account of God's self, but on account of himself (i.e. on account of the angel himself); therefore he loved himself more than God; therefore he sinned mortally . . .[93]

In his reply William explains that the objection is based on a fallacy. Mortal sin comes through that excess of desire which is found in the luxurious, the proud, and the lustful. But there is a natural desire for utility or the conservation of one's nature which is neither pride nor lust.[94] William's reasoning that loving oneself more than God is not culpable is based on premiss (4), namely that in order for an act to be sinful, it must be within one's power to avoid it. But an angel in the first state was not given grace to love God more than himself, since he had only the natural desire for the useful and self-preservation. Consequently, the angel did not sin by loving himself. In his responses to both objections William could have supported his position that the angels existed in a first natural state by attacking the objector's assumption that it is not possible to love God more than self without grace. Instead, William concedes to the objector the thesis that such a love is impossible without grace, but he argues that such love would not be required in a purely natural first state.

This discussion of a natural state leads to the issue of how to distinguish among different meanings of the word "nature." To address this question, William borrows from Boethius three definitions of nature: (1) "the principle of motion through itself and not according to accident"; (2) "the specific difference of every single thing"; and (3) "whatever thing which, since it is, can be understood."[95] In the first sense of nature, the concupiscible power cannot love either God or temporal goods, since it does not act but is acted upon by an extrinsic mover. Nor can free choice be a nature according to the primary significations of the second and third senses of the term. Nevertheless, natures are sometimes named by their effects. Free choice is an effect of either a human or angelic nature. Therefore, insofar as natures are signified by their effects, free choice can be described as a nature. When we discuss how God and temporal goods can be loved naturally by the concupiscible power, we are discussing whether these goods can be loved by free choice.[96] This point clearly shows that the issue of loving God naturally is not just about a natural inclination for happiness, but rather about how the love for God is expressed in the free choice which belongs to both the human and angelic natures.

William is not entirely concerned with that love which is expressed through free choice. He describes self-love as involuntary. We have seen that according to the Augustinian tradition only God should be the object of *frui*. To address the problem of whether the self should be an object of *frui*, William, like Aristotle and Augustine, distinguishes between a permissible self-love and a vicious self-love. Permissible self-love is an involuntary love for the Neoplatonic triad which is being, living, and understanding: "the love by which someone naturally wills good to himself, namely to exist, to live, to understand, and such love tends only to its own conservation, its own utility . . ."[97] This understanding of self-love differs from that of mainstream Augustinian eudaimonism, which holds that one loves oneself only when one loves God more than oneself. For William, self-love is involuntary. Whereas Augustine and Aristotle attribute a proper self-love to the good person alone, William seems to make the permissible self-love nonmoral and common to all. However, he does condemn the disordered self-loves which are called pride or libidinousness.[98] William repeats the standard Augustinian position that in disordered self-love someone loves himself as the highest good and not for the sake of God.

The question at the heart of William's discussion is, "Whether an angel in the first state loved God."[99] To address this question, he distinguishes four types of natural love, which are important for understanding the relationship between loving and the will and the difference between concupiscence and friendship.[100] William first distinguishes between voluntary and involuntary love, and then between two subclasses of each. Involuntary love is divided according to the difference between the good that man shares with the animals, and that good which he possesses because of his reason.

In the discussion about the first kind of involuntary love, which man shares in common with animals, William uses an example which will have a central importance for understanding elective love in later authors.

> However there is a twofold involuntary love: one which we have in common with the animals, by which a man loves himself, that is his life, his salvation, and his health, and the conservation of these, since by such

love we love our members and we love more those which are more necessary, such as the head, for whose conservation we expose all other
members: by such love the animals love themselves . . . Such love cannot
be a sin, since it is not voluntary, nor can it be voluntary . . .[101]

Based upon this example of the parts of the body being sacrificed for the
good of the whole, some later thinkers will argue that just as the hand naturally exposes itself for the sake of the head, so does a man naturally sacrifice
himself for the good of the whole community or for God. William's own discussion of this issue foreshadows other thinkers who will argue that the
whole body (and not the part itself) wills to sacrifice the part. These latter
thinkers will hold that the involuntary natural inclination of an object is only
for its own benefit, and some suggest that such an inclination does not have
a direct bearing on virtuous action. In this early discussion of the example,
William wishes to show that there is an irrational and involuntary love of the
body for its own preservation. Since such love is involuntary, it cannot be
culpable.

The second type of involuntary love belongs only to rational beings.
This love is the desire for the *summum bonum*. William refers to Cicero,
Boethius, Augustine, and sacred scripture to support his thinking that any
desire for good is in some sense the desire for the highest good, which is
God. Every rational creature has an involuntary love for its own highest good.
However, since this desire for one's own happiness is involuntary, it cannot be
sinful.[102] Involuntary loves, rational or irrational, are not subject to praise or
blame. This kind of love shows that for William there is a pre-elective ordering of the will to God. The most notable aspect of his position is his finding
that there are two kinds of involuntary love. Later thinkers will often emphasize one of the two involuntary loves, or attribute them to the will in different
ways. William's understanding differs significantly from the analysis that will
predominate only a few years after his writing.

William distinguishes between two kinds of voluntary love, also. Because
these two types of love have such importance for later discussions, it is worth
reproducing William's text in full:

However voluntary love is divided into two, that is into concupiscence
(*concupiscentia*) and friendship or benevolence (*amicitia sive benivolentia*).
Concupiscence is the love by which we love all that we wish to enjoy
(*frui*) or that we will to have, just as someone is said to love wine, because he desires to enjoy it. The love which is called friendship is that by
which we love all that whose good we will, that is in whose goods we

rejoice (*bonis congratulamur*). By both loves, whether concupiscence or
benevolence, we love God through nature, without the help of grace,
and through grace.[103]

In this distinction between concupiscence and benevolence Williams differs
from Augustine and Hugh by stating that concupiscence is the love by which
we enjoy (*frui*) an object. Whereas the other thinkers use the *uti/frui* distinction to separate love of God from love of creatures, William makes a distinction between that love by which we love God with enjoyment (*frui*) and that
love which rejoices in God's good apart from any benefit to self (*benivolentia*).
The love which is called friendship or benevolence rejoices in another's good
without making it the object of one's *frui*. How does William's distinction
between concupiscence and friendship clarify the natural love for God?[104]
According to William, through the witness of creatures we can know about
the pleasantness (*suavitas*) of God, which is accessible to the human soul.
That love for God which follows naturally from this knowledge is a natural
concupiscence. In addition to this natural concupiscence for God, there is
also a natural friendship for God. It can be shown by natural reason that God
made us and that we did not make him, and that he made the visible world for
us. The love that follows from this knowledge is a love of friendship, for it
loves God's worth and rejoices in his good. By this love of friendship we
would love God's good even if it did not benefit us. William explains this
point by comparing the natural love for God with the love of a father for
his son's teacher. With respect to the teacher, who is the final cause, the love
is free of charge (*gratuitus*), since the father's love is in no way based on his
obtaining benefit from the teacher. Instead, the father is led by the love of the
son to have love for the teacher. Similarly, the love of friendship for God is
not based on any benefit to the lover, but simply on a consideration of God
as the *summum bonum*.

   This position on friendship contains two interesting issues. First, previous writers are often reticent in describing the love for God as friendship.
Augustine does use such language, but it occurs most often as a description
of the relationship between God and Church leaders.[105] The comparison of
love for God with love for a friend becomes more important in the thought
of Thomas Aquinas.[106] Second, whereas Augustine made the *summum bonum*
the object of *frui* so that it could not be used, but only loved for its own sake,
William uses *frui* to describe the love of concupiscence for God, which differs
from friendship, the love of God for his own sake. William may stress the disinterested aspect of love much more than Augustine or Hugh did, but he
nevertheless repeats the Augustinian tradition's emphasis on the necessity of

grace. According to him, it is not possible to love God more than self naturally by either concupiscence or friendship, first, because it is impossible by concupiscence to love another more than self, and second, because love of God more than self is possible only through that supernatural friendship which is charity.

William's first argument states that it makes no sense to distinguish between the object of concupiscence and the lover himself.[107] When someone loves God as best or useful for himself, he loves God just as much as he loves his own self. He loves with the very same love both himself and his soul's good, which is God. This is the love for God which is possible by man's nature. William adds that the same analysis of concupiscence applies to the angels. An example illustrates his point. One cannot love the sweetness of a wine more than the wine itself. Similarly, the angels could not love God through concupiscence, which is enjoying his good, more than they loved themselves. With the love of concupiscence, the object is loved in the same way and to the same extent as the self. In the second argument William states that although God is loved only equally with self through concupiscence, it is possible to love God more than self through the love of friendship. Grace is necessary for this love. William cites no purely philosophical reasons for why such love cannot be natural. He may have Pelagianism in mind, but he does not explicitly mention it. He argues that in order for grace to add something to nature, natural love has to be unable to fulfill the command to love God above everything. Consequently, his position rests on theological rather than on philosophical grounds.

Although William does not allow for a natural voluntary love of God over self, he does allow that considerations of natural reason can lead to a love of friendship for God even if it is not greater than self-love. How does such natural love differ from charity? The difference is not purely in the fact that by charity the love is greater. God can be loved naturally for his own sake, but the considerations of natural reason (*rationes naturales*) are not an efficient cause for loving God more than one's own self. Although William admits that the commandment to love God more than self is written naturally in the heart of man, he denies that a man by his natural powers can love God more than himself, since he must be lifted up by grace.[108]

William's treatment of the natural love for God is important to his successors because he clearly states that there can be a natural love of God which is voluntary and yet does not depend on grace, and because he helps to bring into common usage the terms "concupiscence" (*concupiscentia*) and "friendship" or "benevolence" (*amicitia*) to describe the love for God. These terms allow William to distinguish between that love which cannot love another more than itself and the type of love which can so love another. Finally, William's treatment of the distinction between natural love and charity has a great influence on subsequent thinkers. According to William, both loves have the final good as their object. Moreover, the law to love this highest good is written in everyone's heart. However, it takes a supernatural efficient cause to enable the Christian to have that gratuitous love which fulfills the law. Charity differs from natural love by having God as its efficient cause. All subsequent thinkers will struggle with this issue of how to uphold the possibility of a natural love for God more than self while at the same time believing in the necessity of God's help for fulfilling the command to love God.

In his *Summa de bono,* Philip the Chancellor adopts much of William's vocabulary and his understanding of a natural love which is both elective and natural in that it can be exercised without the special assistance of grace.[109] Although he eventually disagrees with William's conclusion that it is impossible naturally to love God more than self without grace, he seriously considers both William's arguments for this conclusion and the difficulties which stem from the then widely held view that nature is self-directed. Philip's discussion of this last issue is especially important because it offers what seems to be the first clear statement of the *natura curva* as it applies to the question of whether God can be loved more than self:

> Moreover, nature is curved in itself because it returns to itself. Which appears in natural things, for it naturally ceases from the generative act before the nutritive, by the fact that this [the nutritive act] is for the sake of conserving the subject, that [the generative act] for the sake of the species . . .[110]

Under normal conditions nature always prefers its own good to the good of the species. This preference for the individual's good shows that by nature someone loves himself most of all. It is odd that although Philip considers this objection in the context of the natural love of God over self, he never directly responds to it. He addresses the issue to some extent in a later discussion *On Charity* (*De caritate*), where he states that the *natura curva* refers to vice in corrupt human nature, and not to the original state of Adam's innocence.[111] The grace of charity is not contrary to the ordered love which Adam originally possessed, but it is contrary to the love of corrupted nature. Consequently, man in his present state requires grace in order to overcome corrupt nature and love rightly. Philip appears to formulate the position which was to be adopted by Thomas Aquinas, namely that it is only corrupt nature that cannot naturally love God more than self.

Philip's response to William departs from William's views on two major points. First, Philip changes William's understanding of concupiscence. Whereas William had thought that by concupiscence the lover and object are equally loved, Philip uses concupiscence to describe a primarily self-directed love. Consequently, he is hesitant to describe the love for God as concupiscence. Second, with regard to the love of friendship, Philip may be the first to hold explicitly that someone's power to love God more than himself is natural.[112]

As William did, Philip discusses the natural love of God in the context of the angels' first state. He emphasizes the connection between knowledge and love. The knowledge of the angels in this state was purely natural and not aided by grace. The natural love of the angels followed upon the natural knowledge of the good. Philip writes, ". . . the known good (*bonum cognitum*) cannot not be loved."[113] This statement will serve as the basis for Philip's argument that since God can be known naturally to be the *summum bonum,* it follows that by nature he can be most loved as the *summum bonum.* Here at the beginning of the argument, however, Philip only mentions the principle that love follows knowledge.

Next, Philip discusses the motive (*ratio*) for loving. Philip presents William's position, but alters it slightly to make it more relevant to his own discussion. According to Philip, there are those who say that an angel naturally loved itself more than God, and that it loved God as is its own good (*suum bonum*). They arrive at this position because they distinguish between that good which is useful (*utile*) and that which is honorable (*honestum*). Moreover, they say that the motive for loving comes from the one who loves. Consequently, the good which is the object of natural love is the useful good. Therefore, by natural love God is only loved because he is useful to the one who loves. In contrast, only by charity is God loved not for the benefit of the lover but as the *bonum honestum.*[114]

This distinction between the useful and the honorable affects Philip's understanding of concupiscence and friendship. According to his understanding of the terms, "the love of concupiscence (*dilectio concupiscentie*) is that by which we will a thing for ourselves, the love of friendship (*dilectio amicitie*) that by which we will someone's good or that [good] which we love for him . . ."[115] The moral implication of this change can be seen in the connection of *frui* with friendship. Concupiscence becomes suspect. Philip emphasizes that the debate over naturally loving God more than self is also a debate about whether God can be so loved by his own sake. William defines concupiscence as the love whereby we enjoy (*frui*) an object. Philip does not mention *frui* in this context, but instead defines the love of concupiscence as the desire of an object for one's own sake. For him, the love of concupiscence is based on the Augustinian *uti,* which is the love of an object for the sake of the lover. Consequently, his definition of the love of friendship, by which we love the good not for ourselves but for someone else, contrasts with his definition of the love of concupiscence. Whereas the love of concupiscence is based on self-love, the love of friendship wills good for the sake of the person who is loved.

Whereas William used the way in which we enjoy goods to distinguish between the two types of love, Philip distinguishes them according to the ends for which an object is willed: another or oneself. This difference in approach has direct implications for the meaning of the love of concupiscence. According to William, concupiscence involves *frui.* Consequently, it makes no sense to ask whether in the love of concupiscence a lover loves himself more than the object loved. Both the lover and the object loved are loved with the same love, since the object's good is identical to the self's good. In contrast, Philip describes the love of concupiscence as a form of *uti.* The object is loved merely for the sake of the lover. By Philip's definition of the love of concupiscence, the self is loved most of all.

After setting forth his version of the two types of love, Philip is prepared to make his own statement about the way in which God is loved. Philip agrees with William that God can be loved naturally through both the love of concupiscence and the love of friendship.[116] But is there a love of concupiscence whereby God is loved through grace? In contrast to William, Philip states that if God is loved by the love of concupiscence through grace, then he is loved on account of beatitude (*propter beatitudinem*). Consequently, God would be loved not for his own sake, but on account of his usefulness to the lover (*propter utilitatem*). Philip thinks that this love of God as merely useful is untenable if "*propter*" is understood *simpliciter* and not *secundum quid.*

The understanding of "*propter*" as *secundum quid* resembles those later arguments about the object of the love for God which distinguish between God's own goodness and the goodness that the creature possesses by loving God. According to Philip, if "*propter*" is understood to be *secundum quid,* then the love is said to exist on account of the end as it is present in the subject of the love and not in the object of the love. In such a case, God is still the object and the end of the love, but there is also a lesser sense in which the lover's relationship to God in beatitude is the end of the love (*secundum quid*). God is loved most of all, but the self is also loved because its own happiness consists in loving God. This *secundum quid* interpretation of "*propter*" results in a position which is similar to the one we saw in Augustine and Hugh of St. Victor, where the *summum bonum* is identified with the *bonum nostrum.* Although by loving God the individual obtains the greatest benefit to himself, he loves God for God's sake and not the benefit to himself. Philip has clearly retained the framework of the Augustinian tradition.

The tradition had emphasized that although someone loves himself most by loving God more than himself, it is improper to love God for one's own sake. Philip notes that "*propter*" can also be understood *simpliciter*. In such a case, to love God on account of utility (*propter utilitatem*) would be to love him for one's own benefit. Philip argues that such a love would be sinful, since it would make the creature into the principal end of the love. When someone loves an object by the love of concupiscence, the object is loved on account of (*propter*) its benefit to the one who loves. Even if God were to be loved by grace through the love of concupiscence, the benefit of the person loving would be the ultimate end of the love, and it is a sin to make anything other than God into the ultimate end.

Philip's continuity with the Augustinian tradition can be seen especially in his emphasis on the way in which created goods depend on and participate in God's unchanging goodness. He argues that the angels, unlike humans, had a clear knowledge of God's goodness. Consequently, they knew that every created good is good only by participation in him.[117] This argument is based on the Christian and Neoplatonic tradition of participation that stretches back through Augustine to Plotinus and even Plato. Philip retains the Augustinian emphasis on the difference between changeable and unchangeable goods. The angels' good is changeable. Consequently, the angels would have been sinning if in the first state they loved their own changeable goodness more than that of God.

Contemporary discussions of how the angels were created allowed William to distinguish between charity and natural love. Nevertheless, he seemed to fear that a natural love for God over self might make grace irrelevant. In contrast, Philip argues that if in the first state we loved ourselves more than God, then charity would be contrary to nature. If we loved God more than ourselves in the first state, then the gift of charity would complement nature so that we could love rightly and with ease. Philip uses the relationship between art and nature to illustrate his position. Art imitates nature and does not contradict it. Instead, it accomplishes without error that which nature also accomplishes. Similarly, charity accomplishes what natural love accomplishes, but more easily and without error.[118] This emphasis on the congruity between nature and grace becomes popular in the thirteenth century, being adopted by Thomas Aquinas and others. Philip was at least one of the first to formulate it because of the new distinction between natural love and charity.

Philip distinguishes between the two loves by the knowledge on which they are based. The natural love of God follows the love for him as the *summum bonum* whereas charity follows the knowledge of the Holy Trinity and the Incarnation. Knowledge of God as the *summum bonum* is available without the assistance of grace. Consequently, an angelic intellect without grace knew that God is enjoyable (*fruibile*) and not useful (*utile*). Since appetite follows knowledge, it follows that the angels loved God for his own sake. Philip mentions William of Auxerre's objection that someone's knowledge of God as the *summum bonum* does not imply that there is an ability to love God more than self without the assistance of grace. Philip argues that William misunderstands the relationship between nature and grace:

> I respond that in loving God above everything, [nature] is not elevated above itself, just as it is not [raised above itself] in knowing [God], but love is measured according to the mode of knowledge. However, the knowledge of faith is far nobler than natural knowledge. Whence the charity which follows that knowledge is far more noble than natural love . . . [The knowledge of faith] also brings it about that it extends [to him] as to the highest truth, and charity follows this knowledge by reason of movement or of disposition, but not [by reason] of infusion, of which it is to love the highest good, which is elevating through grace and through glory, and this on account of itself. But it is not so in the love that follows [natural knowledge]; for that knowledge was about God according to the works of creation, which knowledge does not elevate the intellect above itself.[119]

According to Philip, the natural love for God and charity differ according to the types of knowledge that they follow. The natural love for God follows the natural knowledge that we have of him through creation, while charity follows from the knowledge of faith.[120] Again we see Philip's insistence that love can only be understood with reference to the *known* good (*bonum cognitum*). Philip also accepts William's claim that God is an efficient cause of charity. Consequently, it is possible to state that there is a natural love of God over self while at the same time holding the importance of grace for charity.

Philip's distinction between the love of concupiscence and the love of friendship helps to standardize the terminology of later discussions. Against William, Philip argues that the person who loves another through the love of concupiscence loves his own self most of all. Consequently, God cannot be loved through grace by the love of concupiscence. Moreover, he is the first to distinguish between nature and grace in such a way as to be able to argue for the natural love of God more than self. The harmony between nature and grace is emphasized. In his arguments, Philip often relies on principles which have clear precedents in the Augustinian tradition, for example, the doctrine of participation and the distinction between God and mutable goods. But Philip also introduces new arguments about the relationship between nature and grace, and the existence of a natural love which follows from the natural knowledge of God as the *summum bonum*.

By the early thirteenth century the discussion of loving God occurs within an Augustinian framework, but further distinctions within this framework make possible a wide variety of differences about questions which the Augustinian tradition never clearly discussed. How does natural love differ from charity? In what sense does corrupted human nature limit the freedom to love? As the scholastics learned to ask new questions, they were forced to answer them in an innovative fashion.

Nevertheless, the basic ethical framework remains the same from the time of Augustine until the end of the thirteenth century, and it will persist even beyond the introduction of Aristotle's ethical texts. All thirteenth-century theologians think that God is the highest good, and that the happiest and most moral activity consists in loving him above all else. But there will eventually be difficulties in spelling out how this wider framework is related to Aristotle's eudaimonism. In the interim period, at least a generation of scholastics will develop their ethical and psychological doctrines by relying primarily on Augustine and such Fathers as John Damascene, whose understanding of the will, in particular, influences the continuation of the debate over natural love which was first instigated by such figures as William and Philip.

CHAPTER 2

Mid-Thirteenth-Century Scholasticism at Paris

The middle of the thirteenth century is a transitional period for the dispute concerning the natural love of God over self. Thinkers were still elaborating issues raised by William of Auxerre and Philip the Chancellor, but in doing so caused new questions to be raised. This development accompanied the final shift towards universities as the most important academic centers. Paris was the most important university, and it soon had a large faculty from many countries and several new religious orders. The most significant of these orders were the Dominicans and Franciscans, and they were the first to have masters of theology at Paris. One master at Paris, namely Alexander of Hales, became a Franciscan and consequently initiated the strong Franciscan intellectual presence at Paris. The *Summa Halesiana* was completed by Franciscans who were influenced by Alexander. In the 1250s Bonaventure began to take his place as not only a great Franciscan but also as one of the greatest theologians of the Western church. This Franciscan tradition, perhaps best represented by the *Summa Halesiana* and Bonaventure, illustrates how the basic understanding of the different types of love was still being worked out. The *Summa Halesiana* is less clear than were William and Philip about the distinction between the natural and the supernatural, while its discussion of love is more lengthy and nuanced. In contrast, Bonaventure's discussion of loving God is admirably clear, emphasizing that humans were created uprightly and consequently that they could love God rightly even without the help of grace.

While it is during this period that Aristotle's *Nicomachean Ethics* is incorporated into theological thought, neither the *Summa Halesiana* nor Bonaventure connect this issue with pagan ethical theories. The Dominican Albert the Great was among the first to study Aristotle's ethical theory seriously, bringing the discussion of loving God to bear on wider issues.[1] For example, he explicitly addresses the question of whether in pagan moral theory a good citizen can prefer the common good to his own good. If so, it seems that without grace someone can prefer a higher good to his own. But does this ability mean that he can without grace prefer God's good to his own? Albert's difficulties over this issue reveal fundamental challenges in reconciling Greek and Roman ethical theories with the Christian tradition. Albert also sees that the problem of loving God has implications for basic issues in moral psychology. Is "natural love" a general orientation of the will towards the good, or is it a result of deliberation and choice? In what sense can the will be said to love the good before deliberation and choice? Albert identifies these as important questions for understanding the views of his predecessors. Moreover, assumptions about these issues are implicit in the *Summa Halesiana* and Bonaventure. Consequently, before examining Albert and the Franciscan tradition on naturally loving God, it will be helpful to look more carefully at some developing features of moral psychology.

I. *THELESIS* AND *BOULESIS*

In addressing the question of whether God can be naturally loved, Albert introduces John Damascene's distinction between *boulesis* and *thelesis*.[2] Both in some way refer to or describe the will. *Boulesis* is from the pagan tradition and seems to be a kind of wishing.[3] *Thelesis* is a Greek Christian word for the will. There is much disagreement among medieval writers and even contemporary scholars over how Damascene differentiates them. In the mid-twelfth century Burgundio of Pisa had translated some of Damascene's work as the *De fide orthodoxa*.[4] Although the distinction between *boulesis* and *thelesis* is confusing in the original Greek, the translation made it even more confusing.[5] Nevertheless, while disagreeing about their definitions, thirteenth-century figures used these words to develop their ideas about the will and human action.

Albert's understanding of these terms informs his explanation of William of Auxerre's position on naturally loving God, but while William knew Damascene's moral psychology, he did not himself discuss *thelesis* and *boulesis*. Philip the Chancellor may have been the first to do so, but he himself did not explicitly relate the terms to loving God. Albert himself misrepresents William's view on loving God, but his interpretation permits us to see how much of the disagreement over the ability to love God naturally was connected to disagreement over moral psychology. To understand how the distinction between *boulesis* and *thelesis* plays into the problem of the natural love of God, we will first look at Damascene's text. Second, we will look at how Albert's interpretation of this text may have prompted his misrepresentation of William's view. Then we will see how subsequent figures develop Damascene's distinction in a way that makes it possible to think more clearly about the natural love of God.

Damascene distinguishes between *boulesis* and *thelesis* in the context of distinguishing between the cognitive and the vital powers of the soul. The will is a vital, appetitive power. He writes:

> . . . *thelesis,* i.e., the will, indeed is itself a natural and vital and rational appetite of all of the components of nature, a simple power . . . *Boulesis,* i.e., the will, is on the other hand a qualitative natural *thelesis,* i.e., the will, namely a natural and rational appetite of anything.[6]

The language of this passage is important for two reasons.[7] First, the will is clearly described as a rational appetite, a description that becomes a standard one. Second, a distinction is made within the will itself, even though it is not clear what this distinction is. Odon Lottin interprets Damascene to say that *thelesis* is a fundamental impulse to the end, whereas *boulesis* is the act whereby we bring ourselves to the end.[8] Étienne Gilson similarly suggests that *boulesis* is the act of the will and *thelesis* is the will itself.[9] It is unclear how Damascene's precise meaning could be determined.[10]

Lottin argues that Albert is one of the few scholastics to correctly understand Damascene as holding that both *boulesis* and *thelesis* are about the end of human action, whereas others falsely associate *boulesis* with the deliberative will.[11] According to Albert, the distinction between the two is in their objects.[12] *Thelesis* is the willing of natural things, such as to be, to live, and to understand. Just as William had defined one kind of involuntary love in terms of the Neoplatonic triad, Albert associates *thelesis* with this triad. In contrast to *thelesis, boulesis* is the willing of those things which are determined by reason. Albert states that by *thelesis* an object is loved according to the delight of concupiscence, and consequently by *thelesis* the lover loves himself most of all.[13] In contrast, *boulesis,* the will that follows reason, calculates with the reason about the useful, the pleasant, the morally worthy [*honestum*], and the good *per se.* This view of calculation shows that even though Albert does say that *boulesis* is about the end, he also relates it, at least indirectly, to deliberation and willing the means.

An unexpected feature of Albert's interpretation is his association of the distinction between *thelesis* and *boulesis* with the distinction between the loves of concupiscence and friendship. He uses similar language to distinguish between the two kinds of reason, namely reason considered as a nature, which is *curva,* and reason considered as reason, which is as deliberative and seeking the good.[14] So the relationship between *thelesis* and *boulesis* seems to be parallel to that between nature and reason. All are concerned about the end, but the latter members of each pair are concerned about that end which is determined by reason. Moreover, these distinctions recall another demarcation of the will, going back at least to the early Dominican Roland of Cremona, namely, the distinction between the natural will and the rational will.[15] The natural will refers to the will as a natural object with an inclination to the good. The rational will refers to the will as being able to choose one thing or another. Other thinkers identify *boulesis* with the rational will, and a suggestion of this connection is present in Albert's thought. His linking of *thelesis* and concupiscence is more unusual.

Albert explicitly relates *thelesis* and *boulesis* to William's position on naturally loving God.[16] Although Albert faithfully recounts William's position that the angels were unable to love God more than themselves by the love of friendship, he gives an incorrect version of William's position on concupiscence. As we have shown, William thinks that it makes no sense to talk about loving an object more or less by concupiscence, since the object's good is identified with the good of the lover according to such love. According to Albert, it is William's belief that through concupiscence the angels loved God more than themselves, since the divine good is more sweet (*dulcius*) than the angels' own good. However, Albert does agree that this love for the divine good is a love of concupiscence; it brings the love for the divine good back into a love for self.

The influence of Albert's own moral psychology on his description of William can be seen in the way he understands William's distinction between the different types of love. As we have seen, William identifies two types of involuntary love, namely the one we share with the non-rational animals and the uniquely human one, and two types of voluntary love, namely concupiscence and friendship. William states that concupiscence is a voluntary love. Moreover, our will to live and to be is that love which is involuntary and shared with the irrational animals. God is loved in a pre-deliberative way only by that love which is particular to humans. William distinguishes sharply between the involuntary desire for life and being and the involuntary desire for happiness, which he sees as a desire for God. He furthermore distinguishes between the involuntary love of God and the voluntary love of God by friendship or concupiscence. But Albert uses *thelesis* in such a way that he connects the involuntary desire for life and being with a concupiscent love of God. His moral psychology causes him to focus more clearly on the question of whether God can be loved more than self by the love of friendship.

Why did Albert connect *thelesis* with a concupiscent love of God? His predecessors did not do so explicitly. According to Philip the Chancellor, who was among the first to carefully delineate *thelesis* from *boulesis,*[17] *thelesis* is the natural will, an appetitive power for that which is according to nature.[18] Philip did not associate *thelesis* with concupiscence, but held that the natural will is a power extending not only to natural goods and life itself, but also to rational goods.[19] Albert thinks that *thelesis* is concerned exclusively with non-rational goods. Philip does not mention William's claim that there is a non-deliberative love of God, but his treatment of *synderesis* foreshadows the later discussions of such love. The term *"synderesis"* has a tortured history and its use differs greatly among thinkers.[20] For Philip, *synderesis* is distinguished from *proheresis*, which is choice, in much the same way that the natural will is distinguished from the deliberative will.[21] But *synderesis* differs from the natural will. First, *thelesis,* which is the natural will, is a power, whereas *synderesis* is a habit.[22] Second and more importantly, *thelesis* extends even to non-rational goods, whereas *synderesis* extends only to rational goods.[23] Consequently, *thelesis* cannot be solely identified with either William's involuntary love that is shared with non-rational animals or the involuntary love of the highest good. It would seem to include both.

The Franciscan John of Rupella separates *thelesis* from the involuntary love for the highest good, although he describes *synderesis* in a way which is a closer approximation of an involuntary love of God.[24] He argues that *thelesis* and *synderesis* can be distinguished on account of their different goods.[25] *Thelesis* is the "natural will moving and inclining the soul to the substantial good of nature or natural good."[26] *Synderesis* is similar, but moving to the highest good (*summum bonum*).[27] Whereas Philip distinguished between the two as power from habit, John thinks that they are the same kind of thing, but that *synderesis* is concerned with the morally worthy (*honestum*), whereas *thelesis* is concerned with being, living, and understanding. Significantly, both John and Albert understand *thelesis* in terms of this Neoplatonic triad. They are also agreed in stating that *boulesis* can be about the end, while John more clearly states that it can be about the means as well. For him, *thelesis* is the natural will, whereas *boulesis* is free choice.[28] John also emphasizes that *boulesis* is the same as the deliberative will, a point that will be taken up by the later Franciscan tradition.

The most important point here is that although John and Albert disagree about the details, they both identify the natural will with an appetite for natural goods and not for the moral good or God. In light of this understanding of *thelesis,* it becomes clearer why Albert would neglect William's view that there is both a voluntary and an involuntary love of God, and that the voluntary love can be either friendship or concupiscence. In this context Albert fails to distinguish plainly between involuntary and voluntary love, and

associates *thelesis* with concupiscence. For him, *thelesis* is only for natural
goods, limiting its scope to that kind of love that is more for the benefit of
the agent than for God.

John's understanding of *thelesis* is not entirely the same as that adopted by
the *Summa Halesiana,* in which *thelesis* is said to correspond to *synderesis.*[29] In
this *Summa, synderesis* is contrasted with free choice in the same way that *thelesis*
is contrasted with *boulesis,* which is identified with the deliberative and elective
will.[30] There seems to be a connection between *thelesis* and higher goods. The
difference between *thelesis* and *boulesis* is also understood as the difference
between the natural will and the rational will. But later in this *Summa* it is
stated that the natural will is concerned with more goods than is *synderesis.*[31]
Consequently, the link between *thelesis* and moral goods should perhaps not
be emphasized. But the *Summa Halesiana* does open the way for an account of
the involuntary (non-deliberative) love of God.

These different positions on the will are directly related to the debate
about loving God, since they involve questions of the agent's possible motivation. All the authors believe that the will has a natural direction to some
good as an end, but they differ over what this direction is and how it is connected to the virtuous life. The different intepretations of *thelesis* help to bring
into relief two perspectives on the way in which the will is ordered to God.
Is the will ordered in a pre-deliberative and pre-elective way only to natural
goods, and is the love of God necessarily deliberative and elective? Or is
there some way in which the will is ordered to God even before deliberation
and choice? It must be emphasized that all these thinkers see the will as
having an orientation to goods which are not ultimately established by
human desires. Human freedom is connected to the ability to distinguish between goods. Moreover, these thinkers affirm in common that God is the
source of all goodness. Consequently, they all believe in some version of an
Augustinian view in which God's goodness explains how any goodness can
be willed. Their disagreement is over whether there is a special prerational
orientation to God and to moral goodness.

II. THE *SUMMA HALESIANA*

The *Summa Halesiana* discusses the natural love of God in the traditional context of the angels' love, initially combining a new understanding of love with
a deference to William of Auxerre's belief that in the state of innocence grace
was necessary to love God perfectly. In the end, however, the *Summa Halesiana*
agrees with Philip that there is a type of natural love for God over self which

follows the natural knowledge that we have of him.[32] It is not always clear in the *Summa Halesiana* whether the term "natural" is used in opposition to the term "gratuitous" or to the term "rational."

The *Summa Halesiana* begins discussing the ordering of the angels' love by asking whether the angels have a naturally ordered love.[33] In the objection of this question, it is argued that it would be disordered and sinful if the angels did not love God more than self in the first state of their existence. In its response, the *Summa Halesiana* follows William of Auxerre in stating that the order of natural love need not correspond to the order of grace, since natural love lacks perfection. But unlike William, the *Summa Halesiana* leaves open the question of whether the angels were held responsible for loving God more than themselves. It states that if they did love God, they did not yet have the ability to sufficiently and completely love God. The discussion refers to the importance of grace for the angels to have an ordered love, but it is reticent about the exact possibilities for natural love.[34]

At this stage, the *Summa Halesiana* distinguishes between gratuitous love and natural love. Natural love is the love of the *summum bonum* for the sake of (*propter*) the lover. Unlike a vicious love that loves a changeable good for the sake of the lover, there is a natural love of the *summum bonum,* although this love for the *summum bonum* is also brought back to love for the creature. In contrast, gratuitous love loves the *summum bonum* for its own sake. The end of this gratuitous love is God.[35] As with Albert, there is a tendency here to associate natural love with the love of concupiscence and charity with the love of friendship. The *Summa Halesiana* follows Philip in defining these loves. The love of concupiscence desires the good of the lover, whereas the love of friendship aims at another's good.[36]

The *Summa Halesiana* next addresses the question of whether by natural love an angel loves itself more than God. It is noteworthy that the question posed is not about the state of innocence *per se* but about natural love in general. The answer to this question explains the phraseology. Unlike William of Auxerre, who lists four types of love, the *Summa Halesiana* lists three: (1) that which is in common with the brutes, (2) that which is innate to rational creatures, and (3) that which is the product of choice. Every animal naturally has the first type of love for himself, by which he wishes to preserve his existence. Since this love is common to the brute animals, there is no innate knowledge or love of God according to this love. This love clearly corresponds to William of Auxerre's non-rational and involuntary love.[37]

The second type of love follows from the natural knowledge of God which is innate to the rational creature.[38] This concept of love presents a problem insofar as many have erroneous ideas about God or believe in many gods. To explain how such persons love God, a further distinction must be made between knowledge according to the common nature (*in ratione communi*) and knowledge of an object according to its proper nature (*in ratione propria*).[39]

Although idolators lack the proper knowledge of God as true, three, and one, even they know that God is an omnipotent first being. They have a knowledge of God according to his common nature even when they have erroneous notions about God according to his proper nature. Similarly, while all men desire happiness, some mistakenly attempt to find their happiness in fleshly pleasures, riches and honors. These individuals have a knowledge of happiness according to its common nature, but not according to its proper nature. The *Summa Halesiana* gives an example to illustrate this point. Someone might have a knowledge of honey according to its common nature by knowing its softness and color. Nevertheless, such a general knowledge still allows for the confusion of honey with bile, which has a similar texture and color. Similarly, there is a common knowledge of God implanted in all men, even though many have a mistaken knowledge of God according to his proper nature.[40]

The *Summa Halesiana* identifies this love of God which follows from the innate knowledge of God with concupiscence, because in this kind of love God and the self are not loved equally.[41] William of Auxerre's argument for this position is mentioned, namely that according to concupiscence there is no distinction between the object loved and the one loving. The *Summa Halesiana* goes further, however, claiming that the different objects of such love cannot be loved more or less than each other, or even equally, because although there are two objects of such love, there is only one love. Consequently, there is no way to compare the love of that object which is a person and the love of that good which is desired for the sake of the person. Both are loved by one and the same love. In this context, the words "greater," "lesser," and "equal" have no meaning. The *Summa Halesiana* differs from William in attributing the love of concupiscence to an involuntary love that precedes choice. William of Auxerre also believed that there is an involuntary desire for happiness in man which is in some way a desire for God, but he did not describe such love as concupiscence, which he thinks can only be a voluntary love. The *Summa Halesiana* applies William's understanding of the love of God through concupiscence to an innate and involuntary love for God.

Whereas the second form of love precedes choice, according to the third type of love an individual can freely choose either a greater or lesser good. The *Summa Halesiana* argues that an angel can love God more than itself by this type of love, but it does not call this love natural. The terminology of the

Summa Halesiana here uses the word "natural" to describe involuntary love only, whereas the love whereby God is loved more than self is called not "natural" but "elective."[42]

Does this elective love require the assistance of grace to be a love for God more than self? In the response to objections, the *Summa Halesiana* argues that while it can be naturally known that God is the highest good, the elective love of God and the knowledge which follows it are necessarily subject to grace. The *Summa Halesiana* does not distinguish at this stage between a natural love and a love dependent on grace. Rather, the identification of an elective love for God with a supernatural love for God can be seen in the response to the objection that since the commandment to love God is written in the mind naturally, this precept can be fulfilled naturally. Like William of Auxerre, the *Summa Halesiana* argues that having the command naturally written in the mind does not entail a natural ability to fulfill it. However, it combines the claim that such an act of love requires grace with a claim not made explicitly by William in this context, namely, that man is obliged to possess the grace: "man is held by free choice to loving out of charity, however free choice does not suffice for this type of love except when it has charity."[43]

The *Summa Halesiana* can also be fruitfully compared with the approach of Philip the Chancellor. The *Summa Halesiana* differs from Philip in its discussion of *natura curva*. We have seen how Philip thinks that *natura curva* refers to fallen nature alone. Although the *Summa Halesiana* does not here use the phrase *"natura curva,"* it does describe nature as *"reflectitur in se,"* which is the normal description of the *natura curva*.[44] How does the *Summa Halesiana*'s treatment of the way in which nature is reflected in itself differ from Philip's understanding of *natura curva*? According to the *Summa Halesiana,* nature is not reflected into itself according to the object which is desired, but according to the motive (*ratio*) for loving, which is the lover himself. The natural desire for God is reflected into itself not because of fallen nature, but rather because natural love is a love of concupiscence, which always desires the lover's own good.[45] Whereas in Philip the *natura curva* describes fallen nature, in the *Summa Halesiana* the *natura curva* is implicit in the very concept of the love of concupiscence.

In a further discussion, the *Summa Halesiana* raises the issue of how God and not a creature can be the object of *frui* if the creature is always the motive (*ratio*) for the natural love for God. It would appear that if a creature loves God on account of (*propter*) its own self, then its own self is the object of *frui*. The *Summa Halesiana* explains that the love of concupiscence does not describe only natural love: there is also a corresponding elective love of concupiscence. If a creature makes himself the end of his love for God according to this elective love, then he makes himself and not God the object of *frui*, and such love is culpable. But if someone loves God on account of his own self out of an involuntary natural love, such love is not culpable, since this love is natural and not a libidinous movement.[46] We should note that the *Summa Halesiana*'s position compares with that of William of Auxerre. According to William, concupiscence is a voluntary love that loves God as good for the lover and consequently makes him the object of *frui*. God and the lover are both loved equally. The *Summa Halesiana,* in contrast, states that a voluntary love of concupiscence always makes its own self the object of *frui* precisely because it loves the object on account of its own self.

We have already discussed the distinction between the innate knowledge of God and the knowledge of faith. Here the contrast is between innate knowledge and the knowledge of God which can be learned through faith and seemingly by reason. God is not the object of elective love in the sense in which "God" is understood to be the common object of all love. We have seen that such love for God is innate, involuntary, and natural. The *Summa Halesiana* explains, "In fact in another way God is called the substance building and ruling everything and perfecting the rational creature by grace and glory; and according to this way [God] is loved by elective love by the good angels."[47] In its treatment of whether the angels can love God above everything by elective love, the *Summa Halesiana* distinguishes between two types of elective love based on those two types of knowledge of God which are not innate, namely that knowledge which is obtained through natural reason, and that knowledge which is obtained through revelation.

So far, the *Summa Halesiana* has seemed reluctant to discuss a love of God over self which is natural in the sense that it does not require grace. But a later passage corresponds almost exactly to Philip's treatment of the distinction between the natural and gratuitous love for God.[48] According to this passage, there are two ways in which God can be loved for his own sake (*propter se*) and more than the lover loves his own self (*prae se ipso*). By the first way, the love follows upon the knowledge of God through faith, whereby God is understood to be the Holy Trinity, who creates, justifies, and glorifies. This knowledge does not come through natural means but through grace. By the second way, the love follows upon the natural knowledge of God as someone who confers happiness. The *Summa Halesiana* suggests that the angels in their first state were able through their free choice to love God more than themselves naturally because they knew him to be this source of happiness. On this issue of elective love the *Summa Halesiana* follows Philip by using ways of knowing God to distinguish between ways of loving God. It is not clear how this natural elective love of God fits in with the earlier skepticism about the ability of the angels in the first state to love God more than self. Perhaps it is significant that in this discussion of natural love the verb "to love" is in the present tense. It could be that the *Summa Halesiana* distinguishes not between the love for God in a purely natural state and the present love for God, but rather between the present love which is based on natural knowledge and the present love which is based on faith. However, it should be recalled that although William of Auxerre's positions were presented with evident sympathy, they were not clearly applied to the natural elective love for God.

Although the *Summa Halesiana* suggests that the natural love of God follows one's knowledge of him as the source of one's own happiness, it does not conclude from this position the further belief that the love for God as the source of one's own happiness is self-oriented. To address this issue, it invokes the distinction between *ratio ut natura* and *ratio ut ratio*. *Ratio ut natura* loves God as the *summum bonum* on account of the innate knowledge of God. The *Summa Halesiana* associates this love with the doctrine of *natura curva*, since it describes such love as "reflected in itself," a phrase traditionally used to describe nature as self-directed. In contrast, *ratio ut ratio* is able to know God as the *summum bonum* in himself, and not as the *summum bonum* which is also beneficial to the lover. Because the *ratio ut ratio* can love God as the *summum bonum* more than self,[49] there is the possibility of a natural love of God over self which follows from the natural knowledge of him as the *summum bonum*. The emphasis here is on God as the highest good strictly speaking rather than on God's being the agent's own good.

How does the *Summa Halesiana*'s discussion of naturally loving God differ from the preceding ones? The first treatment of natural love in the *Summa Halesiana* concludes by following Philip in distinguishing between love for God based on knowledge obtained through reason and love for God based on the knowledge of faith. However, the *Summa Halesiana* is at first also hesitant to describe the former type of love as natural because it uses the word "natural" not only in opposition to "gratuitous" but also in opposition to "free." The *Summa Halesiana* is close to the position of William of Auxerre in its hesitance to attribute to angels in the first state a natural love for God above all things. But the later discussion concludes that such a natural love can be based on a natural knowledge of God. The tension between these two positions shows how the debate over the ability to love God naturally brings into the open a conflict between widely held theories. First, the belief that humans have a pre-deliberative, natural love of God is challenged by a tendency to identify the natural with a self-interested concupiscence. The love of God should not be so self-interested. How can nature be regarded as both directed to God and as selfish? Another second tension results from the

contrast drawn between nature and grace. The deliberative, rational love of
God is not self-interested; since it is reasonable to love God more than oneself, someone should be able to so love God. But how can this conclusion
stand in the face of the Augustinian tradition that regards grace as necessary
for loving God more than oneself? Later thinkers will strive to reconcile these
conflicting elements.

III. BONAVENTURE

Bonaventure came to Paris during the 1230s, studied with Alexander of
Hales, and became a master in the 1250s. One of the greatest theologians of
any period, his work may also have gained influence as a result of his later role
as minister general of his order. Bonaventure's theology is marked by the precise distinctions he makes between the natural love of God and charity and a
much greater consistency than that of his contemporaries and predecessors.
His theory focuses on the simple position that it is right to love God above
everything, and that God makes his creatures so that they can do what is right.
Bonaventure's clarity may have been obtained to some extent by his setting
aside of problems which other thinkers faced.

In some respects Bonaventure's theory of loving God resembles that of
the *Summa Halesiana*, but it is more concerned than the latter with the deliberative love of God. In addition, Bonaventure makes explicit two points
which had been only tacitly present in the *Summa Halesiana*. First, Bonaventure draws out the different meanings of the word "natural." Bonaventure
accepts the distinction between the natural and the deliberative wills, but recognizes that the term "natural" assumes different aspects when placed in
opposition to the terms "deliberative" and "gratuitous," respectively.[50] *Thelesis*
is the natural will and *boulesis* is the deliberative will. Second, Bonaventure
explicitly identifies *thelesis* with *synderesis*, which is concerned with the morally
worthy (*honestum*), thus creating a clear identification of the natural will with
an appetite for moral goods.

How does *thelesis* refer not only to the morally worthy but also to God?
According to Bonaventure, the natural and deliberative loves can both belong
to the same power (*potentia*). The rational will is moved by its desire for happiness. All men have this desire for happiness, although the desire for happiness is understood in different ways. In contrast, the deliberative will desires
this or that particular good.[51] Both wills have the same object, which is the
good. But the natural will is called *synderesis*, which always desires the good,
whereas the rational will is a voluntary adherence to a particular good. The

division of the will into the rational and voluntary wills is not a real division, since there are not two wills in a person. The term "will" used in these two senses refers not to the essence of a will, but to two powers of one will.[52] Bonaventure's position on the natural love for God follows the *Summa Halesiana* in stating that there is a love for God in the natural will. According to Bonaventure, for all men to desire happiness they must in some sense know what happiness is. Consequently, in some sense by their natural will they love God. However, this love is based on a general knowledge of God (*in generali*) and not on a particular knowledge of God (*in speciali*). The fact that many men identify their happiness with honor or money shows that they do not have a particular knowledge of God as their happiness. They love happiness in general but not in particular.[53] Bonaventure emphasizes that the philosophers were unable to know that God is their happiness in particular, because such knowledge requires grace.[54] Nevertheless, the knowledge that God should be loved is required by the natural law and innate to every human being.[55]

Bonaventure identifies a threefold love for God. First, there is that love for God which exists in the natural will; this is the love for God as the source of happiness. Second, there is the love which belongs to elective will, which desires honor or glory for God. Third, there is the gratuitous love which holds the entire will captive (*captivatur ipsa voluntas tua*) in its allegiance to God. We will see that Bonaventure explicitly uses the term "natural love" to describe not only the love which exists in the natural will, but also to the second type of love, which is deliberative and not dependent on grace.[56]

In keeping with tradition Bonaventure treats the question of whether God can be loved by natural love more than self not in his commentary *In tertium librum sententiarum,* where charity is discussed, but in the *In secundum librum sententiarum,* where he treats angelic love. Bonaventure is unambiguous in his assertion that God was loved more than self by both angels and men in their first natural state:

> It must be said that without a doubt at the time of the establishment of nature it was as easy for a man as for an angel (*tam homo quam Angelus habilis*) to love God for his own sake (*propter se*) and above everything (*super omnia*). And this is evident: for it was impossible for him to be upright (*rectum*) otherwise. For the rectitude of the mind consists radically (*radicaliter*) in love. However, the love cannot be upright (*rectum*) if someone loves something more than God, or equally, or [if he loves] something for its own sake, and God for the sake of something else. Therefore if God made man and the angel upright (*rectum*), it is evident that he gave

to each individual the ability to love him, [namely] God, above everything (*super omnia*) and for his own sake (*propter se*).[57]

It is difficult to translate *rectus* properly, but it should be remembered that in the Bible, Augustine, and Bernard, the *rectus* is the counterpart to the *curvus*. *Rectus* means to be straight and upright in an ethical sense. In this light, Bonaventure's argument is clear. Originally God created man as upright (*rectus*). For a man or an angel to be upright, he must love God more than himself. Therefore the first men and the angels in their original state loved God more than themselves not with the aid of grace, but by natural love.

How does Bonaventure respond to the traditional objection of the *natura curva*? Bonaventure is the first author whom we have discussed who attributes the *natura curva* argument to Bernard by name. Indeed, he shows a respect for Bernard's authority. However, his reply to the *natura curva* objection interprets Bernard's *natura curva* in such a way as to make it compatible with his own view that nature was created *recta*.

Bonaventure offers three alternate but mutually incompatible interpretations of the *natura curva*. First, he suggests that Bernard was thinking of the nature which we have in common with the brute animals. Second, he states that even if Bernard was talking about our rational nature, then only the fallen rational nature is intended. Third, he proposes that the *natura curva* could refer to reason because it desires the good for itself (*bonum sibi*). Bonaventure states that, even allowing for this last interpretation, in the state of nature the angel or man desired no good for himself more than he desired God. Consequently, in the first state he loved God on account of God himself and above everything.[58]

The position that even by this love of concupiscence God was naturally loved more than self distinguishes Bonaventure from his predecessors. We have seen that William of Auxerre, Philip the Chancellor, and the *Summa Halesiana* agree that by the love of concupiscence an object is loved for the sake of the one loving. In contrast, Bonaventure thinks that by the love of concupiscence an object can be loved for its own sake (*propter se*). The key to Bonaventure's position is in his understanding of the two loves. The two loves are distinguished not through definitions but through examples: ". . . something is loved by the love of concupiscence (*dilectio concupiscentiae*), just as someone loves wine, or [by the love of] friendship ([*dilectio*] *amicitiae*) as someone loves a companion."[59] The example of wine shows by parallel how an object can be loved in two ways by the love of friendship. First, the drunkard loves wine on its own account (*propter se*). Or the wine can be loved on account of something else (*propter aliud*), as for the sake of health. Similarly,

Bonaventure quotes Aristotle to show that by the love of friendship we can love a companion for his own sake, when we wish good to that companion. But Aristotle also cites a contrasting sort of friendship, in which the companion is loved on account of something else, such as his usefulness. For example, says Aristotle, when we wish our enemies to become good so that they will not hurt us, then we are loving them on account of their possible usefulness to us and not for their own sakes.[60]

In the first state, the angels loved God for his own sake according to both kinds of love, namely, the love of concupiscence and the love of friendship. They desired him for his own sake by the love of concupiscence because he is the highest good (*summum bonum*) and their maker (*summum reficiens*). They willed good to him for his own sake by the love of friendship because they loved him much more than they would love a friend. Whereas previous thinkers had used the phrases "*propter se*" and "*propter aliud*" to distinguish between the love of friendship and the love of concupiscence, Bonaventure uses them to establish distinct categories within both types of love.[61]

Bonaventure holds that the angels in the first state loved God above everything according to both types of love. What does it mean to love an object above everything? We love a friend above everything if we do not let advantage or disadvantage destroy the friendship. Similarly, we love an object above everything by the love of concupiscence when no inconvenience separates us from our object. An example might be the drunkard who clings to drink despite the many disadvantages that it has caused him. According to Bonaventure, such a love for drink would be a love for it above everything. In the first state, the angels loved God above all things according to both the loves of concupiscence and of friendship, since they would let no advantage or disadvantage cause them to end the friendship. In his *fundamenta,* which are collections of arguments and authorities given before his main response to a question, Bonaventure gives two arguments to support the position that God is loved more than self even by the love of concupiscence. In one, he argues that the motive for loving God is not only that God is the highest good, but also that he is the good for the one loving.[62] In the other, God as the delectable love is compared to the delectable object of taste. Just as taste when it is healthy always loves that which is most delectable, so in the first state did the angels love God most of all.

In general, Bonaventure has a predilection for arguments which show God to be the object of *frui.*[63] Bonaventure's *In primum librum sententiarum,* which comments on Lombard's presentation of the *uti/frui* distinction, gives an argument which recalls the first and last books of Augustine's *Confessiones:* ". . . the soul is born for perceiving the infinite good, which is God, therefore it must rest (*quiescere*) in him alone and enjoy (*frui*) him alone"[64] This emphasis on the soul's being created to enjoy God underlies Bonaventure's reply to William of Auxerre's objection that God cannot be loved above everything naturally because nature would be elevated above itself. Bonaventure states that elevation above oneself can be understood in two ways. First, it can be understood with reference to nature's capability (*posse*), and in this way grace is required for nature to be raised above itself. In a second way, however, Bonaventure states that it is possible and natural for nature to be elevated above its own being (*esse*).[65] He writes: ". . . man is naturally born to be elevated above himself, in contemplating and in loving."[66] Bonaventure stresses that the love of God over self is even the natural end for which humans are made.

More than any thinker we have discussed so far, Bonaventure emphasizes the natural ability to love God more than self by both the love of friendship and the love of concupiscence. If the love and enjoyment of God is natural to man, then why distinguish between the natural love for God and that love which is made possible by grace? Bonaventure cites three differences between natural love and charity. These differences are given in a reply to the objection that since the love of God is the most noble love, then it would seem that the natural love of God would be as noble as grace and even meritorious.

According to this first difference between natural love and the love made possible by grace, the two loves are distinguished by their motion:

> . . . in one way such a motion is of grace, in another way it is of instituted nature. It is of instituted nature from a certain facility and rectitude in respect of the good; but it is of grace, since the affection (*affectus*) is held captive in allegiance to Christ, just as understanding (*intellectus*) is through faith. However then the intellect is captive in allegiance to Christ, when it assents to the first truth against what its reason dictates; and so the affection (*affectus*), when it loves that for which it is naturally inclined to love, by the love of Christ it is prepared to hate . . . And such is the affection (*affectus*), which condemns life and honors and everything desirable, and it loves those things that are hateful and injurious to itself on account of God; and this alone is the affection (*affectus*), which is a slave to God, and which God accepts and remunerates; and this is not by nature, but only by grace.[67]

Bonaventure emphasizes that the gratuitous love for God causes more noble deeds than merely natural love because it works against the lover's own inclinations. The person who has faith believes against the inclination of his own reason. Similarly, the person who has charity sacrifices every good to please God. Gratuitous love is superior to natural love because it entails a captivity to Christ. Bonaventure makes it clear that this first difference is more important than the two differences which follow.[68] The second difference between gratuitous and natural love is based on the knowledge of God. On this issue, Bonaventure repeats the doctrine of Philip the Chancellor and the *Summa Halesiana*, namely, that natural love loves God as the highest good who diffuses good through creation, whereas the love of God as he exists in the Three Persons of the Trinity is gratuitous, because the knowledge of the Trinity is gratuitous.

The third difference between natural love and gratuitous love is based on the motive for the love, which is God. Bonaventure first points out that God is the highest good upon which all other goods causally depend, since they exist only through him. Consequently, someone should love God more than himself. Bonaventure uses the argument to show that God as a creator of goods is an object of natural love. However, God is also good simply because he is good, and not because he is the cause of all goods. A love of God inasmuch as he is good is a gratuitous love, and not available by nature. Bonaventure seems to tie this love of God as he exists in himself to Bernard's belief that in the fourth grade of love, where the Christian loves himself only on account of God (*non diligit se nisi propter Deum*). Although Bonaventure thinks that in the first state God was loved naturally more than self or any other good, he adds that only in the state of grace is God loved not just as the cause of all goods, but as he is good in himself.

Bonaventure follows Philip the Chancellor and the *Summa Halesiana* in arguing that God can be naturally loved more than self, while differing from them by holding that God can be loved more than self by the love of concupiscence. He shares in their assumption that even apart from grace humans are constructed in such a way that they can will the highest good more than their own. Regarding the doubt found in the *Summa Halesiana* about whether the angels were required to love God before self, Bonaventure finds with certainty that the angels were upright (*rectum*) in the first natural state; consequently, they had a well-ordered love of God over self.

IV. ALBERT THE GREAT

Albert the Great's approach to the natural love of god differs from those of the Franciscans perhaps in part on account of his different intellectual formation. He belonged to the Dominican order, which had two chairs at Paris but at the time of Albert's studies did not possess a master of theology to rival Alexander of Hales in importance. Albert's discussion of the natural love of God over self is not so clear or elegant as that of Bonaventure. One reason for this difference may be in the quality of the texts. Albert discusses the question in three works, and none is yet in a critical edition. But serious difficulties rest with Albert's thought itself. Albert wavers between views. He mentions Philip and William by name, which is not customary practice. Moreover, he struggles to fit pagan philosophy into the discussion. Unlike Bonaventure, Albert recognizes different views about the possibility of the natural love of God without consistently locating a preference. It may be that Albert is too aware of the problems to broach any solution.

It is probable that Albert first approached the issue in his *Summa de creaturis (ante* 1246). In this brief discussion, he gives a position resembling Bonaventure's. He introduces the example of the good citizen who prefers the good of the political community to his own private good. This example will play a major role in subsequent debates. In the *In secundum librum sententiarum* (*c.* 1246), Albert gives two opinions which he ascribes to William of Auxerre and Philip the Chancellor, respectively; he leans more heavily towards Philip's position that the natural love of God over self is possible. In contrast, by the time of the writing of the *Summa Theologiae* (*post* 1256) Albert has decided in favor of William's negative view.[69]

From his first treatment of the issue, Albert emphasizes that the motivation of human action is of crucial importance for the question. Question 25 of the *Summa de creaturis* discusses angelic will. In the first article Albert addresses the nature of the will in general. In the second article he applies his discussion of the will's nature to the question of whether the angels from their natural power alone can love God. As we have seen, the discussion of angels' willing in this context and period is usually also a discussion about human willing. Albert's approach to this issue requires distinctions not only about the will but also about the word "natural." Albert adopts the traditional distinctions, but he adds one of his own:

> We will, however, distinguish between different kinds of "natural": for, as far as it pertains to the present discussion, there is a natural in a first way, which depends on natural [powers] alone, that is which depends on things which adhere to and constitute nature. There is then a natural, to which nature can reach by its own work, as reason in deliberating and will in loving. And, again, there is a natural which is brought about through custom, without that grace which makes someone acceptable to God (*gratia gratum faciens*) and thus political virtue is called natural.[70]

The first sense of "natural" corresponds to the non-elective desire for the good. Here Albert seems to have in mind *thelesis*. He argues that in this first sense of the word the angels were not able to love God for his own sake (*per se*) and above everything (*super omnia*).

Albert's discussion of the other senses of "nature" appear in the context of his concern for pagan philosophy. They arise in the *sed contra* arguments to the discussion, which often appeal to authorities or widely held beliefs. Here Albert's arguments contain references to the theory of friendship presented by Cicero and Aristotle, which holds that the best sort of friend is not loved on account of utility or pleasure, but for his goodness. Albert considers the extent to which the will can love and how this is related to those political virtues which can be acquired without grace. According to Albert, the very possibility of the best form of friendship implies that the good can be loved for its own sake, and it is a short move from this position to a belief in the possibility of a natural love of God over self.[71] Another argument introduces the case of the good citizen, which was discussed in Aristotle's treatment of friendship. According to Aristotle, someone who has the political virtue of fortitude disregards the danger to his own life on account of the good.[72] Consequently, a man with fortitude by habit prefers another's good to his own. The assumption here is that the virtuous man loves the political community more than himself. Since an angel has natural powers which are superior to a man and it is assumed that God is a greater good than the political community, it follows that the angel should be able to love God for his own sake and above everything.[73]

In this context, Albert demonstrates the challenge that pagan virtue presents to scholastic thought. If one accepts that virtuous pagans can prefer the common good to their own without grace, then it is difficult to argue that God cannot be similarly loved. Albert resolves this problem by turning to the difference between natural love and charity. The ability to love God naturally without grace is not the same as the ability to acquire the virtue of charity without grace: there is a difference between loving God and accepting that grace which God gives in order to make the creature's love meritorious.[74] Although Albert's position agrees with the positions of Bonaventure, the *Summa Halesiana,* and Philip the Chancellor by distinguishing between that natural knowledge which serves as the basis for natural love and that gratuitous knowledge which serves as the basis for charity, the emphasis on merit separates Albert from his predecessors.

In his *In secundum librum sententiarum,* Albert makes a similar reference to what "we read in the books of the philosophers and the stoics," again bringing political virtue into the discussion. The pagans suffered death rather than be separated from the morally worthy (*honestum*); they naturally were able to undergo death for a good which is inferior to God. Consequently, the angels, who are stronger than men, should be able to naturally love God more than themselves. Clearly Albert is greatly impressed by the example of those who preceded Christianity.[75]

In his response to the *natura curva* objection, Albert's approach is similar to that of the *Summa Halesiana* and Bonaventure. According to Albert, St. Bernard was speaking about *ratio ut natura* which is curved, rather than about deliberative reason, which can love another more than itself. Characteristically Albert adds that many people who do not have the virtue of charity are yet able to love something more than themselves.[76]

By the time of writing the questions on charity which belong to the *In tertium librum sententiarum,* Albert has taken a bleaker view of natural love. The *natura curva* doctrine is almost accepted. In his response to the objection that charity is not a distinct virtue, since there is a natural love for God which follows from the natural knowledge of God, Albert states that even if we know that God should be loved more than ourselves, it does not mean that we have an ability to love God more than ourselves. There are many things which we know and yet are not able to do. Albert does state that there are some who say that there is a natural love for God over self, but he argues that since nature is curved it is difficult to believe in the possibility of such a natural love for God. By the love of concupiscence an object is loved for the sake of the lover.[77] By the love of friendship an object is loved for its own sake (*propter se*), but not more than the self. Albert recognizes a weakness in this position, however, because it fails to take into account the virtuous pagans. He writes:

> However, since we read in the books of the philosophers, that there is so great a love for the morally worthy (*honestum*), that the brave, who do not have charity, even commit themselves to dangers, it is difficult to say that no one loves something above themselves, except from charity.[78]

Albert seems torn between the *natura curva* doctrine and the example of the politically virtuous individuals who did not have charity.

Albert replies to two objections which are based on Aristotle and Cicero. These objections state that since the *summum bonum* and the morally worthy can be loved by nature for their own sake, there is no special virtue of charity.[79] It should be recalled that Albert had previously used the same arguments based on Aristotle and Cicero to establish the existence of a natural love for God over self. In the present discussion, Albert notes that in Book I of the *Nicomachean Ethics* Aristotle discusses human happiness (*felicitas*). However,

Aristotle was unaware of uncreated happiness (*felicitas increata*), which is the *summum bonum.*[80] Albert states that the philosophers did not seek the *summum bonum* for its own sake, but rather the good for man (*bonum homini*), which is the good according to civil life. Albert's position on the philosophers has shifted. Whereas previously Albert had thought that the philosophers provided an argument for the ability to love God above all things, here Albert thinks that this argument has importance only for political life. The natural love for one's own political community can be disinterested to some extent, but the love for the highest good cannot.

It should be noted that Albert has not yet completely abandoned his earlier position. Albert does mention those who say that God is loved naturally for his own sake, but he departs from his previous discussions by listing not two but three uses of the word "*propter,*" namely as denoting an object, an efficient cause, or an end. According to Albert, those who say that God is loved naturally *propter se,* are using "*propter*" to signify the object and the end of the love, and not to denote the efficient cause. The extent to which Albert endorses this view is not clear.[81]

In the *Summa Theologiae,* Albert again discusses the natural love of God in the context of the angelic will, this time approaching the question in terms of the *natura curva*. Indeed, Albert claims to be adopting William of Auxerre's position that according to concupiscence the lover loves himself and the object equally. In the *Summa de creaturis* and the *In secundum librum sententiarum* Albert states that by concupiscence the lover loves himself more than the object, but in the *Summa Theologiae,* Albert identifies his version of William's concupiscence with the *natura curva:* "The love of concupiscence (*dilectio concupiscentiae*) belongs to a nature which is always curved in itself (*curva est in seipsa*); and whatever it loves, it twists back to itself (*retorquet ad seipsum*), that is, to its own private good . . ."[82] He then states that this preference for self is not perverse because nature can love another more than itself only with the help of grace. He accepts William's position: "And this solution pleases me, since it is good."[83]

Whereas Albert had previously thought that the good citizen's love for the morally worthy can be used to support an argument which states that God can be loved naturally more than self, Albert now emphasizes the difference between created goods and the *summum bonum*. Civic virtue loves its good out of natural powers because its good is created. In contrast, the *summum bonum* is uncreated and infinitely elevated above all natural creatures. Previously the argument had been that since the uncreated good is so much greater than created goods, if these created goods can also be loved more than one's self, the uncreated good can be loved more than one's self. Now

Albert argues that whereas nature is able to love created things more than itself even out of its own powers, it is unable to love God in this way, since God is elevated infinitely above nature.[84]

This unusual explanation of why it is impossible to love God over self without the assistance of grace may not be anything more than an *ad hoc* solution to a difficult problem, and it was not accepted by any other major thinker. Nevertheless, it is not hard to see how Albert arrived at it. Albert is convinced that the pagans could love the common good more than themselves. Since there are theological reasons for asserting that pagans do not love God more than themselves, a reason has to be given why they can so love the common good without being able to love God. This reason could be found in the objects of love. God is an infinite good, whereas the common good is not. Although Albert's view is *ad hoc*, it is not entirely implausible. He sacrifices a certain theoretical elegance to take into account the importance of grace.

In this text, Albert relied not only on the example of civic virtue to prove that someone can naturally love another more than one's own self, but also used the example of friendship. In the *Summa Theologiae*, Albert still agrees with Cicero that some friendships are founded not on pleasure or utility, but rather on the morally worthy (*honestum*). However, Albert now thinks that a friend is only loved insofar as one "desires in a friend that which he twists back to himself (*retorquet ad seipsum*)."[85]

In a subsequent reply, Albert makes an interesting comment about Aristotelian friendship which underscores the difference between nature and grace. Aristotle states that in a virtuous friendship the friend is loved for that good which is in a friend. If such were the case, then it seems that friendship is not based on self-love. But Albert rejects the argument by recalling Aristotle's statment that someone wishes his friend to be like himself, and to spend days talking with him. Natural love for a friend makes the friend into another self. In contrast, charity elevates a creature above itself. Albert recalls that according to Bernard, charity involves love for God's good for his own sake and adherence to God in one spirit. Consequently, such a union with God differs from any form of natural love.[86] In the last reply, Albert makes makes another attempt at distinguishing among the different uses of "*propter.*" This time Albert states that "*propter*" refers to the efficient cause, the formal cause, and the final cause. God himself is the efficient, formal, and final cause of a creature's loving him. Albert notes that since nature is curved, it is incapable of being the efficient, formal, or final cause of loving God. Although nature does have an inclination for the good of grace, by itself it does not suffice for loving God.

Albert changes his position on the natural love of God because he recognizes the presence of the potentially conflicting ethical and psychological themes. Both Albert and the *Summa Halesiana* tend to associate nature with concupiscence. At the beginning of his career Albert was more willing to argue explicitly that there can be a love for God which is natural in the sense that it is not assisted by grace. Indeed, without grace pagans were able to love the common good more than their own. But his position on the pagans required Albert to come to terms with the common Christian assumption that grace is necessary for the natural love of God over oneself. In the end, Albert was forced to distinguish between the different goods involved, making it possible for him to argue that even though grace is not necessary for so loving the political good, it is necessary for loving God. Whereas the *Summa Halesiana* discussed these issues only inchoately, Albert brought the problems into the open. This may have been necessitated by his greater attention to the ethics of Aristotle and Cicero. In contrast to Bonaventure, who can seem to sidestep conflicting ideas, Albert tries to resolve them.

The early-thirteenth-century debates about the love of God over self have laid the groundwork for later discussions. First, there is now a distinction to be made between natural love, which is based on the natural knowledge of God, and gratuitous love, which is based on faith. Second, although God is recognized as the final cause of both loves, he is the efficient cause of gratuitous love alone. The distinction between natural and gratuitous love will influence later discussions of pagan, and especially Aristotelian, moral philosophy. We have already seen that Albert's difficulty in understanding how pagans without the aid of grace can love the political community more than themselves. Third, different meanings of the word "nature" have been delineated, allowing it to be opposed both to the "deliberative" and to the "gratuitous," and permitting a distinction between fallen human nature and human nature as it was first instituted by God. Fourth, different kinds of love have been clearly identified. Whereas in previous centuries there seemed to be only one concept for love, William of Auxerre introduced both the distinction between deliberative and non-deliberative love and the further distinction between two types of deliberative love, namely the love of concupiscence (*dilectio concupiscentiae*) and the love of friendship (*dilectio amicitiae*). Although different thinkers apply these distinctions differently to the natural love of God, there is a common concern to distinguish between a self-interested love and a disinterested love.

We are now ready to understand the significance of Thomas Aquinas's treatment of the natural love of God over love of self. Thomas adopts much of the vocabulary and many of the concepts of his predecessors. Like Bona-venture, Thomas asserts that the natural love of God over self is possible. Also, like Bonaventure, Thomas talks about *thelesis* and the natural will as desiring happiness and in some sense God; there is a fundamental non-rational ordering of will to God. But in contrast to Bonaventure, Thomas bases the argument for a natural and deliberative love on inclinations which are not only non-deliberative but even non-rational. Like Albert, Thomas states that a pagan can love the common good more than himself. But Thomas uses this civic love to argue that the natural love of God over self is possible. How does he retain the Augustinian belief that grace is necessary for so loving God? He argues that fallen human nature is so injured that it is insufficient for the natural love of God over self unless it is first healed by grace.

CHAPTER 3

Thomas Aquinas

Thomas's original adaptation of Aristotelianism to the Augustinian ethical framework transforms the discussion of the natural love of God.[1] Although Albert the Great looked to Aristotle's ethics in his own thought, this interest had at most a tangential influence on his own understanding of the natural love of God over self. It is not surprising that Albert held some distance between his Aristotelianism and his discussion of loving God, since the problem of loving God has primarily patristic and biblical roots. At least as the final cause of the universe and the most perfect being, Aristotle's Prime Mover is close enough to the Christian God for believers to identify the two, but the Prime Mover plays a different role in the Aristotelian ethics than does God in Christian ethics. Although Aristotle thinks that our highest activity is the contemplation of the Prime Mover, this activity accords with intellectual rather than moral virtue, and there is no obvious analog for the virtue of charity in his ethical theory. Thomas confronted this problem directly. He was a Dominican student of Albert, but he soon surpassed his teacher. In the 1250s he became a teacher himself in Paris. More successfully than Albert, he incorporated Aristotelian philosophy, and especially ethics, into Christian theology. We saw in the first chapter that Neoplatonism provided a congenial ethical framework to Christians because of its metaphysical understanding of the good. Thomas will now make use of Aristotle's metaphysics and physics to undergird a version of Aristotelian ethics which is largely compatible with the Christian and Neoplatonic framework of his time.

The primary concern of this chapter is to show how Thomas's discussion of naturally loving God turns the debate into one about natural inclination and the common good. Thomas's insight is to see the ethical importance of both Aristotle's physical and metaphysical teleologies. Although Aristotle's *Nicomachean Ethics* is presumably consonant with his natural teleology, no explicit connections are presented in the text. In contrast, Thomas develops an understanding of naturally loving God which is explicitly based on Aristotelian teleology, arguing for a natural inclination in everything to act for the

69

good of the universe and its species more than for its own good. Similarly, although Aristotle describes the Prime Mover as the common good of the universe, he does not develop the ethical implications of this position. But Thomas uses the debate over naturally loving God to draw a parallel between the virtuous agent's love of the political common good and his love of God, who is the common good of the universe.

The issue of the natural love of God entangles us immediately in the multiplicity of conflicting interpretations to be found in the vast Thomistic literature. For example, there is much scholarly disagreement over Thomas's understanding of natural inclination and the common good, and whether they play such a central role in his theory as I claim for them. Moreover, there are sharp disagreements over Thomas's understanding of nature and grace. Some scholars deny the possibility of a natural moral order for Thomas, and some even interpret Thomas as saying that there could be no natural elective love of God over self. Since this last disagreement throws into question whether there is even a natural duty to love God, I shall in the first section show how Thomas develops an argument for the natural elective love of God while at the same time he stresses the importance of grace. It will be made clear that in his later writings Thomas's consistently strong emphasis on the possibility of a natural love of God over self depends on his understanding of the common good and natural inclination. In the second section I shall address the literature on the common good in the context of how and why Thomas uses the priority of the common good as an assumption in the argument for the natural love of God. In the third section, I shall address the disputes over natural inclination and self-interest in order to show how Thomas's argument rests on an Aristotelian eudaimonism which is not self-oriented, but based on a natural inclination to prefer the common good to one's own good.

I. THE NATURAL LOVE OF GOD: PROBLEMS AND TEXTS

Although Thomas's position on loving God varies in his early commentary on Lombard's *Sententiae,* from the late 1260s he settles on one basic argument for showing that if human nature were uninjured by original sin, then there would be a natural ability to love God more than oneself. The later writings all emphasize the natural inclination for the common good. Nevertheless, during the twentieth century serious controversy over the role of this love in Thomas's ethical theory has called into question Thomas's understanding of the relationship between nature and grace. In this first section I shall set out these relevant interpretations and look closely at those texts in which Thomas argues for the possibility of naturally loving God. We will see that this natural love does play a consistent and important role in Thomas's ethics, and underscore the importance of the two themes which will be discussed in the second and third sections of this chapter, namely, natural inclination and the common good.

Much of the contemporary discussion about Thomas's understanding of the supernatural was initiated with the publication of Henri de Lubac's *Surnatural* in the middle of the last century.[2] De Lubac's interpretation has clouded the importance of a possible natural love of God in Thomas's ethical theory. Indeed, in his early work de Lubac even denied that Thomas's discussion of the natural love of God concerns morally relevant elective love. According to de Lubac, Thomas's position on the love of God has been obscured by later commentators who imposed their own understandings of the supernatural on Thomas's texts. De Lubac makes two criticisms which directly threaten my reading of Thomas. First, he argues that traditional interpreters of Thomas misunderstand the relationship between natural love and the act of love.[3] According to him, when Thomas discusses the natural love of God, he is talking about the necessary ordering of the will to God and not about an act of the will. Nature is always necessarily determined. The will by its nature loves God on account of its being ordered to God as its final end. This ordering to God is natural in that it is not elective. By its free choice, the will can love God precisely because its choice is not necessitated by nature. Since explicit acts of love are free, it follows that any such act of loving God must not be natural but rather supernatural. Second, de Lubac argues that the traditional interpretation fails to make a distinction between the natural and supernatural end of humans.[4] When Thomas distinguishes between the natural love for God which is based on the communication of natural goods and the gratuitous love for God which is based on the communication of spiritual gifts, he is not speaking of two different motives for loving God. The natural love for God refers merely to the will's nature, whereas the free love for God loves God as the source of beatitude. God could not be the natural object of free human love. De Lubac argues that such a distinction between God as the supernatural end and as the natural end of humans is an invention of later thinkers. In general, de Lubac holds that the misreading of Thomas results from reading later commentators and not returning to the issues which were faced by Thomas himself.

De Lubac's position has had a great influence on contemporary Thomists. For example, Denis Bradley has recently presented a stronger version of the argument that there is a natural, non-deliberative desire for the beatific vision, and that consequently there can be no natural end for man.[5] Nevertheless, there have been strenuous objections to de Lubac. Jean-Hervé Nicolas has developed perhaps the most insightful alternative to his view.[6] He notes that God is both the natural and supernatural end of man and argues convincingly that the supernatural end is a further determination (*surdétermination*) of the natural end of man, continuous with although not identical to it. This point is important because it illustrates how the two ends can be coordinated while at the same time the natural can be considered apart from the supernatural. Moreover, this distinction is consonant with Thomas's manner of distinguishing between God as the source of both natural and supernatural goods, which shall be discussed below. But recent writers frequently do not take into account the criticisms of Nicolas and others.

With respect to the very possibility of a natural elective love for God, M-R. Gagnebet has refuted de Lubac's position.[7] Gagnebet follows de Lubac's suggestion that in order to interpret Thomas it is better to look to Thomas's contemporaries than to later scholastics. But Gagnebet finds that Thomas's contemporaries do discuss the possibility of an explicit act of the will which loves God over self by strictly natural powers. Although Thomas's contemporaries oppose the "natural" to the "rational," in some contexts they oppose the "natural" to the "gratuitous." De Lubac conflates these two usages. Gagnebet also criticizes de Lubac for ignoring the way in which Thomas uses causality and knowledge to distinguish between the elective natural love of God and charity. The natural love of God comes from the lover's natural powers and is directed by the knowledge of God as the source of the good of nature. In contrast, charity is moved efficiently by God and has as its object the source of undeserved and naturally unknowable beatitude. This distinction between natural love and charity presupposes that both loves are elective.

Gagnebet's criticisms of de Lubac have almost completely disappeared from the scholarly literature. Jorge Laporta has even continued to deny that Thomas discusses a love of God which is natural in the sense that it is elective. He insists that according to Thomas the natural is always determined.[8] One of the problems to be taken up in the third section of this chapter will be to show the relationship between the determined love and the free love of God. Laporta does understand Thomas to hold that a natural beatitude is possible and exists in the case of those souls in Limbo who die without either having sinned and earned hell or having been baptized and made worthy of heaven,[9] but he differs from Gagnebet and the commentators by arguing that this natural beatitude would not satisfy the natural desire to see God.[10] The intricacies of the discussion are beyond the scope of this book, but these positions need to be mentioned because the current of contemporary work has been against them and because I shall argue in the rest of this that Thomas held three positions which much of scholarly literature claims he did not hold: first, that God is not only the supernatural end for humans, but also the natural end as well; second, that there is a natural love for God which results from a natural knowledge of God; and third, that if human nature were unwounded by the Fall, then humans could substantially fulfill the command to love God through their own natural powers. Thomas's adherence to these positions can be seen in his arguments for the natural love of God over self.

Thomas's development can be traced from an earlier to a later group of texts. The early *In quatuor libros sententiarum* (1250s) contains two somewhat different treatments of the natural love of God. In these texts he clearly argues for the natural love of God over self, but he has not yet developed his own approach to the issue. The *In secundum librum sententiarum* primarily discusses the love of the angels, whereas the *In tertium librum sententiarum* discusses human love.[11] In six later texts he gives more or less different versions of the same argument, arguing for the natural love of God over self on the basis that there is in every creature a natural inclination for the good of the whole over its own good. In addition, Thomas compares the inclination of the part to the whole with the good citizen's preference for the common good over his own good. This basic argument is not an incidental aspect of his ethics, but is his consistent and novel treatment of the natural love of God. Perhaps the latest full treatment of the issue is in the *Prima Secundae* (1271) of the *Summa Theologiae,* where Thomas discusses the question, "Whether a human being is able to love God above all things from natural powers alone, without grace?"[12] We will use this text to give a preliminary version of Thomas's argument, referring to the other five to shed light on this text. Two of these other presentations of the argument are found in the *Summa Theologiae* itself. In the *Prima Pars* (1268) Thomas discusses the natural love of the angels, and in the *Secunda Secundae* (1271–1272) Thomas compares the natural love of God with charity.[13] Of the remaining three texts, two minor treatments of the natural love of God above everything are found in the *De perfectione spiritualis vitae* (1269–1270) and in the *Quaestiones disputatae de virtutibus* (1271–1272).[14] The final text is *Quodlibet* I (1269), article 3, which addresses the statement, "It seems that the first man in the state of innocence did not love God above all things and more than his own self."[15] After these different texts have been discussed, a final reconstruction of the argument will be given.[16] This final reconstruction should show that much of the literature on Thomas's understanding of the relationship between nature and grace is mistaken. Moreover, it will show the recurring importance of the common good and natural inclination for Thomas's ethical theory.

a. *In secundum librum sententiarum* (1250s)

The text of Thomas's *In secundum librum sententiarum* asks, "Whether an angel in its natural state loved God more than itself and everything else?"[17] Thomas gives two standard *sed contra* arguments and then sets out his twofold response. First, Thomas appeals to the *frui/uti* distinction to show that if an angel did not love God more than itself then it would make God an object of *uti* and a thing an object of *frui*. Such a love would be perverse and not natural. Consequently, for the angel to avoid such perversity in the orginal state, it would have to have loved God for his own sake.[18] Second, Thomas repeats the traditional argument that the commandment to love God above all things was written in the mind of the angel. Thomas adds that this statement is more true of angels than of human beings. Since it would be sinful to act against the law of nature which is written in one's heart, it follows that in the first state God would be loved above everything. He must be discussing elective love, because otherwise the commandment to love God would be irrelevant. It is clear from these two arguments that Thomas is setting himself squarely in the tradition of those who argue for the natural love of God over self. But what is his unique contribution?

In the body of the text Thomas argues that the distinction between love of concupiscence and love of friendship is misunderstood by those who state that God is not naturally loved above everything.[19] While this view does hold that God is naturally loved by both types of love, it denies that by them he is loved more than the self. Thomas now properly defines the two kinds of love. The love of concupiscence seeks the delectable. Since God is more delectable than an angel's own self, the angel in this sense can naturally love God more than itself. But since God is loved on account of his delectability, the angel loves God because the angel enjoys God. It follows then that the angel loves God for the angel's own sake, and that the angel's love for God is directed back towards itself. In contrast to the love of concupiscence, the love of friendship is a love for the other that is founded on a similitude between the lover and the loved one. Thomas here introduces the Aristotelian notion of friendship, but he does not integrate it with the opposing argument. When he turns from the matter of definition to present the opposing position that the angel naturally loves itself more intensely than it loves God, he drops the notion of similitude, only restating the familiar position that the angel can love God more than itself by the love of friendship because it desires a greater good for God than for itself. The argument is that the angel naturally wishes God to be God, although it wishes only a created good for itself. Nevertheless, the angel more intensely desires its own created good than it desires the divine good.

Two remarks need to be made about Thomas's presentation of the opposing argument. First, he does not seem to be giving a strictly historical presentation of any one argument. Instead, Thomas is indicating that even when the traditional distinctions are used to show that God can in some way be loved more than self, the arguments fail to prove an absolute love of God over self. When Thomas refers to adherents of the opposing position he is referring to a general line of argument. Second, the opposing argument is presented in such a way that it is unsuccessful. In presenting the position Thomas gives his own definition of the love of friendship (*amor amicitiae*) as a type of love which is based on similitude. However, the traditional position under attack argued from the type of good and the object to whom the good is willed.

Thomas thus rejects the opposing position because it overlooks the fact that the angels have a love of friendship for God precisely because God's similitude is resplendent in them according to their natural goods.[20] When someone loves another by the love of friendship, he loves the other person on account of the other's good, and not because of the other's usefulness or propensity to give pleasure. When the angel loved God it loved the source of its good, since the angel would not have any good at all if it did not come from God. Consequently, the angel loved God more than itself by natural powers. Thomas here is talking about the love of friendship, which is an elective love.

This text of the *In secundum librum* is important for two reasons. First, Thomas's use of the Aristotelian notion of friendship shifts the focus to the similitude between the lover and the object loved. Second, Thomas points up the dependence of the lover's own good on God's goodness. These two notions of unity with God and causal dependence on God will carry through to later discussions. Though he has not yet attained the full clarity of his later exposition, Thomas has put his finger on a lacuna in his contemporaries' understanding of love. This text, which is generally neglected in the scholarly literature, is valuable because it shows how Thomas first chooses to depart from his contemporaries.

b. *In tertium librum sententiarum* (1250s)

The text from the *In tertium librum sententiarum* begins, "It seems that God should not be loved above everything out of charity."[21] This discussion focuses on charity, which is a love assisted by grace, rather than on natural love. The importance of this discussion for our purposes is that Thomas's argument for the love of God more than self through charity is based on his belief that there is a natural love for God over self. Thomas here gives the same account of the opposing position that he already presented in the discussion on the natural love of the angels. It should be noted that Thomas does not think that humans and angels ever existed without grace.[22] Nevertheless, the discussion of the natural love of God sheds light on other issues. Here it is used to arrive at a clearer understanding of charity.

Whereas in the earlier discussion of an angel's love Thomas based his refutation on a philosophical understanding of the love of friendship, here in the *In tertium librum* Thomas gives a theological argument based on the principle that charity perfects and elevates nature. If by natural love the self were loved more than God, then charity would stand opposed to natural inclination. Consequently, Thomas describes as more probable (*probabilior*) the position that God is naturally loved more than self.[23]

What is the basis of this natural love of God? In this discussion, Thomas sets out for the first time the first the argument that occurs in all his later treatments of the issue: that by a natural love the part tends more to the conservation of its whole than of its own self (*naturali amore pars plus tendit ad conservationem sui totius quam sui ipsius*).[24] There is a close connection between this principle and Thomas's previous emphasis on the dependence of the angelic good on God. Thomas begins by arguing that someone who loves himself finds his own good where it is more perfect. The part loves the whole more than itself because by itself it is imperfect, since it has its perfection only in the whole. By "perfect" Thomas here does not just mean that the good of the whole is better, but that it is complete. The good of the part is incomplete if it is considered by itself; its good only reaches completion in the context of the whole. Thomas uses two examples to illustrate this point. The first example is that of an animal which exposes its arm to danger for the sake of the head. The arm is endangered because the health of the whole body hangs on the head. The second example is that of individuals who expose themselves to death for the conservation of the community. The individual is a part of that whole which is a political community, and so he endangers his own good for the political community, since this community contains his good more perfectly. This use of the part's inclination for the whole, illustrated by at least one of the examples given, appears in each of Thomas's subsequent treatments of the natural love of God over self.

How does this natural love of the part for the whole apply to the individual's love for God?[25] Thomas argues that our good (*bonum nostrum*) exists more perfectly in God than in ourselves, since God is the perfect and first universal cause of goods, including our own. The good that is in us is caused by God and exists more perfectly in him. It follows from this that a human naturally loves God more than her own self. It is not clear at this point in Thomas's development how the natural love of the part for the whole applies to the case of the natural love of an individual human for God. Is a human being somehow part of God, who is a whole? What is clear is Thomas's conviction that just as the good of the part exists more perfectly in the good of the whole, so does the good of a human exist more perfectly in God than in himself.

c. *Prima Secundae* (1271)

The six later discussions of the natural love of God over self all make explicit use of the argument from the relationship between the part and the whole. Perhaps the clearest presentation of this argument is found in the *Prima Secundae* of the *Summa Theologiae*. It is worth quoting this passage in full:

> . . . but to love God above everything is something connatural to man; and even to any creature whatever, not only to the rational one, but to the irrational and even inanimate one, according to that manner of love which can be appropriate to every single creature. The reason of this is that it is natural for every single thing that it desire and love something, for which it is designed by nature: for "every single thing acts as it is designed by nature" (*sic enim agit unumquodque, prout aptum natum est*), as is said in the Second Book of the *Physics*. And moreover it is manifest that the good of the part is for the sake of the (*propter*) good of the whole. Whence every single particular thing, by its natural appetite or love, loves its own proper good for the sake of the common good of the whole universe, which is God. Whence also Dionysius says, in the book *On the Divine Names,* that "God converts all things to the love of himself." Whence a man in the state of integral nature referred the love of himself and similarly the love of all other things to the love of God, as to an end. And thus he loved God more than himself, and above everything.[26]

Thomas concludes the body of the article by stating that in the state of corrupt nature the will cannot love God above everything unless God heals it by grace.[27] In his earlier writings Thomas does not mention that the corruption of human nature makes it impossible to perform the act of loving God naturally.[28] It may be that his reading of Augustine's anti-Pelagian writings leads

him to change his position on the influence of original sin on human abilities.[29] Nevertheless, throughout his career he does maintain that the love of
self over God is not natural but rather contrary to a natural inclination that is
found in every creature.

Because of its emphasis on the love of the part for the good of the
whole, the argument of the above passage resembles that found in Thomas's
In tertium librum sententiarum. However, this text from the *Prima Secundae* uses
Aristotle and Pseudo-Dionysius to make the argument more explicit. The
Physics of Aristotle explains that an individual object has a natural inclination
towards the good of the whole, while Pseudo-Dionysius characterizes God
as the good of the whole universe. We can reconstruct the argument in the
following way:

(1)   Every single thing loves that according to which it is designed by
      nature. (assumption)
(2)   The good of the part is on account of the good of the whole.
      (assumption)
(3)   The part is designed by nature for the good of the whole. (corollary of 2)
(4)   Every part loves the good of the whole more than its own good. (by 1, 3)
(5)   Every creature is a part of the universe. (implicit assumption)
(6)   Every single thing by natural appetite loves its own good on account of
      the good of the whole universe. (by 4, 5)
(7)   The good of the whole universe is God. (assumption)
(8)   In his integral state a human naturally loves God more than himself.
      (by 6, 7)

The five later arguments all have this basic structure, but each parallel passage
contains the own explanations and additions to the argument. Taken together
these passages individually, clarify the primary argument and permit us to see
the consistency with which Thomas's held his basic positions on natural inclination and the priority of the common good.

d. *Prima Pars* (1268)

In the *Prima Pars* of the *Summa Theologiae,* Thomas discusses "Whether an
angel by natural love loves God more than its own self?"[30] In this article
Thomas gives the same summary of the opposing position that was given in
the *In secundum librum sententiarum.* In contrast to the earlier text, which bases
its argument on the similitude between an angel and God, the *Prima Pars* con-

tains Thomas's earliest formulation of his basic argument for the natural love of God.

There are three major differences between the argument of the *Prima Pars* and the *Prima Secundae*. First, the passage from Aristotle takes a different form. Second, Thomas explicitly invokes the example of the good citizen who risks death for the political community. Third, he describes God as the universal good rather than as the common good.

The first difference is in the formulation of (1), which in the *Prima Pars* is much more explicit. After he describes the position of those who deny a natural love of God over self, Thomas writes:

> The falsity of this opinion is manifestly apparent, if someone were to consider in natural things to what a thing is naturally moved: for the natural inclination in those things which are without reason shows the natural inclination in the will of the intellectual nature. Now each single one of natural things, since this itself, what it is according to nature (*quod secundum naturam hoc ipsum quod est*), belongs to another (*alterius est*), it is more principally and more inclined to that to which it belongs (*in id cuius est*), than [it is inclined] to its own self. And this natural inclination is shown from those things which are moved naturally: since "every single thing, just as it is moved naturally, so it is fit by nature to be moved" (*unumquodque, sicut agitur naturaliter, sic aptum natum est agi*), as is said in the Second Book of the *Physics*.[31]

This version of the argument for a natural inclination towards another has two distinctive features. First, it assumes that by nature everything that exists is part of a greater whole. Second, it states that this inclination can be observed. If a natural object can be naturally moved, then it has a natural inclination for such motion. The same text from Aristotle is quoted here as in the *Prima Secundae,* but the verb *agere* is in the passive voice.

In addition to the more complete treatment of natural inclination, the text of the *Prima Pars* also contains a more detailed explanation of how the part naturally prefers the good of the whole to its own good. Thomas gives the two standard examples which are used by his contemporaries, but he relates them in an original manner. First, Thomas explains that the hand naturally and without deliberation sacrifices itself for the sake of the head.[32] Then Thomas states, "And since reason imitates nature, we find an inclination of this sort in the political virtues: for since it is proper to the virtuous citizen that he exposes himself to peril for the conservation of the whole commonwealth; and if a human being were a natural part of this city, this inclination would be natural to him."[33] Thomas here uses the word "natural" in the sense that the "natural" is opposed to the "rational." In this sense of the word, a natural love lacks deliberation, as when a hand risks itself to protect the head. In contrast, a human being is not a "natural" part of the state because he is a deliberative agent. Nevertheless, since he is a part of that greater whole which is the state, and reason imitates nature, the good citizen deliberately chooses to sacrifice himself for the common good. This passage is important because it shows that although there is a difference between elective love and the love of an irrational creature, if elective love follows nature it will imitate irrational creatures in preferring the good of the whole to its own good. Such love is natural according to that meaning of "natural" which is "not supernatural." In the *sed contra* of the article Thomas mentions that the love of God over self is natural in the sense that this love is commanded by the natural law.

The third interesting feature of this text from the *Prima Pars* is its description of God as the universal good (*bonum universale*). Thomas writes, "Since therefore the universal good is God himself, and under this good are contained indeed the angel and man and every creature, since every creature naturally, according to that which it is (*secundum id quod est*) belongs to God . . ."[34] This passage parallels the earlier statement that a creature belongs to another because of what it is according to its nature (*secundum naturam hoc ipsum quod est*). Here Thomas is showing that the individual not only belongs to a natural whole like a species, but that its good belongs to the universal good, which is God.

e. *Secunda Secundae* (1271–1272)

In the *Secunda Secundae,* the treatment of the natural love of God occurs in the discussion of "Whether a man must love God more than himself out of charity?"[35] To answer this question Thomas draws a distinction between the basis for natural love and the basis for charity. Thomas writes, "I respond by saying that we are able to receive a twofold good from God: namely, the good of nature and the good of grace."[36] He first discusses the natural love of God, which is based on the good of nature. This discussion stresses the continuity between the elective natural love of God and that natural love which is possessed by irrational and inanimate creatures. A man's natural love for God is based on the communication of goods that we have from God. Thomas explicitly compares such love with the natural inclination of inanimate objects like a stone. We know the natural inclination of something by observing the way in which it behaves. A stone has a natural inclination to fall. Similarly, we can see that ". . . whatever part has a principal inclination to the common action for the utility of the whole."[37] In the case of humans, such love should be elective. Thomas here uses the example of the good citizen to show how this natural inclination is related to love for the political community. By exercising virtue, the good citizen acts in accordance with natural inclination. This text differs from that of the *Prima Secundae* in that there is no clear distinction between natural inclination and free choice.

This text of the *Secunda Secundae* also illustrates Thomas's use of the common good to explain the love of God. Since he ultimately wishes to discuss charity, he emphasizes that common good which is part of the friendship that the saints have with God and not that which is founded on the communication of natural goods. He writes, "And therefore from charity a man should love God, who is the common good of all, more than himself: because beatitude is in God as in the common and fundamental principle of all who are able to participate in beatitude."[38]

This text presents God as the source of goodness in two ways. First, God is the source of natural goods. The natural love of God over self is based on this natural communication. But God is also the common good of the saints through that friendship which he shares with them. This point distinguishes Thomas from his contemporaries, who distinguished the natural love of God from charity according to the difference in the causal roles that God plays in the two loves, or by the different types of knowledge upon which the two loves are based. He does not deny that the two differences between natural love and charity exist, but he emphasizes the way in which supernatural beatitude is a common good. In this sense, on account of their friendship with God, God is the common good of the blessed. In this text, Thomas does not discuss God as a natural common good.

f. *De perfectione spiritualis vitae* (1269–1270)

How does Thomas's description of God as the common good relate to his description of God as a whole of which creatures are parts? He gives a more detailed account of the way in which God is the common good in the *De perfectione spiritualis vitae,* where he discusses why someone should love his neighbor on account of (*propter*) God. There are two ways in which many things come together (*convenire*). In the first way there is a natural "coming together" (*convenientia*) when there is a carnal generation, as when parents come together to produce children. The second way of "coming together," which is relevant to the love of God and neighbor, is more like that of a political community, in which the members are brought together under one ruler and his laws. According to Thomas, human beings similarly come together in their relationship towards God. Since all humans tend naturally towards beatitude, they are united in their ordering to God as the highest ruler of all, the source of beatitude, and the legislator of all justice.[39]

This ordering of all humans to God shows why God should be loved more than one's own self. This text uses the familiar example of the hand being sacrificed for the head or heart to emphasize that the part prefers the good of the whole to its own good by a natural instinct (*naturali quodam instinctu*). Thomas then explains how this relation of the part to the whole applies to the natural love for God:

> However, in the aforesaid community in which all men are united in the end of beatitude (*in beatitudinis fine*), each single man is considered as a certain part; however the common good of the whole is God himself, in whom the beatitude of all consists. Therefore thus according to right reason and an instinct of nature, every single person orders himself to God just as a part is ordered to the good of the whole: which certainly is perfected through the charity by which a man loves his own self for God's sake.[40]

This passage is important for two reasons. First, it makes a distinction between the whole and the common good of the whole. In this text, Thomas describes the whole as the community of humans and the common good of this whole as God. Second, God is the common good of the whole because the whole is ordered to God. The passage then concludes with a comparison between self-love and the love of one's neighbor. Since both oneself and one's neighbor are loved on account of God, this ordering to God explains how one's neighbor is loved just as oneself.

g. *Quaestiones disputatae de virtutibus* (1271–1272)

Although the *De perfectione spiritualis vitae* discusses natural inclination, it does not distinguish explicitly between charity and the natural love of God. Is God the common good in any natural way? The short text from the *Quaestiones disputatae de virtutibus* sheds light on this question, identifying two ways in which God is loved above all things. Thomas writes, "In one way, according to which the divine good is the principle and end of all natural being (*totius esse naturalis*); and thus not only rational creatures love God above all things, but also brute animals, and inanimate beings, insofar as they are able to love."[41] In this passage, the ordering of nature towards God has a dual role in that God is not only the natural end of all objects but also the principle which directs all objects. In the state of integral nature a human loved God more than herself because of this ordering from and to God. However, sin has corrupted this ordering and the natural love of God over self is impossible without the help of grace. Thomas's emphasis on the necessity of grace might help to explain why he is often reticent in speaking of God as the natural common good. In the actually created world, with the exception of Limbo, God is never only the natural end of man, but both the natural and the supernatural end. Grace is necessary not only to heal corrupted nature, but to raise it up. Thomas distinguishes between the natural way of loving God and that way "according to which God is the object of beatitude, and according to which by a certain spiritual unity a rational society is produced in relation to God . . ."[42] Whereas according to the first way God is the object of natural love, in the second way God is the object of charity. Although the *De perfectione spiritualis vitae* discusses a natural inclination for God, the focus seems to be on how God orders humans to himself through charity. In the *Quaestiones disputatae de virtutibus,* Thomas distinguishes between God's ordering of rational creatures to himself through charity and God's role in making and directing all creatures to himself through nature. Nevertheless, his position is that humans do not in fact love God more than themselves without grace.

h. *Quodlibet* I (1269)

The hypothetical aspect of Thomas's position on naturally loving God is brought out in *Quodlibet* I, art. 3, which is devoted entirely to the statement, "It seems that the first man in the state of innocence did not love God above everything and more than himself."[43] Thomas first responds to this problem by stating his belief that humans never existed in a purely natural state. According to Thomas, both Basil and Augustine believed that Adam was created in a state of grace. Nevertheless, Thomas writes, "But, since it was possible for God that he could create man with purely natural powers, it is useful to consider the extent to which natural love could extend itself."[44] In this passage he clearly states that it would be possible for humans to exist without grace. The state never existed in fact, but thinking about it is instructive for moral psychology. Around this time the quodlibetal question replaces the commentary on Lombard's *Sentences* as the primary place for discussing the natural love of God. But more importantly, this quodlibetal question of Thomas Aquinas resembles the *Prima Pars* in its emphasis on the role of natural inclination as the basis for even a rational love for God.

The emphasis on natural inclination can be seen in two ways. First, Thomas uses the notion of natural inclination to respond to those who say that God is not naturally loved above everything. He writes, "For natural love is a certain natural inclination imprinted on nature by God; but nothing from God is perverse; therefore it is impossible that some natural inclination or love is perverse . . ."[45] If the first man loved God more than himself, then his love would be perverse. Since the consequence is absurd, it follows that he must have loved God more than himself. This passage resembles that passage where Bonaventure argues that if the angels in the first state did not love God more than themselves, it would follow that God would not have created them *recta,* which is impossible. The important difference from Bonaventure, and from all of Thomas's predecessors, is the emphasis on the natural inclination which God implants in all things in order to direct them to himself.

Second, Thomas employs the notion of natural inclination to explain human choice. In the *Prima Pars,* Thomas uses the word "natural" in opposition to "rational." Since art imitates nature, and the part naturally desires the good of the whole, the good citizen's heroic action is a use of reason to imitate nature. The relationship between virtue and natural inclination is not specified, although in the *Secunda Secundae* Thomas does relate the citizen's self-sacrifice to natural inclination. In *Quodlibet* I, Thomas writes, "Whence according to this natural inclination and according to political virtue the good citizen exposes himself to the danger of death for the common good."[46] This clearly shows that political virtue has its roots in natural inclination. In Thomas's ethics, virtuous action requires that reason fulfills the agent's natural inclination by imitating nature.[47] The example of the hand being sacrificed for the head is not contrasted with rational choice, but it is used to illustrate that natural inclination from which the good citizen's choice has its origin. Although the good citizen's self-sacrifice is a good example of the inclination of the part for the whole, the inclination can be seen much more clearly in the sacrifice of the hand for the sake of the head. Thomas writes, "For natural inclinations can be especially known in those things which are naturally acted upon without rational deliberation, for as each thing is acted upon by nature, so it is designed by nature to be acted upon."[48] The hand is sacrificed for the head because it has a natural inclination to be so moved. This example is given because it illustrates the same natural inclination that underlies the love of rational inclinations for those wholes of which they form a part. Since God is the common good of the universe, each part of the universe loves God more than itself to the extent of its ability.[49] Here it is undeniable that Thomas is not describing God as only a supernatural common good. There could be no such common good for irrational creatures. Here he is referring to God as the natural common good.

i. Many Texts, One Argument

With the exception of the passages from the early *In quatuor libros sententiarum,* two features are common to the different texts that have been discussed. First, the natural love for God is described in terms of the inclination of the part for the good of the whole. Second, this inclination is described as a natural inclination. The texts differ in the presentation of the argument, but we can now reconstruct the argument in a final form. Premisses have been revised and explanations of the premisses have been added:

(1) Every single thing that acts naturally is naturally designed for so being acted upon. (assumption)
   (1.1) This natural fitness is its natural inclination.
   (1.2) This natural inclination is imprinted by God.
   (1.3) This natural inclination is an act of love.
(2) A part's own good is found more perfectly in the good of the whole than in itself. (assumption)
(3) The part is designed by nature for the good of the whole. (corollary of 2)
(4) A part has a natural inclination of love for the good of the whole more than its own good. (by 1, 3)
   (4.1) This natural inclination can be seen in the tendency of the hand to sacrifice itself (or be sacrificed) for the sake of the head.
   (4.2) The example of the good citizen shows how a rational creature loves the common good more than his own good according to this natural inclination (or imitating this natural inclination).
(5) Every creature is a part of the universe. (assumption)
(6) Every single thing naturally loves it own partial good on account of the common good of the whole universe. (by 4, 5)
(7) The common good of the whole universe is God. (assumption)
   (7.1) God is the origin of all creatures.
   (7.2) God is the common end of all creatures.
(8) Every single thing naturally loves God more than itself. (by 6, 7)
   (8.1) As a rational creature, a human being in his integral state loves the common good more than his own according to or imitating this natural inclination.

Some changes have been made to the original formulation. (1) has been modi-fied in order to accommodate the passive voice in which Aristotle's statement is most often expressed. (1.1) identifies this natural fitness with natural incli-nation. (1.2) reflects those passages which state that the natural inclination is imprinted upon a creature by God. (1.3) defines natural inclination in terms of love. (2) has been expanded to show that the incomplete good of the part is present in the more complete good of the whole. (4) has been modified in order to emphasize that the love of the part for the whole is a natural inclina-tion. (4.1) describes the hand's natural aptitude for being exposed to danger as an example of the inclination expressed by (4). (4.2) shows that this natural inclination is present in human choice. (6) has been changed in order to emphasize the importance of the common good. (7.1) and (7.2) are added to describe the different ways in which God is the common good of the uni-verse. Despite these revisions, the basic argument is the same. Throughout his writings, Thomas argues for the possibility of a natural love of God over self which is based on a natural inclination of the part for the whole.

The main difference between the views of Thomas and his contempo-raries is now clear. In Thomas's later position, the basic structure of the argu-ment for the natural love of God above everything rests on the natural inclination for the common good of the universe, which is God. Although Thomas uses the non-rational love possessed by creatures in his argument, he distinguishes between such love and the choice of naturally loving God which could be made by humans. The fact that such love could be freely chosen is underscored by Thomas's insistence that such love is not chosen by us because sin has affected the human ability to love God. The difference between natu-ral love and charity is not that charity is elective whereas natural love is not, but rather that God is the source of goods in different ways. Someone loves God through charity because God is the source of supernatural goods. Such love is based on faith or the supernatural knowledge of God, and presup-poses both healing grace and the elevation of the will through the supernatu-ral virtue of charity. In contrast, someone could love God naturally because God is the source of natural goods. This love is connatural to humans, and the inability to so love God more than self is not characteristic of human nature as such, but rather a result of original sin. Finally, Thomas explicitly considers it possible for God to have created humans without grace. In such a state, humans would be able to prefer God to their own good. A careful analysis of the texts on loving God shows, then, that Thomas consistently and expressly held positions which de Lubac and others say originated only with later theologians. Moreover, such texts show the importance of the com-mon good and natural inclination for Thomas's moral theory.

II. The Common Good

Although the common good has the utmost importance for Thomas's ethical and political theory, there is widespread disagreement dating back to the early history of Thomism over what kind of good it is and how it is to be preferred to the individual good.[50] It is important that we understand this issue, since Thomas's argument for the possibility of the natural love of God over self assumes that God and the good of the political community are both common goods which should be preferred to one's own good.

Two aspects of Thomas's theory should appear unusual to contemporary readers. The first is the belief in a supremacy of the political common good. To the medieval and ancient mind, the common good was not just an aggregate of individual goods, but instead a good which was greater than that of the parts taken together.[51] Moreover, this good did not include only the satisfaction of physical needs, but also the administration of justice, public works, military exercises, and education in virtue. There was no precedent for a bureaucratic or liberal state which claimed to be neutral about the true good for humans. The second unusual aspect of Thomas's theory is his description of God as the common good of the universe. Although this position is familiar from Aristotle, Thomas is original in adapting Aristotle's theory of the Prime Mover to the Neoplatonic understanding of participation and thus integrating it with a Christian view of the universe. To explain Thomas's position, I shall first address contemporary disputes in the scholarly literature. Then I shall look at Thomas's texts on the common good, which have both a Neoplatonic and Aristotelian inspiration.

Most of the secondary literature on the common good has concerned Thomas's understanding of the political common good. There are in general two opposing camps.[52] Some argue that the individual good is not entirely subordinate to the common good, since a citizen is not a natural part of the city.[53] Their opponents argue that such an interpretation lacks a full understanding of the importance and dignity of the common good.[54] Much of the confusion over Thomas's meaning may result from the different contexts in which he discusses the common good. Gregory Froelich even argues that the dispute arose because the term "common good" is an equivocal notion. He is certainly right to note that the phrase has to be interpreted in respect to the context in which it is used.[55]

M. S. Kempshall's book *The Common Good in Late Medieval Political Thought* emphasizes the tension present in Thomas's understanding of the common good. Kempshall writes: " . . . Aquinas is very attentive to the potential practical consequences for the individual human being. Where necessary, he is always careful to draw back from making each human being completely sub-ordinate to the political community."[56] Kempshall cites the text on the natural love of the angels from the *Prima Pars* in this connection, since it is argued there that the good citizen's self-sacrifice would be natural "if he were a natural part of the political community."[57] One problem with Kempshall's view is that he does not take into full account those other passages which consider the citizen's self-sacrifice to be based on natural inclination. I would interpret this passage from the *Prima Pars* as merely stating the difference between being a natural part like a hand and being a part of the political community. In this context, humans sacrifice themselves through deliberation and not through naturally determined action. The contrast here is between "natural" and "rational."

Kempshall discusses the elective natural love for God over self in the context of what he describes as "the four metaphysical principles of good-ness." The first principle is that individuals participate in goodness. The second principle is that God, since he is good, communicates his goodness. The third principle involves hierarchy; God in his goodness orders all things hier-archically to himself. The fourth principle is that the common good is the natural object of the intellect and will. Kempshall stresses that according to Thomas each part of the universe is directed by God towards the perfection of the universe, which is a similitude of God's divine goodness.[58] Although Kempshall is correct to identify all of these principles, he does not address how they work together in an argument to love the common good more than one's own self. Nevertheless, I shall argue here and in the next section that these principles help to reconcile Thomas's apparently conflicting statements about the common good.

The two most interesting attempts to reconcile Thomas's texts have been made by Jacques Maritain and Charles de Koninck. Maritain limits the priority of the political common good by specifying that humans are not just individuals but persons, also.[59] A material individual can be part of a whole, but a spiritual individual, which is a person, is himself a whole. Each material individual is ordered to the good of the universe, but a person is created for God alone. Consequently, although humans are ordered to the common good as parts are to the whole, they are not so ordered by reason of their whole selves. Maritain cites Thomas's statement that "[m]an is not ordained to the body politic according to all that he is and has."[60] Maritain thinks that both communism and totalitarianism regarded humans as material indi-viduals rather than as persons.

Charles de Koninck also distinguishes between totalitarianism or com-munism and a Thomistic preference for the common good, but he does so by arguing that God is truly a common good.[61] Without this recognition of God as the common good of the universe, the state is in danger of regarding itself as the complete end of human life. According to de Koninck, Thomas argues that humans are completely ordered to the political common good only as citizens, whereas they are ordered to the common good of the universe by virtue of their whole selves. On this interpretation, God is a genuine common good. Humans are ordered not to the good of the physical universe but to the beatific vision in heaven. But the possession of God in this beatific vision is a common and not a private good.[62] De Koninck limits the political common good not in terms of the person, but in terms of the vision of God as the most important common good.

De Koninck's emphasis on God as the common good seems the most consistent with Thomas's thought. As we have seen, Thomas argues from the ability to love the common good of a political community to the ability to love the common good of the universe. If God were not a true common good, such an argument would not work. De Koninck's analysis falls short insofar as he outlines the argument, but does not tell us what the position means and why it is important. Moreover, because the beatific vision is supernatural it does not inform us about the natural love of God, which follows upon a natural knowledge of God. In what sense is God naturally the common good not only of the universe but also of human beings?

The "common good" is by definition a good that is not private but instead capable of being shared. A private good can be common according to predication.[63] For example, two humans could share the ownership of a house. But this is not properly a common good, namely one good which can extend to many effects. The common good is the final cause to which many goods can be ordered. The common good of the political community is not diminished when citizens maximize their own virtue. Similarly, the order of the universe is not diminished when a creature becomes more perfect, and one saint does not exhaust God when she contemplates him.

The statement that the good citizen should always prefer the common good to his own private good is repeated throughout Thomas's writings. This view has its roots in Aristotle, the Stoic tradition, St. Augustine, and canon law.[64] In the previous chapter we saw that Albert the Great was puzzled about the ability of the good citizen to love the city more than himself. Thomas bases his position on an analysis of the natural ability of an agent to act for the common good. If the citizen were merely a natural part of the political community, then he would love its good more than himself without reason. However, we have encountered Thomas's notion that human reason imitates the inclination of nature; like the natural part, the good citizen loves the political community more than himself. Moreover, no individual good is good by itself apart from the whole of which it is a part. To make a sharp distinction between an individual good and the common good is to misunderstand the dependence of the individual good on the common good. For example, in the political context a citizen's proper good cannot exist apart from the family or the political community. When the citizen deliberates about what is good for him (*bonum sibi*), he needs to recognize that his own good is the good of a part which is ordered to a greater whole.[65] This love is demonstrated in the desire to preserve the city at the expense of one's own private good. The citizen's reason for preferring the common good to his own good parallels the individual's reason for loving God more than himself.

I will argue here that Thomas's understanding of God both as the whole and as the common good of the universe combines Aristotelian and Neoplatonic elements. To understand the basis for Thomas's synthesis, we must look at both his *In metaphysicam Aristotelis commentaria* and his *In librum de divinis nominibus,* a commentary on the *De divinis nominibus* of the Neoplatonic Christian thinker Pseudo-Dionysius.[66] We will turn first to Aristotle.

In Book XII of the *Metaphysics,* Aristotle states that there is a twofold good of the universe.[67] First, there is the good of order among the parts of the universe. Second, there is the separate good, which is the First Mover. Aristotle compares the universe to an army. First, there is the good of the order of the members of the army. Second, there is the good of the leader of the army, which is separate and greater than the good of order. Thomas explains that the good of the leader is more important because the army exists for the sake of the leader.[68] Similarly, the common good which is the order of the universe exists for the sake of the Prime Mover, who is the separate good of the universe.

Not all creatures have the same order to the common good of the universe. In his commentary on this passage, Thomas discusses at length Aristotle's comparison of the universe to a household.[69] The *paterfamilias* rules the family for its common good. The domestic animals and the slaves participate in this good least of all. The sons participate in the common good more, but only on account of the rule of the father. Each member of the family partakes in the common good by performing his own operation. Similarly, each part of the universe through its natural operation partakes in the common good of the universe.[70] Thomas writes: "Just as someone in the household is inclined by the precept of the *paterfamilias* to something, so in some way a natural thing [is inclined] through its proper nature. And the nature itself of every single thing is a certain inclination put into it by the first mover, ordering it to the destined end."[71] Higher natures partake in this common good more completely; lower natures are directed towards the common good through the higher. Plants are ordered towards animals, and animals are ordered towards humans, who are more directly ordered to the common good.[72] Maritain's distinction between persons and material individuals can perhaps be best understood in this context. Persons are like the sons in the family, who are directly ordered to the common good. Material individuals are like the slaves or domestic animals, since they are ordered to God through persons.

When Thomas uses the superiority of the common good to argue for the possibility of a natural love of God, he has in mind Aristotle's description of God as the separate common good of the universe. Nevertheless, "common good" is a notion which includes the intrinsic order of the universe's parts and also the political common good.[73] Both are wholes which are greater than the goodness of their individual parts. Although it is important to stress the superiority of the common good, the dignity of individual humans should not be overlooked. The political common good is not supreme; it is subordinated to the common good of the universe, which is God. Humans are directly ordered to God. De Koninck correctly notes that *intensive* a human can be better than the intrinsic good of the universe because it is by his own intellect and will that he is an image of God.[74] The universe cannot be such an image because the universe does not have its own intellect and will. Nevertheless, *extensive* even the intrinsic common good of the universe is better than that of the individual, since God created many humans and irrational creatures so that there might be a more perfect imitation of his own perfection. Nevertheless, by being directly ordered to God, humans are a more significant part of the universe's imitation of the divine perfection than are irrational creatures.

It is not clear how the description of God as the separate good of the universe accords with that premise of Thomas's argument which states that God is the whole and humans are parts. It might seem more plausible to consider the intrinsic order of the universe in light of the part/whole relationship, but this intrinsic order is entirely directed to the separate good, which is God. Moreover, Thomas links the part/whole relationship to the separate good through the notion of causality. For Aristotle, the Prime Mover is the final cause of the universe. Thomas combines Aristotle's understanding of God as the final cause of the universe with the Neoplatonic Christian understanding of God as the cause in which all creatures participate.

Thomas's application of the part/whole distinction to creatures and God can be seen in his *In divinis nominibus*. There Thomas makes a distinction between the whole which is from the parts (*ex partibus*) and the whole which

exists before the parts (*ante partes*). The whole from the parts is the easier concept to understand. A house is a whole which is made from various material
parts, e.g., bricks and mortar. The whole before the parts is a more difficult
notion. Thomas states that it is Platonic. The house which exists in the mind
of the builder is a whole which exists before the parts.[75] Thomas states, "And
in this way, the whole universe of things, which is as a whole from parts (*ex
partibus*), preexists just as in the primordial cause in the Deity itself . . ."[76] Both
the universe and God can be described as wholes of which the human being
is a part, but they are different kinds of wholes. The universe is the whole (*ex
partibus*) which has as its parts all created things. In contrast, God is the whole
before the parts (*ante partes*) who as the cause of the universe contains the
parts in himself.

In his discussion of God as good in the *De divinis nominibus* of Pseudo-
Dionysius, Thomas asserts that the basis for the love of God is the relationship to God as to a whole. According to Thomas, the love of concupiscence,
since it loves an accidental good, can be reduced to the love of friendship for
the substantial good which is loved.[77] Since we always love our good (*bonum
nostrum*), there are four different loves which correspond to the four different
meanings of "our good." First, there is the love for one's own self. Second,
there is a love for an equal, which has union with the other as the basis of
love. For example, it is on account of a unity that a relative, a fellow citizen,
or even a member of the same species is loved. Third, there is the love of the
whole for the part as a part of the whole's good. For example, a human being
loves his or her own hand as belonging to him. Fourth, and most important
for our discussion, there is the love of the part for the whole. Thomas
explains, "for the part is not perfected except as in the whole (*nisi in toto*);
whence the part naturally loves the whole, and the part of its own accord
(*sponte*) exposes itself for the preservation of the whole."[78]

This preference of the part for the good of the whole comes from the
way in which the whole contains within itself the perfection of the parts. The
whole possesses completely that perfection which the part possesses only
incompletely. The key point is that the whole is superior to the part on account
of this greater perfection. This superiority explains the basis of the love of
the part for the whole. Thomas writes that in such a case:

> . . . the one loving orders his own good to the loved, just as if the hand
> should love a man, this which itself is, would order towards the whole:
> whence it would be wholly [*totaliter*] placed outside itself, since in no way
> something would be left to itself, but it would order the whole to the

loved object [*amatum*] . . . Therefore one must so love God, that nothing is left to himself that is not ordered to God.[79]

According to Thomas, Pseudo-Dionysius describes this ordering of the self to another as ecstasy.[80] In the *Prima Secundae,* Thomas states that there is a kind of ecstasy where the individual is placed outside of himself (*extra se*) in a way (*quoddammodo*) on account of the extrinsic object of the love of concupiscence. However, ecstasy *simpliciter* takes place when the lover loves another's good through the love of friendship. The extrinsic good is loved for its own sake.[81] The *In librum de divinis nominibus* discusses ecstasy in the context of being totally brought outside of oneself by being totally ordered to God. The hand is not totally ordered to another hand because its perfection is not completely found in the other hand. In contrast, the hand is totally ordered to the whole body. Nor does he who loves his hand completely order himself towards the good of the hand.[82] The relation of the imperfect human to the perfect God as a part to the whole is the reason for the whole ordering of the self to God through love.

Although the language of participation is Neoplatonic, Thomas uses this language in a new metaphysical context.[83] According to Thomas, every creature participates not only in its own act of existence (*actus essendi*) but also in God (*ipsum esse subsistens*). Whereas the participation in the act of existence involves a composition between the essence which participates and the existence which is participated, the participation in God does not involve composition. The creature participates in God through similitude. By becoming more perfect it becomes more like God and its exemplar, which is an idea of God. This exemplar causality in turn is related to God's production of the creature and his ordering the creature to himself.[84] No creature is an isolated individual whose perfection is unconnected to God. God is the formal exemplar cause of every creature, and a creature becomes more perfect by more perfectly resembling God.

The *De divinis nominibus* argues that each part of the universe has its good more perfectly in God, who is the cause of the entire universe. The *Metaphysics* present the universe as ordered to God, its separate final cause. Gregory Stevens argues that the first view depends upon the notion of participation, whereas the second depends upon the notion of causation. He writes that these two realms are ". . . not in opposition, but distinct."[85] Stevens goes no further than this, but we may observe that created beings participate in God because they have been created by him. The participation in God through similitude derives from God's being both the first cause and the last end of the universe. God is not just the creator whose ideas are formal exemplar causes; he is also the extrinsic good of the universe. Thomas states that according to the Platonists God is the good of the universe because he is its cause. Although Stevens may be right to distinguish participation from creation, there exists nonetheless an intimate relation between the two.

God is the whole of the universe *ante partes,* since he contains the universe in himself as a builder contains the house in himself. When God creates through his efficient causality, he gives his creatures a likeness to himself. Although a creature desires its own perfection, this perfection is found more fully in God. Thomas's use of Aristotle's doctrine of the twofold good of the universe is in complete harmony with this schema. First, the order of the universe has its own perfection, which consists in being the similitude of God. Second, the good of the universe is God himself. Considering the part/whole relationship in the context of the natural love of God will help to explain how it is possible for the agent to prefer God to his own good, given that his own good is more perfectly contained in God than in himself.

III. Natural Inclination and Self-Love

The previous section established that for Thomas the common good should be desired more than the individual good. But how is it that humans are in fact able to so love God? The previous arguments showed that the common good is greater than the individual good, but they do not completely explain how someone can conform himself to this order. Indeed, although all scholars admit that for Thomas the goodness of God is greater than that of the individual, they give different explanations of how loving the goodness of God fits into the framework of Aristotelian eudaimonism. Some argue that for Thomas the good is desired for its own sake, whereas others understand him to say that God's good is identical with self-interest. To explore Thomas's position, I shall review the most significant disputes in the literature. Then I shall show that Thomas understands Aristotle to say that each individual has an inclination for the common good which is greater than its inclination for its own good. Furthermore, this teleology informs Thomas's notion of the will,[86] which he understands as possessing a natural inclination to prefer God to its own good and thus to act properly in accordance with this natural inclination.

Pierre Rousselot's *Pour l'histoire du problème de l'amour au môyen age* set the tone for twentieth-century scholarship on the relation between self-love and loving God.[87] According to Rousselot, Thomas's position solves a medieval problem exemplified by the rift between the "physical" and the "ecstatic" theories of love. In the first chapter we discussed Rousselot's description of Hugh as adhering to the physical theory, in which self-love and loving God are identified. According to the ecstatic theory, the love of God is violent, free, and opposed to self-love. The *natura curva* objection would seem to be one component of the ecstatic theory, since it holds that the love of God over self is opposed to the inclination of nature. In contrast, according to the physical theory, the love for God follows natural principles. This theory identifies the love of God with self-love. Rousselot argues that Thomas uses Aristotelian principles to put the physical theory on a sure footing.[88]

According to Rousselot, the "physical" theory of love is based on the Aristotelian dictum, "Those notes of friendship which are for another come from those notes of friendship which are for one's own self" (*Amicabilia quae sunt ad alterum venerunt ex amicabilibus quae sunt ad seipsum*). This dictum can be interpreted in two ways. First, it can be understood to mean that self-love is the sentiment from which all other loves originate; the dictum states no more than that self-love is the occasion for that love which is directed towards another. This interpretation is superficial and to some extent compatible with ecstatic theories of love. The second interpretation of this dictum sees self-love as the reason for any sort of love; altruistic inclinations can thus be reduced to self-love. This interpretation is not easy to reconcile with the notion of genuine love of another person for the sake of the other person's own good, but Rousselot thinks that Thomas's understanding of love can explain how this latter interpretation of Aristotle is reconcilable with the notion of the love of God over one's own self.

Rousselot argues that Thomas's understanding of the natural love of God is rooted in the combination of an Augustinian understanding of the natural desire for God and an Aristotelian understanding of unity as the basis for love. According to Rousselot, Thomas believes that the natural desire for God as the ultimate end of human action shows that God is connatural to the human will. God is the universal good and therefore he is also the proper object of human love. In order for someone to achieve his own proper good, he must love God. Thomas agrees with the axiom that all love has its root in self-love, but he enlarges the notion of self to include an orientation of the self towards God. If a human being's happiness were to be understood only in reference to himself alone, then it would be impossible to love another more than one's own self. However, since the human being's own nature is directed towards God, then his true self-love will involve the love of God over self.[89]

Rousselot uses the notion of the natural desire for God to explain Thomas's understanding of the relationship between the part and the whole in the context of the natural love for God. The human being is not a part of God in the spatial sense of the word "part," but rather participates in God's infinite and separate *esse*. According to Rousselot, this participation makes it possible for someone to be truly one with God; and since unity is the basis for love, this unity makes possible the love of God over self.[90]

The two fundamental aspects of Rousselot's approach are thus the emphasis on the part/whole relationship and the understanding of unity as the basis of love.[91] Although the details of his interpretation are often confusing, the general outline is clear. Subsequent scholarship on the natural love of God over self tends to see Rousselot's approach as mistaken. For example, Étienne Gilson argues not only that Rousselot misunderstands Thomas's doctrine on love, but that he also completely misinterprets the relationship between Thomas and his Cistercian predecessors.[92] According to Gilson, at no point was there a medieval distinction between the "ecstatic" and the "physical" theories of love. Even Cistercian mystics such as Bernard held that the love for God is based on the similitude between the self and God. Consequently, they did not hold to the "ecstatic" view that self-love is violently opposed to the love of God over self.

Gilson's interpretation of Thomas sees a continuity between the Thomistic and Cistercian theories of love. Rousselot and Gilson thus disagree on the very basis of love in the writings of Thomas. Whereas Rousselot argues that love has its basis in unity, Gilson argues that love is based on similitude. Consequently, Gilson thinks that Thomas's use of the relationship between the part and the whole is given too much weight by Rousselot. Gilson writes: "The hand is really and literally part of the body; and in this case it is quite true to say that the relation of the particular to the general good is the relation of a part to the whole. But as soon as we leave this biological example and seek one in the social order, then we can no longer hold to the same formula without risking a flagrant over-simplification."[93] A human being is a part only in the sense that his good is an image of the original good, which is God. Since the love for the image is based on a love for the original, there is a correspondence between self-love and the love of God.

Louis-B. Geiger also thinks that Rousselot's interpretation of Thomas overemphasizes the relationship between the part and the whole.[94] Geiger stresses the ability of the human spirit to choose a good objectively and independent from any self-interest. According to Geiger, Rousselot discusses natural appetite and the human will in a monistic fashion, whereas Thomas makes a sharp distinction between the two.[95] Geiger argues that since the good is the proper object of the will, it follows that the will can love the good for its own sake, without referring the good back to one's own good.[96]

According to Geiger, Rousselot never arrives at a truly disinterested love. Since Rousselot understands love for another as an identification of one's own good with the other's good, it follows that Rousselot cannot truly account for self-sacrifice. If there is no real distinction between another's good and one's own good, then all love is a love of concupiscence. Geiger thinks that Rousselot's understanding is rooted in a misunderstanding of Thomas's view of *natura curva*. Rousselot implies that Thomas accepts the belief that nature always desires its own good, and that Thomas solves the problem of love by redefining the lover's "own good." Geiger argues that in Thomas's view nature does desire its own good, but that human reason can go beyond nature by loving another for the other's own sake. Whereas Gilson rejects Rousselot's reliance on unity as a basis for love, Geiger thinks that Rousselot neglects the intellectual ability to love the good for its own sake.[97]

Jean-Hervé Nicolas also criticizes Rousselot's emphasis on the relationship between the whole and the part,[98] and finds that Geiger neglects the role of natural inclination in Thomas's understanding of love. According to Nicolas, the example of the hand sacrificing itself for the body is not convincing but has value insofar as it points to Thomas's understanding of the universe as an immense whole and nature of which the individuals are parts. Since God is the ultimate and universal good, all creatures are directed towards him. God is the common good not only as the final cause of natural objects, but also as the efficient cause which creates them. Irrational objects are directed to him by natural appetite. Unlike Geiger, Nicolas does not place natural appetite and will in opposition. According to Nicolas, the will's love for God is a voluntary realization of the universal order of all creatures to God. Whereas Geiger distinguishes between the natural inclination for one's own good and the voluntary love for God, Nicolas argues for a metaphysical continuity between the two.[99] Nicolas agrees in part with Rousselot that the love for God over self has its basis in the natural ordering of the self to God. The love for God contains by definition the love for God as the good to which one's own good is ordered.

Avitol Wohlman follows Nicolas both in emphasizing the importance of natural appetite for understanding the natural love for God and in criticizing Rousselot's too close identification of God with the self.[100] Wohlman interprets the Aristotelian principle that love for another has its roots in self-love as a mere psychological fact. Even though self-love might be the psychological origin of the love of God, it is certainly not its ontological foundation. He argues against Geiger's emphasis on the object of love. According to Wohlman, every love must have an underlying natural appetite for one's own good (*bien propre*). This love for one's proper good is not a voluntary self-love (*amour de soi*), but instead an inclination which underlies all the acts of the will. The very notion of disinterested love is false, since every love is a love of one's proper good (*bien propre*). Since the will by nature has an inclination to the final end as the agent's own good, it follows that the act of the will must be directed towards that good.

Wohlman's relatively recent work returns to Rousselot's treatment of the connection between unity with God and loving God, but along with the rest of the French scholarly literature, it neglects Rousselot's treatment of the part/whole relationship. This neglect of Thomas's part/whole argument is also present in the English scholarship. For example, although he does not address Rousselot, David Gallagher argues in a recent article that the part/whole relationship is not basic to Thomas's argument for the natural love of God over self.[101] I shall argue that this literature has criticized the wrong aspect of Rousselot's approach. As Gregory Stevens noted before much of the recent literature was published, Thomas's use of the part/whole argument is indeed central to his argument. In the previous section we examined Thomas's understanding of the part/whole relationship in the context of God as the common good. Now we will examine how it relates to his understanding of the will as directed to the universal good. Every creature has a natural inclination which is more for God than it is for its own good. The will of a rational agent is directed in a pre-elective way to the good for its own sake, and most of all to God. The good agent acts in accordance with this inclination.

Thomas's understanding of eudaimonism is based on his view of the will, and his understanding of the will is based on his view of natural teleology. A creature's natural inclination is not for its own perfection merely as its own perfection. Similarly, humans are ordered to their own perfection, but they should not seek it as their own perfection.[102] Thomas explicitly connects the natural desire for one's own perfection and the natural desire for God for his own sake. The natural appetite for one's own perfection is at the same time an appetite for God himself, since all creatures become perfect by being similitudes of God. Consequently, Thomas's understanding of natural appetite depends upon a doctrine of participation such as he outlines in the *In divinis nominibus* and an understanding of the universe's order such as he describes in the *In metaphysicam Aristotelis commentaria*. The order of the intellectual creature is not to any particular good, but rather to the universal good, that is God, since every particular good is good only by participation. Consequently, participation explains the intimate connection between the individual's own good and God. Thomas writes:

I respond by saying that what is good especially befits God. For something is good as it is desirable. Now, everything desires its perfection. However, the perfection and the form of the effect have some similarity with the agent, since every agent makes that which is similar to itself. Whence the agent itself is desirable, and has the nature of the good (*ratio boni*): for this is that which desired from it, that its likeness be participated. Since therefore God is the first effective cause of all things, it is clear that the nature of the good (*ratio boni*) and desirability befit him. Whence Dionysius, in the book *On the Divine Names,* attributes good to God because he is the efficient cause, saying that God is called good, *as the one from whom all things subsist.*[103]

In this passage Thomas clearly states that the *ratio boni* befits God because he is the good in which other goods participate. For Thomas, the good is convertible with being. The *ratio boni* is participated by creatures insofar as they are all beings which are willed, but their being and goodness are dependent on God.[104] Participation is discussed here in light of God's efficient causality. As was shown in the previous section of this chapter, causality explains participation. Creatures participate in God's goodness because they bear a likeness to God as their efficient cause. This conception of participation influences Thomas's interpretation of Aristotelian teleology.

Unfortunately, Aristotle's influence on Thomas's theory of natural inclination has been passed over in the secondary literature. This lacuna is surprising since, as we saw earlier in this chapter, the first premiss (1) of Thomas's argument for the natural love of God is a direct quotation from Aristotle's *Physics:* "Everything that is naturally acted upon is naturally designed for so being acted upon."[105] Thomas's explanation of this premiss in his *In octo libros physicorum* sheds light on his understanding of natural inclination.[106]

This premiss is taken from Book II of the *Physics,* where it is argued that nature acts for an end. By Thomas's count, Aristotle gives five reasons (*rationes*) for this position. Although all five reasons inform Thomas's understanding of natural inclination, the second and the third are most relevant to his use of natural inclination in the argument for the natural love of God. The second reason has special importance because it indicates how we can know that nature acts for an end that is not just self-preservation. As Thomas explains:

. . . and he says that in whatever things there is some end, and all the things that are prior and all the things that follow are acted on by reason of the end (*causa finis*). Granted this, one can argue as follows: just as something is naturally acted upon, thus is it designed by nature (*aptum natum*) to be acted upon: for this, namely "designed by nature" (*aptum natum*), signifies what I call "naturally" (*naturaliter*). And this proposition is convertible, since just as something is designed by nature (*aptum natum*) to be acted upon, thus it is acted upon: but it is necessary to add this condition, unless something impede (it) . . . But those things which come about (*fiunt*) naturally, so are they acted upon in this way because they are led to an end; therefore they are designed by nature to be acted upon (*apta nata sunt agi*) in such a way that they exist on account of an end (*propter finem*): and this is "nature desires an end," namely that it has a natural aptitude for an end. Whence it is clear that nature acts on account of an end (*propter finem*).[107]

By connecting "designed by nature" with "natural desire," this passage shows how we can know that something has a natural object for an end. If an object is naturally acted upon without an impediment, then it has a fitness for being so acted upon. Since the being acted upon is directed to an end, it follows that the object has a fitness for the end. This fitness can be understood as a natural desire or inclination.

This understanding of natural desire sheds light on Thomas's argument for the natural love of God over self, since it connects something's natural fitness (1) with the observation that a hand has a natural inclination to be acted upon for the sake of the whole body (4.1). If there is no impediment, the hand will be moved to endanger itself in order to protect the head. This natural movement shows that the hand has a natural desire for the preservation of the body over its own preservation. It does not seem to matter whether the verb "to act" is in the active or passive voice. Although Thomas sometimes speaks of the hand's "being exposed," he also describes it as "exposing itself." Similarly, (1) is sometimes quoted in the active voice (*agere* rather than *agi*). The voice does not matter so long as there is a natural movement; that is, a movement without an impediment.

The *In libri physicorum* sets forth a comparison between art and nature in order to shed light on this second reason for holding that nature acts for an end.[108] The movement from the prior to the posterior is similar in both art and nature. For example, if a house were made by nature, the order of its making would be the same as it is when the house is constructed by humans. The builders first construct the foundation, then they make the walls, and only last do they put on the roof. Similarly, when nature produces a plant, it first drives the roots into the earth like a foundation. Second, it raises the trunk high like a wall. The branches on the top are placed in order last. Another similarity is in the practice of medicine. Both a physician and nature act for the end of health when they heal a sick person by cooling and heating. Thomas agrees with Aristotle that there is a similarity between goal-oriented human art and the productions of nature.

The third reason for believing that nature acts for an end explains and complements this discussion of the relationship between nature and art. It explains the similarity between art and nature by focusing on the difference between the examples of healing and of building a house. Healing, unlike the building of houses, is an activity that belongs to both art and nature. As explained in the second reason, when a physician heals, he imitates nature. In general, whenever art and nature perform the same activity, they both move from the prior to the posterior in the same way. Since the action of art and nature in such a case is the same, and we know that art acts for an end, it follows that nature acts for an end as well. By heating the patient, the physician is acting for an end precisely because he is following nature, which acts for the end of health by giving the sick person a fever: "art imitates nature."[109]

This discussion of the relationship between art and nature is important because it sheds light on the relationship between the natural inclination of the hand to be sacrificed for the preservation of the head (4.1) and the decision of the good citizen to protect the common good. In the *Prima Pars,* Thomas explains the application of natural inclination to the example of the good citizen by stating, "reason imitates nature."[110] By (1), the hand's endangering itself for the body shows the natural inclination of the part for the whole. The citizen's choice to endanger himself for the poltitical community is an example of art's imitating nature.

In his mature argument for the natural love of God over self, two facts make it clear that Thomas has in mind precisely this passage from the *Physics*. First, (1) is taken from Aristotle verbatim. Second, the notion that art imitates nature is found in a passage that complements and explains (1). Although in the *Prima Pars* Thomas emphasizes the distinction between reason and nature, in *Quodlibet* I he explains the citizen's love for the city as a natural inclination. In general he alternates between contrasting free action with natural inclination and identifying virtuous action with natural inclination. The citizen's natural inclination is just less easily observed than the inclination of the hand.

It has been shown in the previous chapter that all thirteenth-century discussions of the natural love of God over self have to take into account the *natura curva,* which states that nature desires primarily its own good. This doctrine has authority because of its attribution to Bernard. Thomas's understanding of Aristotle's teleology influences his gradual reinterpretation of the *natura curva.* The *In secundum librum* contains Thomas's first treatment of the issue, in which he rejects the principle. He does not yet base this rejection on a theory of natural inclination.[111] The focus in this early passage is on the good as the proper object of the will. By the time of writing the *Prima Pars,* Thomas clearly reinterprets the *natura curva* to mean that nature has an inclination not only for its own perfection, but even more for the perfection of the whole.[112] Thomas's *Quodlibet* I also describes the twofold inclination of nature, although it uses the term *"natura curva"* only as a description of the first inclination, which is for the creature's own perfection.[113]

The *In secundum librum* discusses the *natura curva* as an objection to the thesis that an angel in its first state naturally loved God more than itself. The objection states the principle in the traditional form: *"natura semper in se curva est."* Thomas here attributes this statement to Bernard. The objection argues that since in the first state an angel could only love God from a natural principle, it follows that this love was ultimately self-directed. Therefore the angel loved himself more than God.[114] Thomas's response to this objection is worth quoting in full:

> To the second it should be said that nature is in itself called curved, because it always loves its good. However, it is not necessary that the intention rest in that, which is its own [good], but in that which is good: For unless it be good for itself in some way, whether according to truth, or according to appearance, it would never love it. However, it does not love on account of (*propter*) this, because it is its own [good]; but because it is good: for the good is *per se* the object of the will.[115]

Thomas responds to the objection by stating that although someone always loves his own good, the intention of the love is the good in itself and not the good as it relates to the one who loves. The reason for this intention rests on the relationship between the good and the will. Since the good is the proper object of the will, it follows that the good is loved simply for its own sake. This early treatment by Thomas of the *natura curva,* like its corresponding argument for the natural love of God over self, does not discuss the natural inclination of the part for the good of the whole. The focus is on the agent's will.

In the *Prima Pars,* Thomas responds to the *natura curva* objection by setting natural inclination in the part/whole context. Thomas writes: ". . . nature is reflected in itself, not only as much as to that which is singular to it, but much more to [that which is] common."[116] Thomas continues that the individual is more inclined to the conservation of its species than to its own good. Furthermore, each creature has more of an inclination to the universal good than to its own species. Thomas has turned *natura curva* objection on its head. Previous arguments for the *natura curva* pointed to the fact that an individual is more inclined to its own nourishment, which is good for itself, than to reproduction, which is for the species; previous writers had thought of natural creatures as isolated individuals. Thomas argues here that such an understanding of natural inclination does not recognize the natural object as part of a species and part of the whole universe. Consequently, when it is said that nature is itself curved, this curvature should be understood as towards the species and the universal good.

Whereas in the *Prima Pars* Thomas interprets the *natura curva* to describe an inclination for the good of the whole, in *Quodlibet* I Thomas retains the traditional understanding of the *natura curva* as an inclination solely for the conservation of the individual. However, Thomas argues that the *natura curva* does not exhaust the meaning of natural inclination. It is worthwhile to reproduce the passage in full:

> To the third objection it is to be said that the natural inclination of a thing is dual (*ad duo*), namely for being moved (*ad moveri*) and for acting (*ad agere*); however that inclination of nature which is for being moved (*ad moveri*) is in itself curved back, just as a flame is moved upwards for its own conservation; but that inclination of nature which is for acting (*ad agere*), is not curved back in on itself: for the flame does not act in order to generate a flame for its own sake (*propter se ipsum*), but for the good of the generated [flame] (*propter bonum generati*), which is its form, and to a greater degree for the common good (*propter bonum commune*), which is the conservation of the species. Whence it is clear that it is not universally true that every natural love is in itself curved back.[117]

This passage argues that *natura curva* is the inclination for the individual's own conservation alone, but the difference between the two passages is more apparent than substantial. Both passages argue that the natural inclination for the conservation of the species and the common or universal good is stronger than the inclination for the preservation of the individual. Whereas in the *Prima Pars* the term "*natura curva*" signifies all these inclinations, in *Quodlibet* I the term signifies only the inclination for the individual's preservation. The passages do not disagree on the underlying natural inclinations.

Thomas's belief that each creature desires the common good of the universe more than its own good is present not only in his commentaries and descriptions of the *natura curva,* but throughout his writings, as a basic part of his worldview. Even in his earliest writings he maintains that natural things have an inclination not only to their own perfection, but to the perfection of the whole.[118] In the *In tertium librum,* while discussing the relationship between knowledge and love, he states, ". . . in all things is found a twofold perfection; one by which it subsists in itself; another by which it is ordered to another . . ."[119] In material objects both perfections are finite. By the first perfection, a material being desires its form, through which it is a member of a species. By the second perfection, each material being is ordered to another. For example, heavy objects have a natural inclination towards the center of the Earth. In the case of immaterial beings their perfection is in some way infinite, since in some way the immaterial being can become all things.[120] The twofold perfection of immaterial beings involves both intellect and will. Through its knowledge, an intellect becomes a similitude of any object it knows, since this object is made present in itself. Through its will, the immaterial being is directed towards the good, which is outside of itself.[121] Irrational animals participate to some extent in the perfection of intellect because they have sense cognition. It is a mistake to see the perfection of either immaterial or material beings as merely the perfection of an individual which is unrelated to the rest of the universe.

The inclination of even irrational creatures towards the good of the whole is emphasized in the *Summa Contra Gentiles.*[122] Thomas points out that although these creatures do not themselves possess intelligence, they are ordered by an intellectual substance to a higher end. In one way, an individual's own good (*bonum suum*) can be understood with respect to its individual perfection. For example, an animal desires food so that it can continue to live. However, an individual's own good is also the good of the species. For example, an animal not only desires to live itself, but it also desires to procreate and feed its offspring. Moreover, the natural inclination of the irrational creature is part of the celestial body's own good, inasmuch as it acts as an equivocal cause. Finally, God's own good is every creature's likeness to him. This likeness comes from its being caused by him. The inclination for the individual's own perfection is directed towards the good of others because each individual is part of a whole. Moreover, as a being is closer to God, its own good will be more clearly connected to a common good. All imperfect beings have a natural appetite for their own good as an individual good, but perfect beings seek the good of the species, and even more perfect beings seek the good of the genus. God, as the most perfect being, acts for the good of the whole universe. Thomas states clearly that an individual's own good cannot be considered by itself, but that it is identified with the end of the natural inclination which is given to it by God.

This discussion sheds some light on the disagreement between Nicolas and Geiger over the relationship between natural inclination and willing the good for its own sake. Nicolas is correct to argue that for Thomas there is a continuity between the two. Nevertheless, Geiger is correct to emphasize that a rational being, since it is more perfect than the irrational, has an even greater ability to seek the good of the universe more than its own good.[123] In the *Prima Pars,* Thomas writes, ". . . all things, in desiring their own perfection, desire God himself, inasmuch as the perfections of all things are certain similitudes of the divine being . . ."[124] Here Thomas states that through knowledge a creature is directed to God. This direction to God occurs in three ways. First, rational creatures are directed to God through intellectual and sense cognition. Second, animals are directed to him through sense cognition. Third, sensible beings are directed to him by a higher intelligence. In this manner the whole universe becomes a similitude of God.[125] This notion of the order of the whole universe to God as a similitude is discussed at length in the *Summa Contra Gentiles*.[126]

It is important to note that for Thomas, although this order comes from God, it is not an extrinsic violation of natural inclination. God orders things to himself through that natural inclination which he gives to them. Thomas writes:

> . . . every inclination of anything, either natural or voluntary, is nothing other than a certain impression by the first mover; just as the inclination of the arrow determined towards the target is nothing other than a certain impression by the archer. Whence everything which acts either naturally or voluntarily, as it were of its own accord (*quasi propria sponte*), attains that to which it is ordered divinely.[127]

The difference between the arrow and the natural creature is important. An archer orders an arrow to its end by violating its natural inclination to move downwards. In contrast, God orders a creature to himself by giving the creature its nature. God does not order creatures in the same way that an archer moves an arrow. Providence orders everything to God not through extrinsic violence but through an intrinsic inclination.[128]

Thomas's understanding of the will's order to the good is based on this understanding of natural inclination. To address this connection, it is necessary to discuss the relationship between natural appetite and the will.[129] How does the human will's love for God relate to this natural ordering to God? We have discussed texts in which Thomas distinguishes between the natural ordering to God and the willed love of God. Nevertheless, there is a continuity between the natural inclination of all creatures and the will's order to God.[130]

Every act or even implicit desire of the will is a love for some real or apparent good. The *In tertium librum* contains a discussion of love which distinguishes between natural and elective loves. Thomas here uses the words *"amor"* and *"dilectio"* to mark one from the other. *Amor* is used to signify the passion of love found in sensitive creatures. In contrast, *dilectio* signifies elective love; Thomas notes that the word *"dilectio"* includes *"electio."* Here he states that although *amor* is sometimes used to describe elective love, *dilectio* never describes a sense appetite.[131] This distinction may be important, but Thomas does not stick to it. We have already seen that he makes a sharper distinction between nature and reason in the *In quatuor libros sententiarum* than in his later writings. The later passages which argue for the natural love of God over self apply *dilectio* to irrational and even inanimate creatures.

Thomas does distinguish at all stages between that love which belongs to sense appetite and elective natural love.[132] In some passages, he uses the term "natural love" to signify sense appetite alone. In the *Prima Pars,* he considers an objection which states that the angels cannot have a natural love (*amor naturalis*) since they are intellectual creatures. He responds by saying that intellectual love (*intellectualis amor*) is distinguished from natural love in the sense that the term "natural love" can be used to mean "natural alone" (*solum naturalis*), as opposed to sensitive or intellectual.[133] Nevertheless, the angels do have a natural love in the wider sense of the term, in which "natural" means "not gratuitous."

Thomas frequently distinguishes between nature and reason. For example, in the *Quaestiones disputatae de virtutibus* he discusses whether virtue is natural. Aristotle is invoked to argue that reason is a principle of operation which can choose opposites, whereas nature is ordered to one end. Consequently, since virtue involves choice, it follows that virtue comes from reason and not nature.[134] This distinction between the will and nature is also present in Thomas's early work *Quaestiones disputatae de veritate* (1256–1259), in which he explains that the human will differs from nature because the will is not determined. Since the intellectual creature is closer to God, it is more clearly a similitude of God's dignity. God is in no way moved, inclined, or directed, but he moves, inclines, and directs all creatures. Since the intellectual creature is closer to God, it moves, inclines, and directs itself much more than other creatures do.[135]

In the *Summa Theologiae,* Thomas emphasizes that although the will can direct itself to this or that particular good, by nature it must always desire beatitude. In one passage Thomas uses this distinction to describe two types of love:

Whence the will naturally tends to its ultimate end: for truly every man naturally wills happiness. And from this natural willing all other willings are caused: since whatever a man wills, he wills on account of the end. Therefore the love of the good that a man naturally wills as the end, is natural love: however, the love derived from this, which is of the good which is loved for the sake of the end, is elective love.[136]

This type of passage could account for de Lubac's misapprehension that every use of "natural love" must be distinguished from "elective love."[137] The problem is that Thomas's terminology is not consistent. The traditional distinction is between the *voluntas ut ratio* and the *voluntas ut natura*. The *voluntas ut natura* is determined and directed solely to happiness, which is knowing God and loving him for his own sake. The *voluntas ut ratio* involves the free choice of particular goods. The *voluntas ut natura* is always directed to God, whereas the *voluntas ut ratio* can choose between different means.[138]

We have now catalogued three different significations of the term "natural love" in Thomas's writings. In the first sense, it is used in opposition to rational or sensitive loves. In the second sense, it is used to signify the natural desire for beatitude as opposed to elective choice. In the third sense, it is used to describe the natural as opposed to the supernatural love for God. In discussions of the natural love of God over self, Thomas argues that this latter, elective love is based on natural inclination.

It is important to recognize that Thomas's belief in the possibility of a natural elective God is based on his position that there is a non-rational love or desire for God. Denis Bradley uses the non-rational desire for God as the universal good to argue that there is a natural desire for God as a supernatural end.[139] Steven Long objects that God is not the universal good.[140] According to Long, there is a division between the universal good and God, who is the subsisting good *per se*. He is correct in his main point, which is that this natural desire for God is not as such a desire for the beatific vision. Nevertheless, Bradley is correct to see that the natural desire for the universal good is a desire for God. The relationship here is similar to the relationship between willing God and willing the *ratio boni*. In one respect, the *ratio boni* is common to all beings. But in another respect, God is the *ratio boni*. Similarly, although a distinction can be made between God and some senses of the universal good, Thomas explicitly connects the desire for God with the desire for the universal good.[141] God can be called the universal good both because of his own being and also because of his final causality. It is in these senses that any desire for the good is an implicit desire for God. Moreover, as Gagnebet

pointed out in his refutation of de Lubac, the originality of Thomas's position lies in his understanding that this implicit desire for God is not self-
directed.[142] For Thomas, deliberate acts of the will should be in accordance
with the natural inclination of the will. There can be a natural deliberative
love of God as the natural end because the *voluntas ut natura* has as its object
the universal good, which is God. In addition, although God is the supernatural end of humans, he is also the natural end, and he could have created
a world in which there would only be one natural end, namely himself as the
source of natural goods.

The connection between the natural elective love of God and the will's
natural inclination can be seen in many of Thomas's writings. In the *Prima
Pars,* Thomas links the angels' love to its natural inclination. Every creature is
moved by the first mover, which is God. An angel's free choice is completely
consistent with the fact that God puts a natural inclination in the angel's will.
Thomas states: "And therefore it is not unfitting, if an angel is acted upon,
inasmuch as the natural inclination is put in it by the author of its nature.
However it is not acted upon in such a way that it does not act, since it has
freedom of the will."[143] Natural inclination is clearly compatible with free
choice. In *Quodlibet* I, Thomas uses the rectitude of natural inclination to
show the falsehood of stating that God cannot be naturally loved more than
self. Thomas writes:

> For natural love is a certain natural inclination put in nature by God;
> nothing [from God] is perverse; therefore it is impossible that some
> natural inclination or love be perverse; however a perverse love is that
> someone might love himself more than God by the love of friendship.
> Therefore such love cannot be natural.[144]

If a human's nature were integral, he would be able to love God more than
himself even out of his own natural powers. This ability to so love God is
based on the natural inclination planted in him by God. It is only because of
the weakness of fallen nature that this purely natural love is now impossible
without grace. The natural inclination of the will towards God shows that the
natural elective love of God is possible.

Pierre Rousselot is correct to emphasize the role of the natural desire for
beatitude when explaining the natural love of God over self. However, he is
mistaken in using Aristotle's dictum that love for another comes from self-
love in order to argue that this natural love of God over self comes from the
identification of God with the self.[145] There are two separate issues here.
First, there is the question of whether love for another is really a form of self-

love. Second, even if it is admitted that another can be loved for his own sake and not on account of oneself, there is still the issue of whether anyone can be loved more than oneself. Even though the friend must be loved less than oneself, Thomas's understanding of the love of friendship shows how a friend can be loved for his own sake.

Thomas argues that there is a twofold love because of the twofold way in which love tends towards something.[146] In the first way, the good is loved as an accident. The object of the love is instrumental, since it is loved for the sake of something else. This love is the love of concupiscence. In the second way of loving, the good is substantial; it is loved for its own sake. This second type of love is the love of friendship. Thomas does not interpret Aristotle's dictum that friendship is based on self-love to mean that a friend is always loved for one's own sake. Since the object of such love would be the friend as an accidental good, such love would be a love of concupiscence.

Thomas interprets Aristotle's dictum in two ways. In the *In secundum librum sententiarum,* Thomas argues that the dictum is true merely in the order of generation. One loves oneself before one loves a friend. However, it does not follow that one loves a friend as a means of loving one's own self.[147] Thomas's own words contradict Rousselot's attempt to give a stronger interpretation to this dictum. In the *Secunda Secundae,* Thomas treats the dictum slightly differently. In this passage he argues that the dictum only refers to a good considered in a particular fashion, and not to the whole good (*secundum rationem totius*).[148] This passage might not rule out Rousselot's strong interpretation of the dictum as applied to relations between humans, but it does preclude Rousselot's use of the dictum to explain the love of God.[149]

The love of friendship intends the good of another for itself, and not for the lover. It might be objected that all love of creatures is for the useful (*commodum*), and so consequently all friendship must be a form of self-love.[150] Thomas replies that although the object of love of friendship might be useful to the lover, this usefulness is not the intent of the love.[151] In another text, Thomas argues that according to the highest form of friendship, the friend would be loved even if it were possible that such love were not beneficial to the lover. A good friend is loved precisely because he is good, and not because he is good for one's own self. Friendship does not twist the love of a friend back to self-love.[152]

Both God and rational creatures can be loved by the love of friendship. In neither case is the object of the love the self. The difference between the two cases is in the ordering of the love. Another human is loved less than oneself, whereas God should be loved more than oneself. It is not that love for a human friend is selfish. Instead, the human is loved as an equal human, whereas God is loved as a superior. Although a human loves his friend for the friend's sake, he does not order all his actions to his friend as the final end. In contrast, a rightly ordered love for God requires the ordering of oneself to God entirely (*totaliter*).[153]

The possibility of loving God over self does not depend just on the ability to love another for the other's sake. The friend is loved for his own sake and yet not loved more than oneself. The key for understanding the love of God over self is the natural ordering of creatures towards God as the universal and common good. God is the universal good because he is the final end of all human desires. The will is not ordered to this or that particular good, but instead to the source of all good. It is again important to recognize that Thomas's moral psychology is firmly rooted in his understanding of teleology and participation. Every particular good is good only by participating in God's goodness. [154]

This ordering of the will to the good is the central issue in the controversy between Rousselot and Geiger on the *ratio diligendi*, which has been one of the staples of the scholarly literature on the natural love of God. Geiger criticizes Rousselot's translation and interpretation of the phrase, "For were I to suppose, which is impossible, that God were not the good of man, there would not be the reason for loving" (*Dato enim, per impossibile, quod Deus non esset hominis bonum, non esset ei ratio diligendi*).[155] Rousselot interprets the phrase to mean that God is lovable because he is man's good. This interpretation rests on Rousselot's belief that in Thomistic moral psychology unity is the fundamental basis for love. Consequently, if God's good were not identical with one's own good, God could not be loved. This interpretation is reflected in Rousselot's translation: "Suppose, dit-il, que Dieu ne fût pas le bien de l'homme, l'homme n'aurait aucune raison d'aimer Dieu."[156]

Geiger argues that this position tells us more about Rousselot than about Thomas Aquinas. According to Geiger, Rousselot translates the second member of the phrase to imply that the statement is about the nature of human love. Geiger notes that the statement occurs in the context of the way in which God is the reason for adhering to the order of love in heaven, where those closer to God are loved more than those farther from God. Consequently, the phrase should be understood to mean that God is the whole reason for man's loving others because he is the whole good. The statement is not about whether one's own good must always be loved, but instead about why God is the reason for loving anything (*ratio diligendi*), which is that he is the whole good of humans. If God were not the whole good, then he would not be the *ratio diligendi*.[157]

The trend in the scholarly literature has been to accept Geiger's criticism of Rousselot's translation and interpretation.[158] Nevertheless, Nicolas points out that Geiger neglects the connection between the *ratio diligendi* and one's own good.[159] We have already seen that good is the *bonum nostrum* according to one meaning of the term. This identification between the reason for loving and one's own good is based on Thomas's notion of participation. God is the *ratio diligendi* because he is the *ratio boni*. This is not to deny that the *ratio boni* is shared by creatures. But God is the *ratio boni* in a special sense, because he is the whole good, whereas all creatures are good only by participating in him.

Much of the disagreement over the role of self-interest in Thomas's ethical theory results from confusion over Thomas's understanding of natural inclination and the will. According to him, every creature naturally desires the good of the whole more than its own good. Even the will has such an implicit desire. This implicit desire explains why it is natural for humans to explicitly prefer the common good to their own. This understanding of natural inclination and its relation to the will lies at the heart of Thomas's argument for the natural love of God over self.

Thomas's argument for the natural love of God over self differs from those of his contemporaries in its emphasis on natural inclination and participation. Thomas's new approach to the distinction between charity and natural love is rooted in his innovative understanding of nature.[160] Thomas's contemporaries generally held a version of the *natura curva* which stated that a creature desires its own perfection more than it desires the perfection of any other creature. The debate among these contemporaries was over whether human reason is similar to nature in its desire for its own perfection or whether it can differ from nature in loving God more than the self. Thomas uses his reading of both Aristotle and Pseudo-Dionysius to argue for a completely different understanding of nature in which each created object is directed not only to its own perfection, but even more to the twofold good of the universe, which is the order among the parts and the ordering of the whole universe to God.

The commandment to love God over self belongs to the natural law because of the natural ordering of the individual to God.[161] Whereas Thomas's contemporaries would distinguish charity from natural love by referring to a difference in the knowledge of God or in God's causal role in the love, Thomas distinguishes between the two loves by referring to the different ways in which God is good. First, God is the good of the universe to which all creatures are naturally directed. The human's elective love of God imitates this natural inclination. Second, God gives grace to humans so that they might share spiritual goods with him through a type of friendship. This sharing of spiritual goods does suppose a supernatural knowledge of God as well as God's gift of charity. In this respect, Thomas agrees with his contemporaries. But Thomas emphasizes that charity is based not only in a different knowledge of God, but even more in a different type of goodness. Natural love is based on the fact that a created object's own perfection is found more fully in the Creator. Charity is based on a greater and undeserved kind of perfection.

Thomas's understanding of the relationship between natural love and charity reflects his general understanding of the relationship between nature and grace. Although Thomas thinks that humans never existed in a purely natural state, he discusses what love would be like in such a state in order to show the extent of man's natural powers. On account of the Fall, even these natural powers have been corrupted. Grace perfects nature; it does not destroy it. God's grace does not just add to human nature, but it heals the defects of fallen nature. Fallen man's inability to love God more than self is not natural, since it contradicts the inclination of nature. Every single created being has an inclination to love God more than self.

Thomas's discussion of the natural love of God over self is based on a complex integration of Christian, Neoplatonic, and Aristotelian elements to form a new metaphysical and ethical system. Thomas interprets Aristotle in such a way that Aristotle's text is surpassed even if it is not contradicted. Although Aristotle himself never discusses the love of God over self, Thomas thinks that an argument for the possibility of such love can be based at least partially on the Aristotelian theories of natural inclination and the priority of the common good. Thomas incorporates Aristotle's eudaimonism into a Christian framework in large part by developing Aristotle's understanding of teleology and the Prime Mover as the separate good of the universe. Although Aristotle focuses on the Prime Mover's final causality, Thomas relates the final causality of God to God's creative causality and to a Neoplatonic understanding of participation. This originality allows Thomas to adopt a version of Aristotelian eudaimonism which is primarily ordered to God. A difficulty for subsequent thinkers is the question of whether his theories are in fact compatible with Aristotle and whether he fails to understand the self-interestedness of Aristotelian ethics. These questions are connected to the worry about whether Aristotle can be taken as a guide for Christian ethics.

CHAPTER 4

The University of Paris in the Late Thirteenth Century

By the middle of the thirteenth century there was considerable tension at the University of Paris over the correct use and interpretation of Aristotle.[1] The members of the Arts Faculty held to a radical Aristotelianism which was influenced in large part by the Muslim commentator Averroes. Many theologians reacted strongly against the Arts Faculty's uncritical attachment to this version of Aristotle. Theologians not only had to worry about how to adapt Aristotle's theories, but also had to choose between interpretations of Aristotle. As the previous chapters have shown, Thomas Aquinas and Albert the Great understood Aristotle's ethical theory as at least compatible with Christian ethics. In general, Albert and Thomas used philosophical arguments against those who interpreted Aristotle's philosophy as inconsistent with the Catholic faith. At the same time, they were not afraid to correct Aristotle and to move beyond the discussion of Aristotle's text.

Our question of whether it is possible to naturally love another more than oneself occasioned an important but somewhat neglected dispute between the Arts Faculty and the theologians. Both Henry of Ghent and Godfrey of Fontaines mention this issue as a point of disagreement between philosophers and theologians. Godfrey states the contrast lucidly at the beginning of his *Quodlibet* 10, q. 6 (1289), "Whether a man from the dictate of reason is able to judge that he must love God more than his own self?"[2] The Aristotelian philosophers, whom Godfrey describes as Peripatetics, follow the light of reason alone, whereas the theologians use both reason and faith. One of the principles of the philosophers is their understanding of the familiar Aristotelian dictum, "The notes of friendship that are for another come from those notes of friendship that are for one's own self." This passage is interpreted by the philosophers to mean that self-love is the cause of all love; therefore it must be stronger than the love of anything else. No one can love another more than one's own self. Godfrey contrasts this position with that of the theologians, who believe that all love comes from friendship with God;

consequently, they think that someone must love God above all things.[3] More-over, in this question Godfrey addresses at length the issue of whether even the contemplative should sacrifice his individual good for the political com-munity, since it is held that his own individual good is more important than the common good. The philosophers seem to exalt their own good of con-templation not only over the good of other individuals, but also over the common good.[4]

Henry shows a similar understanding of the relationship between phi-losophers and theologians in his *Quodlibet* 12, q. 13 (1289/90), in which he asks, "Whether someone not hoping in a future life must according to right reason choose to die for the political community?"[5] Henry emphasizes that there is one truth for both philosophy and theology.[6] Although in this ques-tion Henry does not address the love of God over self, he does address the issue of whether someone must love the community more than himself. The issue becomes especially problematic if the person in question is a con-templative.[7] In what sense is the contemplative's good part of the com-mon good?

All the thinkers addressed in this chapter, beginning with two members of the Arts Faculty, namely, Siger of Brabant and Boethius of Dacia, will be concerned with the relationship between self-love and the moral life. Henry reacts to these two thinkers by agreeing with them about the primacy of self-love for political action while at the same time arguing for the natural love of God over self. Godfrey of Fontaines and Giles of Rome defend the priority of God and the common good, Godfrey primarily through his understanding of moral intention, and Giles with a focus on metaphysics. Both reiterate Thomas's original claim that the natural love for God is indicated by the natu-ral inclination of the part to prefer the good of the whole to its own good. James of Viterbo will criticize Godfrey and Giles by drawing on a self-oriented interpretation of Aristotle and his own version of the *natura curva*. The debate between Godfrey and James on the relationship between moral science and theology sheds light on their different views of human nature and its connec-tion to moral obligation.

I. THE ARTS FACULTY

By this time the University of Paris had fully integrated Aristotle's philosophy into its curriculum, although members of the Arts Faculty held positions on Aristotle which were at the very least in tension with Catholic doctrine. In 1270 and 1277 the Bishop of Paris condemned positions which were held by members of the Arts Faculty, and the later condemnation also touched on positions held or later entertained by Thomas Aquinas, Godfrey of Fontaines, and Giles of Rome. In this period we see that Aristotelianism remained problematic for theologians even after Aristotle had become part of the curriculum and notable theologians such as Thomas and Albert the Great had incorporated his theories into their theologies. The most relevant issue for our discussion is the positions which some members of the Arts Faculty took concerning self-love and contemplation.

Godfrey of Fontaines and, to a lesser extent, Henry of Ghent, attributed to the philosophers the position that the good person loves himself more than he loves anyone else.[8] In question 5 of his *Quaestiones Morales* (1273–1274), Siger of Brabant argues explicitly for this position as the clear reading of Aristotle's understanding of friendship and self-sacrifice.[9] Boethius of Dacia subordinates the moral virtues to the philosophical contemplation of God in particular.[10] His praise of the philosophical life makes it difficult to see why one would sacrifice such a life for the common good. Both Boethius of Dacia and Siger of Brabant emphasize the connection between virtue and one's own good.

In question 5, Siger discusses, "Whether someone is able to love another more than himself?"[11] Before answering in the negative, Siger gives two traditional objections, namely that the more lovable should be loved more, and that the part loves the whole more than itself. In connection with the first objection, Siger presents a new argument which is based on the fact that we should give honor to those who are more worthy of it than ourselves. Consequently, such persons should be loved more than ourselves.

In his response to the question, Siger states that Aristotle's description of friendship in Book IX of the *Nicomachean Ethics* shows that it is impossible for one to love others more than oneself.[12] Like Aristotle, Siger identifies two types of self-love based on the distinction between extrinsic goods, which are used by the sensitive soul, and intrinsic goods, which are intellectual. That self-love which loves extrinsic goods most of all is shameful. In contrast, the love of one's own intrinsic intellectual goods is laudable and good. Siger follows Aristotle in claiming that the good person loves himself most of all and is his own friend, whereas the bad person hates himself, since he loves that which is harmful for himself. There is no discrepancy between the good person's intellect and his will.

Does the good person love another more than himself? Siger again refers to the distinction between intrinsic and extrinsic goods. In a sense it is possible to love another more than oneself if one wishes a greater extrinsic good to another. For example, someone might wish a certain honor to another that is not given to himself. Nevertheless, someone always should desire his own intrinsic goods most of all. This greater love for self is based on the connection between unity and love. Siger writes:

> For to whom is a man more united than to himself? And love seems to be a certain union. For from those notes of friendship which are for another extend those notes of friendship which are for oneself.[13]

Siger interprets Aristotle to say that the difference between the good person and the bad person is that the truly good person loves himself properly and therefore is a friend of himself. Responding to the objection that sometimes the good person wills an honor to a more worthy person, Siger replies that the good person would wish that he himself were worthy of the honor. The extrinsic good of honor should be willed to the more worthy person, but the intrinsic good that makes one worthy should be most of all willed to one's own self.

It is important to emphasize that Siger is not arguing for a radically new interpretation of Aristotle or Christian ethics. In his discussion of charity, Thomas uses the same passage from Book IX of the *Nicomachean Ethics* to argue that love for another comes from self-love, and that the good person loves himself more than the bad person does.[14] Moreover, Thomas follows the Christian tradition in arguing that after God, someone should love himself more than anything else.[15] Although the good person might love his neighbor more than he loves his own body, he must not love the neighbor more than his own soul. Siger departs from Thomas in his understanding of the relationship between the virtuous person and the political community, holding that the good citizen seeks his own good most of all.

When discussing the death of the good citizen for the political community, Siger relies on Book III of the *Nicomachean Ethics*, in which Aristotle states that the good citizen wishes to have one great pleasure for himself for a brief time rather than many small pleasures over a long time, and one great good rather than many small goods.[16] Siger states that the good man is killed for the community on account of this great enjoyment. He does not die because he loves the public good more than his own good, but because he loves most of all his own act of virtue. This understanding of the good citizen's relationship to the common good greatly influenced subsequent discussions, and it seems to have been shared by several Averroistic commentaries on Aristotle's ethics.[17] Siger agrees with Thomas Aquinas that the good person loves himself more than his neighbor, but he disagrees with Thomas by stating that the good person also loves himself more than the common good.

The issue of whether God can be loved more than one's own self does not seem to be addressed by Siger. Nevertheless, because Thomas's argument for the natural love of God over self is based on the understanding of God as the common good of the universe, if Thomas's position on the priority of the common good is rejected, then Thomas's argument for the natural love of God must also be rejected. Siger offers an entirely different view of self-interest in Aristotelian ethics.

The second major position—one that Godfrey and Henry associate with the philosophers—is that the contemplative's good is superior to the common good. Boethius of Dacia argues for this position in the *De Somniis* (1270s) and the *De Summo Bono* (1270s). Aubry of Rheims, another member of the Arts Faculty, seems to have been among the first to have so priviledged philosophical contemplation,[18] but Boethius of Dacia is important both for his lengthier defense of the superiority of contemplation and for his influence on subsequent debates. Because Godfrey of Fontaines made careful summaries of the relevant passages from both works of Boethius of Dacia,[19] it seems likely that he has Boethius of Dacia in mind when he mentions the belief that the contemplative must love the good of his own contemplation more than the common good .

In the *De Somniis,* Boethius of Dacia argues that there are three goods for men which are obtained by three different types of action.[20] First, the natural goods are obtained without cognition, by the natural virtues. The highest natural good is the conservation of the individual and the perfection of the species. Second, moral virtue is directed by prudence to the good of political happiness. Third, the highest good available to humans is the perfect knowledge and enjoyment of truth, achieved in contemplation. The discussion here does not directly address the relationship between moral virtue and contemplation, but since Boethius of Dacia so clearly subordinates political happiness to contemplation, it is difficult to see why a philosopher should risk his life through courage if his own death would end his contemplation.

In the *De Summo Bono,* Boethius of Dacia more clearly emphasizes the importance of philosophical contemplation.[21] Boethius gives three arguments for identifying the highest human good with contemplation. First, contemplation perfects the highest power (*virtus*) in man, which is his intellect and reason. Second, the pleasures of contemplation are the most enjoyable. Third, moral virtues are merely means to contemplation. The implication here is that political happiness is merely a means to contemplation. Only the contemplative avoids sinning because only he lives in accordance with nature. In fact, the philosopher loves God most of all:

And since everyone takes pleasure in that which he loves and takes pleasure most in that which he loves most, and the philosopher has the greatest love for the first principle . . . it follows that the philosopher has the greatest enjoyment in the first principle and in the contemplation of his goodness . . . But this first principle, of which we spoke, is the glorious and sublime God, who is blessed for ages of ages.[22]

Boethius of Dacia is describing a moral theory in which the philosopher is not only the most virtuous person, but in which other people's actions are ordered to the philosopher's contemplation. His statement that the most virtuous person loves God the most seems to have Christian associations, but he clearly specifies that it is the philosopher who so loves God. This view has been described as "intellectual aristocratism."[23] There are obvious problems with attempting to reconcile this view with Christian notions of beatification grace. The proposition that only pholosophers can attain true happiness was included by Etienne Tempier, Bishop of Paris, in his condemnation of 1277, of which Boethius of Dacia was a chief target.[24] At least as interesting is the attempt to reconcile this exaltation of intellectual virtue with Aristotle's own understanding of moral virtue. Critics such as Godfrey addressed the issue from both the Christian theological perspective and the Aristotelian ethical perspective.

From an Aristotelian standpoint, Godfrey thinks it difficult to defend the position that the contemplative should sacrifice the good of the political community. According to Boethius of Dacia, political happiness exists for the sake of contemplation, but contemplation exists for its own sake. Suppose that the political community needs a contemplative to participate in a military activity in which he risks his life. What should the contemplative do? If he undertakes the military action, he forgoes contemplation for a time and risks its cessation in the event of his death. If he does not participate in the action, then his behavior conflicts with what is required of the morally virtuous person. This presents an apparent conflict between moral virtue and self-interest.

The Arts Faculty interprets Aristotle in a way which poses two serious problems for its contemporaries. Not only are its views of self-interest and moral virtue open to challenge, but it is suggested that the philosopher can achieve perfect happiness without grace. Boethius of Dacia associates such happiness with loving God, but is he saying that the philosopher loves God more than himself? He never addresses this issue. Although there exists a tension between the traditional Christian outlook and his own view of happiness, it should not be overstated. Indeed, his description of the philosopher's love for God is to a large extent compatible with that of Thomas.[25] Like Boethius, Thomas thinks that the contemplative loves God, but Thomas distinguishes between the contemplation of the philosophers and the contemplation of the saints. The philosophers' love for God has its roots in the natural knowledge of God, and comes entirely from self-love. Their perfection is a perfection of the operation of knowing. In contrast, the perfection of the saints comes directly from the object of their contemplation, which is God. Boethius of Dacia's position is compatible with Thomas's view to the extent that Boethius of Dacia specifies that he is discussing the highest good as it is possible through natural reason. He does not discuss the contemplation of the saints or deny the importance of grace. Boethius of Dacia, however, completely neglects the importance of the common good. Unlike Thomas, he sees political happiness only as a means to contemplation, and he does not discuss God as the common good.

As Godfrey saw, Boethius of Dacia and Siger of Brabant defend an interpretation of Aristotle's ethics which is not only inconsistent with Thomas's interpretation of Aristotle but also with Christian practice. It might be hasty to describe their position as Averroistic, since at least one "Averroistic" commentary on Aristotle's *Ethics* gives a position which resembles the Thomistic account of the natural inclination for the common good.[26] Moreover, their interpretation of the good citizen's sacrifice is shared to some extent by the Franciscan Eustatius of Arras, who is not an Averroist but argues that the good citizen risks death for the political community only because his good is included in the political community.[27] Nevertheless, Siger and some Averroistic commentaries make the stronger claim that this good citizen intends his own good of virtue rather than the good of the political community. This is the main position that will be attacked by Godfrey, while James of Viterbo and John Duns Scotus will use it in their criticisms of the Thomistic argument for the love of God over self.

II. HENRY OF GHENT

Unlike the other thinkers discussed in this chapter, Henry of Ghent does not base his ethical philosophy primarily upon Aristotle. In his ethical discussions as well in the other branches of his philosophy, Henry is original and eclectic.[28] Henry was a secular master and was consulted by the bishop of Paris during the preparation of the 1277 condemnation. Although his discussion of loving God does take into account Aristotle's discussion of friendship, it resembles the earlier scholastic discussions more than those of his contemporaries. As shall be shown, most other major thinkers were directly concerned with Thomas's argument for the natural love of God over self. Even those who disagreed with Thomas felt it necessary to take his position into account. But whereas Thomas's position on loving God is based on the principle of natural inclination and an interpretation of pagan virtue, Henry takes up the earlier tradition by approaching the problem of Aristotelian friendship and the love of God over self in the context of predeliberative love.

Henry's treatment of loving God over self is best understood as having double roots in a moral psychology with strong early scholastic affinities and a political philosophy which is developed at least partially in response to interpretations of Aristotle that privileged self-interest. In response to the question of whether a citizen should sacrifice himself for the common good, Henry emphasizes that the citizen should prefer his own spiritual good to the common good. Nevertheless, Henry combines a belief in the primacy of self-love in the political order with the position that some sort of natural love of God over self is possible. His argument depends upon his moral psychology, which presupposes that God is the primary object of each person's will. Whereas Thomas argued for the love of God based on an order to the common good, Henry is not explicitly concerned with the common good, but with the individual's order to God. To understand Henry's position on loving God, it is helpful to look first at the role of God in his moral psychology and the role of self-love in his political philosophy.

Henry of Ghent gives God an explanatory role in not only his moral psychology but also his epistemology. Indeed, the two roles are connected.[29] According to Henry, God is the *ratio omnis veri et ratio omnis boni*.[30] Every being is desirable for precisely the same reason that it is knowable, namely, by reason of its relation to God through its nature and semblance (*sub ratione naturae et effigie*). Consequently, God is the first and essential object of both the intellect and the will. Henry is not arguing that everyone who knows or wills explicitly knows or wills God. Rather, he claims that God is the ultimate reason for any being's desirability and intelligibility. By reason of their grade in nature, the will and the intellect are determined not towards themselves, but rather to something outside of themselves and also higher than themselves, which is God.

Henry's most careful discussion of the way in which the will has God as its first object occurs in *Quodlibet* 13, q. 9 (1289–1290), "Whether the first and *per se* object of the will is the good under the nature of the good *simpliciter* or under the nature of suitability?"[31] In his answer to this question Henry expounds in a clear fashion his teaching on the relationship between God, the good, and the will. His method is to distinguish among the different senses of good, to explain how each is the object of desire, and then to show that the good in each of its senses ultimately has God as the source of its desirability. These distinctions allow him to conclude that every act of the will is caused by God as its object. Consequently, he argues that although the philosophers understood that everyone desires happiness, they did not realize that this desire is really for God, and that God's goodness can be desired by the agent for God's own sake.

Henry begins his discussion of how the good is desired by distinguishing between two aspects of the terms "good *simpliciter*" and "suitable good." Under the first aspect, the good *simpliciter* is convertible with being, while the suitable good is the object of any non-rational appetite.[32] Understood in this way, neither of these goods is the first object of the will, since they are the objects of a natural (non-rational) appetite. For example, hunger is present not in the will but rather in the irrational appetite. Under the second aspect, the good *simpliciter* is defined as the "enjoyable good," and the suitable good is taken to be the object of rational appetite. The enjoyable good explains why anything is desirable; it is the *ratio boni*. This object of rational appetite can be desired either as a means ordered to another end or as an end itself. In the first case, the suitable good is a particular good which can be ordered to another, whereas in the second case, the suitable good is understood in a general way as happiness. This recognition of even the suitable good as happiness has important repercussions for Henry's understanding of how God's goodness is willed.

Henry states that the good understood as happiness is God himself.[33] God is not only the suitable good taken in a general way, but also the singular good *simpliciter* who is the source of enjoyment. Moreover, God understood as beatitude is that useful good (*bonum commodum*) which must be desired. God's goodness is desired by humans in all these different ways. At this stage in the discussion it might seem that the desire for the *bonum commodum* differs in kind from the others; it is hard to see how the mere desire for what is advantageous can be the same as a desire for God. But Henry says that even the particular useful good (*bonum commodum*) is desired only because of the resplendence of the good *simpliciter* in it. The advantageous good is dependent upon God. Consequently, God plays a causal role as the first object of the human will in all these different ways. There is no willing of a good which is not in some way a willing of God's goodness. Henry writes, "And this is the good *simpliciter* which is the *per se* and first object of the will, since this is the good which is judged good by the will not according to another [good], but rather any good whatsoever is judged good according to this [good] . . ."[34] Not only is God the suitable good taken in a general sense as providing happiness, but he is also the *bonum simpliciter* by which the suitable good is judged. Henry consistently emphasizes the importance of God's final causality in acts of the will.

Henry's position might seem unusual, but it is not that far from the earlier scholastic discussions of a pre-deliberative love of God. Henry gives this position a complexity which it lacked in the earlier discussions, and he emphasizes the final causality of God and the connection between God and happiness: Whenever a rational agent desires happiness in a general sense he is at the same time desiring God. Henry himself does not think that he is original in this respect, since he invokes Augustine's authority to show that every good is good only because it is a semblance (*effigies*) of that true and pure good which is in God. Henry's originality lies in his using this Augustinian understanding of the desire for God in order to criticize the philosophers' understanding of happiness. He remarks that philosophers are ignorant of the fact that God is the good which causes happiness (*bonum beatificans*).[35] Although philosophers recognized that God is the good *simpliciter* in the first meaning of the term, which considers good as convertible with being, they did not understand that God is the good *simpliciter* in the second sense, which is as the enjoyable good (*bonum fruibile*). According to them, the good is merely the object of the appetite. Such a good is only an advantageous good, which is the suitable good (*bonum conveniens*) generally speaking. The philosophers failed to recognize that such good must be grounded in God, for if God were not the ground (*ratio*) of all good, then he would not be desired for his own sake. The philosophers did not understand that God is the first object of the will.

Henry uses his position on desiring God to criticize the ethical theories of pagan philosophers. Every other thinker discussed in this chapter invokes Aristotle as an authority for ethics, but in his discussion of God as an object of the will Henry makes his own course. He criticizes not only philosophers in general, but Aristotle by name as someone who thought that this good is universal by its predication only to the operations of this life. Aristotle had no understanding of grace or true happiness. According to Henry, Plato much better understood this issue, and Aristotle attacked him unfairly.[36] Henry here follows the commentator Eustratius (not to be confused with Eustatius of Arras, the Franciscan theologian) in thinking that Plato was closer to Christian truth in his understanding of God as the good in which other beings participate. Henry's position is not implausible if we keep in mind the Neoplatonic roots of the Augustinian tradition in which he is working. Henry may make distinctions which were not made previously, but his underlying picture is that of the Christian Neoplatonist.

There are two ways in which Henry's *Quodlibet* 8, q. 9 is important for our discussion of self-interest and loving God. First, in it Henry argues that every rational agent has at least an implicit desire for God, and explains in what way a rational agent loves God. Second, in this question Henry shows his independence from Aristotle's ethical theory. Like Godfrey, Henry thinks it necessary to address the problem of whether the good citizen can prefer the common good to his own. But when Henry discusses why the good citizen chooses death to defend the political community, he passes over Aristotelian remarks and states that an individual should prefer his own spiritual good. Unlike Godfrey, Henry has no desire to defend an interpretation of Aristotle as holding that the good citizen must love more than himself both the political common good and the common good of the universe, which is God.

Henry of Ghent's understanding of the common good is best set forth in *Quodlibet* 9, q. 19 (1286), and *Quodlibet* 12, q. 13 (1288–1289). The latter question discusses at length the problem of whether someone should choose to die for the political community. The former question, "Whether the private good should be procured more than the common?",[37] provides a concise account of Henry's position which is helpful for understanding the lengthier treatment in the later *Quodlibet*.

In *Quodlibet* 9, Henry argues that the answer to the question of whether the common good is to be preferred depends entirely on the good involved. First, the private good is sometimes included in the common good.[38] In such a case one must always primarily procure the common good. The potential conflict arises when the private good is not included in the common good. In such a case, the good in question might be either temporal or spiritual. Moreover, sometimes one good will be more necessary than another. For example, if the community has a great need for a temporal good which would require the sacrifice of a similar individual good, the common good should always be preferred. All things being equal, spiritual goods should be preferred to temporal goods, private or public, but there are exceptions. For example, someone might need bread to survive. If procuring the bread causes a decrease in the spiritual good only of some individuals, then one should obtain the bread. Nevertheless, Henry emphasizes that one should never prefer one's own temporal good if procuring this good is detrimental to the morals or faith of the Church.

Henry is clear that the spiritual common good should be preferred to one's own temporal good. Nevertheless, one's own spiritual good should always be preferred most of all:

Surely if both goods are spiritual, then one's own [good] should be procured, since everyone must will some of the good of grace or of glory
more for himself, on account of its eternal endurance, rather than the
greatest [good] for his neighbor, just as someone must will more himself
alone to be saved and everyone else to be damned, than the converse.[39]

This passage and the question as a whole are important more for what they
omit than for what they contain. Thomas thinks that the good of the individual can be understood only in the context of a common good. Henry
differs in the admission that there can be a real conflict between the individual
spiritual good and the common spiritual good, and he argues that when there
is a conflict, the individual should prefer his own spiritual good.

Why does Henry think the individual's good should be so preferred?
One of Henry's arguments has the following form: (1) by charity someone
loves himself more than another; (2) the common good is the good of another;
(3) therefore, someone should love himself more than the common good.[40]
Although the first statement is a commonplace in the medieval period, the
second statement is not, since it would put the love for the common good on
the same level as the love for one's neighbor. All thirteenth-century thinkers
argue that one must prefer one's own good to that of one's neighbor. Those
who emphasize the priority of the common good, such as Thomas Aquinas,
must argue that the common good takes priority in a way that the individual
does not. We have seen that Thomas bases this priority in a natural inclination. But Henry never argues that an individual should have a natural inclination for the common good. In this discussion he almost seems to be thinking
of the common good as the sum of different neighbors' goods. His discussion
seems to be influenced more by practical considerations than by any philosophical understanding of the way in which the individual good is directed
towards the good of the community.

The other central text for Henry's discussion of the common good is
Quodlibet 12, q. 13, in which Henry justifies the citizen exposing himself to
danger without relying on the superiority of the common good to the individual good.[41] This discussion is not about Christian ethics, but rather about
whether the infidels who do not hope for a future life should die for the political community.[42] Henry stresses that on this issue there is not one answer
for the theologian and another for the philosopher, since it is a matter of right
reason (*recta ratio*).

The question excludes the case of a pagan who chooses such a death for
the sake of honor and glory, since in such an instance he would not be dying
for the sake of justice and innocence, but rather for his own boasting and

cupidity.[43] The citizen must actually choose to die for the sake of preserving the community. Rather than mention the common good, Henry remarks that in certain circumstances the citizen is faced with a choice between death for the community or a shameful act, which is a vice. Since vice should always be avoided, then death cannot be avoided in this case. It is noteworthy that Henry phrases this solution in a negative way. The emphasis is not on the individual's choosing a great good, but rather on the avoidance of sin. After making this point, Henry does mention that the choice of death would be a work of moral virtue, and he paraphrases Aristotle's argument that the choice is more happy because of its greatness. Henry explains, "On account of this therefore to die for the political community is not only better *simpliciter* since [it is better for] many, but it is even better for himself . . ."[44] Henry here seems to accept Siger's interpretation of Aristotle, in which the good citizen primarily intends his own good and not the good of the community. It is likely that Henry has the Arts Faculty in mind, since the response to q. 13 stresses the agreement of the philosophers and theologians.

It is probable that Henry is also concerned about the Arts Faculty's exaltation of philosophical contemplation over political virtue. The citizen who chooses death chooses a morally virtuous action for himself. However, the speculative good is still greater. Why should the philosopher choose to sacrifice his good of contemplation in order to save the political community? Henry is uncertain about the correct interpretation of Aristotle on this point, but he argues that in any event Aristotle may not have had a correct view of speculative happiness.[45] Or, Aristotle would probably recognize that the contemplative would have to choose death in order to avoid the greater evil of culpability. When faced with the choice of the contemplative, Henry falls back on the merely negative justification:

> I say therefore to this that both of them, namely both the happy political man and the happy contemplative, are bound by the law of nature (*ius naturae*), and that they would sin and live shamefully, if they were not to choose it. For it is better to die than to live shamefully.[46]

The contemplative's choice of death is better for him not because it allows him to procure a great good, but rather because it avoids an evil.

In his response to the arguments given at the beginning of the question, Henry returns to the problem of the contemplative. Henry had mentioned arguments for the citizen's exposing himself to death which stated that the public good should be preferred to the private and that the part should sacrifice itself for the preservation of the whole.[47] Although these arguments were traditionally used in support of Henry's position, Henry did not use them in his own argument, claiming that these arguments cannot address the problems presented by the Arts Faculty. For example, someone might interpret Aristotle to say that the contemplative has no duty to die for the city because he is not like a mortal man but more like an immortal god.[48] Since his good is not included in the common good, it seems that he should not die for the political community. Moreover, the analogy of the body does not apply to this case. Particular members do not have their own intellect, and consequently they cannot obtain a good that is separate from the body. In contrast, the contemplative's good could be seen as separate from the good of the political community.

Henry does not insist that this interpretation of Aristotle is wrong, although he emphasizes that philosophers err about the end of human life by thinking it can be found in a happiness short of heaven. Whereas other theologians tend to interpret Aristotle to suit their needs, Henry's concern is with the question itself. For the sake of discussion, he grants that the contemplative's happiness is separate from the public good. But he is not chiefly concerned about happiness, since he shifts the discussion from the acquisition of happiness to the avoidance of guilt. Henry writes, ". . . granted that some private positive good of his not be included in that public good, however his private good is included as if negative, namely by the avoidance of shamefulness and the evil of guilt, as has been said."[49] Every human being has an obligation to the public good. Even a hermit requires society to some extent.[50] Only the blessed in heaven are not bound by the obligation to the common good, presumably because they are no longer in need of human society. This negative inclusion of the contemplative's good in the common good shows how the corporeal analogy can be sustained. If every limb did have reason and judgment, it would choose to die if it suffered a greater evil by not making the choice to die. Similarly, the citizen's good includes the public good to the extent that his own good would be diminished if he did not choose to die for the public good.

Henry is willing to admit the priority of the common good only in the sense that an agent would hurt himself by not sacrificing his life for the common good. Unlike his Aristotelian contemporaries, Henry does not mention the greatness of this last act of virtue. This aspect of Henry's theory stems perhaps from his view that the public good and the private good could possibly be in conflict. For his major contemporaries, such conflict is impossible. Thomas and Godfrey think it impossible to consider one's private good as distinct from the common good. But even assuming that there could be such a conflict, Henry takes the traditional position that right action can never really harm the agent. The good citizen might sacrifice even his life for the political community, but he must not satisfy his greatest good, which is virtue. Henry states that although it is right to choose death for the sake of the political community, it is never right to choose spiritual death by sinning. Death for the political community can be chosen to avoid an evil to oneself, but sinning could never procure good for the agent. Henry both agrees and disagrees with the kind of interpretation which Siger of Brabant gives to Aristotle. Unlike Siger, Henry is hesitant to say that the good citizen chooses a great good for himself by dying. Nevertheless, both Henry and Siger think that the good citizen loves himself more than he loves the political community. On this point they both disagree with Thomas's version of Aristotelianism.

Although Henry exalts the individual's own good, even he does not think that the virtuous person primarily prefers his own good as his own good. He does not follow Siger in thinking that all love for a good is based on a unity with oneself. Henry's similar preference for the individual's own good should not cloud for us his insistence that the virtuous person is disinterestedly concerned with the good of another. Recent writers have focused especially on Henry's theory of friendship, which has its roots both in Aristotle and in the Christian tradition expressed by Richard of St. Victor.[51] Henry argues that there are three degrees of friendship. First, someone loves his own good of virtue. Second, this love for one's own virtue is extended to include a neighbor's virtue. Henry identifies the second stage of friendship with Aristotle's dictum that the notes of friendship come from the friendship for oneself. At this second stage, the friend is loved as another self. Henry quotes Richard of St. Victor's *De trinitate* to emphasize that this second stage is not perfect: "No one is said properly to have charity by his private and own love of himself. Therefore it is necessary that love tend to another so that it is able to be charity."[52] The person who loves a neighbor will wish to have a third person love the good that is between them. According to Henry's reading of Richard, perfect friendship, which is the third and highest level of friendship, is impossible with fewer than three persons. Friendship may begin with the love for one's own virtue, but its perfection is found in the love between at least three persons.

Like his contemporaries, Henry must face the same central question on Aristotelian friendship, namely whether all love for another is a form of self-love. But Henry does not approach the issue from an Aristotelian viewpoint. Unlike many of his contemporaries, he does not allow that anyone should love the common good more than himself. Consequently, he will not invoke the example of virtuous pagans to show how it is possible to subordinate one's own good to a greater good. He is more concerned with the way in which God is desired by the will. His fundamental concern is not so much with Aristotelian moral psychology as with his own version of the common thirteenth-century belief that in every human there is a pre-deliberative love for God.

Although the incorporation of Aristotle's moral psychology does not play a determining role in the development of Henry's own thought, in *Quodlibet* 4, q. 11 (1279–1280), he uses Aristotle's dictum on friendship to open his discussion of whether God can be loved above everything by natural love.[53] The prominent place of this objection in his discussion shows how the debate over naturally loving God has by this time become inseparable from a concern with a self-interested interpretation of Aristotle such as that given by Siger of Brabant. The objection which Henry gives follows the basic pattern of Siger's argument: if the notes of friendship all originate with the self, and the origin is loved most of all, then the self is loved most of all. Henry makes a brief *contra* response to the effect that God is naturally loved most of all because he is the highest being, but he recognizes the insufficiency of such a response. His own approach is to first carefully delineate the kinds of love to show that humans have both a pre-deliberative and a deliberative love of God. Each kind of love is given a separate discussion. His approach to pre-deliberative love is more refined than that of his predecessors and relies heavily on his own moral theology, but its resemblance to that of the *Summa Halesiana* is striking. Henry may or may not have had this *Summa* in mind, but his thought belongs to the same milieu, and his discussion of the deliberative love for God resembles that of William of Auxerre, who emphasizes the need for grace. Henry's discussion does not create a new framework in which to consider such natural love. Nevertheless, his own careful description of the different kinds of love, which is connected to his complex moral psychology, gives him a framework in which to reassert his version of the traditional approach.

Henry states that his discussion on loving God will have five parts.[54] The first four parts make distinctions about love which are then applied in the fifth part to the problem of loving God above all. The first two parts describe what love is and how it is present at different levels in, for instance, non-rational creatures, non-rational appetites, and the will. The third part uses the previously established distinctions to state the difference between natural love and free love, which Henry then examines as in the fourth part both being ways of loving God. In the fifth part Henry returns to the main issue, which is whether it is possible for God to be loved above all by each type of love.

In the first part of the question, Henry defines love (*amor seu dilectio*) as "an inclination or motion towards the good."[55] Here Henry is reasserting the traditional doctrine that everything good is lovable. Unless there is an impediment, the lover will in some way move towards the good. Like Thomas, Henry's notion of love is broad, including even non-rational inclinations. For example, unless it is impeded, a heavy body falls towards the earth. How does this non-rational inclination differ from a human being's love for the good? Henry states that the two loves are similar in that they are inclinations to the good, but different in that one is based on knowledge whereas the other is not. Natural love is without knowledge, but voluntary love requires cognition of the object, and consequently it can be impeded by ignorance. A stone always falls to the ground, but a human loves a good only if he has some knowledge of it. Any sort of loving God falls into this latter category. Such love can be either enjoyment (*frui*) or use (*uti*). Both presuppose knowledge.

Although Henry is not the first to talk about the love of an inanimate object such as a stone, it can be difficult to see the connection between a stone's loving the ground and a human's loving God. They are both inclinations to the good, but is Henry correct to give the same description, love, to both? Henry is not saying in this passage that the stone's love and human love are exactly the same kind of thing. In the *Summa Quaestionum Ordinariarum* Henry emphasizes that the word "love" (*amor*) is equivocal.[56] Sometimes the word "love" refers to a passion, whereas at other times it refers to a habit or act of the will. In the *Quodlibet* under discussion, Henry widens the reference to include even the movement of inanimate objects. Henry's concern here is merely to delineate carefully the different meanings of the word.

In the second section of the *Quodlibet* Henry describes different levels of love,[57] distinguishing not just between the way in which animate and inanimate creatures love, but also identifying the different levels of love that can exist in the same creature. According to Henry, natural love is always a love for what is suitable or good for the lover, and is consequently a self-interested kind of love. This love is common not only to humans and the other animals, but also to things without sense. For example, plants have an insensitive appetite for nourishment, whereas animals have a sensitive desire for food. Henry contrasts this self-directed natural love with that which is exercised through free choice.

In the third section of the *Quodlibet,* Henry further explains the difference between the love expressed through free choice and the love exemplified by a plant's desire for nourishment or an animal's desire for food. He argues that the difference between the two types of love is in the different causes of motion. Natural love does not move itself but requires a mover. Henry quotes Augustine's *Confessions:* "My love is my weight: by it I am carried wherever I am carried."[58] Since such motion is caused by another it is involuntary. The other type of love moves itself and is a free act of the will.[59] Henry quotes from Augustine's *In Psalmum Nonum* to argue that voluntary love is not like a weight (*pondus*) but instead like a foot (*pes*). Love is the foot of the soul, since it can follow the suitable good. Voluntary action presupposes self-motion.

But is the will entirely self-moving? According to Henry, the human will has both a natural inclination which is in common with non-rational creatures and an ability to move itself. In the fourth section of his *Quodlibet,* Henry shows that there are two loves in the will, corresponding to the two species of love, namely, the involuntary and the voluntary.[60] Natural love should be distinguished from voluntary love according to its motion to the good. The distinguishing characteristic makes it possible to distinguish between the two different loves in the will itself. First, there is a love that belongs to the *voluntas ut natura;* this love is intellectual, but it precedes deliberation. In the *Summa,* Henry describes natural love as the "root and origin of free love and of all virtuous habits."[61] Natural love is an inclination towards the good in an indeterminate way, and it must precede the elicited act in time since it is like the weight which inclines the agent towards the good. Deliberative love is able to choose a good only because natural love already is inclined towards the good. Thus, natural love is relevant to the discussion of the natural love of God over self. It might seem odd that Henry discusses the other kinds of love at such length in a question more particularly devoted to the natural love of God over self. Indeed, the details of the discussion might be instances of Henry's prolixity. Nevertheless, they are not entirely irrelevant, since errors about the kinds of love could lead to confusion about the ways in which God might be loved more than self. Moreover, Henry in preparing to argue for a discontinuity between the pre-deliberative love of God over self and such deliberative love, which requires grace.

In the fifth and final section of the *Quodlibet* Henry discusses the natural love of God over self in the context of the different kinds of love, including both natural pre-deliberative love and that deliberative love which is natural in the sense that it does not require grace. He turns first to involuntary love. Although his discussion of involuntary love recalls the treatment given by the *Summa Halesiana,* it is more refined and more clearly holds to an involuntary love of God over self. Moreover, Henry thinks that involuntary love is ordered in the same way that voluntary love should be. Every human being has an involuntary love of God over self. How is such love possible? The answer to this question rests in Henry's distinction between the two types of involuntary love, namely the love of good pleasure (*dilectio beneplacentiae*) and the love of good will (*dilectio benivolentiae*).

According to Henry, each type of love has its own good.[62] It is true that the *voluntas ut natura* is directed only to the good *simpliciter,* but the distinction between the two loves rests on the fact that the good *simpliciter* is twofold.[63] First, there is the good *simpliciter* taken in an absolute sense, and second there is the good *simpliciter* which is good for the one who loves. Both are the same good *simpliciter,* but the first is considered without reference to the one who loves, whereas the second is understood in the context of this relationship. By the love of good pleasure someone loves the good *simpliciter* precisely because it is the good *simpliciter.* In addition, by the love of good will the good *simpliciter* is loved because it is good for the person who loves. What is this good *simpliciter* which is loved by every creature with a will? All intellectual beings love their own being and their own nature with a natural (involuntary) love. Nevertheless, Henry will argue that intellectual beings love God even more by such love. To argue for the existence of this love, Henry relies upon his understanding of the will but also upon his belief that all intellectual creatures know God in some way. Love cannot be separated from the knowledge of what is loved. He quotes Augustine's *De trinitate,* "Nothing is loved unless it is known."[64]

God can be known "in particular" and "in universal" (or, generally).[65] If God is loved as known through the beatific vision, faith, or creatures, then he is not loved in an involuntary way. This knowledge of God "in particular," or as an individual, contrasts with knowledge of God "in universal," as the first object of the intellect. God can be known in three ways "in particular." First, he can be known through his essence directly; only the blessed in heaven have this vision of God. Second, Christians can know God "in particular" through faith. Both the blessed in heaven and Christians on earth know God as a beatifying end. Their knowledge presupposes grace. In contrast with the faith of Christians or the vision of the blessed, the third kind of knowledge of God comes through creatures. These three kinds of knowledge exhaust the ways in which God is known "in particular." The love of God which follows these kinds of knowledge is deliberative. The blessed in heaven and Christians on earth both love the Holy Trinity with a voluntary love. Similarly, the man who knows God through creatures can love God deliberatively. When God is loved deliberately, the natural love is relevant only inasmuch as it is perfected and presupposed by the deliberative love.

It is important to emphasize that in this context Henry conflates the philosophers' knowledge of God through reason with that supernatural knowledge which comes from either faith or the beatific vision.[66] All three kinds of knowledge should lead to a voluntary love of God, but Henry is not implying that all permit an equal love and knowledge of God. The philosophers have the general knowledge of God whereas faith and the beatific vision provide a determinate knowledge of God.[67]

The knowledge of the philosophers can be viewed as particular and general at once: although God "in particular" can be known through his creatures, such knowledge is only general as compared to that knowledge which is possessed by Christians and the blessed in heaven. In the *Summa,* Henry argues that although the philosopher's knowledge is particular compared to the knowledge of God common to everyone, it is not particular compared to knowledge through faith. Henry writes:

> . . . man is naturally ordered to a twofold intellectual knowledge, of which one is that which by study and investigation he is able to obtain through purely natural powers, and such knowledge proceeds from God and from creatures, inasmuch as philosophy can extend itself. But the other is that which man is not able to attain except by the gift of the supernatural, with the help of grace and glory, and in both ways it can be made known to man that God exists . . .[68]

How are these different kinds of knowledge related to the natural love of God? That love which is based on the knowledge of God through grace is not relevant to Henry's discussion of natural love. Natural love presupposes natural knowledge. Henry thinks that the natural knowledge of God is twofold.[69] The philosophers have a natural knowledge of God "in particular." But everyone has a natural knowledge of God "in universal."[70] The philosophers' knowledge is the result of a deduction made by reason, but the knowledge common to all is conceived immediately and naturally with the first intentions of being.

The knowledge of God's existence in universal that is possessed by every intellectual creature bears directly on the question of how God is loved in an involuntary way. In his discussion of the natural love of God, Henry more often uses the word "natural" in the sense of "non-rational" than in the sense of "without the help of grace." In the *Summa,* Henry explains that universal knowledge of God is natural knowledge because it is possessed by nature and not through reasoning. This natural knowledge is naturally inserted in us, since God is the first object of the intellect and the will.

The connection between such natural knowledge and Henry's cognitive psychology is clear. God is naturally known because he is the first object of the intellect. Taken as such, God cannot be thought of as nonexistent.[71] Even the pagans had this much knowledge of God, though they erred in the particular.[72] How is God known through such natural love? Henry's discussion of knowledge in the *Summa* lays the groundwork for the quodlibetal discussion of the natural love of God. Henry never completed that part of the *Summa* which was to be about creatures,[73] so we do not have his detailed discussion of the natural love of creatures. In his discussion of knowing God Henry does argue that the natural knowledge of God is always accompanied by the natural love of God. Every creature naturally desires the universal, first, and highest good, which is God. Taking the name "God" in the universal sense, God is known and loved by every intellectual creature.

In *Quodlibet* 4, q. 11, Henry does not contradict what he establishes in the *Summa*, but rather ties the different kinds of knowledge back into his discussion of the two types of involuntary love, namely, the love of good pleasure and the love of good will. The love of good pleasure desires the good *simpliciter* for no other reason than that it is the good. God's existence in universal (*in universali*) is naturally known to be lovable and *per se* good. Consequently, by the love of good pleasure God is loved for his own sake. This is an involuntary love of the will which follows upon the natural knowledge of God in every intellectual creature.

Henry's statement that God is loved for his own sake by the love of good pleasure is ultimately based upon his understanding of the way in which the good in creatures depends upon God. Emphasizing that God is the good in which other goods participate, Henry relates such participation to his own moral psychology, making God the first object of the will as the *ratio boni* and other objects lovable insofar as they participate in the *ratio boni,* which is also the *bonum universale*. Inasmuch as God is the first object of the intellect (*primum cognitum*), he is also known to be the first good, through which everything else is good only by participation. Henry invokes the well-worn phrase of Aristotle: "On account of which everything is such, is that to a higher degree."[74] Every single good is loved on account of its participation in God. Even what is good for the self is loved for God's sake, since God is the *ratio boni simpliciter*. Henry had previously mentioned that in every creature there is an involuntary love for the creature's nature and being. Now he can explain that even the goodness of one's own nature and being is loved because of God. Consequently, God is loved above everything else by love of good pleasure.

By this point in Henry's discussion of the natural love of God over self, certain peculiar features can be seen. First, Henry returns to the earlier scholastic notion of what is proper to intellectual creatures, whereas Thomas had focused on a natural inclination common even to irrational creatures. Even though Thomas Aquinas and Henry both use participation in their argument for the natural love of God over self, their resulting emphases are quite different.[75] Thomas proposes a causal structure for the universe. Although Henry also has a metaphysical understanding of participation, in his discussion of loving God he emphasizes moral psychology. An additional feature of Henry's discussion at this point is his use of the term "natural" in a sense that excludes a deliberative love based on rational knowledge. Henry's discussion of this pre-deliberative love resembles that of the *Summa Halesiana* in many respects, although it is based firmly on Henry's own more carefully developed cognitive and moral psychology.

Henry's discussion of the relationship between self-love and the love of God by love of good pleasure concludes that someone loves God more than himself even through the involuntary love of himself and his own happiness. An objection in *Quodlibet* 4, q. 11, further makes this point,[76] stating that a suicide does not love his own good because of a displeasure connected to it. He wants to kill himself and therefore he turns away from his own good. The implication is that, failing to love his own good, he therefore does not love God, who is his own *ratio boni*. This objection assumes Henry's position that one's own good is loved according to involuntary love for the sake of God. In his response to the objection, Henry agrees with Aristotle that the suicide is looking for some particular good. Moreover, many people undergo great evils in order to have the natural sweetness of merely being alive. Henry's basic position is that everyone, even the suicide, always wills some good, and by so doing they are willing the source of all good, which is God.

Henry's discussion of the natural love of God over self does not end with the statement that God is so loved in an involuntary manner. He recognizes that the involuntary natural love for God above all by love of good pleasure is imperfect, since it is possessed by everyone, including those who lack the moral virtues and charity.[77] Just as the knowledge of God in particular is possessed only by some individuals, so the perfect deliberative love of God is in only some individuals, following that knowledge of God which comes from creatures. The involuntary love of God is based on the will's inclination to the good *simpliciter;* in contrast, deliberate love is for moral goods. Since Henry thinks that there can be some knowledge of God without grace, it might seem that he would recognize a deliberative love of God which can exist without grace. Instead he states that this deliberative love needs to be informed by grace so that it is directed to supernatural goods (*bona gratuita*). Whereas everyone possesses the natural love of God by the love of good pleasure, deliberative love requires a conversion of the will.

To show how it is possible to love God more than oneself by deliberative love, Henry explains that it follows the same order which is present in natural love.[78] Although deliberative love requires grace and involuntary love does not, they both should love according to the same basic order: God, self, neighbor. God is loved above self by the love of good will because he is the *ratio boni* for that good which is pleasing for oneself. But nothing other than God is the *ratio boni*. Moreover, the love of good will is also based on what is pleasing. Consequently, since no creature is the reason (*ratio*) for what is pleasing, it follows that by the love of good will the self must be loved above everything else, with the possible exception of God. Characteristically, Henry does not mention the love for the common good. The involuntary love in every intellectual being follows the same basic order, which is natural not only in the sense that it does not require grace but more fundamentally in the sense that it precedes the use of reason. This natural order explains how some individuals love God by the love of good will, which is also called the love of friendship (*dilectio amicitiae*).

Unlike Thomas, Henry is cautious when discussing the possibility of friendship with God. The fact that some individuals love God by the love of friendship does not entail that they are friends with God in the same way that they are friends with other humans. Strictly speaking there can be no friendship with God, since, as Aristotle notes, friendship requires equality, and a great distance between the parties corrupts friendship. Consequently, it would be improper to say that God is loved by the love of friendship. However, Aristotle does mention a friendship which is based not on equality but on account of the eminence of goodness. For this reason the happy human being is owed praise rather than honor. Similarly, the love for one's parents or the gods cannot be based on equality but rather on goodness.[79] Consequently, the love of friendship is not necessarily a love between equals, but rather a love of the good.

This ability to love the good makes it possible for there to be a deliberative love which follows the same order as the involuntary love of good pleasure. Henry writes:

> For just as by the love of friendship someone loves himself first and *per se* and then extends the love of this sort from himself to another, as was said, by loving first the good that he himself is in his nature and essence and their good which is another, so by the love of good will first he wills for himself the good that is not himself, and then for another.[80]

Someone must love himself more than another because he first loves his own good. The love for another is based on self-love. But the love of God is different in several ways. Henry has already mentioned that the involuntary love of one's own goodness implies an involuntary love of God, in whom one's own goodness participates. The best good is either willing God to be the good which he himself is, which is the highest good (*summum bonum*), or willing other goods for his sake.[81] Henry stresses that God does not need good from creatures, but it is nonetheless appropriate for creatures to ascribe and deliver the good to him. When God is so loved it is by superexcellent friendship (*superexcellens amicitia*).

How does this love of God through friendship differ from the love of good will?[82] Henry argues that even without knowledge the will as a nature (*voluntas ut natura*) is directed to the good *simpliciter*. With knowledge, the will is able to choose freely and love even more. Although the will is inclined to the good *simpliciter*, it cannot lead itself to that good by its own motion. Charity, and consequently grace, is needed for such deliberative love. Why does Henry think that grace is necessary for the deliberative love of God over oneself? As we have seen, there is a long scholastic tradition of distinguishing between that natural voluntary love which is based on a natural knowledge of God and that love which is based on the knowledge of God through faith. Although Thomas thought that grace was necessary for the love of God over self, he held that such love would be possible for someone who is not suffering from the effects of original sin. Henry agrees with Thomas that original sin has corrupted nature so that God cannot be loved more than self without grace, but he seems to take the even stronger position that such love would not be possible even in a state of uncorrupted nature.

Henry's theological approach emphasizes the effects of original sin on human nature. According to Henry, original sin does not affect the order of the involuntary love of God. In both the state of innocence and the state of corruption, God is loved above self and everything else by the natural love of good pleasure.[83] This position is consistent with his moral psychology, which stresses that the will by its nature has the good as its object. Although original sin does not change the order of the love, it corrupts the will so that the will's motion towards the good is weaker. Now lacking its original intensity and perfection of motion, the will is still inclined towards the good *simpliciter*, but not so strongly. Similarly, God is still loved above everything by the love of good pleasure because God can be willed to be himself, and he is most lovable. But the weakening of the will makes it difficult for someone to have a deliberative love of God which is greater than his self-love. Because of sin there is an incongruity between deliberative and natural love.

Does the weakness make it impossible to love God more than self deliberatively and without grace? Henry recognizes that such a love follows a natural order, and pagan philosophers believed in following this order: "Our purpose is to live according to nature."[84] However, nature is ordered to a supernatural end. The excellence of this end makes grace necessary for a properly ordered love of God and self. Henry argues that the most perfect life is to live in accordance with the Christian virtue of charity, which cannot coexist with a state of serious sin. Does he think that the deliberative natural love of God over self would be possible in someone who does not have grace and is not wounded by original sin? Is the excellence of the supernatural end required to show the necessity of grace for such ordered love, or would original sin by itself suffice to explain it?

To understand Henry's position on this point, it is helpful to consider the theological understanding of nature that Henry expresses in his other writings. Henry's attitude to the supernatural resembles that of Thomas in its emphasis on the importance of the supernatural end and the weakness of human nature, but his position on purely natural human abilities is not clearly stated.[85] According to Henry, the philosophers and infidels were able to act in accordance with the rule of prudence, and this natural action was for the sake of God.[86] Philosophers and infidels could possess moral virtues, and by doing so they would attain God as the end of political virtue rather than as the savior and the one who rewards meritorious actions with eternal life. Consequently, while Henry distinguishes between the way in which moral virtues are ordered to God and the way in which the theological virtues are so ordered, he does not consider the possibility of a merely natural end.[87] Thomas held that there are two ends, but he also entertained the possibility of there being only a natural end. Like Thomas, Henry distinguishes between supernatural acts and those natural acts for the sake of God. Henry differs from Thomas insofar as he does not stress the contrast between the two ends or consider the natural end to be possibly sufficient. Finally, Henry shares with Thomas an unusually strong understanding of original sin. According to Henry, original sin is primarily the loss of the rectitude of the will, and secondarily the loss of the supernatural gifts.[88] This position is common enough, except that Henry emphasizes the disorder of the will rather than just the emotions.

Henry does not directly address many of the issues developed by Thomas. Although he is aware of contemporary Aristotelianism, his approach to the problem of the natural love of God over self resembles that of the earlier scholastics more than Thomas Aquinas or the other figures discussed in this chapter. He does address self-oriented Aristotelianism. Although he finds Aristotle's understanding of happiness to be deficient on even a philosophical level because it does not relate happiness to God, Henry more or less accepts as true the self-oriented interpretation of Aristotle on friendship and self-sacrifice. But Henry's overall view is connected to his own cognitive and moral psychology. It is in the context of his moral psychology that Henry resembles Thomas in holding that there is a natural order in which God is preferred to one's own good. But Henry roots this order in something peculiar to the will, namely the inclination to the good *simpliciter*. With Thomas, Henry thinks that grace is necessary for the deliberative love of God over self, but he is not clear on why the grace is necessary. It may be necessary because of the effects of original sin on the will, but the necessity might also be the result of Henry's reluctance to distinguish between a natural and supernatural end. The three other figures to be discussed in this chapter, namely, Godfrey of Fontaines, Giles of Rome, and James of Viterbo, are all directly concerned with the Thomistic arguments over whether there is an inclination in nature to prefer another's good to one's own. Henry's position more or less disappears from view. Nevertheless, his position possesses intrinsic interest because he views deliberative love without grace as self-interested, while at the same time he asserts that the natural involuntary love of the will has a preference for God over self.

III. In Defense of the Thomistic Position: Godfrey and Giles

Whereas Henry of Ghent does not mention the key features of Thomas's argument for the natural love of God over self, Giles of Rome and Godfrey of Fontaines both defend the basic outline of Thomas's position.[89] They base their positions on two original insights of Thomas, namely, (1) that the individual has a natural inclination to prefer the common good to its own good, and (2) that God is the common good of the universe. For both Godfrey and Giles, the ethical understanding of the natural love of God rests on a view of the universe in which each of the parts has an internal order which is more for the good of the whole than it is for its own good. Nevertheless, their approaches differ from each other and from that of Thomas. Neither Giles nor Godfrey focuses on Thomas's particular metaphysical concerns, and neither one explicitly adopts his theological position that humans, because they are corrupted by original sin, are unable to naturally love God most of all. We will discuss Godfrey first because, like Henry, he explicitly addresses the Arts Faculty's interpretation of Aristotle's ethical theory.[90] For Godfrey, the debate over the natural love of God has become a debate over whether Aristotle's eudaimonism is self-oriented.

Whereas Henry is content to reject many aspects of Aristotle's ethics, Godfrey remains a stalwart Aristotelian. Godfrey was a secular theologian who had studied in the Arts Faculty during the difficult period of the 1270s when conflict was rife over Aristotelianism. Godfrey's Aristotelianism has its roots in conflicting sources, however, since he also frequently turns to Thomas.[91] It is important to note that, at least for Godfrey and the Arts Faculty, the disagreements are not simply over what Aristotle thinks, but over what is philosophically correct. Even though Godfrey does not always accept Thomas's interpretation of Aristotle, his Aristotelianism is much closer to that of Thomas than it is to that of the Arts Faculty. This influence of Thomas Aquinas can be seen in the way Godfrey rejects the positions that the virtuous citizen loves most of all his own virtue, and that the contemplative acts against his own interests when he sacrifices contemplation for the common good. Moreover, Godfrey bases his position on an understanding of natural inclination which is similar to that of Thomas. But Godfrey's wider physical and especially metaphysical outlook is very different. He rejects the distinction between essence and existence, and consequently disagrees with much of Thomas's understanding of participation.[92] Consequently, his approach to the natural love of God emphasizes those aspects of Thomas's philosophy which are most evidently Aristotelian.

Godfrey's most interesting treatment of the common good occurs in his discussion of the natural love of God in *Quodlibet* 10, q. 6, but other passages scattered throughout his writings also emphasize the importance of the common good.[93] Godfrey focuses on the Aristotelian doctrine of man as a social animal.[94] Since it is natural for humans to live together, there is nothing proper to a human being which cannot be referred to the common good. The perfection of an individual can only be understood in the context of some community,[95] and the common good is always also the good of the person acting for the sake of the common good.[96] According to the virtue of prudence, it is understood that the acts must be directed to the different communities of which a human being is a part. For example, prudence directs the acts of a human with reference to his membership either in a household or in a city or kingdom. Regarded by the general virtue of justice, the common good is not common in the sense that a general concept is abstracted from particulars, but is like the good of a city or kingdom, some one singular whole which contains, as it were, integral parts.[97] According to Henry, the individual good is sometimes included in the common good only in a negative way. In contrast,

Godfrey thinks that the perfection of individuals through the virtues cannot be understood without reference to that common good which is the object of the moral virtues. Individuals become good precisely by acting for a good which is greater than their own.

Godfrey emphasizes the common good more than Henry possibly because he recognizes that the political common good is not the only or most important common good. Following Thomas, Godfrey describes God as the common good of the universe.[98] Godfrey's resemblance to Thomas here is remarkable. Godfrey holds that there is a desire for this common good, which is naturally implanted (*naturaliter indita*) in the human will.[99] Although the will is indeterminate with respect to partial goods, it is determined to the good *simpliciter*. Consequently, it has a natural order to the universal good and to God.[100] Just as the particular virtues can never be perfect unless they are directed by general justice to the political common good, so the virtues cannot be perfect unless they are directed by charity to God.[101] Godfrey reasons that although the particular virtues are directed to the individual's good, the individual's good requires the political common good. Just as an individual person should be ordered to the political common good, so should every creature, including humans, be ordered to God.

We have looked at several passages which more or less repeat or explain the basic Thomistic position on the common good, but in his *Quodlibet* 14, q. 2 (1298–1299), Godfrey considers the possibility that on a natural level the virtuous person prefers his own good to the political common good.[102] He suggests that the difference between the love for the political common good and the love for God might be not just of degree but of kind.[103] The object of every acquired virtue except for friendship might be loved by the love of concupiscence. Consequently, the good of the political common good might be loved by the love of concupiscence, although God is loved by the love of friendship. In this view, God would be loved by the love of friendship only through charity. It would seem that according to natural reason the common good should be loved less than oneself. It is difficult to reconcile this passage with the others, especially *Quodlibet* 10, q. 6 (1294–1295) and *Quodlibet* 13, q. 1 (1297–1298). In these latter two questions he explicitly affirms and reaffirms the Thomistic position that by the love of friendship the good citizen loves the common good more than his own. Did Godfrey change his mind in this short period? M. S. Kempshall states that Godfrey's position in *Quodlibet* 14 is "no more than a suggestion."[104] But it is hard to know why Godfrey would make such a suggestion. Could it perhaps be that he was worried about the necessity of grace?

Although Godfrey resembles Thomas insofar as he accepts a version of Aristotelian eudaimonism which is not self-oriented, he does not share Thomas's position on the effects of original sin. Godfrey does not suggest that concupiscence has wounded human nature so that the natural love of God over self is impossible. He differs from Henry also by focusing more on concupiscence than on an actual lack of rectitude in the will.[105] According to Godfrey, concupiscence indicates a defect of nature, but this defect is not itself culpable if there is no consent of the will. The only connection between concupiscence and guilt is the fact that concupiscence is the result of the first sin of Adam. Unlike Thomas, Godfrey discusses the *natura curva* primarily in the context of original sin: "For it is not necessary that original sin includes some moral curvature except in potency and in habit. However, such is not repugnant to nature according to itself, as has been said."[106] Godfrey accepts Thomas's view that each part has a natural inclination to the good of the whole more than to the good of itself, but he does not agree that original sin has made it impossible without grace to perform acts which are in accordance with this inclination. Even after original sin, there is a fundamental congruity between nature and morality.

Thomas admits the possibility of a purely natural end, but thinks of it only as a possibility and is always careful to subordinate the natural end to the supernatural. As we have seen, he argues that in the first state grace would have been helpful not only to heal the effects of the Fall, but also to ensure a correct ordering of the passions. But Godfrey is less cautious about discussing the possibility of a purely natural end.[107] According to Godfrey, the rectitude of original justice was in fact supernatural. Nevertheless, it would have been possible for there to be a perfectly natural congruity with the divine reason, coming from man's purely natural powers. In this merely natural state humans would possess the acquired virtues without the theological virtues.

Godfrey's concept of this natural state is related to his distinction between two human ends. According to Godfrey, the two ends of human life are related to the two principal communities to which humans belong. He writes: "And a man, according to his powers, namely intellect and will, is ordered to a twofold perfect life or to a twofold happiness; namely natural according to the human civil life, and supernatural according to heavenly civil life."[108] The acquired virtues are directed towards the natural end, which is the preservation of the political community and the contemplation of God insofar as it is possible in this life.[109] By emphasizing the relative superiority of the intellectual virtues, Godfrey supports his position that even acquired virtue is directed towards God. However, whereas acquired virtue is directed to the contemplation of God in this life, supernatural virtue is directed to the contemplation of God in heaven. Moreover, the difference between the natural and supernatural ends lies in whether the contemplation is obtained through natural or supernatural means.

Godfrey states not only that man is directed to God as a merely natural end, but that a state of completely natural happiness could have been created by God. Moreover, Godfrey holds that the concupiscence resulting from original sin does not destroy the congruence between nature and morality. It is therefore not surprising that when Godfrey turns to the question of whether God can be naturally loved more than self, the discussion treats deliberation and moral decision-making rather than just the pre-deliberative inclination of the will. Godfrey's theological outlook might explain why he does not adopt the more Neoplatonic and Augustinian aspects of Thomas's ethical theory, even though he accepts both Thomas's understanding of natural inclination and his interpretation of Aristotle.

Godfrey's acceptance of the basic elements of Thomas's theory can be seen in his *Quodlibet* 10, q. 6, "Whether a man from the dictate of natural reason is able to judge that he must love God more than himself?" Here he discusses the question of the natural love of God over self in the context of the debate between the theologians and the philosophers regarding Aristotle's dictum that friendship has its origin in self-love.[110] Godfrey argues that the virtuous agent should love both God and the common good more than himself, and he states that this love is the love of friendship. For the most part, Godfrey's first argument for this position restates the position of Thomas Aquinas. But the bulk of the question is an attempt to apply this position to the problems raised by the Arts Faculty's self-oriented interpretation of Aristotle. First, Godfrey considers an objection which resembles Siger's position that the good person intends his own intrinsic good most of all. Godfrey responds to this objection by using the difference between intrinsic and extrinsic goods to explain how the common good is the object of a good citizen's self-sacrifice. Second, he considers the objection that the contemplative's own good is more important than the common good, which at the very least resembles the position of Boethius of Dacia.

Godfrey responds to this objection by drawing on Thomas's distinction between the different ways in which the intellectual and moral virtues make the agent good. Whereas in *Quodlibet* 14, q. 2, Godfrey considers it possible that the political common good is not loved by the love of friendship, in this *Quodlibet* 10, q. 6, he bases his argument on the fact that an agent can naturally and through the love of friendship prefer the common good to his own.

Godfrey does distinguish between the love of friendship properly so called and a wider usage of the term. We cannot love God naturally through the love of friendship properly so called because such friendship exists among those who are in some sense equals.[111] Nevertheless, friendship can be extended to superior and more eminent objects, such as one's parents, one's country, and God. Godfrey departs from Henry by emphasizing the similarity among an individual's relationships with parents, country, and God. All three objects are loved by someone because he has his natural and social being from them. The object of the will is that good which is suitable to the lover (*bonum conveniens*). Consequently, since God is the common good upon which any other good of any being depends, it follows that all beings have an inclination to love God more than self by natural love. God is both the highest good and any being's own best end.

Godfrey's argument is rooted in a Thomistic understanding of natural inclination. Every part of the universe has a natural inclination to prefer the good of the universe to its own good.[112] To support this view, Godfrey mentions the typical examples of the self-sacrifice of the member for the body and of the citizen for the community. These are two instances in which the part prefers the whole to its own good. Since God is the most universal and common good, which contains not only the human good but also the good of every creature, it follows that the natural inclination to love God over self not only indicates a natural tendency common to all creatures, but also makes possible a love which can be naturally elicited by rational creatures. Like Thomas, Godfrey emphasizes the congruity between reason and natural inclination. Godfrey writes: "Otherwise, grace and charity would destroy and not perfect nature or natural inclination."[113] The natural deliberative love of God over self is possessed by creatures who are not oppressed by the weight of sin or curved towards carnal pleasures.

Although Godfrey follows Thomas on the importance of natural inclination for understanding the natural love of God, he points up even more strongly the connection between natural love and charity, which in Godfrey's theology are understood as tending to the same object. The major difference between them is that charity is more perfect than natural love.[114] By both loves another can be loved more than one's own self if one chooses to die for that object. Since the willingness to sustain death is also possessed by the good citizen, it follows that this mode of loving even the political common good is clearly obtainable through natural powers. Godfrey connects love with a willingness to die because Christ himself does so in John 15:13. This reference to the New Testament is just one example of Godfrey's tendency to identify Christian ethics with the ethics of Aristotle.

The natural inclination to the good is a persistent theme throughout Godfrey's writings, and shows the extent of Thomas's influence on later thirteenth-century discussions of ethics. According to Godfrey, the virtues are natural not in the sense that they are present in all humans, but rather because human nature has an inclination to be perfected through them.[115] Just as a heavy object has an inclination towards the earth, so does a human have an inclination to the intellectual and moral virtues. Godfrey bases this position on Aristotle's statement that "everything is naturally inclined to its own perfection."[116] Since the perfection of the intellect and the will consists in contemplation, it follows that contemplation is the object of natural inclination.[117] This natural inclination can help to explain how God is loved more than the self. The will is designed by nature (*apta nata est*) to desire the suitable good that is shown to it by the intellect.[118]

Although Godfrey's understanding of the natural love of God closely resembles that of Thomas, Godfrey does not explicitly follow Thomas in modifying the conclusion to say that God could be naturally loved before self only in an incorrupt state, nor does he contrast original justice with the state of corrupt nature on this issue. In general, Godfrey adopts Thomas's Aristotelianism but does not share Thomas's Augustinian emphasis on the corruption of human nature.

The main novelty of Godfrey's Aristotelian approach lies in his dialectical struggle with objections to the Thomistic account which closely resemble positions held by Siger and Boethius. To object to his own Thomistic argument, Godfrey first refers to that same passage of Aristotle which Siger interprets to say that the good citizen loves his short great act of virtue most of all.[119] The debate over the natural love of God over self has clearly become a debate about whether Aristotle's eudaimonism is self-oriented. Godfrey strengthens the objection from Aristotle with a passage from Augustine stating that even beatitude is desired as one's own good. Therefore, by loving beatitude a human loves himself more than God. Godfrey responds by stating:

> It should be said that since [1] the act has form and perfection from the object; and [2] the object by which God is loved per se and principally is the divine good; and [3] the divine good itself is the greatest [good] *simpliciter;* but [4] the object of love by which someone loves himself loving God and perfected by the virtues is less good; it is clear that [5] the former love is greater and more perfect *simpliciter et absolute;* and thus it seems that [6] I love more God himself perfected than myself perfected by a love of this sort and other virtues.[120]

Godfrey gives briefly here the core of his general strategy, which is to explain "loving more" by looking more closely at the structure of the act by which God or the common good is loved. He will emphasize that God and not the self is the object of someone who loves God.

In order to develop this point further, Godfrey brings an objection against this understanding of the act of love. The objection is based on the distinction between intrinsic and extrinsic goods. Riches and honor are extrinsic goods; an intrinsic good is like virtue, which perfects the agent by inhering in him and shaping him. The objector interprets Aristotle to say that the good person desires most of all the intrinsic good for himself.[121] Godfrey responds to this objection by distinguishing between the ways in which intrinsic and extrinsic goods can and cannot be compared. First, strictly speaking the two goods cannot be compared because of the way in which the intrinsic goodness of an act depends upon the extrinsic goodness of its object.[122] Consequently, the extrinsic good is loved more than any other good. The objector misinterprets Aristotle, who never says that the good citizen prefers his own good to the good of the community. The good citizen despises the other extrinsic goods precisely because he loves the common good more than himself. Second, Godfrey thinks that it is mistaken to ask which good is loved more since they describe different reasons for loving (*ratio dilectionis*) an object. Consequently, the two goods are properly speaking not comparable to each other.[123] Godfrey seems to be making the point that the good of virtue and other goods are not loved similarly, because they are not the same kinds of goods. We can love a relative more than a neighbor by giving more to our relative when both are equally in need. Giving bread and giving alms involve the same type of love. "Loving more" implies a choice between goods: someone loves a person more by giving that person more. Godfrey is pointing out that the loves for two objects, such as one's relative and one's neighbor, are comparable, whereas the love of one's neighbor and the love of one's virtuous almsgiving are not. The agent can choose between loving his neighbor or his relative more, but it would not make sense for him to choose between giving alms and his own virtue. In the same way, it does not make sense for the good agent to choose between dying for the political community and his own act of virtue. In this case, "loving more" does not imply a choice. What then could it mean?

Although the two goods are not comparable as are members of one genus or species, there is some way in which they might be compared.[124] Godfrey states that the good is most properly the end to which the love is ordered. While discussing justice in *Quodlibet* 14, he explains the different ways in which the just act is directed towards the good of the other. Although particular justice is in a way directed to the good of another, like the special moral virtues it is primarily directed to the agent's own good. In contrast, by general justice the agent intends the common good.[125] Acts of general justice are not primarily ordered to the agent's own perfection but instead to the good of the community. In another passage Godfrey states that the prudent human being must intend the other's good if he is to exercise the virtues of justice and friendship.[126] In the question on the natural love of God, Godfrey uses this notion of justice to understand the natural love of another more than oneself.[127] Justice seeks not the good of the agent but rather the good of the one to whom the action is directed. The debt of justice is most owed to one's parents, one's country, and God. Consequently, God is loved for his own sake and not for any goods that follow upon the act of loving God. Somebody who loves God would rather that his own intrinsic good of virtue disappear than that the divine good not exist. Godfrey quotes Aristotle to illustrate this point: ". . . the eager citizen (*studiosus*) as much as soever he loves his own and intrinsic good, however more he chooses to die well and virtuously and not to exist rather than for the common good to perish."[128]

In the beginning of the question, Godfrey distinguished between the Peripatetics who follow reason and the theologians who follow faith enlightened by reason. The former think that the self must be loved most of all, whereas the latter think that God should be so loved. Godfrey is now ready to state that the Peripatetics can be refuted through reason alone, unaided by the light of faith. The Peripatetics' mistake is in their understanding of the relationship between the intrinsic and extrinsic goods. According to Godfrey, a greater intrinsic good is obtained when the greater extrinsic good is loved for its own sake. Godfrey writes:

> But since that intrinsic good has its goodness from the goodness of the object principally loved, therefore I thus will more the greatest good possible to me. I do not however will that [good] first and principally and most of all, since that [good] is not the first and *per se* object of the will, but [I do will] that [good] from which the act of this sort, which is good to me, has its goodness.[129]

If someone loves himself more than God, or loves his own life more than the political common good, he does not love the greatest good for himself. The intrinsic good of virtue is obtained reflexively through loving an extrinsic good. The act which perfects the lover is included reflexively in his act of loving God. The lover loves his own good "as if by consequence and implicitly."[130] Nevertheless, he loves God more than himself. Similarly, the good citizen loves the political community more than himself. It would be impossible for him not to do so, since if he loved himself more he would not be willing to sacrifice his own good for the common good. However, the common good includes his own good. The common good can exist without his good, but his own good cannot exist without the common good. Therefore in order to love himself most of all he would have to will simultaneously his own good to exist and not to exist. Siger's interpretation of Aristotle neglects this dependence of the individual good on the common good.

Godfrey does not criticize Siger's view that the virtuous citizen maximizes his own intrinsic good of virtue by dying for the political community. But he is concerned with the object and intention of the act. The self-sacrifice is the type of act that it is precisely because it is for the sake of the common good. Since the common good is the object of the act, then it follows that the common good is what is willed and loved by the act. In the case of self-sacrifice, the common good is loved even more than one's own existence. The maximization of the citizen's own good results from the act; it does not specify the act in the way that the common good does. Consequently, the self-sacrifice is an act whereby the political community is loved more than the citizen's own good.

Throughout his writings Godfrey emphasizes that the species and first perfection of an operation comes from its object.[131] When there is movement towards whiteness this operation is perfected and named through its becoming white. Similarly, the perfection of beatitude is the highest good, which is its object. Moreover, the malice of an act also comes from the object.[132] Although every good that is love is good for the lover (*bonum sibi*), such love is not always self-love because the self's own good need not be the object of that love.[133] One's own good is willed only reflexively. Godfrey's argument focuses primarily on the structure of the moral act.[134] The Peripatetics misinterpret Aristotle on this point because they are incapable of recognizing that although the good citizen does procure for himself a greater intrinsic good through his death, the object of his act is the common good. Therefore he loves the common good more than himself.

At this point Godfrey's differences from Henry should be clear. First, they differ in their attitudes towards Aristotle. Godfrey and the Arts Faculty both think that Aristotle is right, but differ about the way in which Aristotle should be understood. Henry is willing to admit that Aristotle might be wrong. Second and more importantly, Henry and Godfrey differ about the common good. Unlike Henry, Godfrey thinks that the individual good is always included in the common good. This inclusion is based on the individual's relation to the common good as a part is related to the whole. Godfrey agrees with Henry's view that one should never choose the common good over one's individual good. No one should ever perform a vicious act for the sake of the common good, since this act would make him worse. The difference is that Henry interprets this choice as showing that the citizen must love himself more than the common good, while Godfrey takes it as demonstrating that the individual's love for the common good always includes a love for his own good.

After discussing the intention of the virtuous person who loves the political common good and God more than his own good, Godfrey addresses the problem of whether the contemplative should love the common good more than his own individual good. As we have seen, the relationship between the intellectual and the moral virtues is central for the debates over whether Aristotelian eudaimonism is primarily self-oriented. Consequently, Godfrey needs to address this issue in the context of whether, on a natural level, someone is required to love both God and the common good more than himself. Godfrey sympathizes with Henry's view that by preferring the common good to his own good the contemplative gains a good for himself by avoiding the evil of guilt. Nevertheless, Godfrey thinks that in certain circumstances the exercise of moral virtue can be a greater good than the exercise of the intellectual virtues.[135] Although the contemplative virtues are more perfect in themselves and *simpliciter,* the moral virtues can be more perfect in some cases, just as for a poor man it is better to make money than to philosophize. Godfrey is much closer to Boethius of Dacia than he is to Henry in his justification for this position. According to Godfrey, the contemplative must be willing to abandon contemplation for the common good because the good that he derives from contemplation depends on the common good for its existence. There is no recognition that the political community has any goods which are higher than those of contemplation. Whereas Henry justified the contemplative's sacrifice by appealing to natural law, Godfrey merely points to the physical dependence of the contemplative on the political community.

It is curious that in this passage Godfrey gives such an unsatisfactory account of the way in which the common good includes the contemplative's good. In *Quodlibet* 11, q. 6 (1295/1296), Godfrey's discussion of this issue takes a more Thomistic approach.[136] Thomas had stated that although the intellectual virtues are superior to the moral ones *simpliciter,* moral virtue can be superior *secundum quid.*[137] Intellectual activity is superior to moral activity if they are considered by themselves, but since moral virtue makes someone a good person, sometimes the exercise of moral virtue is superior. Godfrey applies the distinction to the question of whether the contemplative should sacrifice his good of contemplation for the common good. First, Godfrey notes that sometimes contemplation needs to be given up in the face of practical needs. Just as someone would sin if he needed food and refused to eat because the eating would interrupt his contemplation, so he would sin if he refused to conserve the political community for fear of losing the good of contemplation. Second, it is possible to have the intellectual virtues without the moral virtues, but in such a case the intellectual virtues make a human good only *secundum quid.* On the other hand, a human who possesses only the moral virtues is good *simpliciter.* Although the exercise of the speculative virtues is the highest activity, the moral virtues are more eminent *secundum quid* because they are more necessary to the agent.

Godfrey's understanding of the relationship between the contemplative and moral virtues is a clear response to the position of Boethius of Dacia, who thinks that the moral virtues must be subordinated to the intellectual virtues. Godfrey holds that the proper exercise of these virtues depends upon the exigencies of a particular situation. Nevertheless, in this passage Godfrey resembles Boethius more than Thomas Aquinas in that he does not distinguish between philosophical contemplation and the contemplation of the saints.[138]

Godfrey closes his question on the natural love of God over self (*Quodlibet* 10, q. 6) with a refutation of the Peripatetics' interpretation of Aristotle's dictum that "the notes of friendship that are for another are from those notes of friendship which are for oneself."[139] Godfrey argues that there is a difference between that friendship which is among equals and that friendship which is based on a good which includes one's own good. Aristotle's dictum applies to the friendship between equals, but it does not apply to that friendship which is for God. Aristotle and a theologian who understands rightly do not disagree. Godfrey writes:

> Therefore according to this aforesaid way of expounding the speech of the Philosopher, it is clear that it does not differ from the most perfect Christian theologian; rather what Aristotle says, "'The friendly notes that are for another, etc.," seems nothing other than what Christ says, "Love your neighbor as yourself, etc."[140]

According to Godfrey, there is a harmony between the teachings of Christ and of Aristotle. In another passage Godfrey shows at length how Aristotle's discussion of the way in which an act intends the good of another is close to St. Paul's treatment on charity.[141] Godfrey emphasizes the congruity between the natural and the supernatural even more than Thomas Aquinas does.

At the beginning of the question on the natural love of God, Godfrey showed the contrast between the theologians and the Peripatetics on the issue of the natural love of God over self. Godfrey ends his discussion by stating that both parties misinterpret Aristotle. We have seen that both Henry and Siger understand Aristotle to say that the common good cannot be loved over the individual good. Godfrey's Aristotle is much closer to that of Thomas in that Godfrey and Thomas both think that Aristotle's good citizen loves the political community more than himself.

Godfrey uses a Thomistic version of Aristotle's eudaimonism to address the difficulties which are raised by the Arts Faculty's self-oriented interpretation of Aristotelianism. His main contribution to the debate lies in his single-minded focus on the Aristotelian aspects of Thomas's ethics, and his analysis of what it means to love one object more than another. Loving God poses a unique problem for eudaimonism because it is only by loving God more than himself that someone can best love himself. In fact, the agent cannot choose between his real good and loving God. By loving himself more than God the agent loves himself less. If the agent cannot separate loving God from his own good, then in what sense can he be said to prefer God's good to his own? Godfrey draws our attention to the structure of the act in the situation of the citizen who exposes himself to danger for the common good. The object of the act is not the agent's own virtue, but the political common good. The common good is what makes sense of the act and gives the virtue its goodness. Similarly, God is the object of the act of loving him. The act makes sense only because of God's goodness. There is a natural inclination in every human to prefer God's good to his own. The nobility of this object makes the love of God over self possible.

Thomas's influence on the debate over naturally loving God was not limited to Godfrey of Fontaines. Giles of Rome repeats Thomas's emphasis on the natural inclination of the part to the whole. In *Quodlibet* 4, q. 14 (1289), Giles of Rome addresses the question, "Whether a man by natural love should love God more than himself, or conversely?"[142] Unlike Thomas and Godfrey, Giles does not discuss the political common good, but focuses entirely on the relationship between the individual good and God. Giles's treatment is significant because it so clearly addresses the metaphysical issues raised by Thomas's argument.[143]

Giles argues that there are three ways to show that a human must love God more than himself. The first way proceeds from the fact that God is the creator and conserver of all good. Giles begins the argument by stating, ". . . we say that God is more intimate (*magis intimus*) to each thing, than the thing is to itself."[144] This intimacy between God and a creature is based on the special way in which the creature is an effect and vestige or likeness (*vestigium vel similitudo*) of God.[145] To some extent a creature is a likeness of God, not as an impression on wax is in the likeness of the seal, but more as the imprint of the seal on water would be. The impression of the seal remains in the wax after the seal has been withdrawn, but if God ceases to preserve a creature in existence, then the creature disappears. The likeness of a creature to God is more like the imprint of a seal represented in water. Once the seal has been removed, its likeness in the water disappears. Similarly, if God ceased to preserve a creature in existence, it would be annihilated. God is more intimate to a creature than the creature is to itself because God conserves the essence of a creature more than the creature does.

It follows from this causal dependence that the good of a creature is more present in God than in itself. Even if the creature were annihilated, God could make it again. Therefore, if we consider in what respect his good is the conserver and cause of all good, including our own good, we act most badly (*pessime*) if we do not love God more than ourselves, because we know that our good is reserved more in God than in ourselves. Although in this question Giles does not discuss the difference between the pre-elective and elective love of God, he does state that we can erroneously love ourselves more than God. Consequently, Giles is concerned with an elective love of God which is natural in the sense that it does not require grace.

The second way of showing that a human must love god more than himself is based on the fact that ". . . God is the whole good (*bonum totale*), having within himself any good whatever."[146] Although Giles does not mention the standard argument of the good citizen's sacrifice of his life for the political community, he does give a detailed discussion of how the part of the body sacrifices itself for the good of the whole. The law of the greater love of the part for the whole is naturally stamped (*impressus*) by an instinct of nature on the members of our body. In general, this self-sacrificing love of the part for the whole is naturally inserted (*inditus*) into any part. If this were not the case, then the arm would not expose itself to danger or death for the good of the head. Since a part has a natural instinct to sacrifice itself for the whole, and a creature is a certain expression of that whole good which is God, it follows that it is natural for a creature to love God more than itself.

At the end of this argument, Giles briefly discusses Aristotle's dictum about the notes of friendship.[147] According to Giles, this dictum refers only to the love between creatures, which is a love between parts. Consequently, this type of love for another can be based on self-love. Since the love of a creature for God is the love of a part for the whole, it follows that the love for the whole good is entirely different from love for one's neighbor, and cannot result from self-love. Both Giles and Godfrey interpret Aristotle's dictum so as to limit its application only to relations among individuals. It is unclear whether Giles is responding here to Siger's interpretation of Aristotle.

Giles's third argument is based on God's being good through his essence, whereas all other goods are good only by participation.[148] He begins by asserting that our good is good only insofar as it participates in the divine good (*in quantum participat divinum bonum*). Therefore our good is to be loved on account of the divine good (*propter divinum bonum*). The divine good is not loved on account of anything, because it is essentially and *per se* good. Even our neighbor is loved only on account of that society which we share with him in the divine good. Giles then quotes the same Aristotelian phrase we have already seen used by Henry: the reason why anything is such, is that to a higher degree (*propter quod unumquodque, tale et illud magis*). Since we love our own good on account of (*propter*) the divine good, it follows that we must love the divine good more than our own good.

Giles continues the discussion in the context of the difference between the love of neighbor and the love of God. The second objection had stated that if we must love something just because it has more goodness in it, then it would follow that we must love more than ourselves a neighbor who is better than ourselves.[149] We have seen that Siger addresses this problem by stating that we must will the greater extrinsic good of honor for our neighbor while at the same time willing the intrinsic good or virtue more for ourselves. In this third argument, Giles states that we do not have goodness by participating in our neighbor, but rather by our participation in God.[150] Consequently, our good is not to be loved on account of our neighbor as the final good (*finaliter*), but on account of the divine good. God is the final good for the sake of which we must love both ourselves and our neighbor. In his reply to the second objection, Giles also points out that even if our neighbor is better than ourselves, we are not good by participation in his goodness. Only God is the final good which must be loved more than ourselves.

Giles's first objection and reply are also important for their discussion of the relationship between the love of God and the good for one's own self procured by such love. The objection states that God is loved for our own sake, and consequently he must be loved less than ourselves.[151] Giles admits that God is the good of the soul and enjoyed (*frui*) by us. If the argument is that we only love God on account of his own sake (*propter seipsum*), because he is good, then the argument is not relevant to the issue of whether the self is loved more than God, since God is thereby loved for his own sake. If the argument is that God is loved on account of some good which he gives to the lover, then the argument is simply false, since every good is loved for the sake of God.

Giles's argument is significant for the way in which he modifies and emphasizes the metaphysical aspects of Thomas's argument for the natural love of God over self. Giles does not express Godfrey's explicit concern with the self-oriented eudaimonism of the Arts Faculty, nor does he emphasize that God is the common good of the universe. Nevertheless, Giles shares Godfrey's acceptance of Thomas's position on natural inclination, which is that each individual in the universe has a natural inclination to God more than it has to its own good. Moreover, all three associate a well-ordered human love with this natural inclination. But like Godfrey, Giles does not draw attention to the effect of original sin on human nature. Indeed, Giles states that grace is necessary not for the substance of the act of loving God over self, but instead for fulfilling God's intention in giving the command.[152] In holding this position he reflects the less Augustinian stance of Thomas's early writings.[153] Indeed, Thomas's later belief in the constraints of corrupted human nature was unusual for his time, and did not greatly influence his successors.

Giles and Godfrey show the way in which the thirteenth-century concern over Aristotle affects the basic issues underlying debates over the natural love of God. Whereas debates before Thomas's time were focused primarily on moral psychology and pagan virtue, both Giles and Godfrey are concerned with natural inclination. If everything has an inclination to prefer the good of the universe to its own good, then there is room for an Aristotelian eudaimonism which is not overly self-oriented. Giles and Godfrey focus on different aspects of the Thomistic picture. Godfrey describes the way in which an agent intends the divine or common good for its own sake, even when this good is also good for the agent. Giles does not emphasize the nature of moral reasoning, but turns rather to the problem of the different ways that the good pertains to different objects. Each of his three arguments traces the origin of a particular good back to that good which is God. Godfrey and Giles share an underlying teleology in which each part of the universe tends to its own good only by tending to the good of the whole most of all.

IV. James of Viterbo

After Giles of Rome became the prior general of the Augustinian order, his chair at Paris was taken by James of Viterbo. Like Giles, James was an

Augustinian, but he shows no reverence for Giles's thought. In his *Quodlibet* 2, q. 20 (1294/1295), James of Viterbo attacks this whole tradition of arguing for the natural love of God over self on the basis of a part/whole relationship.[154] James restates the position of Siger, that the good citizen loves himself most of all when he dies for the political community. James's originality is that he strengthens or makes explicit the metaphysical and psychological bases for this position through his criticism of Godfrey of Fontaines and Giles of Rome. Moreover, he develops an alternative view of the relationship between nature and grace so that he can reconcile his self-oriented interpretation of Aristotle with Christian ethics.

James begins his discussion of the natural love of God by stating that there are three ways of speaking about the issue. The first way of speaking is to say that the self is loved most of all *absolute,* although God is loved more than self *secundum quid.*[155] The argument for this position is that the self must always be loved first and more intensely. In another way however, God is loved most of all since he is willed to be himself, which is the greatest good. James does not cite sources for this position. L-B. Gillon proposes that James is attempting to express William of Auxerre's position,[156] but this identification is questionable because William does not hold that it is possible to love God over self through natural love. Although James wishes to record this argument, he does not think it relevant to contemporary debates. James dismisses this first position by stating, "But this way of speaking does not please others."[157] The argument is not mentioned again.

The third way of speaking about the issue, too, is completely dropped by James later in this discussion. According to this third approach, God is naturally loved more than self in the state of integral nature, whereas in the state of corrupted nature the self is always naturally loved more than God, unless nature is healed by grace.[158] This third position seems to be that of Thomas Aquinas. We have seen that both Giles and Godfrey use the Thomistic argument for the natural love of God over self without discussing in any detail the effects of the Fall.[159] It is interesting that James isolates Thomas's conclusion about the effect of the Fall on the natural love of God over self from the Thomistic arguments for such love. While the first and third approaches are not considered any further, they serve to frame the focus of the debate. First, we see that James is aware of positions which did not influence his major contemporaries or the subsequent history of the discussion. Second, James passes over Thomas's concern with the corruption of human nature. By the end of the thirteenth century, the most important issues in the debate over the natural love of God over self have shifted to (1) the relationship between the part and the whole, and (2) the congruity between nature and grace.

James now turns to the second way of speaking about the issue, which is the position of Giles and Godfrey that a human being loves God more than himself *simpliciter et absolute*. He states that this opinion is held by many. Three arguments are given for this position. The first is based on the connection between charity and natural love.[160] As Godfrey argued, if someone loved himself naturally more than God, then such love would be perverse and contrary to charity. The second argument is founded on the connection between reason and natural inclination. Both James and Godfrey use the phrase "*ex dictamine rationis.*" From reason, a human judges that he should love God more than himself. Unless such natural love existed, natural inclination would be opposed to reason. These first two arguments closely resemble arguments given by Godfrey in *Quodlibet* 10, q. 6.[161] The third argument appeals to the different manners in which God is the causal, whole, and final good (*bonum causale, totale, et finale*). This is the same one given by Giles of Rome, and James often uses Giles's own language when explaining it. Nevertheless, during the discussion of God as the whole good (*bonum totale*) James mentions the example of the good citizen who wills to die for the political community, an issue that Giles does not bring up. As we shall see, James's understanding of the good citizen will play an important role in his interpretation of Aristotle's ethics. Moreover, his treatment of all three arguments foreshadows the change he will effect in the nature of the debate over loving God. In his response to the first two arguments he will attack the Thomistic position on the relationship between nature and grace, and the attempt to base ethics on natural inclination. His response to the third argument will attack the Thomistic understanding of natural teleology, in which everything has an inclination not just for its own perfection, but even more for the perfection of the whole universe.

James begins his own discussion of the issue by referring to the traditional distinction between the love of friendship and the love of concupiscence.[162] Although some of the other late-thirteenth-century thinkers discussed in this chapter do not put emphasis on these two loves, the distinction between them had been a standard part of the discussion for the previous generation. James adheres to the traditional understanding of the love of friendship as willing another's good, and the love of concupiscence as willing a good for the sake of a person, whether it be for oneself or another. Nevertheless, James is unusual in his insistence that the good loved by the love of concupiscence may be either an end or a means to an end (*finis vel ad finem*).

How are these two loves related to the love of God and self? Non-rational creatures cannot love God by the love of friendship, although they do love him by the love of concupiscence since every creature has a natural desire to be a similitude of God. Rational creatures love God both by the love of friendship, when they will him to be God and the highest perfection, and by the love of concupiscence when they wish to be conjoined to him through similitude and participation. The self is also loved by both types of love. Someone loves himself by the love of friendship when he wills himself some good, and by the love of concupiscence when he wishes to be, to live, to understand, etc.[163]

James agrees with Henry and Godfrey that strictly speaking there is no friendship with God since there is no equality on which to base the friendship.[164] Nevertheless, God is still loved by the love of friendship because the relationship between a creature and God is greater than friendship. James adds that there is also no friendship with self, since friendship is based on union with another through similitude, whereas someone by himself is a unity. Nevertheless, taken in a broad sense there is a friendship with oneself and with God. James does not think that because there is strictly speaking no friendship with an object, the object cannot be loved by the love of friendship. Somebody can love another by the *amor amicitae* without being the friend of the object of his love.

According to James, there are three ways of understanding the question of whether God is naturally loved more than one's self. First, God could be loved more by the love of concupiscence, whereas the self is loved by love of friendship.[165] James argues that if the question is understood this way it makes no sense, because it would be like asking whether the self is loved more than beatitude. The two loves are not comparable. A second way of approaching the question would be to ask whether by the love of concupiscence God is loved by the self more because the divine good (*bonum divinum*) is greater than one's own good. The divine good (*bonum divinum*) could thereby be loved in two ways. First, the divine good could be God himself. James points out that then it would not be loved by the love of concupiscence. Nothing desires the good of another thing for the other's own sake, because the perfection of one thing cannot be the perfection of another. Second, the divine good (*bonum divinum*) is called good because it is a similitude of God. The good of a creature is a divine good precisely because it is a similitude of God. James points out that thereby the divine good would be loved to the same extent that the good of the creature is loved. Everything loves God in this fashion.

James eliminates these two lines of argument to turn to the third possibility, that the question of the natural love of God over self is really a question about the love of friendship, and in particular about whether someone can love God more than self for the sake of God. James gives two arguments to show that the self is always loved more than God by such natural love.

The first argument is based on the connection between love and unity. It begins with the premiss that love follows the mode of natural being. Being a thing and being one come from the same source.[166] For example, by natural being Socrates through his humanity is one with himself and Plato; likewise, he is a thing himself and (in some sense) something other than himself. Love causes such a unity with another. James argues, "Whence, just as someone loves both himself and another, thus through love he is said to be one with himself and with another."[167]

According to natural being, a thing cannot be another more than it can be itself, since it is itself through numerical identity, whereas it is another only through conformity or likeness (*per conformitatem vel similitudinem*).[168] Additionally, the thing is a being more through the numerical identity than through conformity. Since love follows being, one loves another because the other is in some way conformed to the self. Consequently, the other cannot be loved more, since a human being always has numerical identity with himself, whereas his union with another is based only on a likeness. Therefore a human being must love himself more than any other human or even God.

The emphasis on union in this argument is important. In his *Quodlibet* 1, q. 8 (1293/1294), James argues that the *ratio boni* comes from unity.[169] Something is desired only insofar as it is suitable and similar to the one who desires it. Since James thinks that an object is lovable precisely insofar as it is one with the lover, it clearly follows that a human loves himself more than anyone else.

James's second argument for the view that through the natural love of friendship the self is loved more than God is based on the fact that charity elevates nature.[170] It is clear how the natural love of God by the love of concupiscence is so elevated. By this love God is naturally loved as the *bonum universale,* and by charity he is loved as supernatural beatitude. The natural love of God through the love of friendship can only be elevated by order and mode. Consequently, charity must reverse nature. If God were loved only for his own sake and more than one's own self naturally, then how could such love be elevated? James here offers an argument to show that a human can love God more than himself through charity. Just as natural love follows the way of natural being, so does grace follow the way of gratuitous being. Through grace a human is made divine. God loves himself more than anything else. Through grace a human becomes one with God and shares God's love. Consequently, through charity a human can love God more than any other thing, including his own self.

According to James, the orders of nature and grace are inverse.[171] James interprets Aristotle's dictum on friendship in the same way that Siger does, but James thinks that the dictum must be modified if supernatural love enters the discussion. James writes:

> For natural love tends first and more to itself than to God. Whence, with respect to this love, what the Philosopher said is true, namely that the notes of friendship which are for another, come from those notes of friendship which are for oneself. But gratuitous love, which is charity, is opposite (*econverso se habet*); since first and more it tends more to God than to the neighbor or itself, thus according to this love the notes of friendship which are for oneself or a neighbor, come from those notes of friendship which are for God.[172]

James modifies the Aristotelian dictum in the way that Godfrey suggests that the theologians do. James, Giles, and Godfrey all interpret this dictum to mean that the love of a neighbor has its basis in self-love. The disagreement is about the application of this dictum to God. Since Giles accepts the Thomistic notion that every creature has a natural inclination to love God more than itself, he thinks that Aristotle's distinction is irrelevant to the discussion of the love for God. Godfrey even thinks that the dictum does not apply to the love for one's parents or the common good. In contrast, James thinks that Aristotle's statement refers to any purely natural love, including the natural love for God.

Why does James take this position? It is significant that after mentioning Aristotle, James brings St. Bernard of Clairvaux into the discussion.[173] There seems to be a connection between Bernard's *natura curva* and James's understanding of human nature. This grafting of Siger's Aristotle onto the *natura curva* position is strange, since the historical sources are so different. Nevertheless, James is correct to pull together the two views. If nature is primarily self-directed, as the *natura curva* position asserts, and Aristotle discusses nature rather than grace, then it would not be surprising for Aristotle to have a self-directed understanding of human love. James takes Bernard's position to be that all natural love is self-directed. James's discussion focuses on Bernard's account of the four grades of love. According to the first grade, a man loves himself on account of himself. According to the second grade, a man loves

God on account of himself. In the third grade, a man loves God on account of God. According to the fourth and highest grade of love, a man not only loves God on account of God, but he loves himself on account of God. According to James's interpretation of Bernard, the first two grades pertain to natural love, whereas the third and fourth require grace. There is no disagreement between Aristotle's dictum and Bernard's first two grades of love.

James does not object to linking Aristotelian eudaimonism with natural inclination, but he does object to identifying either with Christian ethics. Whereas Godfrey thought that Aristotle's dictum about friendship was compatible with Christ's own understanding of love, James argues that it describes only a non-Christian order of love. Without criticizing Aristotle, James contrasts Aristotelian and Christian ethics. He can distinguish yet maintain both positions because of his view on nature and grace. The Thomists see them as complementary, but James attacks this position by challenging the Thomistic understanding of natural inclination.

James's replies to the six objections that open the discussion in *Quodlibet* 2, q. 20, highlight important problems with the Thomistic approach to the natural love of God. The first two objections come from Godfrey. In the first objection, it is argued that nature would be perverse if it were contrary to charity. James responds by distinguishing three different senses of the phrase "natural love."[174] In the first sense, natural love is that which operates by its own powers without the assistance of grace. In the second sense, natural love is for the end, as opposed to elective love, which chooses the means to the end. In the third sense, natural love is what is receptive to grace in a rational creature. In this third sense, charity perfects that rational nature which is capable of receiving it. But James states that the second sense in which natural is opposed to elective love, pertains most to the question. This view is unexpected because, as we have seen, both Giles and Godfrey focus their discussions on elective love. Nevertheless, James sees this non-elective love as the crux of the matter, arguing that charity replaces natural love by making it stop. Natural love is imperfect; consequently, when charity is exercised the natural love remains only in aptitude. If natural love is imperfect, then it would seem to be perverse. James avoids this problem by distinguishing between what comes from perversity and what comes from a defect or impotence. Natural love is not perverse, but it needs to be perfected and elevated by grace if God is to be loved more than self. James draws a comparison with the knowledge of God through reason and faith. The natural knowledge of God is not perverse, but rather impotent and deficient. Faith perfects natural knowledge by elevating it.

The second objection, also from Godfrey, claims that if God cannot be loved naturally more than self, then reason would dictate what nature is incapable of performing. James responds by agreeing with the consequent.[175] Reason states that God is the most knowable being, and yet we cannot know God naturally in this way. Moreover, all the precepts of the natural law can be known through reason, but they cannot be fulfilled without the help of God's grace. Godfrey thinks that there should be a congruity between natural powers and what reason dictates, whereas James asserts that through reason we can know that we have duties which we are unable to fulfill through our natural powers. The obligation to love God most of all can be known through reason, but the very existence of the obligation does not imply that there is a natural ability to fulfill it. Godfrey thinks that "ought" implies "can," whereas James denies this implication, at least on a natural level.

James's understanding of the relationship between nature and grace allows him to hold both that nature is self-directed and that a natural ethics is based on natural inclination. James's criticisms of the Thomistic understanding of natural inclination are connected to his belief that unity is the basis of love. Nature is primarily self-directed because everything seeks its own perfection most of all. Grace does not take away the connection between love and unity; rather, it makes the Christian one with God. But this unity occurs only on a supernatural level.

The third, fourth, and fifth objections are all taken from Giles of Rome's consideration of God's goodness. James attacks the Thomistic understanding of the natural level by attacking in order those objections which are based on Giles's arguments for the natural love of God over self. The third objection argues from God as the causal good (*bonum causale*), more intimate (*intimior*) to the creature than it is to itself. This view is inconsistent with James's position not because it bases love on something other than unity, but because it states that even on a natural level someone has a unity with God which is greater than his union with his own self. James's reply focuses on two different uses of the word "*intimus*."[176] James admits that with respect to the causality of a creature's conservation in existence God is more intimate to the creature than it is to itself. This is true because God is the cause of the creature, whereas the creature is not the cause of itself. But if intimacy is considered as flowing from union or unity, every creature is more intimate to itself that it is to God. Since a creature is united to itself most of all, it will love itself most of all. James simply denies that there is such a natural connection between an individual and God.

The fourth objection is based on the notion of God as the whole good (*bonum totale*). This argument is central to the Thomistic approach to the natural love of God. James responds by stating that a part is included in the whole in two ways.[177] In one way the part is one thing with the whole. In this sense the part loves the whole with a love equal to that by which it loves itself, since they are both one. In another sense, the part can be considered as different (*diversa*) from the whole. Inasmuch as the part is different from the whole, it loves itself more than the whole. This objection captures the central issue of the debate, which is whether natural inclination is primarily self-directed.

To reject the Thomistic position, James must address the examples of the hand sacrificing itself for the body and the good citizen sacrificing himself for the good of the community. James first attacks the doctrine that creatures have a natural inclination to love the whole more than themselves.[178] When the good of a part is sacrificed for the good of the whole, this sacrifice is caused not by the natural appetite of the part, but rather by the natural appetite of the whole which uses the parts. The hand or arm does not expose itself to danger. On the contrary, the whole body exposes such less worthy parts to danger in order to protect a more noble (*nobilior*) part like the eye. Similarly, in the universe God permits evil among the parts on account of the good of the whole universe. Whereas the Thomists think that the part has impressed within itself a natural instinct for the good of the universe, James thinks that the part is ordered to the whole primarily by an external orderer; the two views of Aristotelian eudaimonism differ correspondingly. In the Thomistic view, the natural inclination is for the good of the whole, and Aristotelian eudaimonism is a theory which states that the virtuous individual is perfected through preferring the good of the whole to his own good. In James's view, natural inclination is primarily for the good of the individual. Consequently, Aristotelian eudaimonism is a theory which describes how the virtuous agent is concerned with maximizing his own perfection.

James uses his self-directed interpretation of teleology to support the belief that the citizen who exposes himself to danger for the political community is acting primarily for his own benefit.[179] Henry held this view because he thought that only God could be preferred to one's own good. Siger held it because he based love on unity, and everyone is one with himself. James's view is closer to that of Siger. There are two ways in which such citizens intend their own benefit. One type of citizen endangers himself for glory and for the praise of the political community. Using the same terminology as Siger, James notes that praise and glory are extrinsic goods. Another type of citizen exposes himself to danger for the good of virtue. This citizen endangers himself not because he loves the community more than himself, but rather because he loves the good of virtue, which pertains to his own perfection (*pertinens ad perfectionem hominis*). Indeed, he loves himself even more than the citizen who acts for praise and glory loves himself, since virtue is an intrinsic good, whereas praise and glory are merely extrinsic goods. Such a virtuous citizen loves the good of the community more than the good of his own body, which he is prepared to sacrifice; however, he does not prefer the public good to the good of virtue. This is clear from the fact that such a citizen would not expose himself to the loss of the good of virtue for the sake of the political community. Godfrey agrees with this last statement, but he thinks that the common good always includes the individual good.

The fifth objection is based on the principle of God as the final good. James's version of this argument is not from Giles, in that James does not discuss participation. However, Giles's conception of participation in this context is itself based on finality. The objection states that God is the final good precisely because every created good participates in God and is to be loved for the sake of that divine good. James's response to this objection applies to any position that would hold that an individual naturally prefers his external end to his own good. He does not attack the Thomistic belief that every creature is ordered to an end other than itself, but he denies that such an ordering implies that a creature can naturally prefer the end to himself.

James argues against this view in two ways. First, he attacks the objection's use of the phrase, "But that on account of which everything is such, is more" (*Sed propter quod unumquodque est, et ille magis*).[180] Although something is more (*magis*) in an absolute sense, it does not follow that it is more to us. James again makes the distinction between that which is most lovable in itself and that which is most lovable to us, explaining it here in greater detail. We do not always love those things that are better, but instead we love those that are more joined to us (*nobis coniunctores*). God is the most lovable thing (*maxime diligibilis*) because he is the most good (*maxime bonus*). However, since a man is naturally most one (*maxime unus*) to himself rather than to God, it follows that by natural love he loves himself more than God. Giles's argument does prove that God is the most lovable absolutely speaking, but it does not prove that God is the most lovable to man by natural love. Moreover, James has already shown in what sense every creature loves the good on account of God. His general position on this issue is connected with his view that although God orders everything to the end as an external agent, each creature naturally acts for its own good. There is a difference between God's view and that of the creature. From an impartial view, the end, which is God, is most important. Nevertheless, each creature naturally desires its own perfection most of all.

James's second criticism of the argument is based on the two different uses of the preposition "*propter*," which correspond to the different types of love. The first use of *propter* is to refer to an end (*finis*).[181] In this way, to be loved *propter* as an object is to be loved as an end. Consequently, the object of the love is loved by the love of concupiscence. In this sense, it is correct to assert that a human loves his own good on account of (*propter*) God. But by such love God is desired as one's own end. Consequently, in this fashion a human cannot love God more than himself. The other use of *propter* is to refer to the moving cause (*causa movens*) of the love. In this sense someone can love a human on account of (*propter*) another, as when someone loves a servant on account of (*propter*) his lord. The love for the servant has the love for the lord as its moving cause. In this sense someone will love his friend on account of (*propter*) himself, since the love for the friend has its origin in self-love. Such love is the love of friendship. James replies by again giving his interpretation of Aristotle's dictum, that by natural love the self is the source of all other love and therefore superior to all other love. Only by charity can God be loved more than self.

James's understanding of the natural love of God over self not only differs from that of Thomas and his followers but also disagrees with Henry of Ghent's understanding of Aristotelianism. Henry and James agree with Siger that the good citizen loves himself more than the political community, but by separating the issues concerning the natural love of God from those concerning the common good Henry is able to argue for the natural love of God over self. James is anomalous in grafting Siger's interpretation of the good citizen onto St. Bernard's understanding of *natura curva*. By nature, every human loves himself more than the political community and God. It is only through grace that God is loved above everything, and this supernatural love of charity becomes the source for a heightened love of self and neighbor that is subordinated to the love of God. The self-directed eudaimonism of Aristotle is both correct and yet inconsistent with Christian ethics. James defends his position on the basis of his innovative view of the orders of nature and grace. For both, unity is the basis of love. Nevertheless, on a natural level each individual is most of all united with itself, and consequently it acts primarily for its own good. It is only on a supernatural level that someone can prefer God's love to his own, and the order of this love depends on the fact that he has been made one with God through grace.

V. The Conflict over Moral Science:
James and Godfrey

During the last few years of the thirteenth century, both Godfrey and James return to what had become the two basic issues of their debate over naturally loving God, namely (1) whether grace and nature are congruous, and (2) whether natural inclination is most of all for the agent's own good. In his *Quodlibet* 13 (1297/1298), q. 1, Godfrey addresses the question, "Whether the science of theology is a speculative science?"[182] Godfrey's concern is James's *Quodlibet* 3 (1295/1296), q. 1, which asks, "Whether the science of Sacred Scripture is speculative or practical?"[183] In the course of this question James makes statements about the relationship between moral science and theology which Godfrey finds unpalatable. One issue at stake is whether moral science is directed to the love of God over self. This debate over moral science is partially a debate over the relationship between nature and grace.

In his discussion of the nature of theology, James of Viterbo defends Giles of Rome's thesis that theology is an affective science.[184] This understanding of theology complements James's view that happiness consists in loving rather than in knowing.[185] According to James, theology is best understood as an affective science because its end consists in loving God.[186] Moreover, it is the only science that has this love as its end *simpliciter et absolute*. James recognizes that this view of theology faces the problem that the philosophers, too, think that God should be loved, yet they did not have faith. Therefore the love of God seems to be the end of moral science as well as of theology. James argues that there are three differences between the moral science of the philosophers and theology.

The first difference between moral science and theology is that theology more principally intends the love of God.[187] James uses the relationship between metaphysics and theology to illustrate this point. Metaphysics does not regard as a subject just God, but rather God considered as the most perfect being, or as the cause or principle of being. In contrast, theology considers as a subject God in relation only to himself. Similarly, moral science considers the love of God as the principle among possible actions and as the end of such actions that are not the love of God, but it is not directly concerned with the love of God for his own sake. Theology is principally concerned with the love of God, and considers other possible actions only insofar as they relate to the love of God.

The second difference between theology and moral science is that moral science is ordered to the love of God only insofar as such love can be obtained through natural principles or the acquired virtues.[188] Theology is ordered to that love which can be obtained through supernatural help, namely charity. James differs from Godfrey in his account of the acquired and infused virtues. James contrasts legal justice, which considers all virtues as directed towards the common good, with charity, which is directed towards God. In *Quodlibet* 3, q. 21, James argues that there are both infused and acquired moral virtues which are based on the different ends of human action. Acquired legal justice is the form of the acquired virtues since it is directed towards the common good.[189] Infused justice is directed to the supernatural common good, which is God. In a more important way, infused friendship, or charity, is the form of the virtues. The acquired virtue of friendship moves the agent to seek the good more freely than justice does, but the good sought remains only natural happiness. The infused virtue of friendship is charity, which seeks the good of supernatural happiness. James will go on to write, "Inasmuch therefore as infused virtue is superior to acquired [virtue], so theology is more perfectly ordered to love than moral [science is]."[190]

The third difference between theology and moral science is that moral science is ordered to the love of God by the love of concupiscence, whereas theology is ordered to the love of God by the love of friendship.[191] The philosophers knew that God should be loved. Aristotle mentions that friendship with God is impossible, but the Platonists did have some knowledge of this friendship, although they did not understand it well. The philosophers thought that God should be loved as an end, and consequently they discussed only how God is loved by the love of concupiscence. Through grace we are called sons and friends of God. This friendship with God is charity, to which end Holy Scripture is ordered. Although according to such friendship God is loved by both types of love, he is loved most of all by the love of friendship.

In his *Quodlibet* 13, q. 1, Godfrey argues that theology is both a speculative and a practical science. At the end of the discussion Godfrey brings up James's belief that both theology and moral science are practical, but in different ways.[192] According to this position, the moral philosopher (*moralis philosophus*) is concerned with the love of God as the end, who is the principle of all possible actions. According to moral science, all love for another, including the love of God, comes from self-love. In contrast, the theologian (*theologus*) is concerned with the love of God through charity. By such supernatural love a human loves God more than himself, and charity, which is infused, is the source for his self-love and love of others. Godfrey is clearly referring to James here, and he even paraphrases James's modification of Aristotle's dictum on friendship.

According to Godfrey, James's understanding of the contrast between the moral philosopher and the theologian has some truth to it.[193] First, moral science and philosophy do consider different types of possible actions. Second, natural friendship and supernatural friendship with God through charity do differ importantly, in that the first comes from natural powers whereas the other comes through the infusion of a supernatural habit. Moreover, the two types of friendship are ordered to different common goods, namely, the natural common good, which is the object of legal justice, and the supernatural common good, which is the object of charity.

Godfrey distinguishes between James's understanding of the difference between the two types of friendship and his own.[194] James is correct to distinguish between the virtues involved in the different types of friendship, but Godfrey states that there is also a difference between the different goods involved. Natural friendship comes from sharing the natural goods, whereas the friendship with God through grace is based on sharing the goods of supernatural beatitude. This supernatural beatitude cannot be known by reason, but rather by faith. It is clear from this that theology is more noble than moral science, although both sciences consider the love of God. Godfrey's emphasis on the sharing of goods shows how he can hold the position that God is loved more than self naturally and supernaturally while at the same time distinguishing between the two loves. Godfrey offers an alternative understanding of the main difference between natural and supernatural friendship, namely, that when grace elevates nature it does not change the natural order, but rather elevates nature to an end which cannot be obtained from purely natural powers.

Godfrey's criticism of James's position on nature and grace has three parts. First, Godfrey attacks James's understanding of the relationship between nature and grace. Second, he attacks James's understanding of the relationship between the intellect and the will. Third, Godfrey uses the part/whole argument to correct James's belief that the self must be loved most of all because of the lover's union with himself.

First, Godfrey's argues that if a human naturally loved himself more than God, then his nature would not be perfected by grace, since nature would not be ordered to God as its happiness. James states that the natural love of self over God is perfected by the supernatural love of God over self. Godfrey remarks that these two loves are not related as the imperfect to the perfect, but rather as simple contraries. James's comparison of the relationship between the natural knowledge of God and faith is also misleading. The natural knowledge of God is imperfect, but it is not repugnant to faith. Godfrey writes:

> For just as we are designed by nature (*nati*) to love God supernaturally through charity and naturally, thus also we are designed by nature (*nati*) to know him through supernatural faith and through natural reason; however, these do not stand together, that as far as it concerns God I know him to be three supernaturally and through faith and that I know

him not to be three through natural reason; nor are natural and super-natural reason repugnant.[195]

The Trinity is not known naturally, but nonetheless the Trinity is not naturally denied. The natural knowledge of God is compatible with the supernatural knowledge of God. Similarly, natural love is not directed to a different end than charity; the two are compatible. Otherwise, charity would be opposed to natural inclination.

Godfrey's second criticism is that James misunderstands the relationship between natural reason and will.[196] James thinks that although natural reason orders that God should be loved more than self, the command of reason cannot be fulfilled without the help of grace. Godfrey responds that the will by nature is inclined to the judgment of reason. On account of its liberty the will might not follow natural reason, but it has the ability to do so. "Ought" implies "can" if the "ought" is known through natural reason. Godfrey thinks that Aristotle agrees with this position.

The third criticism is directed against James's belief that a human loves himself most of all because he is more one with himself than he is with another.[197] According to Godfrey, James cannot simultaneously hold the belief that unity is the basis of love and the belief that reason commands someone to love God more than himself even if he cannot follow reason through his natural powers alone. So long as nature remains, the agent will be most of all one with himself and consequently according to reason he will love himself most of all.

Moreover, Godfrey argues that if love required strict unity, then right reason could never command that another be loved more than the self, but he thinks that the relationship of the individual as a part to God as a whole solves this problem. Every particular being is a part of that whole which is God because God contains and conserves all being in himself through his power and perfection. Consequently, all being is united with God as a part is united to the whole. Every part naturally loves the good of the whole. At this point Godfrey criticizes James's understanding of the connection between union and friendship:

> Therefore because the union which is *per se* required for friendship is not the union which consists solely in the conjunction of the natural prin-ciples of some being as it is something existing singularly according to itself, but as it is a certain part of some whole. For this reason, even the natural inclination includes this, that the good of the part should be

ordered to the good of the whole and that each individual thus should love his own self as he is some one singular being according to nature, just as he arranges what is the principal good and the principal object of the ordered will in an order to the good of the community. So what is included in this is that the part loves the common good more than the private inasmuch as [the part] orders even the private good to the common good, but not conversely . . .[198]

Although Kempshall thinks that Godfrey's reply to James is based on the transforming power of love, Godfrey's argument is clearly based instead on the already existing order of the part to the whole. Love does not change the relationship, but rather follows the relationship. The union which forms the basis for love is not just a union of the principles of being, but rather that union which consists of the natural order of the private good to the common good.

James thinks that the universe consists of individuals who seek their own benefit. According to this position, when the good citizen dies for the political community, he loves his own good of virtue more than the good of the political community. Godfrey argues that James is right in thinking that the citizen gains for himself a great good by dying, but mistaken in thinking that the citizen attends to this good.[199] The object of the citizen's action is not his own virtue, but the public good. The personal virtue results from and is expressed in the act. Godfrey consistently emphasizes that although the common good includes the individual good, the common good is not loved for the sake of the individual good. Rather, each individual has implanted within himself an inclination for the common good.

This dispute over moral science indicates the focal points of the debate in the thirteenth century over the Thomistic view of the natural love of God over self. As we saw in chapter 3, one of Thomas's most important innovations was his attempt to base ethics on a natural inclination which is not primarily self-directed. This view of natural inclination is central for understanding the nature of Aristotelian eudaimonism as reconcilable with Christian ethics. James interprets nature as primarily self-directed and consequently views moral philosophy as self-directed and theology as directed towards God. According to Godfrey, the natural inclination of each creature is primarily to the good of the whole, and the order of grace is in conformity with the order of nature. Theology does not conflict with natural moral knowledge, although it is primarily concerned with how through grace the moral virtues lead to eternal life. Both James and Godfrey think that Aristotle accurately describes natural ethics, but they disagree over whether in Aristotle's ethics the agent prefers his own good most of all.

It is interesting that neither of them take into account Thomas's emphasis on the corruption of human nature which is due to original sin. The Thomistic view of natural inclination became the focus of later discussions, but Thomas's equal insistence on the corruption of human nature had only a marginal presence.

The argument between Godfrey and James over the nature of moral science underscores the most important issues raised by the thinkers of this chapter. First, what is the basis of love? Siger and James think that all natural love stems from self-love, whereas Henry, Giles, and Godfrey emphasize the natural inclination of the part for the whole. Henry applies this argument only to the natural love for God, since he does not think that it works for the political community. The second major issue concerns the relationship between charity and natural love. Henry does not distinguish clearly between elective natural love and charity, perhaps because he does not think that a purely natural end for humans is possible. In contrast, Godfrey argues that the two are congruent. The natural love of God is for God as an object that can be known naturally, whereas charity requires supernatural knowledge and the communication of spiritual goods. James of Viterbo argues that the self is loved most of all by natural love, whereas God is so loved only through charity. This position allows James to incorporate the Arts Faculty's interpretation of Aristotle's ethics into his understanding of moral science, but Godfrey shows that this position leads to serious difficulties concerning the relationship between nature and grace.

At the end of the thirteenth century, the fundamental philosophical issue has become whether a natural moral philosophy is primarily self-interested. Earlier discussions were about moral psychology. These later discussions do include moral psychology, but they more deeply consider the entire worldview which is presupposed by positions in moral psychology. Thomas's emphasis on natural inclination and the Arts Faculty's self-directed interpretation of Aristotle have altered and deepened the debate. The fundamental issue is no longer just the way in which the will is ordered to God, but the way in which every creature is ordered to God. Henry's position is more traditional and he does not take Aristotle as a completely reliable guide. His view is philosophically interesting in that he responds to a self-directed Aristotelianism without adhering completely to his own version of Aristotle's ethics. Among those who do rely on Aristotle there are two alternative approaches, which show two different ways of being an Aristotelian eudaimonist. The first, which was chosen by James, accepts Aristotle's authority in the realm of philosophical morality, but then contrasts this self-interested philosophical morality with Christian ethics. The second, and more or less Thomistic, position holds that grace perfects nature in such a way that the demands of philosophical morality cannot conflict with Christian ethics. On this approach, all creatures are inclined by nature to prefer God to their own good. James, Godfrey, and Giles agree that Aristotle is a reliable guide to philosophical moral science, and that such morality is based on natural inclination. They differ over whether this natural inclination is self-interested, and whether it is opposed to grace. All seem to accept the belief that Aristotelian ethics is based on natural inclination. These two controversies, namely that over natural inclination and that over nature and grace, help to put Scotus's ethical theory in its historical context.

CHAPTER 5

John Duns Scotus

John Duns Scotus's teaching on the natural love of God over self brings us to the final chapter in the history of thirteenth-century discussions of the issue. Scotus was eventually recognized as one of the great Franciscan theologians and his followers were influential well into the seventeenth century. Although his writings on loving God show a great familiarity with the theologians at Paris, his background as a Franciscan and an Oxonian would not have encouraged much sympathy for Thomas Aquinas and his followers. At Oxford, Franciscans such as John Pecham and William of Ware were more influenced by theologians such as Bonaventure and Henry of Ghent. These and other thinkers discussed in the previous chapters left unresolved three main issues in the debate over the natural love of God. The first issue is the metaphysical basis for the natural love of God over self. Whereas such earlier writers as Philip the Chancellor and Bonaventure had thought that the ability to love God over self had its basis in reason, Thomas Aquinas emphasized the conformity between natural inclination and the natural love of God over self. According to Thomas, a human's natural love for God is like the natural love of a part of a whole for the good of the whole. Later writers who did not adhere to this theory of natural inclination, such as Henry of Ghent and James of Viterbo, were skeptical about the natural ability to love God over self. The difference between Thomas and his immediate predecessors was mostly about whether the ability so to love God comes from nature or reason. The dispute between the later supporters of Thomas's position, namely, Godfrey of Fontaines and Giles of Rome, and their contemporaries, such as Henry and James, was more about whether an individual by nature loved most himself or the common good.

This disagreement about natural inclination leads to the second major issue left unresolved by Scotus's predecessors: Is Aristotelian moral psychology compatible with the natural love of God over self? Thomas Aquinas and his followers thought that it was. But in the Arts Faculty Siger of Brabant had championed an interpretation of Aristotle which stated that the virtuous individual loves his own self more than the common good. The differences among the late-thirteenth-century writers we have studied were not so much about their acceptance or rejection of Aristotle as about the interpretation of Aristotle. James of Viterbo and, to some extent, Henry of Ghent applied their understanding of Aristotelian moral psychology to the natural love of God when they stated that by nature the self is loved more than God. Although they did not excuse such love, they did argue that the proper order of love, according to which God is loved more than self, can only come about through grace.

James's emphasis on the limits of human nature raises the third major question: Does "ought" imply "can" on the natural level? If not, then does this inability to act correctly come from human nature itself, or is it the result of original sin? Godfrey of Fontaines followed in the tradition of Philip the Chancellor when he used the claim that there is a natural love of God over self to justify the belief that there is a corresponding natural ability to love God in this way. Thomas Aquinas took the more nuanced view that only after the Fall are human beings unable to fulfill the command to love God over self. James and Henry argue that this inability to love God more than self has its basis in human nature. James explicitly states that "ought" in no way implies "can" on a natural level.

To understand Scotus in context and correctly, these three issues must be kept in mind, namely the relationship between the natural love of God and natural inclination, the compatibility of Aristotle's moral psychology with the love of God over self, and the question of whether the obligation to love God more than self implies a natural ability to do so. The recent proliferation of literature on Scotus's ethics has produced no agreement on whether Scotus accepts Aristotelian moral psychology, and Scotus's understanding of natural inclination has frequently been oversimplified. Consequently, before discussing Scotus's own texts, it will be helpful to consider some of the recent disputes.

I. Contemporary Disagreements over Scotus

Two areas of scholarly disagreement have special interest for the question of whether God can be naturally loved above self. First, there is a debate over whether Scotus looks on Aristotle's ethical theory as incomplete or whether he entirely rejects Aristotelian ethics. Second, there is disagreement over the relationship between the moral law and the divine will. Is Scotus's understanding of natural law generally consistent with that of previous thirteenth-century thinkers, or does Scotus opt for a position which would base ethical commands only on the will of God?

The contemporary discussion of Scotus's attitude towards Aristotle centers on Scotus's understanding of the distinction between will and nature, as well as on Scotus's teaching that the will has not only an *affectio commodi* (tendency for the beneficial), but also an *affectio iustitiae* (tendency for the just). The first issue is important because Scotus develops his understanding of the contrast between nature and freedom in a commentary on Aristotle's *Metaphysics*. According to Scotus, Aristotle himself distinguishes between a natural potency, which has a tendency to only one act, and a rational potency, which is indeterminate with respect to a part of opposite actions.[1] The range of scholarly opinion on Scotus's interpretation is indicated by Allan Wolter's own scholarly development. Originally Wolter had argued that Scotus was appropriating Aristotle's authority to provide support for his own, different position.[2] Wolter's final position is that Scotus did in fact interpret Aristotle correctly even though he greatly expanded the doctrine.[3] According to this latter view, Scotus's position is not at variance with that of Aristotle, but it is more complete. This distinction between rejecting Aristotle and completing Aristotle should be kept in mind when interpreting texts in which Scotus expounds positions that are not found in Aristotle. An additional distinction should be made between Scotus's own version of Aristotle and the historical Aristotle. Although Scotus's own position might actually conflict with that of Aristotle, it does not necessarily follow that Scotus thinks that there is a conflict. The scholarly literature is relatively silent on this last distinction, but it is important. Contemporary attempts to contrast Scotus with the historical Aristotle do not show that Scotus develops his own ethics as an alternative to that of Aristotle.

The relationship between Scotus's understanding of the will and Aristotelian ethics becomes more problematic when Scotus's theory of the will's two *affectiones* is introduced. Briefly, Scotus's distinction between the two *affectiones* derives from his distinction between two different goods.[4] The *affectio commodi* is a tendency for the *bonum sibi* (good for the self), whereas the *affectio iustitiae* is a tendency for the *bonum in se* (good in itself). Marilyn McCord Adams, John Boler, and Thomas Williams all identify Aristotelian eudaimonism with the *affectio commodi*.[5] John Boler makes the further claim that Scotus's distinction between the *bonum sibi* and the *bonum in se* makes it impossible for him to adopt an Aristotelian ethics.[6] Boler's claim is problematic since, as we have seen in chapter 3, Thomas Aquinas himself makes this distinction, and it would be foolhardy to say that Thomas rejects Aristotelian ethics. Moreover, with respect to the wider claim about the delegation of Aristotelian ethics to the *affectio commodi,* nowhere does Scotus himself make this claim. Mary Elizabeth Ingham has defended the consonance of Scotus's theory with Aristotelianism.[7] Although her position is developed as a criticism of Williams, it makes the wider point that interpretations which see Aristotle's ethics as incompatible with that of Scotus presuppose a particular interpretation of Aristotle which Scotus would reject.

The disagreement over Scotus's attitude towards Aristotelianism informs the debate over Scotus's voluntarism. There has been a long tradition of interpreting Scotus to say that the natural law has its basis only in God's will.[8] The proponents of this view often infer from this claim the additional belief that considerations of human nature are largely irrelevant to an understanding of moral claims. Allan Wolter and Mary Elizabeth Ingham have argued that Scotus's historical context and emphasis on right reason (*recta ratio*) show that Scotus was not a radical voluntarist.[9] Scotus, like other medievals, used a rational consideration of human nature to buttress claims about the natural law. Thomas Williams has added a further twist to the issue by arguing that voluntarism as a theory of moral obligation does not entail any epistemological views.[10] It could be true both that God's will is the sole source of moral obligation and that humans can learn about this law through reasoning about human nature. Nevertheless, Williams denies that Scotus thinks human nature entails moral precepts.[11]

In general, the voluntaristic interpretation of Scotus has been predominant, and accompanied by a neglect of the importance of human nature for Scotus's ethics. Many writers suggest that Scotus is altogether hostile to the notion of an ethical inclination of human nature. For example, in an article on the natural love of God, Rudi te Velde writes, "Scotus appears to regard the will's natural inclination as self-centered, and, without the *affectio iustitiae,* closed off from the moral domain of what is intrinsically good."[12]

This brief survey of the scholarship shows that any exposition of Scotus's ethics must necessarily take sides on controverted questions. I will argue that the general understanding of Scotus as being hostile to natural inclination is to some extent true, although it is imprecise. Scotus has a more nuanced view of human nature and natural inclination than is generally attributed to him.

II. Natural Inclination

The natural love of God over self is discussed at length in Book 3, d. 27 of both Scotus's *Opus Oxoniense* and his *Reportata Parisiensia.*[13] Since the argument in these passages presupposes Scotus's theory of natural inclination, the natural law, and original sin, these three topics will be considered in order. Moreover, the discussion of these topics will provide a basis for justifying positions on especially controverted issues in the scholarly literature. After these issues have been clarified, it will be easier to expound the two passages in which Scotus explicitly discusses the natural love of God over self.

Although Scotus's view of ethics is not generally presented as based on natural inclination, in at least two passages Scotus does identify a good act as an act in accordance with natural inclination. In the *Opus Oxoniense,* Book 2, d. 7, q. un., Scotus discusses whether a bad angel necessarily wills evil. Scotus argues that since the bad angels are still good in their nature, they are able to act in accordance with their natural inclination. Since acts which accord with natural inclination are good, the bad angels do not necessarily will evil.[14] In the *Reportata Parisiensia,* Book 2, d. 7, q. 3, Scotus relates the question of whether the bad angels can will good to whether they can naturally love God:

> An angel from purely natural powers is able to love God above everything . . . Therefore a natural inclination is able to incline an angel to this, that it love God above everything, since no accident happening to a nature can incline the nature more to another, than [can] the whole weight of nature to that to which the nature inclines. Therefore, if the obstinacy in the angels is to such a degree through this, which remains habitually in a bad act, the angel is able in other things to have a completely morally good act.[15]

This passage is interesting for understanding the natural love of God, but it is not of central importance because Scotus does think that the angels probably not only habitually but also actually elicit the bad act, and that they in fact do not love God more than themselves.[16] The importance of this passage is that it reinforces that passage in the *Opus Oxoniense* which states that a moral act is in accordance with natural inclination. Neither of the two passages mentioned has played a role in the scholarly debate over Scotus's understanding of the relationship between natural inclination and moral obligation. One reason may be that they do not reflect Scotus's typical mode of expression. Scotus's great commentator Francis Lychetus notes that the passage from the *Opus Oxoniense* seems to contradict other positions found in the same work. Nevertheless, Lychetus states, ". . . if the Doctor [Scotus] is rightly understood, no contradiction will appear."[17] Although I do think that in these passages Scotus may be simply following contemporary usage, there is some truth to Lychetus's view, since the will is directed to God because of its nature. To support this argument, I will first present the different meanings of the word "natural" as discussed by Scotus. Second, I will apply Scotus's understanding of the relationship between the will and nature to his theory of the two *affectiones* and love. Finally, I will evaluate the question of what an individual might choose to love as his natural end.

Although Scotus distinguishes will from nature, he argues that there are three ways in which the will is called "natural."[18] First, nature can be understood as a relation following upon the will's potency to its proper perfection. Second, the term "natural" can distinguish the natural will from that will which is informed by grace. Third, the will's choice of an act which is to the advantage of the agent [*ad commodum*] can be called natural. By this meaning, the natural will would be contrasted with the free choice of an act which in some sense is opposed to the agent's own benefit. The first and third meanings are important when discussing the will's natural inclination. In the first meaning, an elicited act is excluded, thereby also excluding a selfish act. According to the third meaning, the will actually elicits an act with the intention of becoming more perfect.

Scotus applies these three different meanings of the word "nature" to natural love, as well. Scotus argues that although in a broad sense there are three different natural loves, properly speaking there are only two.[19] According to the first meaning, natural love could be the inclination for that natural good which goes along with its nature. Scotus is reluctant to describe such an inclination as love, although he concedes that it might be described as "habitual love" (*dilectio habitualis*). According to the second meaning, natural love is an elicited act in accordance with this natural inclination; this act elicits what is to the agent's own benefit (*commodum*). "Natural" in this second meaning is the counterpart to the third meaning of "natural" as applied to natural will. Both describe an elicited act which is directed to the self. In the third meaning, natural love is distinguished from supernatural love. This third meaning of "natural love" clearly corresponds to the second meaning of "natural will." Although the meanings of the term "natural" appear in a different order in the two passages, their correspondence is clear. Scotus not only distinguishes between the natural and the supernatural, but he also distinguishes between the natural inclination for perfection and that elicited act which conforms to this inclination.

Scotus's distinction between the natural inclination for perfection and the elicited act for perfection helps to explain passages in which Scotus differentially evaluates acts that conform to natural inclination. There appears to be a contradiction. To avoid confusion, a distinction needs to be made between two meanings of the term "conformity." An action could conform to natural inclination because it perfects the natural agent, or an action could conform to natural inclination because it has this perfection as its primary intention. To understand this contrast more clearly Scotus's understanding of the difference between nature and will must be explained.

Scotus's discussion of the traditional distinction between the will as free and the will as a nature (*voluntas ut natura*) shows the novelty of his moral psychology. Whereas other writers had stated that the *voluntas ut natura* was directed towards happiness, Scotus emphasizes that there is a twofold *voluntas ut natura.*[20] By the first meaning, the *voluntas ut natura* signifies the will's natural inclination to its proper object. By the second meaning, it signifies the will's natural tendency to follow other appetites. The first way is the more interesting because the *voluntas ut natura* is neutral with respect to the motive for the will's natural direction to its proper object. An act elicited in accordance to this natural inclination could be directed to an object either for the object's good or for the sake of the agent.

This natural inclination of the will for its own perfection is not a separate property that belongs to the will, but instead it is a relation between the will and its perfection.[21] If the will is understood correctly, its perfection will also be understood. The two cannot be separated without a contradiction. The will's natural inclination is both like and unlike the natural inclination of a stone to fall towards the earth. The natural inclination of the stone is similar to the will in that the stone's tendency to fall towards the earth is not something separate from the stone, but rather it is the relation of the stone to the center of the earth, where it will achieve its proper perfection.[22] Like the stone, the will's natural inclination for perfection is not in reality distinct from its nature.

The difference between the natural inclination of the will and that of the stone illustrates the peculiar difficulties that arise with respect to the notion of the will's natural inclination. The stone by necessity tends towards the earth. It will fall unless impeded. In contrast, although the will's natural inclination is also a passive potency to its perfection, this perfection is obtained through indeterminate and therefore freely elicited acts.[23] Scotus thinks that this distinction between the potency of the will and the natural potency of an object like a stone is found in Aristotle's *Metaphysics,* where a distinction is made between non-rational and rational potencies.[24] A non-rational potency is oriented to only one action because it is a merely natural potency. The will is a rational potency, which is indeterminate with respect to different and incompatible actions. The will's freedom is precisely this rational potency of the will to contradictories.[25]

This distinction between nature and liberty is accompanied by a distinction between two appetites of the will. The first appetite is for its own perfection, while the second appetite is the ability to will freely.[26] The first appetite is a natural inclination and not an elicited act. A stone has no choice about seeking the center of the Earth; it necessarily seeks its own perfection. A free agent can elicit an act which either is conformed to this natural inclination for perfection or is opposed to it.[27] For example, by natural appetite an agent wills to avoid death.[28] Nevertheless, the martyrs act against this appetite when they freely choose to die. The agent's ability to act independently of the natural inclination for perfection makes human freedom possible. Scotus is not arguing that the martyr's perfection is accomplished through choosing death; on the contrary, the martyr gives up his own perfection by so choosing. It would be helpful for us if Scotus had explained whether the martyr or the person who dies for the political community actually gains a greater good than he would have otherwise. Scotus never goes into the detail that his predecessors do on this point.[29] Scotus's recognition of this type of choice shows that his ethical theory cannot rest entirely on natural inclination, since the natural inclination of the martyr appears to run counter to the virtuous action. With respect to this understanding of the way an act accords with natural inclination, Duns Scotus shares James of Viterbo's view that natural inclination is opposed to a morally obliged action. Nevertheless, Scotus, unlike James, does not think that human choice is limited by natural inclination.

How is the martyr able to freely give up his own perfection? Scotus does not say that it is easy for the agent to act against his natural inclination. Everyone wills happiness. When necessary, the just human being is able to choose death freely by acting against this inclination, but his choice is accompanied by difficulty. The contexts in which Scotus describes the individual's self-sacrifice as contrary to natural inclination display a clear opposition between the desire for perfection and the elicited choice. Scotus may think that although the just person would be less perfect if he did not sacrifice himself, this act of self-sacrifice does limit the just person's desire for perfection. If the agent dies he will not be able to continue his virtuous action. This interpretation of Scotus is strengthened by Scotus's argument that the freedom of the will is in the agent's ability to moderate his own desire for happiness.[30] When discussing the difference between the good and the bad angels, Scotus notes that they both have the same natural inclination for happiness, but that the inclination of the good angels is stronger because their natural perfection is stronger. The good angels differ from the bad in that they freely obtain their happiness by acting in accordance with a higher rule. Scotus generally emphasizes that the desire for happiness must be moderated by a higher rule or a higher will. Whether the agent is an angel or a human, a moral agent's perfection consists in being able either to seek happiness on its own or to follow a higher rule or will that puts a restraint on this search. Therefore, perfection is obtained by not having an immoderate desire for happiness or one's own perfection.

The distinction between the advantageous (*commodum*) and the just (*iusti*) plays a central role in Scotus's understanding of how the desire for happiness is moderated.[31] Created freedom requires an ability to will in accordance with the rule of justice, which is given by a higher will. St. Anselm had developed a thought experiment in which an angel is created with only the desire for happiness and without a desire for rectitude. This angel would not be free since it could seek only its own happiness. Anselm gives the example to show a necessary connection between freedom and rectitude.[32] Scotus interprets this thought experiment as making the stronger claim that freedom requires an ability to choose between the advantageous and the just. If an angel were created so that it would necessarily seek happiness, then its ability to perform meritorious actions would be no greater than that of a cow. [33]

The distinction between the advantageous and the just forms the basis for Scotus's distinction between the two *affectiones* (tendencies) of the will.[34] The *affectio commodi* (tendency for the advantageous) is a tendency to act in accordance with the agent's natural inclination for happiness, whereas the *affectio iustitiae* is the ability to act freely in accordance with a higher rule. The distinction between the two *affectiones* does not entail that natural inclination is curved in on itself, but instead that a free choice is not right (*rectus*) in the same way that a natural appetite is. Scotus explains:

> But the free appetite is not right from the fact that it is conformed to some inferior right thing, but from this, that it wills that which God wills it to will. Whence those two *affectiones,* for the advantageous (*commodi*) and the just (*iusti*), are ruled by [*per*] a superior rule, which is the divine will . . .[35]

What sort of justice is the object of the *affectio iustitiae*? Scotus is not implying that every will contains moral justice, or that justice is infused in it by God. Instead, every will has an innate justice precisely because the will is free.[36] Properly speaking, justice is the habitual rectitude of the will by which someone wills the good of another. The agent acts for himself justly when he thinks of himself as another person.[37] The *affectio iustitiae* is the ability of the will to choose a good which is not ordered to the agent's own self (*non ordinatum ad se*). In contrast, the *affectio commodi* refers to the tendency to will a good only because it is good for one's own self.[38]

Although there has been controversy over the subject in the scholarly literature, Scotus clearly states that the *affectio iustitiae* is a necessary condition for liberty.[39] As a nature, the will has an inclination for the advantageous in the way that every other nature does. The *affectio iustitiae* is the ability of the will to act against this natural inclination. Animals do not have freedom precisely because they can seek only what is advantageous for themselves.[40]

Scotus's emphasis on the connection between the *affectio commodi* and natural inclination raises the question of whether the *affectio commodi* is always selfish. According to the more traditional interpretation, which is represented perhaps most notably by Allan Wolter, the *affectio commodi* seems to be entirely for the agent's own advantage.[41] The *affectio iustitiae* is a check on selfishness. But according to Thomas Williams' interpretation, the *affectio commodi* is merely the intellectual appetite as conventionally understood.[42] Someone can sin not only by loving himself too much, but also by loving a friend too much. Such a love is according to the *affectio commodi* even though it is not selfish. There is truth to both interpretations. Williams is correct to note that the *affectio commodi* is not always selfish, but Wolter is surely right in noting that the *affectio commodi* is connected directly to the will's natural inclination, and that a nature always prefers its own good to that of another. The primary self-orientation of nature does not imply that the natural inclination is always selfish. Someone may will his neighbor's good as *commodum*. Sin arises not only from self-love but also from an inordinate love of others. Nevertheless, no one can prefer another good to his own if he wills according to the *affectio commodi*. It is only in accordance with the *affectio iustitiae* that someone can love another more than oneself, and the only possible object of such love is God.

To better understand these issues, it is important to consider how the two *affectiones* play a central role in the interplay among the desire for happiness, the love of God, and self-love. By the *affectio iustitiae* the good agent desires happiness not for his own sake, but rather for God. There is a sharp contrast between the *bonum sibi* (good of the agent) and the *bonum in se* (good in itself).[43] Scotus does not deny that the *bonum sibi* is an object of desire, but he argues that it must be subordinated to a higher good. Those who are bad desire happiness immoderately.[44] Although the bad angel's first sin was pride, the second sin consisted precisely in this disordered lust for its own beatitude.[45] To understand how the first sin of pride led to the second sin of immoderate desire for happiness, it is necessary to return to the difference between the love of friendship and the love of concupiscence.

The two loves are distinguished by their different objects. Scotus states in one place that by the love of friendship the good is willed for the sake of the one to whom it is willed, whereas by the love of concupiscence the good is willed for the lover's own sake.[46] From this point of view the love of concupiscence appears to be self-centered. This distinction is to some extent misleading because it does not show the dependence of the love of concupiscence on the love of friendship.[47] The love of concupiscence may love a good because that good is willed to someone who is already loved by the love of friendship. Consequently, not every act of love of concupiscence is selfish, even though the good is not loved for its own sake but by the *affectio commodi*. The love of concupiscence is the love of a good for the sake of another, whereas the love of friendship is the love of the other for the other's own sake. For example, someone could love a bottle of wine by love of concupiscence when he gives it to a friend who is loved by the love of friendship. Every good that is loved by the love of concupiscence presupposes a person who is the object of the love of friendship.

The dependence of the love of concupiscence on the love of friendship is important because it shows how moral order and disorder cannot be the result of the love of concupiscence alone; rather, there must be a previously disordered love of friendship. The order of the love of friendship determines the order of the love of concupiscence.[48] God cannot be the object of a too great love of friendship, since, as we will see, God must be loved above all things because he is the complete source of goodness. The first sin of the angels, which was pride, occurred when they loved themselves by the love of friendship. This sin of the angels contrasts the correct ordering of the love of friendship to God rather than to self. Human sin is more complicated. According to Scotus, Adam's first sin was on account of the love of friendship which he had for his wife.[49] Scotus is careful to note that he is not stating that Adam sinned because of any impure desires he had for Eve. Presumably these desires would be instances of the love of concupiscence, and Adam would have erred thereby only in loving himself most by the love of friendship. Instead, Adam loved his wife excessively by the love of friendship and thereby broke the command of God not to eat the apple. Adam's sin was not the result of a disordered sense appetite, but of that love of friendship which led him to share Eve's fate.

Even though Adam's sin involved an inordinate love of friendship for Eve, Scotus makes it clear that after God the self must and should be loved more than another. Adam did not love Eve more than himself. Following Augustine, Scotus thinks that there are ultimately only two highest objects of love: God and the self. Why must the self be loved more than another?

Scotus here argues that such love is based on natural inclination. According to Scotus, this natural inclination explains the famous dictum of Aristotle, that the notes of friendship for another come from those notes of friendship which are for one's own self. Contrary to the more extreme tradition of the *natura curva,* Scotus holds that natural inclination does not render the love of God over self impossible. As described by Scotus, natural inclination causes the love for self to be greater than the love for any other creature, but it is not necessarily greater than the love for God.[50]

What is the source of this natural inclination? In another passage Scotus argues that there are two reasons (*rationes*) for loving, which are goodness and unity.[51] Each of the objects which can be loved most of all, namely, God and the self, respectively exemplify the two highest reasons for loving. In God, who is the infinite good, there is an infinite reason of goodness (*ratio bonitatis*) for loving God. Consequently, there is a reason to love God more than anything else. However, the self has the highest degree of unity with itself, which is identity (*identitas*). Scotus writes, "Indeed, anyone is naturally inclined to the love of self after the infinite good. Natural inclination is always right (*recta*) . . ." Scotus agrees with James of Viterbo's position that on account of identity (*identitas*), which is the greatest degree of unity, the individual naturally loves itself more than others. Scotus departs from James by stating that the good can independently be an object of love. Consequently God, as the highest good, can be loved even more than self. Nevertheless, the identity (*identitas*) that the agent has with his own self can result in the disordered love of self over God.

Scotus's insistence that the proper order of human love follows natural inclination is difficult to reconcile with his teaching that acts which follow natural inclination are in accordance with the *affectio commodi,* and that freedom occurs only because an object can be loved for its own sake by reason of the *affectio iustitiae.* Two points should be kept in mind. First, we have already seen that Scotus gives different meanings to the term "natural inclination." With regard to the *affectiones,* Scotus thinks that the natural inclination of the will to its own perfection includes both the *affectio commodi* and the *affectio iustitiae.* Nevertheless, the *affectio commodi* is more properly described as a natural inclination, since the inclination for one's own happiness is shared by non-rational creatures.[52] The rectitude of natural inclination to the highest degree and principally (*maxime et principaliter*) is for the ultimate end and not for a lesser good. Since the *affectio iustitiae* makes it possible to love God more than self for his own sake by the love of friendship, it follows that to love God more through the *affectio commodi* than through the *affectio iustitiae* would violate this natural rectitude, since the self would be the primary object of the love.

Scotus's reluctance to specify the application of the different senses of "natural inclination" has caused difficulty for generations of interpreters. For example, in one passage Scotus writes, ". . . sin is against nature, that is, against that act which it is designed by nature (*natus est*) to be elicited in accord with and conforming to (*concorditer et conformiter*) natural inclination."[53] We have already discussed passages in which Scotus argues that sin occurs when the just is neglected on account of the natural inclination for one's own happiness. This passage contrasts sin with natural inclination. How can these passages be reconciled? Lychetus argues that in the latter passage "natural inclination" can be understood in three ways.[54] First, an act against nature is an act against the right dictate of natural reason. This suggestion does not seem very helpful, since it says nothing about the connection between right reason and nature. Second, Lychetus suggests that nature is inclined to that more perfect act which requires the appropriate circumstances. This suggestion has some value because it indicates the connection between sin and imperfection. Third, Lychetus says that a sin also can be said to be against nature since there is a lack and privation of good. This third way of understanding natural inclination is the most helpful because it reinforces the connection between sin and imperfection. A good act is in accordance with natural inclination because it perfects the agent's nature. Consequently, an act which takes away such perfection will be against natural inclination.

In those passages where Scotus disparages acts in accord with natural inclination, he is describing an act which has as its aim the agent's own perfection rather than the divine goodness. However, the agent does not perfect himself by acting in this way. These acts do agree with the natural inclination which all creatures have for their own perfection, but the agent is different on account of the freedom which enables him to love God more than his own happiness. This love is the perfection to which the free will is naturally inclined.[55]

Why is the will so inclined to love God? The recent literature on Scotus's understanding of the command to love God does not take into account the underlying explanation of such love, namely, that God is the most perfect nature (*ratio*) of the adequate object of the will, which is being.[56] Scotus argues against Henry of Ghent that God is not the first adequate object of someone's intellect in this life.[57] Nevertheless, it can be said that being is the common adequate object of the intellect. The concept of being is univocal for Scotus, and is common to both God and creatures. Scotus's rejection of Henry's position affects his moral theory. Rather than arguing that God is known and loved as the first object of the intellect and the will respectively, Scotus argues that God is the most perfect instance of what can be known and loved. If philosophers do not see that human happiness requires the vision of God's essence, it is because the human soul is difficult to know.[58] God is the most lovable object of all and the will is designed (*nata*) to love most of all the highest good, which is God.[59]

According to Scotus, every act is designed by its nature (*natus est*) to be ordered to the ultimate end.[60] If there were no ultimate end, the regress would go on infinitely. Scotus, following his theological predecessors, with the exception of James of Viterbo, appeals to the *Posterior Analytics*:

> . . . among things which can be willed (*volibilia*) something is to be willed (*volendum*) on account of itself (*propter se*); since, if whatever thing [is willed] on account of another thing (*propter aliud*), the process would go on infinitely: indeed nothing will be supreme; because what is willed (*volendum*) on account of something else (*propter aliud*) is to be willed (*volendum*) less than the something else on account of which (*propter quod*) it is to be willed (*volendum*), [as is explained] in the first book of the *Posterior Analytics*.[61]

The will is ordered to God in a special way as the highest good. Again following Augustine, Scotus uses the word *frui* to describe this love of God as the highest good.[62] Every intellectual nature is designed by nature (*nata est*) to be joined through its will to this most desirable object (*summum appetibile*). This union with God is a necessary condition for the perfection of the intellectual creature.[63]

Scotus's discussion of the *volibile* and the *appetibile* in the abovementioned passages reflects the confusing vocabulary of his moral psychology. For example, the word *"volibile"* is rarely if ever used by his predecessors.[64] The *volibile* is the potential object of an act of *velle*. Scotus frequently uses the words *"velle," "diligere,"* and *"amare"* interchangeably. When Scotus discusses an act of love, he is almost always talking about an act of the will and not an act of the sense appetite. For Scotus, *velle* is the same as *diligere,* and the *volibile* is the same as the *diligibile*. Moreover, although the *appetibile* can be an object of the sense-appetite, Scotus follows common usage, which has its roots in the Latin translation of Aristotle, in using the word to refer to any possible object of the will.[65] The *volibile* is also the *appetibile*. It must be kept in mind that in Latin the word *"velle"* means not just to will but also to wish.[66] Only the good can be willed. Any act of the will is an act of desire or an act of love, even though sometimes the sense-appetite is said to desire or to love. The highest object of the will, which is God, is similarly the highest object of love and desire. The *supremum volibile* is the same as the *supremum appetibile*.

How does the will love the supreme good more than itself if the will is not one with the supreme good? We have seen that Scotus thinks that both goodness and unity are reasons (*rationes*) for loving. In loving God, these two reasons are connected. By loving God the will is joined to something nobler than itself. God is so much greater than the creature that through the appetite a creature can be more joined to God that to itself.[67] This appetite for God is based on the inability of the will to be satisfied in anything other than God. Like other potencies, the will has a first adequate object. The potency of sight cannot be satisfied by anything other than the most beautiful visible thing. Similarly, being (*ens*) is the first adequate object of the human intellect and will. Consequently, the will can only be quieted in the most perfect being, which is God. The ability of the free agent to love God more than anything else can be shown from a consideration of God's infinite goodness. An ordered will is able to love a greater good more than another. The infinite good includes more goodness than any one thing. Therefore, the ordered will is able to love the infinite good most of all, and is unable to be satisfied in anything other than this infinite good.[68] Scotus's argument for the will's natural orientation towards God is based on the two Augustinian themes of *frui* and *quiescere*. Since the soul cannot find rest in anything other than God, its happiness consists in making God the object of its *frui*.[69]

Every will, including God's own will, can only be satisfied by God. Scotus is so certain of this point that he uses it as an argument against the position that there are two Gods. If there were two Gods, named "A" and "B" respectively, then both Gods would have an infinite and right (*recta*) will. However, each God would also be infinitely lovable. Consequently, B, since he is an infinite good, would be infinitely lovable by A, and A would have to love B infinitely, which would be more than himself. However, it would be impossible for A to love another more than himself, since anything loves itself more than another, unless it is a part or an effect of the other.[70] Therefore there cannot be two Gods. Scotus makes the further consideration that if there were two Gods, then every will would have to love more than one infinite good. The plurality of infinite goods would share more in the reason of goodness (*ratio bonitatis*) than the one infinite good by itself. However, if more than one infinite good is required for the will's satisfaction, then it does not find rest in one infinite good. Since we know that the will does find its rest in one infinte good, the premise that there are two Gods must be false.[71] These arguments are important because they show that the reason (*ratio*) for loving God is his infinite goodness, to which the will is directed by its nature. If a free creature does not make God the object of his *frui,* then that creature lacks a perfection that he was made to have.[72] But the choice is only between the creature's own self and God.

Scotus's understanding of God as the most perfect instance of the common adequate object of the will explains why it is necessary to love either God or self most of all. Like Augustine, Scotus argues that there are at bottom two choices. First, there are those who make themselves the object of *frui;* they love themselves most of all through the love of friendship. In contrast, the good love God more than themselves. God and not their own act is the object of their *frui.*[73]

At this point the contrast between Scotus's understanding of natural inclination and the Thomistic position can be clarified. First, unlike those who adhere to the Thomistic understanding of natural inclination, Scotus frequently speaks of natural inclination in a disparaging way, and he often describes bad actions as inordinately following the natural inclination for perfection. Nevertheless, at other times Scotus associates moral action with natural inclination. A second and more important difference between Scotus and the Thomistic view is that Scotus is above all worried that the free agent will seek his own happiness immoderately. This concern is explained by the third and most important difference. Whereas those who follow Thomas on this issue think that all creatures have a natural inclination to seek the good of the universe more than their own good, Scotus makes a sharp distinction between irrational and free creatures. According to Scotus, a free creature can love God more than itself precisely because it is free. While the free will finds its own perfection in loving God more than itself, other natures are not perfected in this way. We will explore this most important innovation of Scotus when we discuss his explicit arguments for the natural ability to love God more than self. But first, we need to consider the relationship between the natural law and the love of God, and the relationship between original sin and the ability to fulfill the natural law.

III. THE LAW OF NATURE AND ORIGINAL SIN

Scotus's distinction between nature and freedom influences his understanding of the natural law. Thomas Aquinas stresses the connection between natural law and physical human nature.[74] In contrast, Scotus makes a sharp distinction between those precepts which are strictly speaking a part of the natural law and those which are merely consonant with them. According to Scotus, the natural law most strictly speaking involves practical principles known from their terms, and all that follows necessarily from these practical principles.[75] The emphasis is entirely on reason. Since these principles follow from reason alone, they are the same for every intellectual creature in every state of life. There can be no variation.

The first practical principle of human action is to love God above everything. Scotus even suggests that there is an inclination in us to follow this principle. The precept to love God over self is known from its terms because God is the highest good and therefore the most lovable.[76] There can be no question of "voluntarism" with respect to this precept to love God, since Scotus argues that this law is prior to the determination of even the divine will.[77] Scotus's seventeenth-century commentator Anthony Hickey worried that this doctrine could be misunderstood, since strictly speaking no law can regulate or oblige the divine will.[78] Nevertheless, Scotus's statement that the law is prior to the will is important, because God cannot change it. Moreover, God cannot refuse to love himself. Since the command to love God over self is known from its terms, it must hold in every possible situation.

Since the precept to love God is known from its terms, its truth cannot be hidden by unruly passion or a disordered will. Scotus argues that even the bad angels know that they should love God more than themselves.[79] They might not act in accordance with this knowledge, but they cannot deny it any more than they could deny those speculative principles which are known from their terms. Scotus emphasizes that bad choices cannot blind reason. Since the principles are known from their terms and the conclusion is known syllogistically, the intellect's assent is forced.[80] With respect to God the argument is presumably as follows: The best object must be loved over everything; God is the best object; God must be loved over everything.[81] The intellect necessarily assents to the conclusion. Consequently, vicious habits cannot hide its truth from the intellect.

What does this first practical principle actually prescribe for human action? Scotus thinks that the command to love God may be misleading, because the precept does not so much command the love of God as it prohibits the hatred of God.[82] Someone might not be able to love God if he has other activities which keep him busy. Nevertheless, the hatred of God is always wrong. Since this hatred is instantiated through sin, Scotus emphasizes that the just human being must will not to exist rather than to dishonor God by sinning mortally. Moreover, someone should permit himself to be killed by God rather than to sin.[83] The contrast between the individual's own perfection and right action is perhaps shown most strongly by this example, in which the individual attains his final end only by choosing not to exist.

It is important to understand that although the command to love God is contained in revelation, Scotus thinks that it is known through its terms and not from revelation. When Scotus argues for the rationality of the Bible, one of the claims is that the Bible contains the precept to love God more than anything.[84] Marilyn Adams has stated that Scotus's moral psychology comes in part from the theological need to account for the love of God over self.[85] From Scotus's point of view, the influence runs in the other direction. Scotus's own position is that, philosophically speaking, the command to love God is the most easily known part of the natural law. Consequently, Scotus uses his philosophical understanding of this precept to illustrate the rationality of the Christian faith.

Scotus differs from his predecessors in arguing that not only is loving God the principal part of the moral law, but it is also the only principle that is strictly speaking part of the natural law. The first two commandments, and possibly the third, strictly belong to the law of nature because they can be deduced from this precept to love God. Moreover, loving God is the only act which cannot be against right reason, since any moral act other than loving God has a moral goodness that depends upon the situation of the agent or the circumstances of the act.[86] By the same token, the hatred of God is the only act which is incapable of being good in any circumstance.[87] Loving God is good from its object alone, which is the infinite good. Consequently, God can never be loved too much. The distinction between nature and freedom can be seen in Scotus's understanding of how only loving God belongs to the natural law strictly speaking. Whereas Thomas had argued that the human body puts certain obligations on human agents, Scotus's emphasis is primarily on the relation between the free will and God, who is the most perfect nature (*ratio*) of being, which is the common adequate object of the will. To Scotus, all other considerations are secondary.

Scotus's understanding of the relationship between the primary and secondary tables of the law shows the primary importance which Scotus gives to the command to love God. The first table consists of those three precepts which prohibit offenses against God, whereas the second table consists of the seven precepts which prohibit offenses against one's neighbor. Medieval theologians had difficulty in explaining how in the Old Testament God approved apparent violations of the law. For example, Abraham was prepared to kill his son Isaac, and the Jewish people appeared to steal Egyptian property when they left Egypt. Thomas had argued in a roundabout manner that these actions were not against the precepts of the second table. Thomas had no other choice, since he thought that these precepts were rooted in human nature.[88] Since Scotus is mostly concerned about the relationship between the human will and God, he does not think that these precepts strictly belong to the law of nature. Consequently, God can dispense with them. Both Thomas and Scotus agree that God cannot dispense with the natural law. The difference is that Thomas tries to show that the apparently forbidden actions do not actually violate the ten commandments or the natural law, whereas Scotus strictly speaking restricts the natural law to the precepts of the first table and argues that God can dispense with the second table.[89]

Scotus's understanding of the first table also exemplifies his belief that the precept to love God and its corollaries are the only necessary parts of the natural law. Scotus doubts whether the third commandment, which prescribes the Sabbath observance, is part of the natural law. Strictly speaking, there is no need to worship God on any one particular day. Nevertheless, it does not follow from this that there is no command to worship God on any particular day. Similarly, the duty to sacrifice to God is merely contingent. Although it is consonant with the love of God, it is not known without knowledge of God's will.[90] Scotus thinks that the only simply necessary practical principles are those which are directly ordered to the ultimate end, which is God's own goodness. The secondary precepts are not immediately ordered to God. The activities forbidden by them are incompatible with loving God only because God is the one who has forbidden them.[91]

Can the precept to love God be fulfilled without the assistance of grace? Thomas Aquinas followed Augustine in insisting that the inheritance of original sin includes a concupiscence which makes certain good actions impossible. Because of man's fallen nature, grace is a necessary condition for the love of God over self. Henry emphasized the effect of original sin on the will. In contrast, Scotus has a much weaker understanding of original sin.[92] According to Scotus, the difference between the sinner and someone in a purely natural state is that the sinner lacks justice. The sinner owes a debt to God. This debt is a relation to God, and it does not corrupt the will. Scotus refuses to attribute *curvitas* to the fallen will.[93] According to Scotus, original justice is a tranquility among the powers of the soul. In such a state the sensitive appetites would not lead the will astray. Nevertheless, the loss of this rectitude did not take away the liberty of the will. God made the human will *recta* in its purely natural state, and this natural rectitude cannot be taken away by sin. The ability to choose freely is an innate property of the will that cannot be separated from it.

This emphasis on liberty leads Scotus to affirm that "ought" implies "can."[94] Thomas clearly states that the implication does not hold for man's fallen nature alone. The real debate on this issue was between Godfrey of Fontaines, who held that the command to love God proves a natural ability to do so even in man's present state, and James of Viterbo, who argued that there is no reason to think that a precept's moral obligation shows that it can be observed naturally. Scotus sides with Godfrey on this issue. According to Scotus, God commands only the possible.

Scotus argues that even someone without grace is able to love God properly. To argue against the belief that without charity all actions are sinful, Scotus states that a pagan could act justly to his neighbor and also have a more vehement love of God than many Christians who exist in a state of grace. Scotus is not suggesting that the pagan's works are more meritorious than those of the Christian, since the pagan does not have grace. Consequently, the Christian's works have more value to God even though they may have less moral goodness. Nevertheless, although he does not merit heaven, through loving God the pagan is able to avoid sin.[95]

Scotus does not say whether anyone in the actual world ever loves God more than self without grace. The above passage implies that some pagans might. Nor does Scotus show how to reconcile the view that an individual can freely choose any action with the belief that an individual requires grace to act virtuously.[96] In one passage Scotus even argues that everyone who tries to obey the natural law receives grace.[97] Lychetus explains this passage by stating that although Scotus thinks that there is no way to avoid actual sin without grace, this is because the avoidance of sin entails the acceptance of grace.[98] If someone loves God more than himself naturally, then God will oblige him to accept grace. If the grace is rejected, then the agent sins mortally. On Lychetus's reading of Scotus, the connection between grace and the avoidance of sin is a part of the order which God establishes, but there is no necessary connection between them. Lychetus's reading of Scotus is strengthened by a passage in which Scotus claims that God is always prepared (*semper paratus*) to give grace to those who follow the law in their hearts.[99]

This position of Lychetus addresses some difficulties, but it is hard to square with Scotus's assertion that while we can know whether we love God more than ourselves, we cannot know whether we have supernatural love through grace or merely a natural love of God.[100] If in the actual world the love of God over self were always accompanied by charity, then we could in fact know ourselves to be in a state of grace.[101] Scotus uses this latter argument to establish the possibility of a purely natural love of God over self, but he admits that it depends upon the theological premise that no one can know whether he is in grace. Scotus's primary reasons for thinking such love possible are philosophical. When considering his philosophical arguments, it is important to remember that for Scotus original sin does not prevent a moral agent from fulfilling the natural law.

III. Main Argument for the Natural Love
of God over Self

Scotus's sustained treatments of the natural love of God over self occur in his *Opus Oxoniense,* Book 3, d. 27, and his *Reportata Parisiensia,* Book 3, d. 27. Both discussions are concerned with whether there is a theological virtue to love God above everything. To show that there is such a virtue, in both discussions Scotus first shows that the act is right, and that it has God as its formal object (*formalis ratio obiectiva*). Only then does he criticize the traditional arguments for the natural love of God over self and explain his own.[102] To understand why Scotus devotes so much of his discussion of the supernatural virtue of charity to natural love, we will first consider Scotus's understanding of the relationship between natural love and infused charity. Second, we will discuss Scotus's objections to his predecessors. Finally, we will examine Scotus's positive arguments for the natural love of God over self. The present discussion will rely primarily on the *Opus Oxoniense,* since Allan Wolter has published a corrected version, but we will note relevant discrepancies in the *Reportata.*

The issue of whether charity is needed for a natural love of God accounts for the third and fourth of Scotus's four objections to his own position in the *Opus Oxoniense.* The third objection argues that if an agent can love God more than himself, then no theological virtue of charity is necessary, since the ability to act in such a fashion exists without the habit.[103] Scotus concedes this objection but argues that the habit of charity is not superfluous because charity adds an intensity to the act.[104]

Scotus's extended discussion of charity in the *Ordinatio* Book 1, d. 17, explains what it means for the habit of charity to add to the substantial intensity of an act.[105] Scotus lists five ways in which a habit could be involved in an act, but he at last settles on two of them. According to the third way, which he seems to favor, the habit is an active partial cause (*causa partialis activa*) of the act.[106] In this case, the will would be the total cause in respect to the generation of a habit, but once the habit is established there are two causes. According to the fourth way, which is less favored by Scotus, a habit is not an active principle of the act, but it does incline the will.[107] Scotus compares the habit to the gravity which inclines an object to its proper place. Scotus expands this image later on to describe how a habit by itself does not suffice for an action, whereas an active potency is both a necessary and sufficient condition for action. Nevertheless, when the habit concurs with the active potency in the operation of an act, the operation is more perfect than an operation performed by the active principle alone.[108]

In the parallel discussion of the *Lectura,* Scotus does not go into detail concerning the different ways a habit may be involved in an act, but he does emphasize the concurrence of the natural will with the habit.[109] In a purely natural state, the will would have a less perfect act than the will has when informed by charity. The will alone does not cause the intention of the love; the will and the habit do so together. The description of the habit as a weight is explained in greater detail here, in two ways. In the first way, charity could be understood as a weight that sufficiently moves the action. Scotus thinks that this description of charity as a weight is incompatible with free will. In the second way, charity could be compared to the weight that inclines someone's hand down when he holds a rock. Although the weight is not sufficient for the movement, the weight does concur with the movement by making the act more intense. Charity works similarly to incline the will to act. To further explain this position Scotus suggests a thought experiment in which someone can will wood to burn. If a flame occurred from the burning, then the action of burning would be caused both by the will and the flame. Like charity, the flame would cause an action to be more intense even though it is not necessary for the action.

In both the *Ordinatio* and *Lectura* Book 1, d. 17, and in the *Opus Oxoniense* Book 3, d. 27, Scotus states that charity causes a geometrically and not an arithmetically proportionate superiority in the act.[110] An individual who has an arithmetically superior will in relation to someone else becomes geometrically superior once he has been aided by grace. An example will illustrate this point.[111] Suppose that Mother Theresa without charity can elicit an act of love that is around level 4, whereas a simple diocesan priest can only bring himself up to level 2. The theological virtue of charity increases this disproportion. With it, Mother Theresa's charity increases to level 8, but the poor priest only increases to level 4. Whereas before there had been only two levels between them, now there are four levels. This new disproportion results not from the difference between the wills, but from God's grace. Scotus is so fond of this notion of geometrical proportion that he also uses it to describe the relationship between infused and acquired faith. The infused faith of different individuals is geometrically proportionate to their natural abilities. According to Scotus, the supernatural virtues are not superfluous precisely because they create this geometrical disproportion between different individuals.[112]

It is important for our purposes that Scotus is discussing the intensity of one and the same act. The infused virtue of charity adds to the intensity of the act, but it does not change the natural act. This close affinity between charity and love brings us to the fourth objection raised by Scotus against his own position in the *Opus Oxoniense,* Book 3, d. 27.[113] If God can be naturally loved above all, then a natural habit of loving God can be acquired. This habit of loving God would seem to be of the same species as the habit of charity. If the two habits are of the same species, then how can they be distinguished from each other? Scotus argues in the *Opus Oxoniense* that the two habits can be distinguished because their efficient causes belong to different species.[114] We have seen in previous chapters that in the thirteenth century the difference in efficient causes is a standard way of distinguishing between charity and natural love. For Scotus in this passage it also seems to be the most important distinction.

One obstacle to understanding Scotus's view on natural love and charity is the variety of descriptions he gives of the difference between the two. In the parallel passage of the *Reportata,* Scotus admits that the two habits do not differ on account of their objects, but he states that they still differ formally. In the *Opus Oxoniense,* Scotus emphasizes that their efficient causes differ, but he adds that charity is by nature more perfect. Even if natural love were infused by God, it would be less perfect than charity.[115] The superior perfection of charity can be understood in two ways. First, charity more delectably inclines the will to love God. It is not clear in what way the perfection of the habit would make it differ formally, and Scotus does not explain this matter. Second, natural love produces only a natural friendship according to which God is loved as a private good for the lover (*ut bonum privatum sibi*). Charity is, in contrast, an infused friendship whereby God is loved as the common good (*ut bonum commune*). This last distinction between the private good and the common good is curious because Scotus generally does not follow his predecessors in describing God as the common good. Moreover, the *Reportata* does not explain why charity makes God to be the common good, or how this difference in goods makes the species of love different. It must be kept in mind that even in the *Reportata* Scotus agrees that charity and natural love share the same object. Consequently, the distinction between the common good and the private good does not entail that the private good is the object of natural love whereas the common good is the object of charity.

In his *Quodlibet,* q. 17, Scotus devotes the entire question to distinguishing between natural love and charity. However, his approach here differs from that found in the passages already discussed. In the *Quodlibet,* Scotus argues that the specific difference between natural love and charity could be that charity is meritorious whereas natural love is not.[116] What does it mean for charity to be meritorious? According to Scotus, God has made charity the reason for his acceptance of an individual.[117] Merit does not imply an actually

existing thing which is cause in the individual. Instead, merit expresses a relationship between the individual and God's will.[118] In this quodlibetal discussion, Scotus does not bother to emphasize the different efficient causes of
natural love and charity, and he does not discuss their intensity. The difference is something external to the act itself, namely, its being meritorious.

Scotus has great difficulty in distinguishing between charity and natural
love. The close connection between the two shows why Scotus must involve
the natural love of God in his treatment of charity. Since charity just intensi-
fies an already possible natural act, Scotus must discuss the natural act before
he discusses charity. What was Scotus's motive for saying that natural love
and charity do not have different objects? We have already shown that Thomas
distinguishes between natural love, which follows from God's natural goods,
and charity, which follows from a sharing in spiritual goods. This distinction
allows Thomas to delineate clearly between charity and natural love. But as
we shall see, Scotus thinks that Thomas commits a grave error by connecting
the object of happiness with what is advantageous for the individual. Scotus
closely identifies natural love with charity in part because he wants to avoid
any theory which would make either love have happiness as its object.[119]

In the *Opus Oxoniense,* Scotus distinguishes three different ways that God
could be the formal object of love (*formalis ratio obiectiva*).[120] First, God himself (*secundum se*) could be the object. Second, the formal object could
be good considered as good for the one loving (*inquantum bonum conveniens
amanti*). Third, God could be loved as the infinite God in whom the lover
participates. The *Reportata* lists the points slightly differently. First, Scotus
notes the view that God is loved as the end and principle of nature and also
as our highest supernatural beatitude.[121] This position is close to Thomas.
(Although Thomas's own opinion may have been more nuanced, for conve-
nience we will simply identify this view with Thomas.) Second, the *Reportata*
considers the position that God as the object of love could be simultaneously
good in itself and good for us (*summum in se et in comparatione ad nos*). The
understanding of God as a participated good is an instance of this position.
We have already seen that many thinkers use participation to justify the natural love of God over self.

Scotus's main objection to Thomas's opinion is that God in himself is
most perfect and the reason for loving; his perfection does not consist in a
relation to any other being. Scotus argues that if someone's charity regards
God with respect to his most perfect lovability (*diligibilitas*), then it cannot
have as its object God's beatifying that person, since God's perfection does
not consist in beatifying the creature.[122] In the *Reportata,* Scotus adds that if
God were loved only as the source of goods, then this love would pertain to

the *affectio commodi,* whereby God would be loved for the sake of the lover only and not because God is good in himself. However, we should also love God by the *affectio iustitiae,* since we would love him even if he were not our good.[123] This counterfactual expresses a clear difference between Thomas and Scotus. Since Thomas thinks that God is loved as the source of goods, it is not clear whether God would be loved if he were not such a source. Presumably Thomas rejects such a situation as impossible. If God were not the source of goods, then there would be no good at all. But Scotus finds a deeper issue here. Although this possibility were realized, if we consider it, we are led to the conclusion that God would still have to be loved. Consequently, the reason for loving God is not that he is the source of goods. Scotus also refuses to associate charity with the *affectio commodi.* According to Scotus, charity perfects the *affectio iustitiae,* whereas hope perfects the *affectio commodi.*[124] Hence Scotus does relate the *affectio commodi* to an important theological virtue. This aspect of Scotus's thought should moderate the general tendency of scholars to identify good actions with the *affectio justitiae.* At the same time, this recognition of the importance of one's own advantage with regard to the virtue of hope can also underscore the distinct disinterestedness of charity, which in this respect is very much unlike hope. Scotus argues against what he regards as Thomas's too close identification of charity and one's own good. Indeed, he gives further variations on Thomas's opinion, but the replies return to the same theme: the reason for loving God cannot be God's relation to something other than himself.

Scotus raises similar objections to the position that the formal object of the love of God is God considered as both good in himself and good to us. According to this view, God is the object of love both as the infinite good and as the good in which we participate. Scotus first argues that from this point of view the love of God actually has two objects, which is impossible.[125] Moreover, if we were like Aristotle's Intelligences and did not participate in God's goodness, we would still be required to love God more than ourselves. Consequently, our loving God should not be based on the notion of participation. On this point Scotus departs from most of his predecessors. His primary goal is to ensure that the only motive for loving God is God's infinite goodness and not God's relation to any creature.

Scotus begins the exposition of his own view by distinguishing the three different ways in which there can be a formal object of charity:

> . . . I say that the object (*ratio obiectiva*) of an act or a habit of charity can be understood in three ways: first, which according to itself it is designed by nature (*nata est*) to be the final reason (*ratio terminandi*) [of the act]

per se; or second, which is some reason (*ratio*) preceding some act on account of which the act is designed by nature (*natus est*) to be elicited in respect to the object; or third, which accompanies the act itself, rather as if it follows the elicited act itself.[126]

The first meaning alone describes the formal object properly and strictly speaking. To show that God himself is the formal object of the virtue of charity, Scotus relies on the principle that the will has being as its first adequate object. But an intellectual or volitional power that has a first adequate object can only find its satisfaction in the most perfect nature (*ratio*) of its adequate object. The will and the intellect are directed to the whole of being as both their end and their motive. The most perfect nature of being (*perfectissima ratio entis*) is found only in God. Consequently, the will is satisfied only with the most perfect being in itself as its object. God is this most perfect being not insofar as he is related to other creatures, but in himself.[127]

According to the second way in which God can be the formal object of charity, God's relation to us can provide us with a reason for loving. God shows that he loves us by creating us, redeeming us, and beatifying us. These actions of God all provide a reason for loving him. Although charity does not depend on these objects, it combines them all together when it regards God not only as simply good (*bonum honestum*), but as communicating his goodness to us. Scotus quotes St. John: "Let us love God because he first has loved us."[128] According to the third way in which God can be the formal object of charity, God is loved as the ultimate end. In this meaning God's beatifying us is the object of love. Although the love does not depend on God's so acting, the object of our love is also the object which makes us happy.[129]

Scotus accepts that God is loved on account of his goodness to us, but he does not think that this goodness is the formal object of our love for him. The formal object of the love must be God in himself and not God in any relation to us. Scotus uses the example of vision to show how a potency can be related to its adequate object. If there were a most perfect adequate object of sight which gave the eye the power to see, then the eye would be completely happy in loving this object. This visual beauty would be the adequate object of vision, and loved for its own sake. Because the visible object gave sight, there would be a further reason for loving it. Moreover, the satisfaction that results from the viewing is also good in itself. Nevertheless these secondary reasons do not take away from the importance of the primary object. Similarly, the primary object of loving God is his own goodness, and not his goodness in beatifying the lover. Those who accept Thomas's claim that the object of charity is God as the source of beatitude take this least important reason for loving God and make it primary.

Scotus departs from his predecessors in believing that God in himself is the highest instance of the primary adequate object of the will. Consequently, any theory that wishes to justify the love of God in terms of natural or super-natural gifts, or even the metaphysical doctrine of participation, is insufficient for him. Scotus thinks that we can love God in himself apart from any connection he has to us. The will is the basis for such love. Scotus's emphasis on the orientation of the will to God also explains why he criticizes those predecessors who think that the love of God is rooted in a natural inclination which is shared with creatures that are not free.

In his discussion of whether God can be loved over self without an infused virtue, Scotus presents two opposing approaches. According to the first approach, which is close to that of Henry of Ghent and James of Viterbo, nature is determined only to one thing, which is its own being rather than God's being. Since natural appetite seeks only what is suitable for itself (*convenientem sibi*), the natural appetite cannot love God more than itself.[130] In this connection, Scotus mentions in the *Reportata* Aristotle's doctrine that friendship requires unity between the friends.[131] According to the contrasting position, which seems to be the Thomistic view as set forth by Godfrey of Fontaines, any part naturally loves the whole more than itself, and consequently by natural inclination God is loved more than self.[132] These first two arguments are about differing interpretations of nature. In the *Opus Oxoniense,* Scotus argues in addition that since every rational nature loves happiness above all, it follows that every rational nature loves the beatific object, which is God, more than itself.[133]

If Scotus does not directly attack the first view that nature is directed to the self, this is not surprising. According to Scotus, the debate is not about nature but about free will. Scotus may disagree with the conclusion that God cannot be loved over self, but he does accept the view of nature as tending primarily towards its own perfection. The bulk of Scotus's attention is given to explaining and then refuting the argument that even non-rational creatures love God more than self.

The difference between Godfrey's presentation of the argument and Scotus's is striking. Godfrey attempted to show that the natural inclination for the common good was present not only among non-rational creatures but also in the political realm, where the good citizen sometimes chooses to die for the common good. Scotus leaves out the case of the good citizen, which is not surprising since on Scotus's view the action would be explained with reference to free will rather than to nature. As Scotus presents the argument, the part's preference for the good of the whole exists both in the macrocosm (*in maiori mundo*), which is the universe, and in the microcosm (*in minori mundo*), which is the human being. For example, according to Scotus, in the macrocosm water sometimes moves upwards against its proper place in order to avoid a vacuum. By moving upwards it prefers the good of the universe to its own natural inclination. In the microcosm, Scotus gives the familiar example of the hand's desire to sacrifice itself for the preservation of the head. In both cases the part loves the whole more than itself.[134] Since the creature participates in the divine goodness, it follows that it must love the divine goodness more than its own goodness.

Although Scotus touches on the main themes of the Thomistic argument, the description of the water's natural inclination shows both that Scotus presents the argument inaccurately and, consequently, where he will attack it. As Scotus presents the argument, the water's upward movement for the good of the universe is against its natural inclination. On the Thomistic view, the natural inclination is precisely what would cause a creature to intend the universe's good more than its own. Scotus's objection to the Thomistic argument is in fact an objection against the Thomistic understanding of natural inclination. Scotus points out that the water moves downwards because of its form. Consequently, any upwards movement for the good of the universe would be against its natural inclination downwards. The water does not love the good of the universe more than its own good; rather, the ruler of the universe orders the parts in such a way that they bring about the well-being of the universe.[135]

Scotus's choice of the upwards movement of the water to illustrate the Thomistic argument is interesting precisely because this example does not seem to occur in Thomas, Godfrey of Fontaines, or Giles of Rome. Nevertheless, on their own principles these thinkers would have to agree with Scotus and admit that the water is moved against its own natural inclination.[136] It would seem then that they would also be forced to agree that, to bring about the good of the universe, an external orderer violates natural inclination. James had previously argued for the view that the action for the good of the whole is brought about by an external order and not natural inclination. Scotus's brilliance lies in his choice of an example where the contrast between natural inclination and the common good is apparent.

Nevertheless, this argument only works in combination with other views. Thomists admit that the diversity of the universe requires that some parts of it fall short of their perfection; still, the inability of these parts to act according to their natural inclination does not imply that this inclination is to the perfection of the individual alone. For example, a stag's inclination to live might conflict with a lion's inclination for food.[137] Or, the inclination of a member of a species for its life might conflict with the preservation of the species as whole. These two facts can be accepted even when one thinks that the inclination of the stag is not primarily for itself but ultimately for the species or the universe. Similarly, individuals such as Judas have an inclination to love God even though their failure to do so is ordered to the good of the whole.[138] The ultimate difference between the Scotist and Thomist positions is not whether providence requires that some creatures do not achieve their natural end, but whether their inclination is only to this end as their own individual end.

Like James, Scotus is also unconvinced that the self-sacrifice of the hand shows anything about natural inclination or even about self-sacrifice. According to Scotus, the human being is the agent who sacrifices the hand for the sake of the head. Scotus writes:

> . . . whatsoever consideration (*ratio*) shows that God loves more the well-being of the universe, or even his own well-being, than the well-being of any one part; and loves the well-being of the principal part more than the well-being of the less principal part . . . considered according to its own inclination, [a part] never exposes itself to nonexistence for the sake of another.[139]

Moreover, Scotus argues that the whole argument rests on a misunderstanding of the relationship between creatures and God. A creature is not related to God as a part is related to a whole, even though a creature is an effect of God and it participates in him. Unlike Thomas and his followers, Scotus does not describe God as the common good of the universe.

In the *Opus Oxoniense,* after discussing the Thomistic arguments Scotus turns to the argument which sees the natural desire for happiness as an instance of the natural love of God. Scotus mentions the case of a suicide in this context.[140] Henry considers the suicide's rejection of happiness as an objection to Henry's own belief that all creatures have a non-deliberative love of God since they love the *ratio boni.* He replies that the suicide does not hate happiness, since death is desired in order to avoid misery. Henry's doctrine of the natural non-deliberative love of God represents a long tradition, and Scotus takes up this view of suicide as support for the argument that all humans naturally love God since they love happiness. Scotus agrees that everyone loves happiness, but he argues that happiness does not need to be loved more than anything else. Moreover, love for general happiness does not entail a love of God in particular, even though there is a sense in which God is happiness. Scotus not only rejects any theory of natural love based on natural inclination, but also passes over the subject of non-deliberative love, which both Henry of Ghent and the *Summa Halesiana,* written by members of Scotus's own order, treated at length.[141] Scotus's position is novel in that it is based entirely on the notion of the free choice of a moral agent endowed with both intellect and will. Scotus rejects any description of loving God over self that is based on natural inclination or a natural non-deliberative love.

Scotus himself presents two arguments for the natural love of God over self. The first argument invokes right reason (*recta ratio*). The second argument is based on the example of the good citizen who risks his life for the political community. Scotus agrees with his predecessors that this example has probative force, but disagrees with Thomas and his followers about how the argument works.

Scotus's first argument reasons from the hierarchy of being.[142] Among things which are essentially ordered, there must be one supreme thing (*aliquid supremum*). Presumably love is an essentially ordered act, since Scotus argues that there is a highest love and a most lovable object of love. Natural right reason (*ratio naturalis recta*) identifies this most lovable object with the infinite good. If this were not the case, then charity, which loves God above all, would contradict right reason and not be a virtue. As we have seen, Scotus thinks that "ought" implies "can." Consequently, if reason dictates an action to the will, it follows that the will can so act. If this were not the case, then the will would be naturally bad or not free.[143] Scotus stresses that the ability to fulfill a moral precept is a necessary condition for any freedom, whether it be human or angelic. He illustrates this point with an example which is close to Bonaventure's argument about the angels' state of innocence. Since the angels could only elicit a right act (*rectum actum*), it follows that they must have been able to fulfill right reason's dictate to love God more than themselves.

The invocation of essential order in this context is striking because it shows the interrelation of Scotus's moral and metaphysical ideas. An essential order is the ordering of a sequence by a priority and posteriority which are essential and not just accidental. According to Scotus, in any essential order the posterior must be less perfect than the prior.[144] It is not certain what type of essential order Scotus has in mind in his discussion of the natural love of God. At different periods of his career, Scotus treated different examples of essential order. For example, the essential order of eminence occurs only in the *Tractatus de primo principio,* which is a later work than the *Opus Oxoniense.*[145] Consequently, the essential order under discussion in the *Opus Oxoniense* is probably not that of eminence. The essential order of ends, however, which

Scotus discusses at length in the *Tractatus de primo principio,* would seem to be relevant to the love of God.[146] The final end is also an efficient cause, since it moves by being loved. Moreover, this final end is more good than the effect which it causes.[147] Like Thomas, Scotus follows Aristotle in stating that art imitates the order in nature.[148] Scotus departs from Thomas in the strength of his emphasis on the difference between the irrational order of nature and the ordering of intellectual creatures to God. Nevertheless, Scotus clearly states that the essential order of the will to God is rooted in nature. The will is essentially ordered to God as the ultimate end and the only appropriate object of *frui.*[149]

Despite this discussion of essential order, the overall structure of this argument is not complicated. First, Scotus shows that right reason commands the love of God over self. Second, he argues that the command shows that there is a natural ability to love God in this way. The first part of the argument need not be lengthy because the truth of its conclusion is known from its terms. It is clear that the most lovable object should be loved the most. The second part of the argument follows directly from the freedom of the will. Unlike his predecessors, Scotus does not need to put much effort into explaining the precept because he thinks that it is easily known from its terms.

In the *Reportata,* Scotus gives a shorter version of the argument which simply assumes that natural reason dictates that there is something which should be loved above everything.[150] The *Reportata'*s discussion of God as the most perfect instance of the will's common adequate object occurs in the context of whether it is right (*recta*) to love God above everything.[151] In this discussion, Scotus emphasizes that every power with a common adequate object is designed (*nata*) to have a most perfect act relating to the supreme instance of what is contained under its common adequate object. For the will, this act is loving God. Again there is an order of the objects of love. God is at the highest rank, and all other objects are posterior.

Aristotle's example of the good citizen is used by Scotus to show that an individual can choose a greater good over his own private good. Whereas Thomas and Godfrey had used this example to show that there is a natural inclination to love the common good more than the private good, Scotus, as we should expect, separates the discussion of the good citizen's free choice from that of natural inclination. He does not use the example to illustrate the natural inclination of the citizen, but rather to show the extent to which free choice can be exercised. Since Aristotle did not assume that the good citizen who dies for the community will be rewarded in the afterlife, it follows that the good citizen's death deprives him of the good and even of his political virtue.[152] Scotus claims elsewhere that through the natural law it is known that God is a judge.[153] Consequently, it would seem that there must be some reward for virtue or punishment for vice. Scotus also claims that virtue is its own reward.[154] The good citizen is thus not in such a bad state as it would seem from the discussion on the natural love of God over self. Scotus emphasizes that the good citizen wills himself to perish so that the public good is conserved. Since the individual is able to prefer the political good to his own private good, it follows that he should likewise be able to prefer the divine good. This example of the good citizen buttresses belief that the free individual can follow the dictates of right reason even when his own good is thereby lost.

Scotus considers as an objection to his view the thesis that the good citizen really loves most of all his own virtue rather than the public good.[155] James had used this interpretation of Aristotle to show that humans by nature are inclined to their own perfection. Although Scotus agrees with James's understanding of natural inclination, Scotus disagrees with James's attempt to use natural inclination to explain the act of the good citizen. According to Scotus, the good citizen clearly wills his nonexistence to protect his political community from evil. Consequently, the common good is loved more than the act of virtue. On Scotus's view the willingness to die for another shows that the other is loved more than oneself. In another passage, Scotus compares the citizen who suffers death for the political community with the human being who chooses to expose himself to death by following the divine law.[156] This self-exposure to death shows the greatness of the love.

Although Scotus does not accept the Thomistic understanding of natural inclination, he does agree with Thomas and his followers that the natural love of God is compatible with Aristotle's understanding of friendship. Of the arguments against Scotus's position presented at the beginning of the *Opus Oxoniense,* Book 3, q. 27, we have discussed the latter two, which involve the connection between natural love and charity. The former two attempt to use Aristotle to argue against the possibility of a natural love of God over self. The first of these objections is that love is a type of friendship, and since friendship is only between equals, there can be no friendship with God.[157] The second objection is based on a paraphrase of Aristotle's famous dictum on friendship: ". . . those notes of friendship for another are measured from these, which are for oneself." If friendship for another is measured by friendship for oneself, then it follows that the love for another cannot be greater than self-love. The second objection adds that friendship is based on unity, and that it is impossible for something to be more one with the lover than the lover is with himself. Consequently, the love of God over self is impossible.[158]

Scotus takes a standard approach to the first objection when he states that the meaning of "friendship" must be expanded so as to apply to friendship with God. Whereas Henry had called this friendship "superexcellent" (*superexcellens amicitia*), Scotus describes it as "superfriendship" (*superamicitia*). Equality is not the lone basis for friendship, since friendship presupposes the simply good (*honestum*). Since God's good is lovable most of all, it follows that charity can be a type of friendship with God.[159]

In his discussion of Aristotle's dictum Scotus addresses more particularly the connection between goodness and unity as bases of friendship. Whereas James of Viterbo and Siger of Brabant had both understood Aristotle's dictum to mean that unity is the basis for friendship, Scotus argues that the dictum only describes a sign of friendship between equals. One recognizes that one loves a friend when one desires the same goods for a friend that are also desired for the self. This dictum cannot be applied to God, because friendship is not based entirely on unity, but rather on both unity and goodness. With regard to the love for God, the lack of unity with God is compensated for by the magnitude of God's goodness.[160] Like many of his predecessors, Scotus thinks that Aristotle's moral psychology is compatible with the natural love of God over self. But Scotus's interpretation of Aristotle rests on Scotus's own view that God is the infinite goodness which alone can quiet the human will.

The natural inclination of the human will to become perfect through loving God should not be forgotten in this context. For Scotus, friendship with God is the only possible type of friendship whereby the friend is loved more than the self. Scotus is not arguing that the greater good must always be loved more, since only in God's case is the goodness enough to overcome the lack of unity between the lover and the object of love. This point is emphasized by Scotus in other passages. For example, when discussing Aristotle's dictum Scotus argues that the self is loved immediately after God, and that the first disorder of sin must always be a *love of friendship* for the self. Moreover, there is never an obligation to love another more than oneself even if the other person is better. For example, while discussing whether someone is obliged to love the Blessed Virgin Mary more than one's own self, Scotus emphasizes that after God someone must love himself most of all. Otherwise, someone would hate another's sin more than his own, and end up fleeing the other person's sin more than his own.[161] The reason for this self-love is unity, "since love is founded in unity."[162]

When discussing whether God is the formal object (*ratio formalis*) of the will, Scotus emphasizes that God can be loved more than self only because he is the most perfect being. The relevant issue is whether the formal object of loving God is God in himself. It could be objected to Scotus's position (namely, that God in himself is the object of charity) that if it were true, then the greater good would be loved more, and a better person would have to be loved above one's own self.[163] In the *Reportata,* the objection even states that someone would have to love the apostle Peter more than his own self, since Peter is better (*maius bonum*).[164] Scotus responds that the question is not about a difference of greater or lesser ordered goods, but rather about the supreme member of the order. The power of sight has as its object colors which are more or less, but those which are more do not satisfy the power of sight. There is an infinite good which alone satisfies the will.[165] This good is not more good but the highest good (*summum bonum*). Peter's greater grace does not satisfy my will completely; only God's goodness can.[166]

With this relationship between God and the will in mind, it is possible to explain how Scotus can argue both that sin is an act in conformity with natural inclination and that sin violates natural inclination. Sin conforms to natural inclination in the sense that nature always seeks its own perfection. By loving her own perfection more than God, an agent sins. Only God can satisfy the will. Sin is committed when the will loves something other than its proper object more than that object. Consequently, the sin is not just against reason, but against the very nature of the will. Scotus's disparaging remarks about natural inclination occur in those contexts in which he argues against the conflation of free agency with merely natural inclination. His more positive remarks about natural inclination may reflect the relation between the nature of the will and God, its final end. The natural law does not follow from our physical nature, but rather from the will's order to God.

Scotus's discussion of the natural love of God shows both the innovative character of his ethical theory and the continuity of Scotus with his predecessors. Although Scotus has sometimes been described as rejecting a nature-based ethics, he differs from his predecessors not so much by refusing to see morality as based on human nature, but rather by giving an absolute priority to the rational nature of human beings. According to Scotus, the natural inclination of inanimate and non-rational creatures is not a guideline for the elicited choices of a rational agent. The only *per se* part of the natural law is the precept to love God over self, since this precept is known from its terms. By its very structure the will is ordered to love the most lovable object, which is

God. Scotus does not embrace a "divine command ethics," because no divine command could dispense with the first two or three precepts of the ten commandments. Neither does Scotus adhere to a theory of natural law, like that of Thomas and his followers, in which not only the human intellect but also the human body provides the basis for natural law. Although according to Scotus natural law is concerned in a secondary way with marriage and bodily life, strictly speaking the natural law is that which requires both angels and human beings to love God more than self.

Although Scotus does emphasize freedom more than his predecessors had, he does not argue that the will is free to choose simply any good as the highest object of its love. Like his contemporaries, Scotus argues that an individual must either love himself most of all or God most of all. No creature can love any other creature more than itself, even if the object of love has more goodness than the lover himself has. Scotus's innovative emphasis on free choice is shown in the sharp delineation he makes between natural inclination and freedom. Scotus agrees with James of Viterbo that every nature seeks its own perfection, but does not follow James's belief that Aristotelian ethics is similarly based on a project of self-perfection. According to Scotus, Aristotle himself makes the distinction between natural objects, which seek their own perfection alone, and rational potencies, which can freely choose between contradictories. This ability to choose something other that one's own perfection allows the agent to have a tendency for justice (*affectio iustitiae*) in addition to the tendency for the useful (*affectio ad commodum*). But this tendency for justice does not mean that moral obligation has no relation to the good of the agent. Scotus emphasizes that the love of God over self comes from the essential order of the intellect to God. Although the agent should not love her own perfection more than God, the agent in fact procures her own perfection by loving God over self. In this respect Scotus agrees not only with his immediate predecessors but with an explicit Christian tradition going back at least to Augustine.

Scotus resembles his predecessors in the Aristotelian scholastic tradition more strongly than scholars have recognized. He does not isolate morality from happiness and self-interest. Just like many of his predecessors, he argues that everyone must love herself most of all after God and the common good. Moreover, it is not merely that she should love herself more than other individual beings, but that she must. According to his moral psychology, the will can only will at most one of two ends: the self or God. In addition, he follows his predecessors in holding that the natural law has its basis in human nature. Human beings are bound to love God more than themselves because of the types of creatures that they are. If philosophers cannot prove that happiness requires the vision of God's essence, this is because of the poverty of knowledge about the soul, and not because the soul can find happiness elsewhere.

Scotus differs from most of his predecessors in that he strongly contrasts the desire for happiness with the desire for what is just. The two are not unrelated, but they are neatly distinguished. He emphasizes that happiness must be subordinated to justice in moral action. This tension between happiness and justice indicates the complex relationship that Scotus's ethics has to previous ethical theories. Just as his predecessors did, Scotus emphasizes that happiness is connected to human nature, and that humans have an inclination to happiness. Moreover, he follows the tradition which contrasts free action with natural action. He is innovative in that he contrasts the free virtuous action with the natural inclination for happiness, and foreshadows the tendency of modern ethics to focus only on reason, which is peculiar to human beings, and to ignore that which humans share with other animals.[167]

Nevertheless, Scotus's approach remains squarely teleological. Indeed, he gives the last new argument concerning the natural love of God because he still works in the tradition in which arguments must be given for the position that someone can prefer another good to his own. He thinks that the will has a direction towards certain goods which are preestablished. In contrast, some later medievals argued that free choice implies an ability to will anything whatsoever. Accordingly, thinkers with such a notion of freedom no longer need to address the same arguments concerning the natural love of God over self. Contemporary libertarian views are much closer to the views of these late medieval thinkers than they are to those of earlier thinkers.[168] For example, William of Ockham's understanding of freedom is based largely on a liberty of indifference between alternatives. He thinks that evil can be willed; at any rate, he holds that there is an act of will which is not for a real or apparent moral good, or useful good, or even a pleasurable good.[169] A corollary to this position would seem to be that there is an act of the will which is not an act of love. Moreover, according to William the will is not only free with respect to such goods, but it is also free to will another's happiness more than the happiness of the person willing.[170] Both of these views indicate a notion of freedom which is stronger than those held by the authors discussed in this book, including that of Scotus. The very existence of a debate over the possibility of natural love of God implies that positions about free choice are not merely about indeterminism, but about greater issues concerning human nature and moral obligation.

Conclusion

If most of the authors discussed in this book are correct, it is simply mistaken to consider the good of the individual in isolation from his order to something else, whether it be God or even the political community. Moreover, this order must be understood in the context of a wider theory of human nature. Modern and contemporary attempts to isolate the individual's good from that of others rest on assumptions which are not accepted in most of ancient philosophy and the high medieval tradition. Considering this history of the medieval debate over naturally loving God, we can now see that the figures addressed in this book raise and clarify distinctions about eudaimonistic ethics which present important challenges for contemporary ethics.

From the inception of their tradition, most Christian thinkers have recognized at least some compatibility between their ethical views and those of the ancient philosophers. Although at first Christians were more influenced by Neoplatonic ethics, in the thirteenth century they attempted to incorporate Aristotelian ethics into the previously existing patristic framework. During the first flourishing of the universities, theologians learned to distinguish more carefully between the orders of nature and grace. With the reception of Aristotle's *Nicomachean Ethics,* philosophers and theologians applied this distinction to ethical theory and moral psychology.

Some thinkers, such as Siger of Brabant and James of Viterbo, thought that Aristotle's eudaimonism was based on a self-love which is in disharmony with the Christian duty to love God more than oneself. In their view, although Aristotle correctly describes the natural order, there is a conflict between the natural and the supernatural. Another approach, perhaps best exemplified by Henry of Ghent, was to suggest that Aristotle's ethical theory was in some relevant respects mistaken. But the two most important thinkers, namely Thomas Aquinas and John Duns Scotus, thought that Aristotelian ethics, although incomplete, was at least compatible with the duty to love God. Both think that humans are harmoniously directed to an ultimate end which is not up to an individual's choice; they differ on how the order to this end is founded. Thomas thinks that the will's inclination is like that of other natural things; by nature everything prefers the common good of the universe, namely God, to its own good. Humans are incapable of such ordering without grace only on account of their fallen nature and the overall weakness which comes from being both material and spiritual.[1] Scotus thinks that natural things have a primary inclination towards their own good. Humans can act independently of this inclination insofar as they have a rational potency, namely the will, which makes possible the choice of the just for its own sake. Together with Thomas and the other thinkers, Scotus also holds that the individual cannot prefer any other person's good to his own unless that person is God. Moreover, one's good is attained through so preferring God's good.

Which medieval thinkers provide the best interpretation of Aristotle? One important lesson of this survey is that older philosophical texts are to some degree undetermined with respect to later discussions. I have not argued that any one figure, such as Thomas, James, or Scotus, gives an accurate interpretation of Aristotle, but I hope to have shown that the attempt to return directly to Aristotle's ethics without reading the medievals is at best unwise, since many of our present concerns about whether eudaimonism is egoistic have their remote roots not in Aristotle himself but in his later followers.

Neither is it clear who gives the most successful argument for his own position. Generally speaking, each thinker's argument depends upon wider views which they argue in another context, if they argue for them at all. For example, Scotus and Thomas disagree over naturally loving God because they have different understandings of natural inclination and human willing. It is difficult to judge them from a strictly contemporary standpoint because their views of nature and the will presuppose both a teleological understanding of nature and a conception of freedom which differs greatly from contemporary doctrines of "free will." It seems to me that Thomas's understanding of free choice is not too different from that of Aristotle.[2] The will is simply our rational appetite for the end of achieving happiness through loving God, and our freedom consists in the ability to act knowingly for this end. The Thomistic argument for loving God largely rests on an Aristotelian account of human flourishing and an understanding that the actions which constitute this flourishing need not be self-directed. Godfrey of Fontaines emphasizes the most Aristotelian aspects of Thomas's thought, and consequently focuses on the issue of intention. God's good is the object of our love and it is greater than our own good. Consequently, it is loved more. Although I have argued that Scotus himself is not guilty of separating morality from happiness, his distinction between nature and will at least prepares the way for an understanding of the will which separates it from ordinary teleology. Indeed, for Scotus the will seems to have a twofold teleology, one which is self-directed and another which is directed to the just. The will has an inclination of its own which explains how someone acts for the sake of the just. This separation of willing from natural teleology perilously foreshadows modern and contemporary "volitions" which are somehow *sui generis*.[3]

In the genealogy of modern and contemporary concepts, medieval philosophy reintroduced distinctions which would become important for contemporary philosophy. Medieval thinkers were forced by their religious outlook to mine the ancient texts for principles and ideas which would help to reconcile the agent's own good with that of others. In the rise of a Christian intellectual tradition, thinkers were required to develop issues which at best are only briefly or implicitly treated in ancient ethics. Although there has been a revival of interest in ancient virtue theories during the past twenty-five years, the great importance of the medieval tradition is not always understood or explained.

The contemporary problem of reconciling morality and self-interest is in large part a result of the shift to a modern scientific worldview. According to most premodern philosophers, what a particular human should do is intrinsically connected with what it means to be human. Bernard Williams writes, ". . . we must admit that the Aristotelian assumptions which fitted together the agent's perspective and the outside view have collapsed. No one has yet found a good way of doing without those assumptions."[4] It is important to recognize not only that we no longer share many assumptions which were held by ancient philosophers, but also that the ancient philosophers themselves did not adequately address how these assumptions relate to ethics.[5] Medieval thinkers made these problems explicit and argued different possibilities for resolving them.

Moreover, the medieval debates show how our understanding of eudaimonism is intrinsically connected to a theory of motivation. My reasons for stating in the introduction that it is anachronistic to describe medieval thinkers as egoists or altruists in a contemporary sense should now be more clear. Most medievals make the distinction between willing another's good for one's own sake and willing it for the sake of the other person. They hold that the will is ordered to a good which is really in the world. The good is the kind of thing that can be willed. Moreover, willing the good results in the agent's achieving his own good. There is a distinction between willing what is good for the agent and willing it under that description. Although the virtuous agent may sometimes will what is good for his own sake, he need not always do so. Indeed, in many cases he wills what is good for himself only by willing another's good for the other person's sake. Modern and contemporary psychological egoists argue that all actions are fundamentally self-interested, whereas altruists argue that some are not. Their distance from the medieval discussion of loving God has its roots in a new understanding of human willing. As we have seen, before the fourteenth century most philosophers thought that the will has a direction to the good which is more to one's own good than to that of another individual. Although another person's good can be desired for its own sake, it cannot be desired more than one's own. Later debates about human freedom often swing between extremes. On one side, later medievals such as Ockham thought that humans have a "liberty of indifference" by which they can will anything whatsoever. This notion of freedom becomes prevalent in contemporary libertarian theories, but other modern thinkers argue that all actions are done for the sake of satisfying one's own desires.

Earlier philosophers are concerned with whether and how someone could obtain his own good of virtue by preferring that of another. Some later libertarians assume that right action might not be in the interest of the agent, but they do not need to argue for the possibility of preferring another's interests to one's own, since it is implicit in their understanding of freedom. Alternatively, later psychological egoists assume that all willing must be self-interested. They often use this understanding of motivation to support ethical egoism in which right action is the same as self-interested action. Consequently, the issue for these groups of later thinkers is not the relationship between eudaimonism and self-love, but whether good actions are altruistic or egoistic. At the very least, the altruistic theories hold that there can be a balancing of one's interests whereby someone wills another's good. According to these theories, it is quite possible that by willing another's good there is no reflexive benefit to the agent. For example, in his classic *The Possibility of Altruism,* Thomas Nagel argues that willing another's good is much like willing good for one's own future self.[6] In both cases someone is willing a good which is not at the present moment good for him. His position is that someone else's interests by themselves provide an objective reason for action.

The new difficulty over how to understand acting for another's interests should cause us to recall the more significant question of what it would mean for someone else's good to be preferred to one's own. Whereas most contemporary altruists think that by acting for the sake of another, one's own good is at least sometimes sacrificed, medievals do not. They do not fall into this position because they either implicitly or explicitly make a distinction between internal and external goods. Sometimes the virtuous agent sacrifices external goods such as wealth and honor, but by doing so he does not sacrifice his own internal good of virtue, which is by far the most important. For example, the virtue of justice involves a mean between one's own good and that of another. Someone who acts unjustly may increase the amount of money that he has, but he sacrifices his own intrinsic good of virtue, which is ultimately what is good for him. Consequently, by acting unjustly he harms himself.

Although medieval eudaimonism assumes that virtuous action is good for the agent, the more influential forms should not be described as egoistic because they hold that someone can will the good for its own sake. In its more standard form, premodern eudaimonism is not about aiming at one's own good, but about achieving one's own good through virtuous activity.[7] Richard Kraut's distinction between substantive and formal egoism is based on this point.[8] According to him, modern and contemporary theories are formally egoistic in that they require an agent to seek his own happiness. But by substantive egoism ancient theorists can argue that an agent's happiness can be used to evaluate his action, even when the agent himself should or need not do so.

In the introduction I indicated that for most medievals there is no conflict between the virtuous life and another's good. Nevertheless, in the course of the book we have seen that the possibility of such a conflict was raised. It is important to recognize that this possible conflict is quite different from that with which later philosophers are concerned. Although medievals doubt that there can be a conflict between the development of moral virtue and the common good, there is a problem with intellectual virtue. On Boethius of Dacia's view, moral virtue is ordered to intellectual virtue, which is simply superior. Why should someone engaged in contemplation sacrifice this activity for the sake of some political necessity? For the thirteenth-century thinker, this question threatens the congruity between virtuous action and the interests of others by asking whether the shared political good is subordinate to the private intellectual good of the philosopher. The question becomes not whether the good life harms the philosopher, but whether the philosopher's good life might deprive the political community of his assistance. Following Thomas, Godfrey distinguishes between an agent's good simply speaking and that good which is available in a particular situation. Strictly speaking, one is better off doing philosophy than helping the political community. Nevertheless, there are situations in which one is better off forsaking philosophy. One who neglects his political community when there is grave danger misunderstands where his own good lies. Consequently, when considering how an agent flourishes, it is important to consider what kind of flourishing is possible in a particular situation.

The contrast between the premodern and contemporary views of self-sacrifice is important. For medievals, the challenge is to explain how the contemplative's self-sacrifice is in fact in his own interest. They do not countenance the possibility that someone can be required to act in a way that stunts his own perfection. Given the modern and contemporary tension between morality and self-interest, it is easy to see why scholars such as Kraut give an alternative explanation of the tension between political and intellectual virtue. Kraut writes, "I take Aristotle to agree that in certain circumstances I should *not* develop the virtue that is best for me—theoretical wisdom—even though doing so would clearly be in my best interest."[9] The agent is not performing an act that is bad for him, but is rather choosing, in certain circumstances, some inferior good. Notice that Kraut is introducing here a conception of obligation which is not rooted in the agent's good. What sort of obligation is this? What is its basis, if not to help the agent to achieve his ultimate end? Thomas and Godfrey do not face this difficulty because they relate obligation to the agent's good. They avoid the tension between intellectual and moral virtue by making the distinction between what is good for the agent simply speaking and what is good for him in particular circumstances. It may be that in a particular set of circumstances developing theoretical wisdom is not in an agent's best interest.

We have seen that for the medievals the good life is that by which someone achieves the end towards which he is ordered. Thomas and his followers emphasize that this direction is a natural inclination much like that of even non-rational living creatures and inanimate bodies. Presumably the virtuous person does not need to have a full understanding of how his virtue is related to natural inclination. Nevertheless, a theoretical account of virtue depends on a recognition of its importance. Teleology is no longer widely accepted. How is it possible to retain a eudaimonistic virtue theory without it? Could such a theory be Thomistic or even Aristotelian? Some contemporary virtue theorists defend the truth of moral reasoning by granting a special status to "practical reasoning," so that such reasoning has its own autonomy without the need to ground moral judgments in either human nature or metaphysics.[10] This position is distinct from the medieval one in which it is true both that the agent can reason without a theoretical understanding of human nature or metaphysics and that such a theoretical understanding ultimately explains why and how the judgments are true

Although Scotus's ethical theory now has little influence compared to that of Thomas, it might seem to have more resources for dealing with the modern and contemporary denial of teleology. Scotus bases his ethics not on the bodily nature which is shared with other creatures, but on the will's own inclination to what is just. His theory sets up a greater dichotomy between non-rational creatures and humans than did previous thinkers. Scotus's understanding of freedom rests in the same fashion on the distinction between the will's natural inclination for happiness and its ability to act for justice. Finally, Scotus's ethics depend on a hierarchical view in which the natural law is primarily about loving God. Like Thomas, Scotus presupposes a teleological view of human nature. But whereas Thomas sees human nature as continuous with non-intellectual creation, Scotus sees it as discontinuous.

Nevertheless, Thomas's understanding of natural inclination depends on his position that God is the separate good of the universe to which everything else is ordered. Like Aristotle, he thinks that final causality requires the existence of a First Mover. In Thomas's ethical theory, God has several roles, of which two are important for our purposes. First, there is that most important obligation to love God above everything else. Second, there is the natural inclination which everything has for the common good, which is internally the perfection of the universe and externally God. This natural inclination to the common good explains why Thomas's eudaimonism is based on nature and yet is not selfish. Moreover, it ultimately explains why there is no conflict between the true good of different rational individuals. Since they are all immediately directed to God as the common good, there is no conflict between their ultimate ends. God is the kind of good that can be shared.

This coordination of human ends can also be seen in Thomas's understanding of the political common good. Each member of the political community is ordered to a common good which is not the aggregate of individual goods, but which can be shared at the same time by everyone. A state made up of individuals who do not share in a common good cannot justify someone dying on its behalf. Nevertheless, if the goods of different citizens ultimately conflict, someone must be willing to prefer another citizen's good to his own. It is the common good which ensures the harmony between virtuous action and one's own good.

Alasdair MacIntyre has also pointed out the difficulty in achieving a genuine political common good in our contemporary economic and political climate.[11] If the political common good is overemphasized in our age of disunified and bureaucratic nation-states, then there is the danger of a statist or totalitarian "good" which is not shareable by the members of the community. Charles de Koninck has explained the difficulties with restricting the common good to its political context.[12] First, it is God who ultimately ensures the coordination of individual goods because he is actually or at least potentially the common good of every living human. As the Thomist school notes, we should love our neighbor because God is our common good. If the common good were only political, it is ultimately not clear why someone should care about individuals outside of one's own community, or whether there could be ultimately conflicting political common goods. More seriously, in the age of Nazism and communism, de Koninck emphasized that by refusing to recognize God explicitly as the common good the state runs the danger of making itself absolutely supreme.[13] In contrast, the state recognizes its limitations when it recognizes that its citizens are ordered to a common good which is more important than the political.

If all goods were private, there could be a genuine conflict between virtue and self-interest. Traditional eudaimonism would be impossible to defend. Nevertheless, there is the danger of regarding the political common good as the highest good. One of Thomas's greatest insights was to recognize that God is a genuine common good. Even those medievals who denied that God is a common good emphasized that one's obligation to God is far more important than political obligations.

Consequently, it was possible for them to hold both that the moral life is not self-directed and that there exists an objective ultimate end which is more important than any human community. Where contemporary eudaimonistic theories have often presented the choice as between an inadequate individualism and an oppressive statism, the medieval debates over naturally loving God achieved unusually sophisticated thinking about eudaimonism and its relationship to theories about human nature and motivation.

Notes

Introduction

1. For an example of one such discussion which does not address the important philosophical issues see Richard Kilwardby, 2 Sent., q. 145, in *Quaestiones in librum secundum sententiarum*, ed. Gerhard Leibold, Bayerische Akademie der Wissenschaften, Veröffentlichungen der Kommission für die Herausgabe ungedruckter Texte aus der mittelalterlichen Geisteswelt, 16 (Munich: Bayerische Akademie der Wissenschaften, 1992), 389–395.

2. For attempts to wrestle with these issues, see David O. Brink, "Self-Love and Altruism" in *Self-Interest*, ed. Ellen Frankel Paul, Fred D. Miller, Jr, and Jeffrey Paul, 123–157 (Cambridge: Cambridge University Press, 1997); David Schmidtz, "Self-Interest: What's In It for Me?" in *Self-Interest*, 107–121.

3. J. B Schneewind, "The Divine Corporation and the History of Ethics," in *Philosophy in History: Essays on the Historiography of Philosophy*, ed. Richard Rorty, J. B. Schneewind, and Quentin Skinner (Cambridge: Cambridge University Press, 1984), 178.

4. Jesus Christ is not an exception, since he is a divine person who has assumed a human nature.

5. For a recent defense, see Michael Smith, *The Moral Problem* (Oxford: Blackwell, 1944), 92–129. For a critical discussion, see Philippa Foot, *Natural Goodness* (Oxford: Clarendon Press, 2001), 5–24.

6. Thomas Nagel, *The Possibility of Altruism* (Oxford: Clarendon Press, 1970); Elliot Sober and David Sloan Wilson, *Unto Others: The Evolution and Psychology of Unselfish Behavior* (Cambridge, Mass.: Harvard University Press, 1998).

7. For a historical and conceptual look at egotism that precludes the attribution of egotism or altruism to medieval thinkers, see Alasdair MacIntyre, "Egoism and Altruism," in *The Encylopedia of Philosophy*, vol. 2, ed. Paul Edwards (New York: Macmillan, 1967), 462–466.

8. Alasdair MacIntyre, "The Relationship of Philosophy to Its Past," in *Philosophy in History: Essays on the Historiography of Philosophy,* ed. Richard Rorty, J. B. Schneewind, and Quentin Skinner, 31–48 (Cambridge: Cambridge University Press, 1948); John Henry Newman, *An Essay on the Development of Christian Doctrine*, 6th ed. (Notre Dame, Ind.: University of Notre Dame Press, 1989), 33–54.

9. Aristotle *Physica* 2.1.192b8–34.

10. Aristotle *Eth. Nic.* 9.4.1116a1–2. For the importance of this dictum, see Pierre Rousselot, *Pour l'histoire du problème de l'amour au moyen âge*, Beiträge zur Geschichte der Philosophie und Theologie des Mittelalters, Bd. 6, Hft. 6 (Münster: Aschendorff, 1908), 6. Rousselot gives this dictum in one of its standard versions. The Latin translation of Robert Grosseteste in the *recensio pura* states, "Amicabilia autem quae ad amicos et quidem amicicie determinantur, videntur ex hiis que ad se ipsum venisse." See Aristotle, *Ethica Nicomachea*, trans. Robert Grosseteste, ed. René Antonin Gauthier, vol. 26, fasc. 3 of *Aristoteles Latinus*, Corpus Philosophorum Medii Aevi (Leiden: Brill; Brussels: Desclée, 1972), 328.

11. Aristotle. *Eth. Nic.* 9.8.1169a18–26. For the translation, see Aristotle, *Nicomachean Ethics*, trans. Terence H. Irwin (Indianapolis: Hackett, 1985).

12. David Bostock, *Aristotle's Ethics*. (Oxford: Oxford University Press, 2000), 172–179. For an attempt to interpret Aristotle such that the agent does not maximize his own good, see Richard Kraut, *Aristotle on the Human Good* (Princeton, N.J.: Princeton University Press, 1989), 78–154. For an interpretation of Aristotle as broadly altruistic (not in a particularly modern sense), see Paul Schollmeier, *Other Selves: Aristotle on Personal and Political Friendship* (Albany: SUNY Press, 1994). For the position that Aristotle is neither an egoist nor an altruist, see especially Julia Annas, *The Morality of Happiness* (Oxford: Oxford University Press, 1993), 249–262, 322–325; Arthur Madigan, "*Ethic. Nic.* 9.8: Beyond Egoism and Altruism," in *Essays in Ancient Greek Philosophy IV: Aristotle's Ethics*, ed. John P. Anton and Anthony Preus (Albany: SUNY Press, 1991), 73–94. Madigan's essay is a revised version of an article of the same title originally published in *The Modern Schoolman* 63 (1985): 1–20.

CHAPTER 1

The Augustinian Tradition and the Early Scholastic Background

1. John M. Rist, *Augustine: Ancient Thought Baptised* (Cambridge: Cambridge University Press, 1994); Alasdair MacIntyre, *Whose Justice? Which Rationality?* (Notre Dame, Ind.: University of Notre Dame Press, 1988), 146–163.

2. Anders Nygren, *Agape and Eros,* trans. Phillip F. Watson (Philadelphia: Westminster Press, 1953). For contemporary discussions, see Gerald W. Schlabach, *For the Joy Set Before Us: Augustine and Self-Denying Love* (Notre Dame, Ind.: University of Notre Dame Press, 2002), 4–12; Darlene Fozard Weaver, *Self-Love and Christian Ethics* (Cambridge: Cambridge University Press, 2000), 48–52.

3. Ethelbert Stauffer, "ἀγαπάω," in *Theologisches Wörterbuch zum Neuen Testament,* vol. 1, ed. Gerhard Kittel (Stuttgart: Kohlhammer, 1933), 20–34. His article is translated in *Theological Dictionary of the New Testament,* vol. 1, ed. Geoffrey W. Bromiley (Grand Rapids, Mich.: Eerdmans, 1964), 35–55. See also Victor Warnach, "Agape in the New Testament," in *The Philosophy and Theology of Anders Nygren,* ed. Charles W. Kegley (Carbondale: Southern Illinois University Press, 1970), 143–155.

4. Matt 22:37–41. See also Deut 6:5; Lev 19:18. The translation is taken from the Revised Standard Version, Catholic Edition. For the Greek text, I have used Nestle-Aland, 26th ed., in Kurt Aland et al., eds., *Novum Testamentum Graece et Latine* (Stuttgart: Deutsche Bibelgesellschaft, 1984). Its Latin text is that of the New Vulgate. For the Old Vulgate, I have used Augustine Merk, *Novum Testamentum Graece et Latine* (Rome: Pontifical Biblical Institute, 1957). For *agape,* see especially Ferdinand Prat, "Charité," in *Dictionnaire de Spiritualité,* vol. 2 (Paris: Beauchesne, 1953), cols. 508–523; Gottfried Quell, "ἀγαπάω," in Kittel, *Theologisches Wörterbuch,* vol. 1, 20–34.

5. Gustav Stählin, "φιλέω," in *Theologisches Wörterbuch zum Neuen Testament,* vol. 9, ed. Gerhard Friedrich (Stuttgart: Kohlhammer, 1973), 153–156. Stählin's article is translated in the corresponding volume of Bromiley.

6. Jn 15:13.

7. Stählin, "φιλέω," 116–117.

8. Hélène Pétré, *Caritas: Étude sur le vocabulaire latin de la charité chrétienne,* Spicilegium Sacrum Lovaniense, 22 (Louvain: Spicilegium Sacrum Lovaniense, 1948), 92.

9. John M. Rist, *Eros and Psyche: Studies in Plato, Plotinus, and Origen,* Phoenix Supplementary Volumes, 6 (Toronto: University of Toronto Press, 1964), 195–212; 217–218.

10. For a criticism of Nygren's understanding of the Greek Fathers, see Rist, *Eros and Psyche,* 195–220; idem, "A Note on Eros and Agape in Pseudo-Dionysius," *Vigiliae Christianae* 20 (1966): 235–243. For a criticism of Nygren's whole approach, see idem, "Some Interpretations of Agape and Eros," in *The Philosophy and Theology of Anders Nygren,* ed. Charles W. Kegley (Carbondale: Southern Illinois University Press, 1970), 156–173. For criticisms of Nygren's view of Augustine, see John Burnaby, "Amor in St. Augustine," in Kegley, *Philosophy and Theology of Anders Nygren,* 174–186; Oliver O'Donovan, *The Problem of Self-Love in St. Augustine* (New Haven, Conn.: Yale University Press, 1980), 10–18. For a Thomistic criticism of Nygren, see Joseph Pieper, *Love,* trans. Mary Frances McCarthy and Richard and Clara Watson, in *Faith, Hope, Love,* 7th ed. (San Francisco: Ignatius Press, 1997), 210–232. "But what if Dionysius' Eros is in fact equivalent or somewhat near equivalent to Agape? Then, since terms are less important than ideas, it will be hard to accuse Dionysius of introducing alien doctrines when he merely describes proper doctrines by another name." Rist, "Note," 236

11. "Augustine has tried to bring about a fusion of very heterogeneous elements in his doctrine of Caritas, a fusion of ancient eudaemonism with Christian love, of the desire of Eros with the devotion of Agape. The meaning of this synthesis is, in brief: *the Christian Commandment of Love gives the final answer to the question of ancient philosophy about the 'highest good.'* In this union the Christian idea of love is the losing partner, and that is simply because ancient thought is allowed to put the question." Nygren, *Agape and Eros,* 503. For views which are more sympathetic to Augustine, see John Burnaby, *Amor Dei: A Study of the Religion of St. Augustine* (London: Hodder and Stoughton, 1938), 25–83; O'Donovan, *Self-Love in St. Augustine,* 10–22.

12. Augustine, *De moribus ecclesiae catholicae* 1.3.4 (CSEL 90, 6–7). "PL" will be the abbreviation used for Migne's *Patrologia Latina,* "PG" for Migne's *Patrologia Graeca,* "CCL" for *Corpus Christianorum, Series Latina,* and "CSEL" for *Corpus Scriptorum Ecclesiasticorum Latinorum.*

13. "Deus igitur restat quem si sequimur, bene; si assequimur, non tantum bene, sed etiam beate vivimus." *De mor. eccl.* 1.6.10 (PL 32, 1315). Cf. De *mor. eccl.* 1.3.5 (PL 32, 1312). For a discussion, see Burnaby, *Amor Dei,* 85–92.

14. For a reconstruction, see Étienne Gilson, *Introduction a l'étude de saint Augustin,* Études de Philosophie Médiévale, 11 (Paris: Vrin, 1929), 211–219.

15. "Eligimus enim Platonicos omnium philosophorum merito nobilissimos, propterea quia sapere potuerunt licet inmortalem ac rationalem vel intellectualem hominis animam nisi participato lumine illius Dei, a quo et ipsa et mundus factus est, beatam esse non posse; ita illud, quod omnes homines appetunt, id est vitam beatam, quemquem isti assecuturum negant, qui non illi uni optimo, quod est incommuntabilis Deus, puritate casti amoris adhaeserit." Augustine, *De civititate dei* 10.1 (CCL 47, 271–272). For the influence of Plotinus's theory of love on Augustine, see Rist, *Augustine,* 188–191.

16. *De civ. dei* 10.3 (CCL 47, 275).

17. *De civ. dei* 10.16 (CCL 47, 286); *De civ. dei* 10.18 (CCL 47, 293). Cf. *De civ. dei* 19.1 (CCL 48, 657).

18. *De civ. dei* 10.2 (CCL 47, 274).

19. "Non amas certe nisi bonum quia bona est terra altitudine montium et temperamento collium et planitie camporum, et bonum praedium aomoenum ac fertile, et bona domus paribus membris diposita . . . Quid plura et plura? Bonum hoc et bonum illud. Tolle hoc et illud, et uide ipsum bonum si potes; ita deum uidebis, non alio bono bonum, sed bonum omnis boni." Augustine, *De trinitate* 8.3(4) (CCL 30, 271–272).

20. "Quapropter nulla essent mutabilia bona nisi esset incommutabile bonum. Cum itaque audis bonum hoc et bonum illud quae possunt alias dici etiam non bona, si potueris sine illis quae participatione boni bona sunt perspicere ipsum bonum cuius participatione bona sunt (simul enim et ipsum intellegis, cum audis hoc aut illud bonum), si ergo potueris illis detractis per se ipsum perspicere bonum, perspexeris deum. Et si amore inhaeseris, continuo beatificaberis." *De trinitate* 8.3(5) (CCL 50, 273). Cf. *De civ. dei* 11.9 (CCL 48, 330); *De civ. dei* 11.13 (CCL 48, 333).

21. "Eadem quippe trinitate fruendum est ut beate vivamus . . ." *De trinitate* 8.5(8) (CCL 50, 277–278). For God as the *summum bonum,* see *De trinitate* 8.3 (5) (CCL 50, 273–274.).

22. ". . . quia fecisti nos ad te et inquietum est cor nostrum, donec requiescat in te." Augustine, *Confessiones* 1.1 (CCL 27, 1).

23. *Conf.* 13.9(10) (CCL 27, 246).

24. Burnaby, *Amor Dei,* 94.

25. *Conf.* 13.26(41) (CCL 27, 226–227). Phil 4:17. Cf. *Conf.* 13.27; 13.34(49) (CCL 27, 267; 272). For God as the *summum bonum* and happiness of the soul, see *Conf.* 13.2(2)–13.3(4) (CCL 27, 242–244). For God as the rest of the soul, see *Conf.* 13.35–38(50–53) (CCL 27, 273).

26. Augustine, *De doctrina christiana* 1.3(3) (CCL 32, 8).

27. "Frui est enim amore inhaerere alicui rei propter se ipsam. Uti autem, quod in usum venerit, ad id, quod amas obtinendum referre, si tamen amandum est. Nam usus inlicitus abusus potius vel abusio nominanda est." Augustine, *De doctr. christ.* 1.4(4) (CCL 32, 8).

28. *De doctr. christ.* 1.4(4)–1.5(5) (CCL 32, 8–9).

29. Burnaby, *Amor Dei,* 113–135.

30. *De doctr. christ.* 1.22(20–21) (CCL 32, 16–17). Jn 13:34; 15: 12.17. Cf. Rist, *Augustine,* 162–166.

31. "Magnum autem aliquid adeptum se putat, si etiam sociis, id est aliis hominibus, dominari potuerit. Inest enim uitioso animo id magis appetere et sibi tamquam debitum uindicare, quod uni proprie debetur deo. Talis autem sui dilectio melius odium uocatur. Iniquum est enim, quia uult sibi seruire, quod infra se est, cum ipse superiori seruire nolit, rectissimeque dictum est: '*Qui autem diligit iniquitatem, odit animam suam*' . . ." *De doctr. christ.* 1.24(23) (CCL 32, 18–19). Ps 10:6. Cf. *De trinitate* 8.6(9) (CCL 50, 283–284); *De trinitate* 14.14(18) (CCL 50A, 445–446). For discussions, see Raymond Canning, *The Unity of Love for God and Neighbour in St. Augustine* (Leuven: Augustinian Historical Institute, 1993), 116–166; O'Donovan, *Self-Love in St. Augustine,* 37–59; Rist, *Augustine,* 189–190.

32. *De doctr. christ.* 1.22(21) (CCL 32, 17–18). Cf. *De trinitate* 8.7(10) (CCL 50, 284).

33. "Et si deus omni homine amplius diligendus est, amplius quisque deum debet diligere quam se ipsum. Item amplius alius homo diligendus est quam corpus nostrum, quia propter deum omnia ista diligenda sunt, et potest nobiscum alius homo deo perfrui, quod non potest corpus, quia corpus per animam uiuit, qua fruimur deo." *De doctr. christ.* 1.27(28) (CCL 32, 22).

34. For a summary of the controversy and attempted solutions, see Canning, *Unity of Love,* 79–115; Rist, *Augustine,* 159–168.

35. Canning, *Unity of Love,* 109–115. See for example *De doctr. christ.* 1.33.37 (CCL 32, 27).

36. "Fruimur enim cognitis in quibus uoluntas ipsis propter se ipsa delectata conquiescit; utimur uero eis quae ad aliud referimus quo fruendum est." *De trinitate* 10.10(13) (CCL 50A, 327).

37. *De trinitate* 10.5(7) (CCL 50A, 320–321).

38. *De trinitate* 10.11(17) (CCL 50A, 330).

39. *De trinitate* 14.14(18)(CCL 50A, 446).

40. ". . . quod ea re frui dicimur, quae nos non ad aliud referenda per se ipsa delectat ; uti uero ea re, quam propter aliud quaerimus . . ." *De civ. dei* 11.25 (CCL 48, 344). Cf. *De civ. dei* 11.24 (CCL 48, 345); *De civ. dei* 15.7 (CCL 48, 460–461).

41. For example, *De civ. dei* 19.4 (CCL 48, 664–669). For an alternative view of Augustine's early writings, see F. B. A. Asidieu, "The Wise Man and the Limits of Virtue in the *De beata vita*: Stoic Self-Sufficiency or Augustinian Irony?" *Augustiniana* 49 (1999): 215–234.

42. *De civ. dei* 19.3–4 (CCL 48, 662–669). For an earlier variant position, see Augustine, *De libero arbitrio* 2.19(191–192) (CCL 29, 271).

43. "Nam et amor ipse ordinate amandus est, quo bene amatur quod amandum est, ut sit in nobis uirtus qua uiuitur bene. Unde mihi uidetur, quod definitio breuis et uera uirtutis ordo est amoris . . ." *De civ. dei* 15.22 (CCL 48, 488).

44. Canning, *Unity of Love,* 20–25.

45. "Non enim caro sine anima concupiscit, quamvis caro concupiscere dicatur, quia carnaliter anima concupiscit. Tunc erit justus sine ullo omnino peccato, quia nulla lex erit in membris ejus repugnans legi mentis ejus (Rom 8:23), sed prorsus toto corde, tota anima, tota mente diliget Deum, quod est primum summumque praeceptum." Augustine, *De perfectione justitiae hominis liber* 8.19 (CSEL 42, 18, 300–301).

46. Support for this interpretation can be found in *De trinitate* 10.7(9) (CCL 50A, 322).

47. ". . . unde est in hominibus charitas Dei et proximi nisi ex ipso Deo? Nam si non ex Deo, sed ex hominibus, vicerunt Pelagiani: si autem ex Deo, vicimus Pelagianos." Augustine, *De gratia et libero arbitrio liber unus,* 18.37 (PL 44, 905). Cf. *De peccatorum meritis et remissione* 2.5.5 (CSEL 60, 75); *De natura et gratia* 59.69 (CSEL 60, 285).

48. Alister E. McGrath, *Iustitia Dei: A History of the Christian Doctrine of Justification,* 2nd ed. (Cambridge: Cambridge University Press, 1998), 74–75.

49. Jasper Hopkins, *A Companion to the Study of St. Anselm* (Minneapolis: University of Minnesota Press, 1972), 16–28; R.W. Southern, *Saint Anselm: A Portrait in a Landscape* (Cambridge: Cambridge University Press, 1990), 71–87.

50. Anselm of Canterbury, *De casu diaboli* 4, in *Opera Omnia,* ed. Francis Sales Schmitt (Seckau and Edinburgh, 1938–1961), vol. 1, 240–242. See Imelda Choquette, "Voluntas, Affectio and Potestas in the Liber de Voluntate of St. Anselm," *Mediaeval Studies* 4 (1942): 64–70; John R. Sheets, "Justice in the Moral Thought of St. Anselm," *The Modern Schoolman* 25 (1948): 132–139; G. Stanley Kane, *Anselm's Doctrine of Freedom and the Will,* Texts and Studies in Religion, vol. 10 (New York: Mellen Press, 1981), 61–108.

51. Phillippe Delhaye, "Quelques aspects de la morale de saint Anselme," *Spicilegium Beccense,* vol. 1 (Le Bec-Hellouin: Abbaye Notre-Dame du Bec; Paris: Vrin, 1959), 401–423; Robert Pouchet, *La rectitudo chez saint Anselm: Un itinéraire Augustinien de l'ame à Dieu* (Paris: Études Augustiniennes, 1964), 187–197; Kane, *Anselm's Doctrine,* 107–108. For an alternative interpretation, see Eugene R. Fairweather, "Truth, Justice, and Moral Responsibility in the Thought of St. Anselm," in *L'homme et son destin d' après les penseurs du moyen âge, Actes du premier congrès international de philosophie médiéval Louvain-Bruxelles, 28 Août–4 Septembre 1958* (Louvain: Éditions Nauwelaerts; Paris: Béatrice-Nauwelaerts, 1960), 385–391.

52. For a treatment of the connection between *rectitudo* and freedom, see especially Bernd Goebel, *Rectitudo, Wahrheit und Freiheit von Anselm von Canterbury: Eine philosophische Untersuchung seines Denkansatzes,* Beiträge zur Geschichte der Philosophie und Theologie des Mittelalters, nf. 56 (Münster: Aschendorff, 2001), 363–502.

53. Anselm of Canterbury, *Monologion* 68 (*Opera,* vol. 1, 78–79); idem, *Cur deus homo,* praefatio (*Opera,* vol. 2, 42–43).

54. Anselm, *Monologion* 16 (*Opera,* vol. 1, 30–31). For the view that Anselm accepts Augustine's Neoplatonic metaphysics, including participation, see Hopkins, *Compan-*

ion to St. Anselm, 127–135. For controversies over Anselm's attitude towards Augustine's Neoplatonism, see Francis Sales Schmitt, "Anselm und der (Neu-)Platonismus," *Analecta Anselmiana* 1 (1969), 39–71; Kurt Flasch, "Der philosophische Ansatz des Anselm von Canterbury in Monologion und sein Verhältnis zum Augustinischen Neuplatonismus," *Analecta Anselmiana* 2 (1970): 1–43.

55. Anselm, *De casu diaboli* 23–24 (*Opera,* vol. 1, 269–272). See Kane, *Anselm's Doctrine,* 183–184.

56. Anselm, *Cur deus homo* 2.1 (*Opera,* vol. 2, 97–98); *Monologion* 69 (*Opera,* vol. 1, 79–80).

57. Rousselot, *L'amour au moyen âge,* 43–49. See also Artur Michael Landgraf, "Charité," in *Dictionnaire du spiritualité,* vol. 2 (Paris: Beauchesne, cols. 1953), 578–579. For a criticism of Rousselot's distinction, see Étienne Gilson, *The Spirit of Medieval Philosophy,* Gifford Lectures 1931–1932, trans. A. H. C. Downes (Notre Dame: University of Notre Dame Press, 1991), 289–303.

58. See Marcia L. Colish, *Peter Lombard,* Brill's Studies in Intellectual History, 41 (Leiden: Brill, 1994), vol. 2, 500; Richard E. Weingart, *The Logic of Divine Love: A Critical Analysis of the Soteriology of Peter Abailard* (Oxford: Clarendon Press, 1970), 172–173; Rousselot, *L'amour au moyen âge,* 74. For the "cultured distaste" of Hugh of St. Victor for Abelard, see D. E. Luscombe, *The School of Peter Abelard: The Influence of Abelard's Thought in the Early Scholastic Period* (Cambridge: Cambridge University Press, 1969), 183–197.

59. Rousselot, *L'amour au moyen âge,* 72–75.

60. Peter Abelard, *Commentaria in epistolam Pauli ad romanos* 3.7.13 (CCL, Continuatio Mediaeualis, 11, 202). For discussions, see Rousselot, *L'amour au moyen âge,* 73–74; Étienne Gilson, *La Théologie mystique de Saint Bernard,* Études de Philosophie Médiévale, 20 (Paris: Vrin, 1934), 183–189; Weingart, *Logic of Divine Love,* 171–172; John Marenbon, *The Philosophy of Peter Abelard* (Cambridge: Cambridge University Press, 1997), 300–301.

61. "Ex his itaque beati Augustini uerbis aperte declaratur quae sit uera in aliquem ac sincera dilectio, ipsum uidelicet propter se, non propter sua diligit." *Commentaria in epistolam Pauli ad romanos* 3.7.13 (CCL, Continuatio Mediaeualis 11, 202).

62. There are two main theories about why Abelard focuses on disinterested love. Gilson, *Saint Bernard,* 186–188, suggests that we look to Heloïse. Weingart, *Logic of Divine Love,* 171, note 1, argues for the less interesting but more plausible view that Abelard's emphasis on disinterested love is connected to his soteriology.

63. For the position that Hugh was a consistent adherent to both the "physical" and the "ecstatic" theories of love, see Roger Baron, *Science et Sagesse chez Hugues de Saint-Victor* (Paris: Lethielleux, 1957), 190–191.

64. Peter Lombard, *Sententiae in IV libris distinctae* 3.27.2, in *Sententiae in IV libris distinctae,* Spicilegium Bonaventurianum, 4–5 (Rome: Collegium S. Bonaventurae, 1971, 1981), vol. 2, 162–163. For Hugh's influence on Peter's teaching regarding charity, see Colish, *Peter Lombard,* vol. 2, 500–502.

65. "Geminam nobis sacra Scriptura charitatem commendat; Dei videlicet et proximi. Charitatem Dei ut sic ipsum diligamus ut in ipso gaudeamus. Charitatem

proximi ut sic ipsum diligamus, non ut in ipso, sed ut cum ipso gaudeamus in Deo. Hoc est, ut Deum diligamus propter se ipsum; proximum autem propter Deum." Hugh of St. Victor, *De sacramentis fidei christianae* 2.6 (PL 176, 528–529).

66. Rousselot, *L'amour au moyen âge,* 46–47; Landgraf, "Charité," 578.

67. "Si vere diligitur, diligitur ubicunque invenitur. In seipso, in proximo, intus et foris, et sursum et deorsum, longe et prope . . . Mel propter seipsum diligitur. Favus autem propter mel diligitur; et si forte videris favum non habentem mel, vides receptacula ubi mel esse debuerat, et dotes vacua esse; et non placet tibi, quia arida sunt, et cupis mel illic esse quod diligis; et si venerit, amplius diligis. Ita dilige Dominum Deum tuum, qua dulcedo est ipse, et bonitas et veritas. Proximum autem tuum dilige, quia receptaculum est dulcedinis, bonitatis, et veritatis . . ." *De sacramentis* 2.6 (PL 176, 530).

68. "Nemo carnem suam odio habuit." Eph 5:29. The psalm is 10:6. *De sacramentis* 2.7 (PL 176, 531–532). Cf. Augustine, *De doctr. christ.* 1.23–24(23–25) (CCL 32, 18–20).

69. *De sacramentis* 2.8 (PL 176, 534–535).

70. Colish, *Peter Lombard,* 500–504; Landgraf, "Charité," 579.

71. Peter Lombard, *Sententiae* 1.1.2–3 (SB 4, 56–61).

72. *Sententiae* 3.27.1–8 (SB 5, 162–168).

73. "Caritas est dilectio qua diligitur Deus propter se, et proximus propter Deum vel in Deo." *Sententiae* 1.27.2 (SB 5, 162).

74. For a discussion of love in the works of Bernard, see Joseph Ries, *Das geistliche Leben in seinen Entwicklungsstufen nach der Lehre des Hl. Bernard* (Freiburg im Breisgau: Herder, 1906), 168–213; Gilson, *Saint Bernard,* passim; Pacifique Delfgaauw, "La nature et les degrés de l'amour selon S. Bernard," in *Saint Bernard théologien: Actes du Congrès de Dijon, 15–19 septembre 1953, Analecta Sacri Ordinis Cisterciensis* 9 (1953): 234–252; G. R. Evans, *The Mind of St. Bernard of Clairvaux* (Oxford: Clarendon Press, 1983), 107–137.

75. Rousselot, *L'amour au moyen âge,* 29–55; Landgraf: "Charité," 576–578. It should be noted that Bernard's theory of love is seen as containing aspects of both the "physical" and the "violent" approaches. See also Rousselot, *L'amour au moyen âge,* 88–89. For a discussion of Bernard and the "physical" theory of love, see Delfgaauw, "L'amour selon S. Bernard," 240–243. For a harsh criticism of Rousselot, see Gilson, *Medieval Philosophy,* 289–303. For a discussion of Augustine, *natura curva,* and the physcial theory of love, see O'Donovan, *Self-Love in St. Augustine,* 148–152.

76. Bernard, *Sermones super cantica canticorum* 24.6, in *S. Bernardi Opera,* vol. 1, ed. Jean LeClerq, Charles H. Talbot, and H. M. Rochais (Rome: Editiones Cistercienses, 1957), 157. See also *Super cantica* 24.7–8 , in *Opera,* vol. 1, 158–162; *Super cantica* 36.5, in *Opera,* vol. 2, 7; *Super cantica* 80.3–4, in *Opera,* vol. 2, 279–280; *Sermones de diversis* 12.1, in *Opera,* vol. 3, 127–128; *De diversis* 32.3, in *Opera,* vol. 3, 220; *De diversis* 40.4, in *Opera,* vol. 3, 237; *De diversis* 103.4, in *Opera,* vol. 3, 373.

77. See especially Nygren's discussion of Augustine and *"curvatus,"* *Agape and Eros,* 485, note 3.

78. "Non relicto superiore bono, curvare te ad inferius bonum . . . Esto bene utens rebus inferioribus, et eris recte fruens bono superiore." Augustine, *Sermo* 11.3, in

Sermones de vetere testamento (CCL 41, 279). For an extensive treatment, see Augustine, *Sermo* 21.8–10 (CCL 41, 283–286). See also Augustine, *Ennarationes in Psalmos* 37.10 (CCL 38, 389); 50.15 (CCL 38, 610–611). See Nygren, *Agape and Eros,* 485–488.

79. Bernard, *De diligendo deo* 8.23, in *Opera,* vol. 3, 138–139. See also *De diligendo* 15.39, in *Opera,* vol. 3, 152. See Delfgauuw, "L'amour selon S. Bernard," 240–241.

80. *De diligendo* 8.25, in *Opera,* vol. 3, 139.

81. "Amat ergo iam Deum, sed propter se interim, adhuc non propter ipsum." *De diligendo* 9.26, in *Opera,* vol. 3, 140. See also *De diligendo* 15.40, in *Opera,* vol. 3, 152–153.

82. "Iste est tertius amoris gradus, quo iam propter seipsum Deus diligitur." *De diligendo* 9.26, in *Opera,* vol. 3, 140. See also *De diligendo* 15.39, in *Opera,* vol. 3, 153.

83. *De diligendo* 10.27–28, in *Opera,* vol. 3, 142.

84. "Ego puto non ante sane perfecte impletum iri: 'Diliges Dominum Deum tuum ex toto corde tuo, et ex tota anima tua, et ex tota virtute tua,' quousque ipsum cor cogitare iam non cogatur de corpore, et anima eidem in hoc statu vivificando et sensificando intendere desinat, et virtus eiusdem relevata molestiis, in Dei potentia roboretur." *De diligendo* 10.29, in *Opera,* vol. 3, 143–144. Mk 12:30. See also *De diligendo* 15.39, in *Opera,* vol. 3, 153. For the position that such love will not exist before the resurrection of the body, see *De diligendo* 10.30–33, in *Opera,* vol. 3, 144–147.

85. Artur Michael Landgraf, "Studien zur Erkenntnis des Übernatürlichen in der Frühscholastik," *Scholastik* 4 (1929): 1–37; 189–220; 353–389; idem, *Dogmengeschichte der Frühscholastik,* vol. 1/1 (Regensburg: Friedrich Pustet, 1952), 141–201. For bibliography, see Z. Alszeghy, "La teologia dell'ordine soprannaturale nella scolastica antica," *Gregorianum* 1950 (31): 414–450. For the relationship between charity and the supernatural, see Landgraf, "Charité," 574–578.

86. Reginald Garrigou-Lagrange, "Le Problème de l'amour pur et la solution de Saint Thomas," *Angelicum* (1929): 83–124; Delfgaauw, "L'amour selon S. Bernard," 237–239.

87. Delfgaauw, "L'amour selon S. Bernard," 235–240.

88. For a summary of the developments, see L-B. Gillon, "Primacia del apetito universal de Dios según Santo Tomás," *Ciencia Tomista* 63 (1942): 328–342; M-R. Gagnebet "L'amour naturel de Dieu chez Saint Thomas et ses contemporains," *Revue Thomiste* 48 (1948): 397–412.

89. "Utrum angelus in primo statu diligebat Deum." William of Auxerre, *Summa Aurea* 2.2.4, vol. 1, ed. Jean Ribaillier, Spicilegium Bonaventurianum 17 (Paris: Éditions du Centre National de la Recherche Scientifique; Rome: Collegium S. Bonaventurae, 1982), 40. For a summary of William's position, see Gillon, "Primacia," 330–332; Gagnebet, "L'amour naturel de Dieu," 398–400; Landgraf, "Studien," 377–378; idem, *Dogmengeschichte,* 197; idem, "Charité," 577–578.

90. *Summa Aurea* 2.2.1 (vol. 1, 32–33; 34–35).

91. "Si sic, ergo ex caritate diligebat eum, quoniam sola caritate sic diligitur Deus. Si non, ergo ommittebat hoc preceptum quod erat scriptum in mente sua: *Diliges Dominum Deum tuum* etc." *Summa Aurea* 2.2.1 (vol. 1, 33)

92. "Ad aliud dicimus quod angelus diligebat Deum in primo statu quantum debebat et sicut debebat, ex eis que data erant ei, id est ex naturalibus; diligebat ergo Deum angelus quantum debebat et sicut debebat diligere tunc, non tamen diligebat eum simpliciter quantum debebat <vel> tenebatur diligere, in quantum habebat mandatum caritatis scriptum in mente sua: tenebatur ergo eum diligere ex caritate, sed nonnisi prius accepta gratia." *Summa Aurea* 2.2.1 (vol. 1, 34).

93. "Item in primo statu angelus aut diligebat Deum propter se et super omnia, aut non. Si sic, ergo ex caritate, quoniam meliori modo non potest diligi Deus. Si non, <non> diligebat Deum propter se Deum, sed propter se, id est propter se angelum; ergo magis diligebat se quam Deum; ergo peccabat mortaliter . . ." *Summa Aurea* 2.2.1 (vol. 1, 33).

94. *Summa Aurea* 2.2.1 (vol. 1, 34).

95. "Primo modo dicitur 'natura principium motus per se et non secundum accidens.' Secundo 'uniuscuiuslibet rei specifica differentia.' Tertio 'quaelibet res que, cum sit, intelligi potest.'" *Summa Aurea* 2.2.1 (vol. 1, 37). Cf. Boethius, *De persona et duabus naturis* 1 (PL 64, 1341–1342).

96. *Summa Aurea* 2.2.1 (vol. 1, 37). Cf. Aristotle, *Physica* 2.1 (192b21–23).

97. "Amor naturalis sui est ille amor quo aliquis vult naturaliter sibi bonum, scilicet esse, vivere, intelligere, et talis amor non tendit nisi ad conservationem sui, ad utilitatem sui . . ." *Summa Aurea* 2.2.2 (vol. 1, 38). For the sources of this triad, see M. J. Edwards, "Porphyry and the Intelligible Triad," *Journal of Hellenic Studies* 110 (1990): 14–25.

98. *Summa Aurea* 2.2.2–3 (vol. 1, 38–40).

99. "Utrum angelus in primo statu diligebat Deum." *Summa Aurea* 2.2.4 (vol. 1, 40).

100. In making these divisions William is following Geoffrey of Poitiers. However, the fourfold division of love probably was so influential because it was presented by William. At any rate, Geoffrey's division of love is only in manuscript form, and according to Landgraf we do not know his position on the natural love for God because the manuscript is so corrupt as to be unreadable. See Landgraf, "Charité," 577.

101. "Est autem duplex dilectio involuntaria: una quam habemus communem cum brutis, qua homo diligit se, id est vitam suam, salutem, et sanitatem, et conservationem istorum, quoniam tali amore diligimus membra nostra et magis diligimus magis necessaria, ut capud pro quo conservando exponimus cetera membra: tali dilectione diligunt se bruta . . . Talis dilectio non potest esse peccatum, quoniam non est voluntaria, nec potest esse voluntaria . . ." *Summa Aurea* 2.2.4 (vol. 1, 42).

102. *Summa Aurea* 2.2.4 (vol. 1, 42). Cf. Cicero, *De natura deorum* 1.17; Boethius, *De consolatione philosophiae* 3.2 (PL 63, 724); Songs 3:1; Augustine, *Soliloquies* 1.1.2 (PL 32, 869).

103. "Dilectio autem voluntaria dividitur in duas, scilicet in concupiscentiam et amicitiam sive benivolentiam. Concupiscentia est dilectio qua diligimus omne illud quo frui appetimus vel quod habere volumus, sicut aliquis dicitur diligere vinum, quia

appetit frui eo. Dilectio que dicitur amicitia est qua diligimus omne illud cuius bonum volumus, id est cuius bonis congratulamur. Utraque dilectione, sive concupiscentia, sive benivolentia, diligimus Deum per naturam sine adiutorio gratie et per gratiam . . ." *Summa Aurea* 2.2.4 (vol. 1, 43).

104. *Summa Aurea* 2.2.4 (vol. 1, 43).

105. Michael Sherwin, "'The Friend of the Bridegroom Stands and Listens': An Analysis of the Term *Amicus Sponsi* in Augustine's Account of Divine Friendship and the Ministry of Bishops," *Gregorianum* 38 (1998): 197–214; G. G. Meersseman, "Pourquoi le Lombard n'a-t-il pas conçu la charité comme amitié?" in *Miscellanea Lombardiana* (Turin: Pontificio Ateneo Salesiano, 1957), 165–174.

106. For a history of the issue, see especially Richard Egenter, *Gottesfreundschaft: Die Lehre von der Gottesfreundschaft in der Scholastik und Mystik des 12. und 13. Jahrhunderts* (Augsburg: Filser, 1928).

107. *Summa Aurea* 2.2.4–5 (vol. 1, 41–44). Cf. Augustine, *De doctr. christ.* 1.27 (28) (CCL 32, 22).

108. *Summa Aurea* 2.2.4–5 (vol. 1, 43–44). In the *adventiculum post capitulum 5,* it is explained that charity and the natural love for God are of different species. The species is not only about acting, but about acting easily. Since the act of charity loves good with more prodigality and liberality, it belongs to a different species than the act of natural love. *Summa Aurea* Appendix IV (vol. 2, 721).

109. For Philip's position, see Gillon, "Primacia," 334–337; Gagnebet, "L'amour naturel de Dieu," 400–401; Landgraf, "Studien," 380–384; idem, *Dogmengeschichte,* 197–199; idem, "Charité," 578.

110. "Item, natura in se curva est quia ad se reflectitur. Quod apparet in naturalibus, prius enim cessat ab actu generativa naturaliter quam nutritiva, eo quod hec sit propter subiectum conservandum, illa propter speciem . . ." *Summa de bono,* ed. Nikolaus Wicki, Corpus philosophorum Medii Aevi Opera philosophica Mediae Aetatis selecta, 2 (Bern: Francke, 1985), vol. 1, p. 86 Since the structure of the *Summa de bono* is exceedingly complex, references will be to volume and page.

111. *Summa de bono,* vol. 2, 731.

112. Philip always uses the plural when discussing adherents to William's position and distinctions. It is not clear to me whether he is merely following the medieval custom of not naming disputants, discussing William's followers or positions that have not been handed down to us, or whether he might also be discussing the position of Geoffrey of Poitiers. Certainly Geoffrey, like William, distinguished between love and concupiscence.

113. ". . . bonum cognitum non potest non diligi." Philip the Chancellor, *Summa de bono,* vol. 1, 86.

114. *Summa de bono,* vol. 1, 88.

115. "Dilectio concupiscentie est qua nobis volumus rem, dilectio amicitie qua volumus bonum eius vel ei quod diligimus . . ." *Summa de bono,* vol. 1, 89.

116. *Summa de bono,* vol. 1, 89.

117. *Summa de bono,* vol. 1, 90.

118. *Summa de bono,* vol. 1, 90.

119. "Respondeo quod in diligendo Deum super omnia non elevatur supra se, sicut nec in cognoscendo, sed mensuratur dilectio secundum modum cognitionis. Longe autem nobilior est cognitio fidei quam cognitio naturalis. Unde caritas que sequitur illam cognitionem longe nobilior est dilectione naturali . . . Facit etiam cognoscendo tendere in ipsum tamquam in summam veritatem, et hanc cognitionem sequitur caritas ratione motus aut dispositionis, sed non infusionis, cuius est diligere summum bonum quod est elevans per gratiam et per gloriam et hoc propter se. Sed non sic est in cognitione naturali et dilectione subsequente; cognitio enim illa fuit de Deo secundum opera creationis, que cognitio non elevat intellectum supra se." *Summa de bono,* vol. 1, 91.

120. *Summa de bono,* vol. 1, 91–92.

CHAPTER TWO
Mid-Thirteenth-Century Scholasticism at Paris

1. Georg Wieland, "The Reception and Interpretation of Aristotle's *Ethics*," in *The Cambridge History of Later Medieval Philosophy,* ed. Anthony Kenny, Norman Kretzmann, and Jan Pinborg (Cambridge: Cambridge University Press, 1982), 660–661.

2. Albert the Great, *Summa de creaturis,* t. 4, q. 25, a.1, in *Opera Omnia,* ed. Auguste Borgnet, 38 vols. (Paris: Vivès, 1890–1899), vol. 34, 487–488; idem, *Summa Theologica,* p. 2, q. 4, q. 14 (vol. 33, 196–198).

3. Vernon J. Bourke, "Human Tendencies, Will, and Freedom," in *L'homme et son destin d' après les penseurs du moyen âge, Actes du premier congrès international de philosophie médiéval Louvain-Bruxelles, 28 Août–4 Septembre 1958* (Louvain: Éditions Nauwelaerts; Paris: Béatrice-Nauwelaerts, 1960), 77.

4. John Damascene, *De fide orthodoxa:* Versions of Burgundio and Cerbanus, ed. Eligius M. Buytaert, Franciscan Institute Publications, 8 (St. Bonaventure, N.Y.: Franciscan Institute, 1955).

5. Odon Lottin, *Psychologie et morale aux XIIe et XIIIe siècles,* 6 vols., 2nd ed. (Louvain: Abbaye de Mont César; Gembloux: Duculot, 1942–1960), vol. 1, 423.

6. ". . . 'thelesis (id est voluntas) quidem est ipse naturalis et vitalis et rationalis appetitus' omnium naturae constitutivorum, 'simplex virtus,' . . . 'Bulisis (id est voluntas) autem est qualitativa naturalis thelesis' (id est voluntas), scilicet naturalis et rationalis appetitus 'alicuius rei.'" Damascene 36.8–9 (Buytaert, 135–136). See Maximus the Confessor, *Opusculum I ad Marinum* (PG 91, 12–13).

7. Vernon J. Bourke, *Will in Western Thought: A Historico-Critical Survey* (New York: Sheed and Ward, 1964), 59.

8. Lottin, *Psychologie,* vol. 1, 396.

9. Etienne Gilson, *History of Christian Philosophy in the Middle Ages* (New York: Random House, 1955), 601, note 72.

10. For an attempt to explain the Greek text, see Michael Frede, "John of Damascus on Human Action, the Will, and Human Freedom," in *Byzantine Philosophy and its Ancient Sources,* ed. Katerina Ierodiakonou (Oxford: Clarendon Press, 2002), 63–95.

11. Lottin, *Psychologie,* vol. 1, 403–404. Another excellent discussion of the difference between Albert and his contemporaries can be found in Dionys Siedler, *Intellektuelismus und Voluntarismus bei Albertus Magnus,* Beiträge zur Geschichte der Philosophie und Theologie des Mittelalters, Bd. 36, Hft. 2 (Münster: Aschendorff, 1941), 19–23. See also Geoffrey C. Reilly, *The Psychology of Saint Albert the Great Compared with That of Saint Thomas* (Washington, D.C.: The Catholic University of America Press, 1934), 76–77.

12. "... *thelesis* enim natualis voluntas est ad ea quae sunt naturae: et talia vult Angelus; qui vult esse, vivere, et intelligere ... Et similiter etiam vult ea quae determinantur ex ratione, quoniam sunt bona, et non tantum ex natura: et illorum est voluntas quae dicitur *boulesis.*" *Summa de creaturis* t. 4, q. 25, resp. (vol. 34, 487). Cf. *Summa Theologiae* p. 2, t. 4, q. 14, resp., ad 1–2 (vol. 33, 197–198). This section of the *Summa de creaturis* is also known as *"De iv coaequavis."*

13. *Summa de creaturis,* t. 4, q. 25, a. 2, resp. (vol. 34, 489).

14. 2 Sent. d. 3, K, art. 18, ad 5 (vol. 27, 98).

15. Siedler, *Intellektuelismus,* 21; Ephrem Filthaut, *Rolan von Cremona O.P. und die Anfänge der Scholastik im Predigerorden: Ein Beitrag zur Geistesgeschichte der älteren Dominikaner* (Vechta: Albertus Magnus, 1936), 109.

16. 2 Sent. d. 3, K, a. 18, resp. (vol. 27, 98). Cf. *Summa Theologiae,* p. 2, t. 4, q. 14 (vol. 32, 200).

17. Lottin, *Psychologie,* vol. 1, 400–401; Siedler, *Intellektuelismus,* 20–21.

18. Philip the Chancellor, *Summa de bono,* ed. Nikolaus Wicki, Corpus philosophorum Medii Aevi Opera philosophica Mediae Aetatis selecta, 2 (Bern: Francke, 1985), vol. 1, 160.

19. *Summa de bono,* vol. 1, 195.

20. Lottin, *Psychologie,* vol. 2, 10–349; Timothy C. Potts, "Conscience," in *The Cambridge History of later Medieval Philosophy,* ed. Norman Kretzmann, Anthony Kenny, and Jan Pinborg (Cambridge: Cambridge University Press, 1982), 689–690.

21. Philip, *Summa de bono,* vol. 1, 162. For Philip's understanding of *synderesis,* see Lottin, *Psychologie,* vol. 2, 138–157; Potts, "Conscience," 690–695.

22. Philip, *Summa de bono,* vol. 1, 199.

23. Philip, *Summa de bono,* vol. 1, 195.

24. For John's view of the distinction between *thelesis* and *boulesis,* see Lottin, *Psychologie,* vol. 1, 401–402; Siedler, *Intellektuelismus,* 21–22. For his understanding of *synderesis,* see Lottin, *Psychologie,* vol. 2, 167–178.

25. John of Rupella, *Tractatus de divisione multiplici potentiarum animae* 2.24, ed. Pierre Michaud-Quantin, Textes Philosophiques du Moyen Age, 11 (Paris: Vrin, 1964), 98–99; idem, *Summa de anima* 79, ed. Jacques Guy Bougerol, Textes Philosophiques de Moyen Age, 19 (Paris: Vrin, 1995), 212–214.

26. "... thelesis autem est voluntas naturalis mouens naturaliter et inclinans animam ad bonum substanitiale nature siue naturale." *Tractatus* 2.24, 99.

27. *Tractatus* 2.24, 98; *Summa de anima* 119, 287. In the latter work John states that *synderesis* is about the morally worthy (*honestum*). For the distinction between *honestum* and *utile* in Cicero, see Robert Combès, ed., introduction to Cicero, *Laelius de amicitia* (Paris: Société d'Édition 'Les Belles Lettres', 1971), xxix–xxxviii.

28. *Tractatus* 2.43, 119–120; Ibid., 2.46, 122; *Summa de anima* 119, 286–287.

29. For the *Summa Halesiana*'s understanding of *thelesis* and *boulesis,* see Lottin, *Psychologie,* vol. 1, 403; Siedler, *Intellektuelismus,* 22. For the *Summa Halesiana*'s understanding of *synderesis,* see Lottin, *Psychologie,* vol. 2, 178–187.

30. Alexander of Hales (attributed), *Summa Theologica* (Quaracchi: Collegium S. Bonaventurae, 1928), n. 388 (vol. 2, 465–466). Because of the complexity of the *Summa Halesiana,* references will be to number.

31. *Summa Halesiana* 418 (vol. 2, 493).

32. For the *Summa Halesiana*'s position, see Gagnebet, "L'amour naturel de Dieu," 404–405; Landgraf, "Studien," 385–386; idem, *Dogmengeschichte,* 200. There is also a lengthy discussion of the natural love of God in an objection and reply to the question of whether there was a purely natural first state, in *Summa Halesiana* 505, obj. 6 and ad 6 (vol. 2, 728, 731–732). However, this discussion occurs in the treatise *De coniuncto humano,* which is an addition to the *Summa* that relies heavily on the writings of Bonaventure. It is assumed to have been written by an unknown disciple of Bonaventure, although it may have been written by William of Miltona. It seems to me that this discussion of loving God in particular was taken almost directly from Bonaventure. For a discussion of the authorship of the *Summa Halesiana,* see Victor Doucet, "The History of the Problem of the Authenticity of the Summa," *Franciscan Studies* 7 (1947): 26–41; 274–312. For the *De coniuncto humano,* see especially 294–295, 310–311.

33. "Utrum dilectio naturalis sit ordinata in angelo." *Summa Halesiana* 164 (vol. 2, 216).

34. *Summa Halesiana* 164, sol. (vol. 2, 216); see also I, ad 1–3 (vol. 2, 216).

35. *Summa Halesiana* 164, II, ad 1 (vol. 2, 216–217).

36. *Summa Halesiana* 165, resp. (vol. 2, 217).

37. *Summa Halesiana* 166, sol. (vol. 2, 218).

38. *Summa Halesiana* 166, sol. (vol. 2, 218).

39. *Summa Halesiana* 26, ad 3 (vol. 1, 44). Cf. solutio (vol. 1, 43–44) and *Summa Halesiana* 24, resp. (vol. 1, 36).

40. *Summa Halesiana* 26, ad 3 (vol. 1, 44).

41. *Summa Halesiana* 166, sol. (vol. 2, 218).

42. *Summa Halesiana* 166, sol. (vol. 2, 218). Cf. Aristotle, *Ethica Eudemia* 2.10.1226b6–8; for a discussion of *praeoptare* (*prohairesis*) in this passage, see Michael Woods, commentary, in Aristotle, *Eudemian Ethics: Books I, II, and VIII,* trans. and comm. Michael Woods, 2nd ed. (Oxford: Clarendon Press, 1992), 143–144.

43. ". . . tenetur homo ex libero arbitrio ad diligendum ex caritate, non tamen sufficit liberum arbitrium ad huiusmodi dilectionem nisi cum habet caritatem." *Summa Halesiana* 166, ad 2 (vol. 2, 219).

44. *Summa Halesiana,* 166, contra b (vol. 2, 218).

45. *Summa Halesiana* 166, ad b (vol. 2, 219).

46. *Summa Halesiana* 169, sol. (vol. 2, 221–222).

47. *Summa Halesiana* 174, sol. (vol. 2, 227).

48. *Summa Halesiana* 175, sol. (vol. 2, 227).

49. *Summa Halesiana* 175, ad 2 (vol. 2, 227). Cf. *Summa Halesiana* 26 (vol. 1, 43).

50. For Bonaventure's theory on the will and its relation to love, see Jean Rohmer, *La Finalité morale chez les théologiens de Saint Augustin à Duns Scot* (Paris: Vrin, 1939), 201–207. For Bonaventure's general understanding of love, see Z. Alszeghy, *Grundformen der Liebe: Die Theorie der Gottesliebe bei dem Hl. Bonaventura,* Analecta Gregoriana, 38 (Rome: Gregorian University, 1946). For Bonaventure's understanding of *thelesis* and *boulesis,* see Lottin, *Psychologie,* vol. 1, 403; Siedler, *Intellektuelimus,* 22. For Bonaventure's view of *synderesis,* see Lottin, *Psychologie,* vol. 2, 203–210; see also Douglas C. Langston, *Conscience and Other Virtues: From Bonaventure to MacIntyre* (University Park: Pennsylvania State University Press, 2001), 21–37.

51. Bonaventure, *In secundum librum sententiarum* dist. 2, d. 24, p. 1, a. 2, q. 3, resp., in *Opera Omnia* (Quarrachi: Collegium S. Bonaventurae, 1882–1902), vol. 2, 566. For Bonaventure's understanding of *thelesis* and *boulesis,* see not only this article, but also *In tertium librum sententiarum,* d. 17, a. 1, q. 2, sed contra obj. 3 (vol. 3, 364).

52. 2 Sent. d. 24, p. 1, a. 2, q. 3, resp. (vol. 2, 566).

53. 4 Sent. d. 49, p. 1, a. un, q. 1, resp.; q. 2, ad 1.2.3. (vol. 4, 1000–1003). For the importance of grace, see also 2 Sent., d. 28, a. 2, q. 1, ad 3 (vol. 2, 683).

54. 2 Sent. d. 28, a. 2, q. 1, ad 2 (vol. 2, 683). Cf. 2 Sent. d. 28, a. 1, q. 1, resp. (vol. 2, 675–676).

55. 2 Sent., d. 39, q. 2, resp. (vol. 2, 904). For Bonaventure's understanding of the natural law, see John F. Quinn, "St. Bonaventure's Fundamental Conception of Natural Law," in *S. Bonaventura: 1274–1974* (Grottaferrata: Collegio S. Bonaventure, 1973), vol. 3, 571–598.

56. 2 Sent. d. 5, a. 3, q. 1, ad 4 (vol. 2, 155).

57. "Dicendum, quod absque dubio tempore naturae institutae tam homo quam Angelus habilis erat ad diligendum Deum propter se et super omnia. Et hoc patet: impossibile enim erat, eum aliter esse rectum. Rectitudo enim mentis consistit radicaliter in amore. Amor autem rectus esse non potest, si aliquid diligat supra Deum vel aeque, vel aliquid diligat propter se, et Deum propter aliud. Si ergo Deus fecit hominem et Angelicum rectum, patet, quod unicuique dedit habilitatem ad amandum se, Deum, super omnia et propter se." 2 Sent. d. 3, p. 2, a. 3, q. 1, resp. (vol. 2, 125). See Alszeghy, *Gottesliebe,* 109–124.

58. 2 Sent. d. 3, p. 2, a. 3, q. 1 ad 1 (vol. 2, 126). For the present need for grace, see 2 Sent. d. 27, a. 1, q. 2, ad 6 (vol. 2, 658).

59. ". . . aliquid diligi dilectione concupiscentiae, sicut aliquis amat vinum, vel amicitiae, sicut aliquis amat socium." 2 Sent. d. 3, p. 2, a. 3, q. 1, resp. (vol. 2, 125).

60. 2 Sent. d. 3, p. 2, a. 3, q. 1, resp. (vol. 2, 125). Aristotle, *Top.* 3.1.116a30–34; *Eth. Nic.* 8.2.

61. 2 Sent. d. 3, p. 2, a. 3, q. 1, resp. (vol. 2, 125–126).

62. 2 Sent. d. 3, p. 2, a. 3, q. 1, fund. 2–3 (vol. 2, 125).

63. 2 Sent. d. 3., p. 2, a. 3, q. 1, fund. 5 (vol. 2, 125). Augustine, *De diversis quaestionibus lxiii* 30 (CCL 44A, 38).

64. ". . . nata est anima ad percipiendum bonum infinitum, quod Deus est, ideo in eo solo debet quiescere et eo frui." 1 Sent. d. 1, a. 3, q. 2, resp. (vol. 1, 41).

65. 2 Sent. d. 3, p. 2, a. 3, q. 1, ad 2 (vol. 2, 126).

66. ". . . homo naturaliter natus est elevari supra se, contemplando et amando." 2 Sent. d. 3, p. 2, a. 3, q. 1, ad 2 (vol. 2, 126).

67. ". . . motus iste aliter est gratiae, aliter est naturae institutae. Naturae institutae est ex quadam habilitate et rectitudine respectu boni; gratiae vero est, quia captivatur affectus in obsequium Christi, sicut intellectus per fidem. Tunc autem captivatur intellectus in obsequium Christi, quando contra illud quod ratio sua dictat, assentit primae veritati; sic et affectus, quando id ad quod diligendum naturaliter inclinatur, amore Christi paratus est odire . . . Et talis est affectus, qui contemnit vitam et honores et omne desiderabile, et amat odientes se et laedentes propter Deum; et hic est solus affectus, qui Deo famulatur, et quem Deus acceptat et remunerat; et hic non est a natura, sed solum a gratia." 2 Sent. d. 3, p. 2, a. 3, q. 1, ad 3 (vol. 2, 126).

68. 2 Sent. d. 3, p. 2, a. 3, q. 1, ad 3 (vol. 2, 126).

69. For an analysis of Albert's texts on this issue, see H.-D. Simonin, "La Doctrine de l'amour naturel de Dieu d'après le Bienheureux Albert le Grand," *Revue Thomiste* 36 (1931): 361–370. Simonin argues that the *Summa de creaturis* gives Albert's final position, since it is most closely resembles the position of Thomas. For a contrary view, which is argued to be more in accordance with the dates of the texts, see Gagnebet, "L'amour naturel de Dieu," 401–404. For dating Albert's works, see especially James A. Weisheipl, "The Life and Works of Albert the Great," in *Albertus Magnus and the Sciences: Commemorative Essays* (Toronto: Pontifical Institute for Mediaeval Studies, 1980), 13–51. For the dates of the *Summa de creaturis* and Book Two of the *Sentences,* see 22. See also Odon Lottin, "Problèmes concernant la 'Summa de creaturis' et le Commentaire des Sentences de saint Albert le Grand," *Recherches de théologie ancienne et médiévale* 17 (1950): 319–328. For evidence that the *Summa Theologiae* was written later than 1256, see 34. Gagnebet dates the *Summa Theologiae* as 1274. For a summary of Allbert's teaching on the end of moral reasoning, see Rohmer, "La finalité morale," 51–96. See especially 63–70. For the relationship between the *Summa de creaturis* and the *Summa Theologiae,* see Hieronymus Wilms, *Albert the Great: Saint and Doctor of the Church,* trans. A. English and P. Hereford (London: Burns, Oates & Washbourne, 1933), 116–118. For Albert's general understanding of love, see Guy Guldentops, "Les amours d'Albert le Grand," in *Les passions dans la philosophie médiévale,* ed. G. Jeanmart (forthcoming).

70. "Distinguemus tamen multipliciter naturale: est enim naturale primo modo dictum, quantum ad praesens pertinet, quod dependet ex solis naturalibus, hoc est, naturae adhaerentibus et constituentibus eam. Est iterum naturale, ad quod potest natura opere suo pertingere, ut ratio ratiocinando, et voluntas diligendo. Est iterum naturale, quod per assuetudinem inducitur sine gratia gratum faciente: et sic dicitur virtus politica naturalis." *Summa de creaturis,* t. 4, q. 25, resp. (vol. 34, 489).

71. For Cicero, see *Summa de creaturis,* t. 4, q. 25, a. 1, contra 3 (vol. 34, 488). For Aristotle, see contra 2, 4–5 (vol. 34, 488–489). See Aristotle, *Eth. Nic.* 9.8.1169a18–35.

72. Scholastics frequently describe the cardinal virtues as "political" virtues.

73. *Summa de creaturis* t. 4, q. 25, a. 2, contra 2 (vol. 4, 488).

74. *Summa de creaturis* t. 4, q. 25, a. 2, ad 1 (vol. 34, 489).

75. 2 Sent. d. 3, K, a. 18, contra 4 (vol. 27, 98). For the concept of *honestum* in Albert's moral psychology, see Colleen McCluskey, "Worthy Constraints in Albertus Magnus's Theory of Action," *Journal of the History of Philosophy* 39 (2001): 518–524.

76. 2 Sent. d. 3, K, a. 18, ad 5 (vol. 27, 98).

77. 3 Sent., d. 27, A, a. 1, ad 3 (vol. 28, 509)

78. "Tamen quia legitur in libris Philosophorum tantam esse dilectionem honesti, ut etiam fortes periculis se committant, qui tamen charitatem non habent, difficile est dicere, quod nemo diligit aliquid supra se, nisi ex charitate: et ideo tunc revertendum est ad priorem solutionem." 3 Sent. d. 28, A, a. 1, ad 3 (vol. 28, 509).

79. 3 Sent. d. 28, A, a. 1, obj. 2–3 (vol. 28, 508).

80. 3 Sent. d. 27, A, a. 1, ad 1.2 (vol. 28, 509).

81. 3 Sent. d. 27, A, a. 1, ad 1.2 (vol. 28, 509).

82. "Dilectio concupiscentiae est naturae, quae semper curva est in seipsa: et quidquid diligit, ad seipsam retorquet, hoc est, ad bonum proprium et privatum . . ." *Summa Theologiae* p. 2, t. 4, q. 14, resp. (vol. 32, 200).

83. "Et haec solutio mihi placet: quia bona est." *Summa Theologiae* p. 2, t. 4, q. 14, resp. (vol. 32, 200).

84. *Summa Theologiae* p. 2, t. 4, q. 14, ad 3 (vol. 32, 201).

85. "Ad aliud dicendum, quod amicitia fundata super honestum, non diligit amicum nisi aliquid concupiscat in ipso quod retorquet ad seipsam." *Summa Theologiae* p. 2, t. 4, q. 14, ad 4 (vol. 32, 201).

86. *Summa Theologiae* p. 2, t. 4, q. 14, ad 6–7 (vol. 32, 201). Cf. Aristotle, *Eth. Nic.* 8.4.

CHAPTER 3
Thomas Aquinas

1. For a description of his method, see Alasdair MacIntyre, *Whose Justice?*, 164–182.

2. Henri de Lubac, *Surnaturel; études historiques.* Études publiées sous la direction de la Faculté de Théologie S.J. de Lyon-Fourvière, 8 (Aubier: Éditions Montaigne, 1946). For a summary of de Lubac's position on the love of God, see Gregory Stevens, "The Disinterested Love of God according to St. Thomas and Some of His Modern Interpreters," *The Thomist* 16 (1953): 326–328. For a bibliography of the issue up to 1950, see Alszeghy, "La teologia," 414–450.

3. de Lubac, *Surnaturel,* 231–260.

4. Ibid., but see also de Lubac, *Surnaturel,* 449–471.

5. Denis J. M. Bradley, *Aquinas on the Twofold Human Good: Reason and Human Happiness in Aquinas's Moral Science* (Washington, D.C.: The Catholic University of America Press, 1997). Bradley seems to argue that the natural endlessness of man

follows from the fact that the beatific vision fulfills the natural desire for God. For criticisms of Bradley, see Steven A. Long, "On the Possibility of a Purely Natural End for Man," *The Thomist* 64 (2000): 211–237; Peter A. Pagan-Aguiar, "St. Thomas Aquinas and Human Finality: Paradox or *Mysterium Fidei?*" *The Thomist* 64 (2000): 374–399.

6. Jean-Hervé Nicolas, *Les profondeurs de la grace* (Paris: Beauchesne, 1969), 331–397.

7. For a summary of Gagnebet's criticisms, see Stevens, "Disinterested Love," 327–328. I have not been able to find a response by de Lubac to these particular criticisms. He seems to be silent on the issue in his later writings. For example, see Henri de Lubac, *The Mystery of the Supernatural*, trans. Rosemary Sheed (New York: Herder and Herder, 1967). Nevertheless, it may be difficult to reconcile even de Lubac's general interpretation of Thomas with Thomas's texts on naturally loving God.

8. "Cet amour naturel n'est pas du tout une activité consciente et libre, il subsiste dans les damnés autant que dans les justes." Jorge Laporta, *La destinée de la nature humaine selon Thomas d'Aquin*, Études de la Philosophie Médiévale, 55 (Paris: Vrin, 1965), 117, n. 39. Cf. Laporta 46, note M. Laporta's interpretation would seem to have difficulty in explaining how the inability to naturally love God over self is a result of original sin. For a criticism of Laporta on this point, see Nicolas, *Profondeurs*, 354, n. 29.

9. Laporta, *La destinée*, 119–120. See especially 120, nn. 52–53.

10. Laporta, *La destinée*, 91–104. See also Nicolas, *Profondeurs*, 380–386; Bradley, *Human Good*, 424–481. Two older works on the natural desire to see God are William R. O'Connor, *The Eternal Quest* (New York: Longmans, Green, 1947) and James E. O'Mahoney, *The Desire of God in the Philosophy of St. Thomas Aquinas* (Cork: Cork University Press; New York: Longmans, Green, 1929).

11. 2 *Sent.*, d. 3, q. 4, in *Scriptum super libros sententiarum*, ed. Pierre Mandonnet and M. F. Moos (Paris: Lethielleux, 1929–1947), vol. 2, 125–128. 3 *Sent.*, d. 29, q. 1, a. 3 (Lethielleux, vol. 3, 927–930). For dating, see Jean-Pierre Torrell, *Saint Thomas Aquinas*, vol. 1, *The Person and His Work*, trans. Robert Royal (Washington, D.C.: The Catholic University of America Press, 1996), 332.

12. "Utrum homo possit diligere Deum super omnia ex solis naturalibus sine gratia." *Summa Theologiae*, I–II, q. 109, a. 3. For dating the parts of the *Summa*, see Torrell, *Saint Thomas Aquinas*, 145–147, 333. The text is taken from the Leonine edition as reprinted by Marietti. The page number will not be given because of the number of editions with different pagination.

13. *S.T.*, I, q. 60, a. 5; *S.T.*, II–II, q. 26, art. 3.

14. *De perfectione spiritualis vitae*, c. 14, in *Opera Omnia* (Rome: Commissio Leonina, 1884–), vol. 41, B 86. *Quaestiones diputatae de virtutibus*, q. 4, a 1, ad 9, or, *De Spe*, a. 1, ad 9, in *Opera Omnia* (Parma: Petrus Fiaccadori, 1852–1873; repr. New York: Misurgia, 1948–1950), vol. 8, 620.

15. "Videtur quod primus homo in statu innocencie non dilexerit Deum super omnia et plus quam seipsum." *Quodlibet* I, a. 8 (Leonine, vol. 25, 187–189).

16. For a collection and translation of nine relevant texts, see Stevens, "Disinterested Love," 515–523. His selection of the relevant texts differs slightly from the

one in this chapter. First, Stevens does not include the text from the *In secundum librum sententiarum*. Second, he gives two additional texts, which are from *In librum beati Dionysii de divinis nominibus expositio,* lect. 9, n. 406 and lect. 10, nn. 431–432, ed. Ceslaus Pera (Turin: Marietti, 1950), 134–135 and 142–143. Since these two texts discuss premisses of the argument more than the argument itself, their exposition will be delayed until the third section of this chapter.

17. "Utrum angelus in statu suo naturali dilexerit Deum plus quam se et omnia alia." 2 Sent., d. 3, q. 4 (Lethielleux, vol. 2, 125).

18. 2 Sent., d. 3, q. 4, sc. 1–2 (Lethielleux, vol. 2, 125–126).

19. 2 Sent., d. 3, q. 4, sol. (Lethielleux, vol. 2, 126).

20. 2 Sent., d. 3, q. 4, sol. (Lethielleux, vol. 2, 126–127). For the importance of similitude in Thomas's theory of love, see especially H-D. Simonin, "Autour de la solution Thomiste du problème de l'amour," *Archives d'histoire doctrinale et littéraire du moyen âge* 6 (1931): 174–274.

21. "Videtur quod Deus non sit super omnia diligendus ex caritate." 3 Sent., d.. 29, q. 1, a. 3 (Lethielleux, vol. 3, 927). For a discussion of this text, see Stevens, "Disinterested Love," 516–517.

22. For the angels, see 2 Sent., d. 4, q. 1, a. 3 (Lethielleux, vol. 2, 136–139); *S.T.,* I, q. 62, a. 3. For humans, see 2. Sent., d. 20, q. 2, a. 3 (Lethielleux, vol. 2, 515–518); *S.T.,* I, q. 95, a. 1; *De malo,* q. 4, a. 23, ad 1 [n. 22] (Leonine, vol. 23, 113).

23. 3 Sent., d.. 29, q. un., a. 3, sol. (Lethielleux, vol. 3, 929).

24. 3 Sent., d. 29, q. un., a. 3, sol. (Lethielleux, vol. 3, 929).

25. 3 Sent., d. 29, q. 1, a. 3, sol., in *Opera Omina* (Paris: Vivès, 1871–1872), vol. 9, 458.

26. "Diligere autem Deum super omnia est quiddam connaturale homini; et etiam cuilibet creaturae non solum rationali, sed irrationali et etiam inanimatae, secundum modum amoris qui unicuique creaturae competere potest. Cuius ratio est quia unicuique naturale est quod appetat et amet aliquid, secundum quod aptum natum est esse: *sic* enim *agit unumquodque prout aptum natum est,* ut dicitur in II *Physic.* Manifestum est autem quod bonum partis est propter bonum totius. Unde etiam naturali appetitu vel amore unaquaeque res particularis amat bonum suum proprium propter bonum commune totius universi, quod est Deus. Unde et Dionysius dicit, in libro *de Div. Nom.,* quod *Deus convertit omnia ad amorem sui ipsius.* Unde homo in statu naturae integrae dilectionem sui ipsius referebat ad amorem Dei sicut ad finem, et similiter dilectionem omnium aliarum rerum. Et ita Deum diligebat plus quam seipsum, et super omnia." *S.T.,* I–II, q. 109, a. 3, resp. Aristotle, *Ph.* 2.8.199a10; Pseudo-Dionysius the Areopagite, *De divinis nominibus,* 4, in Beate Regina Suchla, ed., *Corpus Dionysiacum,* I, Patrische Texte und Studien, 33 (Berlin: de Gruyter, 155). Various Latin versions of this quotation from Pseudo-Dionysius, which do not exactly correspond to that of Thomas, can be found in *Dionysiaca,* vol. 1 (Paris: Desclée de Brouwer, 1937), 201. "*Nata*" is the Latin translation of Aristotle's *péphuke.* A more literal translation of the whole phrase would be "for which it is born to be apt."

27. "Et ideo dicendum est quod homo in statu naturae integrae non indigebat dono gratiae superadditae naturalibus bonis ad diligendum Deum naturaliter super

omnia; licet indigeret auxilio Dei ad hoc eum moventis. Sed in statu naturae corruptae indiget homo etiam ad hoc auxilio gratiae naturam sanantis." *S.T.*, I–II, q. 109, a. 3, resp. Cf. *In Epistolam ad Romanos*, cap. 2, lect. 3, n. 216, in *Super Epistolas S. Pauli Lectura*, ed. Raphael Cai (Marietti, 1953), vol. 1, 39.

28. 2 Sent., d. 28, q. 1, art. 3 (Lethielleux, vol. 2, 724–726); *Quaestiones de ueritate*, q. 24, art. 14 (Leonine, vol. 22, 722–724).

29. Henri Bouillard, *Conversion et grâce chez S. Thomas d'Aquin*, Études publiées sous la direction de la Faculté de Théologie S.J. de Lyon-Fourvière, 1 (Aubier: Montaigne, 1944), 92–122. For the development of Thomas's doctrine of *gratia sanans*, see Bernard J. F. Lonergan, *Grace and Freedom: Operative Grace in the Thought of St. Thomas Aquinas*, ed. J. Patout Burns (London: Darton, Longman, and Todd; New York: Herder and Herder, 1971), 46–55. For the importance of grace and loving God for Thomas's moral theory, see my "The Augustinianism of Thomas Aquinas's Moral Theory," *The Thomist* 67 (2003): 279–305.

30. "Utrum angelus naturali dilectione diligat Deum plus quam seipsum." *S.T.*, I, q. 60, a. 5. For a discussion of this text, see Stevens, "Disinterested Love," 520–522.

31. "Sed falsitas huius opinionis manifeste apparet, si quis in rebus naturalibus consideret ad quid res naturaliter moveatur: inclinatio enim naturalis in his quae sunt sine ratione, demonstrat inclinationem naturalem in voluntate intellectualis naturae. Unumquodque autem in rebus naturalibus, quod secundum naturam hoc ipsum quod est, alterius est, principalius et magis inclinatur in id cuius est, quam in seipsum. Et haec inclinatio naturalis demonstratur ex his quae naturaliter aguntur: quia *unumquodque sicut agitur naturaliter, sic aptum natum est agi*, ut dicitur in II *Physic.*" *S.T.*, I, q. 60, a. 5, resp.

32. *S.T.*, I, q. 60, a. 5, resp.

33. "Et quia ratio imitatur naturam, huiusmodi inclinationem invenimus in virtutibus politicis: est enim virtuosi civis, ut se exponit mortis periculo pro totius reipublicae conservatione; et si homo esset naturalis pars huius civitatis, haec inclinatio esset ei naturalis." *S.T.*, I, q. 60, a. 5. For a list of parallel texts and sources of the sacrifice for the common good, see I. Th. Eschmann, "A Thomistic Glossary on the Principle of the Preeminence of the Common Good," *Mediaeval Studies* 5 (1943): 123–165. For the historical context, see Ernst H. Kantorowicz, "*Pro Patria Mori* in Medieval Political Thought," *American Historical Review* 56 (1951): 472–492. For the imitation of nature by reason, see especially *Sententia libri politicorum, prologus* (Leonine, vol. 48, A69). For a discussion of the issue, see Benedict M. Guevin, "Aquinas's Use of Ulpian and the Question of Physicalism Reexamined," *The Thomist* 63 (1999): 613–628 at 623–628; Stephen L. Brock, *Action and Conduct: Thomas Aquinas and the Theory of Action* (Edinburgh: T & T Clark, 1998), 114–127. Brock's work is especially helpful for understanding the connection between virtuous action and natural inclination.

34. "Quia igitur bonum universale est ipse Deus, et sub hoc bono continetur etiam angelus et homo et omnis creatura, quia omnis creatura naturaliter, secundum id quod est, Dei est . . ." *S.T.*, I, q. 60, a. 5, resp.

35. "Utrum homo debeat ex caritate plus Deum diligere quam seipsum." *S.T.,* II–II, q. 26, a. 3. For a discussion of this text, see Stevens, "Disinterested Love," 523.

36. "Respondeo dicendum quod a Deo duplex bonum accipere possumus: scilicet bonum naturae, et bonum gratiae." *S.T.,* II–II, q. 26, a. 3, resp.

37. ". . . quaelibet enim pars habet inclinationem principalem ad actionem communem utilitati totius." *S.T.,* II–II, q. 26, a. 3, resp.

38. "Et ideo ex caritate magis debet homo diligere Deum, qui est bonum commune omnium, quam seipsum: quia beatitudo est in Deo sicut in communi et fontali omnium principio qui beatitudinem participare possunt." *S.T.,* II–II, q. 26, a. 3.

39. *De perfectione spiritualis vitae,* cap. 14 (Leonine, vol. 41, B 86). For a discussion of this chapter (numbered in the older editions as chapter 13), see Stevens, "Disinterested Love," 519.

40. "In praedicta autem communitate qua omnes homines conveniunt in beatitudinis fine, unusquisque homo ut pars quaedam consideratur; bonum autem commune totius est ipse Deus in quo omnium beatitudo consistit. Sic igitur secundum rectam rationem et naturae instinctum, unusquisque se ipsum in Deum ordinat sicut pars ordinatur ad bonum totius: quod quidem per caritatem perficitur qua homo se ipsum propter Deum amat." *De perfectione spiritualis vitae,* cap. 14 (Leonine, vol. 41, B 86).

41. "Uno modo, secundum quod bonum divinum est principium et finis totius esse naturalis; et sic amant Deum super omnia non solum rationalia, sed et bruta animalia, et inanimata, inquantum amare possunt . . ." *Quaestiones disputatae de virtutibus,* q. 4, a. 1, ad 9 (Parma, vol. 8, 620). For a discussion of this text, see Stevens, "Disinterested Love," 518–519. For a general discussion of some issues, see Bernard James Diggs, *Love and Being: An Investigation into the Metaphysics of Thomas Aquinas* (New York: Vanni, 1947).

42. ". . . secundum quod Deus est objectum beatitudinis, et secundum quod fit quaedam societas rationalis ad Deum quadam spirituali unitate . . ." *Quaestiones disputatae de virtutibus,* q. 4, a. 1, ad 9 (Parma, vol. 8, 620).

43. "Videtur quod primus homo in statu innocencie non dilexerit Deum super omnia et plus quam seipsum." *Quodlibet* I, a. 8 (Leonine, vol. 25.2, 187). For a discussion of this text, see Stevens, "Disinterested Love," 519–520.

44. "Set, quia possibile fuit Deo ut hominem faceret in puris naturalibus, utile est considerare ad quantum se dilectio naturalis extendere possit." *Quodlibet* I, a. 8, resp. (Leonine, vol. 25.2, 188). Thomas's source for Basil is not clear, and Augustine never established an authoritative position on this issue, which was only made explicit in the twelfth and thirteenth centuries. See the notes to the Leonine edition, vol. 25.2, 187 and 184. Thomas elsewhere also argues that in the original state grace preserves the order of the parts of the soul. For the history of this debate, see Artur Michael Landgraf, *Dogmengeschichte,* 43–50. Although Thomas may be referring to what will later be described as the state of pure nature, he may also use "*in puris naturalibus*" to refer to the state of original justice, but abstracting from the influence of grace. See Thomas de Vio Cajetan, *Commentaria in Prima Secundae,* q. 109, art. 2 (Leonine, vol. 7,

293); Domingo Bañez, *Comentarios inéditos a la prima secundae de Santo Tomás*, q. 109, art. 2, ed. Vincente Beltrán de Heredia (Madrid, 1948), vol. 3, 34.

45. "Dilectio enim naturalis est quedam naturalis inclinatio indita nature a Deo; \<a Deo\> nichil autem est peruersum; inpossibile est ergo quod aliqua naturalis inclinatio uel dilectio sit peruersa . . . " The text continues, ". . . peruersa autem dilectio est ut aliquis dilectione amicicie diligat plus se quam Deum; non potest ergo talis dilectio esse naturalis." *Quodlibet* I, a. 8, resp. (Leonine, vol. 25.2, 188).

46. "Vnde et secundum hanc naturalem inclinationem et secundum politicam uirtutem bonus ciuis mortis periculo se exponit pro bono communi." *Quodlibet* I, a. 8, resp. (Leonine, vol. 25.2, 188).

47. *S.T.*, II–II, q. 130, a. 1, resp.; q. 133, a. 1, resp. Cf. Josef Pieper, *The Four Cardinal Virtues*, trans. Daniel F. Coogan, Lawrence E. Lynch, and Richard and Clara Winston (Notre Dame, Ind.: University of Notre Dame Press, 1966), 167–168, 230 n. 50.

48. "Inclinationes enim naturales maxime cognosci possunt in hiis que naturaliter aguntur absque rationis deliberatione: *sic* enim *agitur unumquodque* in natura *sic aptum natum est* agi." *Quodlibet* I, a. 8, resp. (Leonine, vol. 25.2, 188).

49. "Manifestum est autem quod Deus est bonum commune totius uniuersi et omnium partium eius; unde quelibet creatura suo modo naturaliter plus amat Deum quam se ipsam, insensibilia quidem naturaliter, bruto uero animalia sensitiue, creatura uero rationalis per intellectualem amorem, qui dilectio dicitur." *Quodlibet* I, a. 8, resp. (Leonine, vol. 25.2, 188–189).

50. L-B. Gillon, "Le sacrifice pour la patrie et la primauté du bien commun," *Revue Thomiste* 49 (1949): 242–253.

51. For a perceptive discussion of the contemporary political problem of understanding the common good, see Alasdair MacIntyre, *Dependent Rational Animals*, The Paul Carus Lectures, 20 (Chicago: Open Court, 1999), 129–146; "Politics, Philosophy, and the Common Good," in *The MacIntyre Reader*, ed. Kelvin Knight (Notre Dame, Ind.: University of Notre Dame Press, 1998), 235–252; originally published as "Politica, filosofia e bene commune," *Studi Perugini* 3 (1997): 9–30. See also Yves Simon, *A Critique of Moral Knowledge*, trans. Ralph MacInerny (New York: Fordham University Press, 2002), 75–87.

52. For a summary of the controversies, see Gregory Froelich, "The Equivocal Status of the *Bonum Commune*," *The New Scholasticism* 63 (1989): 38–42.

53. The most representative of this camp is I. Th. Eschmann, "In Defense of Jacques Maritain," *The Modern Schoolman* 22 (1945): 183–208. For a similar and more contemporary view, see John Finnis, *Aquinas: Moral, Political, and Legal Theory* (Oxford: Oxford University Press, 1998), 219–254.

54. Charles de Koninck, *De la primauté de la bien commun contre les personalistes* (Québec: Éditions de l'Université Laval; Montréal: Éditions Fides, 1943); "In Defence of Saint Thomas: A Reply to Father Eschmann's Attack on the Primacy of the Common Good," *Laval théologique et philosophique* 1.2 (1945): 9–109. For de Koninck's estimation of Eschmann, see p. 52: "Indeed I recognize the distinct though unenvied polemic

advantage of his faulty Latin, his shallow acquaintance with philosophy and theology, when allied to such unclouded confidence." For similar critiques of Finnis, see Lawrence Dewan, "St. Thomas, John Finnis and the Political Good," *The Thomist* 64 (2000): 337–374; Steven Long, "St. Thomas Aquinas through The Analytic Looking-Glass," *The Thomist* 65 (2001): 291–299.

55. Froelich, "Equivocal Status," 42–57. Eschmann argues that the common good is primarily political, and other conceptions are therefore analogical ("Jacques Maritain," 108). A more thorough treatment is André Modde, "Le Bien Commun dans la philosophie de saint Thomas," *Revue Philosophique de Louvain* 47 (1949): 221–247. For the understanding of God as the common good, see especially 223–228. For de Koninck's refutation of Eschmann's belief that God is not a common good in the full meaning of the term, see his "In Defence," 42–69.

56. M. S. Kempshall, *The Common Good in Late Medieval Political Thought* (Oxford: Clarendon Press, 1999), 129.

57. ". . . et si homo esset naturalis pars huius civitatis, haec inclinatio esset naturalis." *S.T.,* I, q. 60, a. 5. Kempshall, *Common Good,* 128–129.

58. Kempshall, *Common Good,* 79–86.

59. Jacques Maritain, *The Person and the Common Good*, trans. John J. Fitzgterald, (Notre Dame, Ind.: University of Notre Dame Press, 1966).

60. *S.T.*, I–II, q. 21, a. 4, ad 3, quoted in Maritain, *Person*, 71.

61. De Koninck, "In Defence," 92–97.

62. De Koninck, "In Defence," 73–78.

63. *De veritate*, q. 7, a. 6, ad 1 (Leonine, vol. 22, 207).

64. Eschmann, "Thomistic Glossary," 124–139. For Aristotle, see *Eth. Nic.* 1.2.1094b10–11.

65. *S.T.*, II–II, q. 47, a. 10, ad 2. See de Koninck, *De la primauté*, 25–26.

66. Modde, "Le Bien Commun," 228–232; Stevens, "Disinterested Love," 523–532. For the influence of Pseudo-Dionysius on Thomas, see Fran O'Rourke, *Pseudo-Dionysius and the Metaphysics of Aquinas,* Studien und Texte zur Geistesgeschichte des Mittelalters, 32 (Leiden: Brill, 1992).

67. "We must consider also in which of two ways the nature of the universe contains the good and the highest good, whether as something separate and by itself, or as the order of the parts. Probably both ways, as an army does; for its good is found both in its order and in its leader, and more in the latter; for he does not depend on the order, but it depends on him." Aristotle, *Metaph.* 10.1075a12–16, trans. W. D. Ross, in *The Basic Works of Aristotle* (New York: Random House, 1941), 885–886.

68. *In metaphysicam Aristotelis commentaria*, l. 12, lect. 12, n. 2631, ed. M-R. Cathala and Raymond M. Spiazzi, 2nd ed. (Turin: Marietti, 1971), 612. See also, *De spiritualibus creaturis*, a. 8, resp., ed. Leo W. Keeler, Pontifica Universitas Gregoriana, Textus et Documenta, Series Philosophica, 13 (Rome: Gregorian University, 1946), 93–94.

69. "For all are ordered to one end, but it is as in a house, where the freemen are least at liberty to act at random, but all things or most things are already ordained for them, while the slaves and the animals do little for the common good, and for the

most part live at random; for this is the sort of principle that constitutes the nature of each." *Metaph.* 12.10.1075a19–23 (886).

70. "Huiusmodi enim gradus diversimode se habent ad ordinem domus, qui imponitur a patrefamilias gubernatore domus. Filiis enim non competit ut faciant aliquid causaliter et sine ordine; sed omnia, aut plura eorum quae faciunt, ordinata sunt. Non autem ita est de servis aut bestiis, quia parum participant de ordine, qui est ad commune. Sed multum invenitur in eis de eo quod contingit, et causaliter accidit. Et hoc ideo quia parvam affinitatem habent cum rectore domus, qui intendit bonum domus commune. Sicut autem imponitur in familia ordo per legem et praeceptum patrisfamilias, quae est principium unicuique ordinatorum in domo, exequendi ea quae pertinent ad ordinem domus, ita natura in rebus naturalibus est principium exequendi unicuique id quod competit sibi de ordine universi." *In metaphysicam Aristotelis commentaria,* l. 12, lect. 12, nn. 2633–2634 (Marietti, 612–613). See also *De veritate,* q. 8, a. 4, resp. (Leonine, 22.1, 149). For a brief discussion, see Eschmann, "In Defense," 191, n. 14.

71. "Sicuti enim qui est in domo per praeceptum patrisfamilias ad aliquid inclinatur, ita aliquid res naturalis per naturam propriam. Et ipsa natura uniuscujusque est quaedam inclinatio indita ei a primo movente, ordinans ipsam in debitum finem." *In metaphysicam Aristotelis commentaria,* l. 12, lect. 12, n. 2634 (Marietti, 613).

72. *In metaphysicam Aristotelis commentaria,* l. 12, lect. 12, n. 2632 (Marietti, 612).

73. De Koninck, "In Defence," 46.

74. De Koninck, "In Defence," 31–41. De Koninck discusses several texts, but see especially *S.T.,* I, q. 93, a. 2, ad 3.

75. *In librum de divinis nominibus,* c. 2, l. 1, n. 113 (38–39).

76. "Et in hunc modum tota rerum universitas, quae est sicut totum ex partibus, praeexistit sicut in primordiali causa in ipsa Deitate." *In librum de divinis nominibus,* c. 2, l. 1, n. 113 (39).

77. For this distinction, see especially David M. Gallagher, "Person and Ethics in Thomas Aquinas," *Acta Philosophica* 4 (1995): 56–62.

78. ". . . non enim est pars perfecta nisi in toto, unde naturaliter pars amat totum et exponitur pars sponte pro salute totius." *In librum de divinis nominibus,* c. 4, l. 9, n. 406 (135).

79. ". . . ipsum suum bonum amans ordinat in amatum; sicut si manus amaret hominem, hoc ipsum quod ipsa est in totum ordinaret, unde totaliter extra se poneretur, quia nullo modo aliquid sui sibi relinqueretur, sed totum in amatum ordinaret . . . Sic ergo aliquis debet Deum amare, quod nihil sui sibi relinquat, quin in Deum ordinetur." *In librum de divinis nominibus,* c. 4, l. 10, n. 432 (142–143).

80. *In librum de divinis nominibus,* c. 4, l. 10, n. 433 (143).

81. *S.T.,* I–II, q. 28, a. 3, resp. See Albert Ilien, *Wesen und Funktion der Liebe bei Thomas von Aquin,* Freiburger theologische Studien, 98 (Freiburg: Herder, 1975), 143.

82. *In librum de divinis nominibus,* c. 4, l. 10, n. 432 (143).

83. My argument here follows John F. Wippel, *The Metaphysical Thought of Thomas Aquinas: From Finite Being to Uncreated Being,* Monographs of the Society for Medieval

and Renaissance Philosophy, 1 (Washington, D.C.: The Catholic University of America Press, 2000), 94–131. For the connection between participation and ethical theory, see Bradley, *Human Good*, 108–128.

84. Wippel, *Thought of Thomas Aquinas*, 592.

85. Stevens, "Disinterested Love," 426. Stevens, n. 204, bases this distinction on the distinction between participation and creation in Louis-B. Geiger, *La participation dans la philosophie de S. Thomas d'Aquin*, Bibliothèque Thomiste, 23 (Paris: Vrin, 1953) 379, and Cornelio Fabro, *Participation et causalité selon S. Thomas d'Aquin* (Louvain: Publications Universitaires de Louvain; Paris: Éditions Béatrice-Nauwelaerts, 1961), 357.

86. For this connection, see Gallagher, "Person and Ethics," 52–55. For Thomas's understanding of the will, see especially David M. Gallagher, "Thomas Aquinas on the Will as Rational Appetite," *Journal of the History of Philosophy* 29 (1991): 559–584.

87. For a summary of Rousselot's position, see Stevens, "Disinterested Love," 308–313.

88. Rousselot, *L'amour au moyen âge*, 1–6.

89. Rousselot, *L'amour au moyen âge*, 10–12; 15–19. For the role of Augustine, see 35–37.

90. Rousselot, *L'amour au moyen âge*, 12–14. For Thomas's understanding of participation, see Fabro, *Participation*; Geiger, *Participation*; Rudi A. te Velde, *Participation and Substantiality in Thomas Aquinas*, Studien und Texte zur Geistesgeschichte des Mittelalters, 46 (Leiden: Brill, 1995); Wippel, *Thomas Aquinas*, 94–131.

91. "He [Rousselot] has given only the main lines of his own interpretation, and, as a result, there is some doubt on the full and exact meaning of some of his statements." Stevens, "Disinterested Love," 312.

92. Gilson, *Spirit of Medieval Philosophy*, 269–303. For a summary of Gilson's view, see Stevens, "Disinterested Love," 313–317.

93. Gilson, *Spirit of Medieval Philosophy*, 284.

94. Louis-B. Geiger, *Le problème de l'amour chez saint Thomas d'Aquin*, Conférence Albert le Grand, 1952 (Montréal: Institut d'Études Médiévales; Paris: Vrin, 1952). This silence about participation in the explanation of the love for God is curious because Geiger is one of the great authorities on Thomas's understanding of participation.

95. Geiger, *Le problème de l'amour,* 37.

96. Geiger, *Le problème de l'amour,* 86.

97. Geiger, *Le problème de l'amour,* 26, 35, 43–44, 124–126.

98. Jean-Hervé Nicolas, "Amour de soi, amour de Dieu, amour des autres," *Revue Thomiste* 56 (1956): 17–23.

99. Nicolas, "Amour de soi," 26–28; 33–34; 42.

100. Avitol Wohlman, "Amour du bien propre et amour de soi dans la doctrine Thomiste de l'amour," *Revue Thomiste* 81 (1981): 203–234. For the neglect of the part/whole relationship, see 207–208, n. 8. Wohlman argues that the part/whole relationship is only a visualization for understanding the finality of natural inclination, and bases this belief on L-B. Gillon, "L'argument du tout et de la partie après saint Thomas d'Aquin," *Angelicum* 28 (1951): 205–223 and 346–362. Although this article

shows how the relationship was used by later writers, it is not clear how Gillon is supposed to prove Wohlman's point about Thomas Aquinas. For Wohlman's criticism of
Rousselot, see Wohlman, "Amour du bien propre," 207, 233.

101. David M. Gallagher, "Desire for Beatitude and Love of Friendship in
Thomas Aquinas," *Mediaeval Studies* 58 (1996): 36. It seems to me that Gallagher, too,
neglects Thomas's position that God, as the common good of the universe, alone is
the ultimate end. See Gallagher, "Person and Ethics," 62–70.

102. Scott MacDonald has used Thomas's teleological position that an individual's being is directed to its perfection in order to argue that Thomas is a kind of egoist. "Thus, Aquinas's natural teleology applied to human beings appears to yield to a
sort of psychological egoism." Scott MacDonald, "Egoistic Rationalism: Aquinas's
Basis for Christian Morality," in *Christian Theism and the Problem of Philosophy*, ed.
Michael Beaty, Library of Religious Philosophy, 5 (Notre Dame, Ind.: University of
Notre Dame Press, 1990), 332. MacDonald thinks that Thomas's teleological view
implies that each individual acts for its own perfection. Although the perfection of
the good agent is consistent with that of others and God's goodness, the individual
primarily is concerned with his own good. MacDonald does not directly discuss the
part/whole relationship, but he writes, ". . . when human beings seek the good of the
family or the city they see it as part of their own good" ("Egoistic Rationalism," 339).
It seems that in his view the individual sees the common good as part of his own
good. The order is reversed. I think that MacDonald explicitly makes the same mistakes which to a lesser extent underlie many scholarly treatments of Thomas's understanding of eudaimonism and self-interest. These mistakes are (1) the failure to recognize the metaphysical foundations of Thomas's ethics, and (2) a misunderstanding
of natural inclination and its relation to the will.

103. "Respondeo dicendum quod bonum est praecipue Deo convenit. Bonum
enim aliquid est, secundum quod est appetibile. Unumquodque autem appetit suam
perfectionem. Perfectio autem et forma effectus est quaedam similitudo agentis: cum
omne agens agat sibi simile. Unde ipsum agens est appetibile, et habet rationem boni:
hoc enim est quod de ipso appetitur, ut eius similitudo participetur. Cum ergo Deus
sit prima causa effectiva omnium, manifestum est quod sibi competit ratio boni et
appetibilis. Unde Dionysius, in libro *de Div. Nom.*, attribuit bonum Deo sicut primae
causae efficienti, dicens quod bonus dicitur Deus, *sicut ex quo omnia subsistunt.*" *S.T.*, I,
q. 6, a. 1, resp. See *In librum de divinis nominibus* c. 4, l. 3, nn. 121, 314–317 (101, 103–104).

104. For the *ratio boni*, see John F. X. Knasas, *Being and Some Twentieth-Century
Thomists* (New York: Fordham University Press, 2003), 248–283.

105. Aristotle, *Ph.* 2.8.199a10. For a discussion of this passage in the context of
the relationship between nature and art, see Friedrich Solmsen, *Aristotle's System of the
Physical World: A Comparison with His Predecessors*, Cornell Studies in Classical Philology,
33 (Ithaca, N.Y.: Cornell University Press, 1960), 115–116.

106. *In octo libros physicorum Aristotelis*, lib. 2, c. 8, lect. 13 (Leonine, vol. 2, 92–93).

107. ". . . et dicit quod in quibuscumque est aliquis finis, et priora et consequen-
tia omnia aguntur causa finis. Hoc supposito sic argumentatur. Sicut aliquid agitur

naturaliter, sic aptum natum est agi: hoc enim significat quod dico *naturaliter*, scilicet *aptum natum*. Et haec propositio convertitur, quia simul aliquid aptum natum est agi, sic agitur; sed oportet apponere hanc conditionem, nisi aliquid impediat . . . Sed ea quae fiunt naturaliter, sic aguntur quod inducuntur ad finem; ergo sic apta nata sunt agi, ut sint propter finem: et hoc est naturam appetere finem, scilicet habere aptitudinem naturalem ad finem. Unde manifestum est quod natura agit propter finem." *In octo libros physicorum Aristotelis*, lib. 2, c. 8, lect. 13, n. 3 (Leonine, vol. 2, 93).

108. *In octo libros physicorum Aristotelis*, lib. 2, c. 8, lect. 13, n. 3 (Leonine, vol. 2, 93).

109. ". . . in iis vero quae contingit fieri et ab arte et a natura, ars imitatur naturam, ut patet in sanitate, ut dictum est: unde si ea quae fiunt secundum artem, sunt propter finem, manifestum est quod etiam ea quae fiunt secundum naturam, propter finem fiunt, cum similiter se habeant priora ad posteriora in utrisque. Potest tamen dici quod haec non est alia ratio a praemissa; sed complementum et explicatio ipsius." *In octo libros physicorum Aristotelis*, lib. 2, c. 8, lect. 13, n. 4 (Leonine, vol. 2, 93).

110. ". . . ratio imitatur naturam . . ." *S.T.*, I, q. 60, a. 5, resp.

111. 2 Sent., d. 3, q. 4, ad 2 (Lethielleux, vol. 2, 127).

112. *S.T.*, I, q. 60, a. 5, ad 3.

113. *Quodlibet* I, a. 4, ad 3 (Leonine, vol. 25.2, 189).

114. "Praeterea, secundum Bernardum, natura semper in se curva est. Sed dilectio angelorum in primo statu non fuit nisi ex principio naturali. Ergo tota in amantem reflectabatur, ut quidquid diligerent angeli propter seipsos diligerent; et ita non Deum supra se diligebant." 2 Sent., d. 3, q. 4, obj. 2 (Lethielleux, vol. 2, 125).

115. "Ad secundum dicendum, quod natura in se curva dicitur, quia semper diligit bonum suum. Non tamen oportet quod in hoc quiescat intentio quod suum est, sed in hoc quod bonum est: nisi enim sibi esset bonum aliquo modo, vel secundum veritatem, vel secundum apparentiam, nunquam ipsum amaret. Non tamen propter hoc amat quia suum est; sed quia bonum est: bonum enim est per se objectum voluntatis." 2 Sent., d. 3, q. 4, ad 2 (Lethielleux, vol. 2, 27).

116. " . . . natura reflectitur in seipsam non solum quantum ad id quod est singulare, sed multo magis quantum ad commune . . ." *S.T.*, I, q. 60, a. 5, ad 3. Notice here that the accusative is used (*in seipsam*), whereas in the previous and following versions the ablative is used (*natura in se curva*). I do not see that ultimately there is much difference in content.

117. "Ad tercium dicendum quod inclinatio rei naturalis est ad duo, scilicet ad moueri et ad agere; illa autem inclinatio nature que est ad moueri, in se ipsa recurua est, sicut ignis mouetur sursum propter sui conseruationem; set illa inclinatio nature que est ad agere, non est recurua in se ipsa: non enim ignis agit ad generandum ignem propter se ipsum, set propter bonum generati, quod est forma eius, et ulterius propter bonum commune, quod est conseruatio speciei. Vnde patet quod non est uniuersaliter uerum quod omnis dilectio naturalis sit in se recurua." *Quodlibet* I, a. 3, ad 3 (Leonine, vol. 25.2, 189).

118. Oliva Blanchette, *The Perfection of the Universe according to Aquinas: A Teleological Cosmology* (University Park: Pennsylvania State University Press, 1992).

119. "... quod in rebus omnibus duplex perfectio invenitur ..." 3 Sent., d. 27, q. 1, a. 4, resp. (Parma, vol. 7.1, 297).

120. "... et utraque perfectio in rebus materialibus terminata et finita est; quia et formam unam deteminatam habet, per quam in una tantum specie est; et etiam per determinatam virtutem ad res quasdam sibi proportionatas inclinationem habet et ordinem, sicut grave ad centrum. Ex utraque autem parte res immateriales infinitatem habent quodammodo, quia sunt quodammodo omnia ..." 3 Sent., d. 27, q. 1, a. 4, resp. (Parma, vol. 7.1, 297).

121. "Patet ergo quod cognitio pertinet ad perfectionem cognoscentis, qua in seipso perfectum est: voluntas autem pertinet ad perfectionem rei secundum ordinem ad alias res ..." 3 Sent., d. 27, q. 1, a. 4, resp. (Parma, vol. 7.1, 297).

122. *Summa Contra Gentiles*, III, 24 (Leonine, vol. 14, 62–63). See de Koninck, *De la primauté*, 9–12; Ilien, *Wesen und Funktion*, 31.

123. The problem with MacDonald's description of Thomas as an egoist should also now be clearer. Not only does this description of Thomas as an egoist seem anachronistic, but it also overlooks Thomas's teaching that something does not tend towards its own perfection as its own perfection. Although it is true that in Thomas's teleological understanding of nature each individual is directed towards its own perfection, MacDonald passes over Thomas's belief that each individual's perfection is directed towards God. For egoism and altruism, see my Introduction and Conclusion. See also Cyril Harry Miron, *The Problem of Altruism in the Philosophy of St. Thomas*, The Catholic University of America Philosophical Studies, 41 (Washington, D.C.: The Catholic University of America Press, 1939), 20.

124. "... omnia, appetendo proprias perfectiones, appetunt ipsum Deum ..." *S.T.*, I, q. 6, a. 1, ad 2.

125. For the similitude with God, see *S.T.*, I, q. 4, a. 3.

126. *Summa Contra Gentiles*, I, 29; III, 23–32. See also 3 Sent., d. 27, q. 1, a. 4, resp. (Lethielleux, vol. 3, 868–869).

127. "... omnis inclinatio alicuius rei vel naturali vel voluntaria, nihil est aliud quam quaedam impressio a primo movente; sicut inclinatio sagittae ad signum determinatum, nihil aliud est quam quaedam impressio a sagittante. Unde omnia quae agunt vel naturaliter vel voluntarie, quasi propria sponte perveniunt in id ad quod divinitus ordinatur." *S.T.*, I, q. 103. art. 8, resp.

128. *S.T.*, I, q. 103, a. 1, ad 3.

129. For a general treatment, see Gustaf J. Gustafson, *The Theory of Natural Appetency in the Philosophy of St. Thomas*, The Catholic University of America Philosophical Series, 84 (Washington, D.C.: The Catholic University of America Press, 1944); Laporta, *La destinée*, 23–46; Ilien, *Wesen und Funktion*, 25–146; Bénézet Bujo, *Die Begründung des Sittlichen: Zur Frage des Eudämonismus bei Thomas von Aquin* (Paderborn: Ferdinand Schöningh, 1984), 93–122, 138–152.

130. Gustafson, *Natural Appetency*, 68–113; Nicolas, "Amour de soi," 13–21; Ilien, *Wesen und Funktion*, 53–74; Bujo, *Die Begründung*, 138–152.

131. 3 Sent., d. 27, q. 2, a. 1, resp. (Lethielleux, vol. 3, 874). See also *S.T.*, I–II, q. 26, a. 3.

132. For the existence of a natural elective love, see especially Nicolas's criticism of Laporta in *Les profondeurs,* 354, n. 29.

133. *S.T.,* I, q. 60, a. 1, ad 1.

134. *Quaestiones disputatae de virtutibus,* q. I, a. 8, resp. (Parma, vol. 8, 561).

135. *Quaestiones disputate de veritate,* q. 22, a. 4, resp. (Leonine, vol. 22.3, 620).

136. "Unde voluntas naturaliter tendit in suum finem ultimum: omnis enim homo naturaliter vult beatitudinem. Et ex hac naturali voluntate causantur omnes aliae voluntates: cum quidquid homo vult, velit propter finem. Dilectio igitur boni quod homo naturaliter vult sicut finem, est dilectio naturalis: dilectio autem ab haec derivata, quae est boni quod diligitur propter finem, est dilectio electiva." *S.T.,* I, q. 60, a. 2, resp. For a parallel passage, see *De veritate,* q. 22, a. 5 (Leonine, vol. 22.3, 621–626).

137. De Lubac, *Surnaturel,* 249–260.

138. See especially *S.T.,* III, q. 18, a. 4. Gagnebet, "L'amour naturel de Dieu," 33–49; Wohlman, "Amour du bien propre," 209–212; Bradley, *Human Good,* 445–446.

139. Bradley, *Human Good,* 457–471.

140. Long, "Possibility," 221–226.

141. For example, see *S.T.,* I, q. 60, a. 5, resp.; I–II, q. 9, a. 6, resp. See de Koninck, "In Defence of Saint Thomas," 53–69.

142. Gagnebet, "L'amour naturel de Dieu," 35–39.

143. "Et ideo non est inconveniens si angelus agatur, inquantum inclinatio naturalis est sibi indita ab Auctore suae naturae. Non tamen sic agitur quod non agat; cum habeat liberam voluntatem." *S.T.,* I, q. 60, a. 1, ad 2.

144. "Dilectio enim naturalis est quedam naturalis inclinatio indita nature a Deo; <a Deo> nichil autem est peruersum; inpossibile est ergo quod aliqua naturalis inclinatio uel dilectio sit peruersa; peruersa autem dilectio est ut aliquis dilectione amicicie diligat plus se quam Deum; non potest ergo talis dilectio esse naturalis." *Quodlibet* I, a. 8, resp. (Leonine, vol. 25.2, 188).

145. Rousselot, *L'amour au moyen âge,* 7. For Thomas's use of this dictum, see Klaus Hedwig, "Alter Ipse: Über die Rezeption eines Aristotelischen Begriffes bei Thomas von Aquin," *Archiv für Geschichte der Philosophie* 72 (1990): 253–274.

146. *In librum de divinis nominibus,* c. 4, l. 10, n. 428 (142). For a helpful discussion, see Ilien, *Wesen und Funktion,* 112–119.

147. 3 Sent., d. 29, q. 1, a. 3, ad 3 (Lethielleux, vol. 3, 930).

148. *S.T.,* II–II, q. 26, a. 3, ad 1.

149. De Koninck, *De la primauté,* 60–61.

150. 2 Sent., d. 3, q. 4, obj. 3 (Lethielleux, vol. 2, 125).

151. 2 Sent., d. 3, q. 4, ad 3 (Lethielleux, vol. 2, 127).

152. 3 Sent., d. 29, q. 1, a. 4, ad 2 (Lethielleux, vol. 3, 930). See also *In librum de divinis nominibus* c. 4, l. 10, n. 430 (142).

153. *In librum de divinis nominibus* c. 4, l. 10, n. 432 (143).

154. *S.T.,* I–II, q. 9, a. 6, resp. See also *De veritate,* q. 24, a. 7, resp. (Leonine, vol. 22.3, 697–698).

155. *S.T.,* II–II, q. 26, a. 13, ad 3.

156. Rousselot, *L'amour au moyen âge,* 14.

157. Geiger, *Le problème de l'amour,* 120–122.

158. Nicolas, "Amour de soi," 25, n. 1; Bujo, *Die Begründung,* 175–176.

159. Nicolas, "Amour de soi," 25, n. 1.

160. Gagnebet, *L'amour naturel de Dieu,* 414–415. Although Thomas is the first to clearly connect an appetite within irrational creatures with the natural and elicited love of God, at least one previous thinker had hinted at this position. See Robert Grosseteste, "Cur Deus Homo," ed. Servus Gieben, *Collectanea Franciscana* 37 (1967): 122–123. I would like to thank Edward P. Mahoney for this reference. For a natural love possessed by everything, which has its intention from the Prime Mover, see Albert the Great, *Super Dionysium de divinis nominibus,* cap. 4, in *Opera Omnia,* ed. Bernhard Geyer and Wilheim Kubel (Monestarium Westfalorum: Aschendorff, 1951–), vol. 37.1, 227–228. I would like to thank Guy Guldentops for drawing this to my attention. For the connection between animals and the natural law, see especially Michael Bertram Crowe, "St. Thomas and Ulpian's Natural Law," in *St. Thomas Aquinas, 1274–1974: Commemorative Studies* (Toronto: Pontifical Institute of Mediaeval Studies), vol. 1, 261–282.

161. For the relationship to the natural law, see especially 2 Sent., d. 3, q. 4, sc 2 (Lethielleux, vol. 2, 126); *S.T.,* I, q. 60, a. 5, sc. For a discussion of how the precept to love God is a most certain and evident part of the natural law, see *S.T.,* I–II, q. 100, a. 1. For the connection between the natural law, religious duties, and the natural love of God, see David M. Gallagher, "The Role of God in the Philosophical Ethics of Thomas Aquinas," in *Was ist Philosophie im Mittelalter?* ed. Jan A. Aertsen and Andreas Speer, Miscellanea Mediaevalia, 26 (Berlin: de Gruyter, 1998), 1024–1033.

CHAPTER 4
The University of Paris in the Late Thirteenth Century

1. See especially Ferdinand van Steenberghen, *La philosophie au XIIIe siècle,* 2nd ed. (Louvain-la-Neuve: Éditions de l'Institut Supérieur de Philosophie; Louvain: Edition Peeters, 1991); C. H. Lohr, "The Medieval Interpretation of Aristotle," in *The Cambridge History of Later Medieval Philosophy,* ed. Norman Kretzmann, Anthony Kenny, and Jan Pinborg (Cambridge: Cambridge University Press, 1982), 80–98; Georg Wieland, "Happiness: The Perfection of Man," in Kretzmann et al., *Cambridge History of Later Medieval Philosophy,* 673–686. For a historiography of this issue, see Bonnie Kent, *Virtues of the Will: The Transformation of Ethics in the Late Thirteenth Century* (Washington, D.C.: The Catholic University of America Press, 1995), 1–38.

2. "Utrum homo ex naturalis rationis dictamine habeat iudicare quod magis debeat diligere Deum quam se ipsum." Godfrey of Fontaines, *Quodl.* 10, q. 6, in *Le dixième quodlibet,* ed. Jean Hoffmans, Les Philosophes Belges, 4.3 (Louvain: Institut Supérieur de Philosophie, 1931), 318. For the date, see John F. Wippel, *The Metaphysical Thought of Godfrey of Fontaines* (Washington, D.C.: The Catholic University of America Press, 1981), xxviii. This question, along with part of Godfrey's *Quodl.* 10, q. 1, Henry of Ghent's *Quodl.* 12, q. 13, and James of Viterbo's *Quodl.* 2, q. 20, are translated in *The*

Cambridge Translations of Medieval Philosophical Texts, Vol. 2: Ethics and Political Philosophy, ed. Arthur Stephen McGrade, John Kilcullen, and Matthew Kempshall (Cambridge: Cambridge University Press, 2001), 257–306.

3. "Inter differentias quae ponuntur inter theologos qui sequuntur dictamen rationis secundum illustrationem luminis supernaturalis et fidei et inter peripateticos qui sequebantur dictamen rationis solum secundum illustrationem rationis naturalis, haec est una quod secundum principem illius sectae, scilicet secundum Aristotelem, ut dicit nono Ethicorum: amicabilia quae sunt ad alterum veniunt ex amicabilibus quae sunt ad seipsum . . . ergo secundum eos primo et plus aliquis diligit seipsum quam quemque alium. Sed secundum theologos, amicitia qua quis diligit seipsum debet procedere ex amicitia qua quis diligit Deum; et sic secundum theologos homo primo et magis debet Deum diligere quam se ipsum." Godfrey, *Quodl.* 10, q. 6 (PB 4, 318). For Godfrey's interaction with the Arts Faculty, see Wippel, *Godfrey of Fontaines,* xviii–xix.

4. Godfrey, *Quodl.* 10, q. 6 (PB 4, 324–325).

5. "Utrum non sperans vitam futuram debeat secundum rectam rationem eligere mori pro re publica." Henry of Ghent, *Quodl.* 12, q. 13, in *Opera Omnia,* vol. 16, ed. J. DeCorte (Leuven: Leuven University Press, 1987), 67. For the date, see Raymond Macken, introduction to Henry of Ghent, *Opera Omnia,* vol. 5, ed. Raymond Macken (Leuven: Leuven University Press; Leiden: Brill, 1979), xvii.

6. "Sicut enim quod verum est apud quosdam, verum est apud omnes, nec est aliquid verum secundum philosophiam veram quod non sit verum secundum theologiam, nec e converso, sicut et de eo quod rectum est aut faciendum secundum rectam rationem, et sic in ista quaestione non debet aliter sentire bonus theologus quam sentiret verus philosophus, nec e converso . . ." Henry, *Quodl.* 12, q. 13 (*Opera,* vol. 16, 68).

7. Henry, *Quodl.* 12, q. 13 (*Opera,* vol. 16, 72–78).

8. Georges de Lagarde, *La naissance de l'esprit laïque au déclin du moyen âge,* 3rd ed., vol. 2 (Louvain: Nauwelaerts, 1958), 28–50; idem, "La Philosophie sociale d'Henri de Gand et Godefroid de Fontaines," *Archives d'histoire doctrinale et littéraire du moyen âge* 14 (1945): 92–93.

9. Siger of Brabant, *Quaestiones Morales,* q. 5, in *Siger de Brabant, Écrits de logique, morale, et de physique,* ed. Bernardo Bazán, Philosophes Médiévaux, 14 (Louvain: Publications Universitaires; Paris: Béatrice-Nauwelaerts, 1974), 103–105. For a discussion, see Fernand van Steenberghen, *Maître Siger de Brabant,* Philosophes Médiévaux, 21 (Louvain: Publications Universitaires; Paris: Vander-Oyez, 1977), 388–389. For the date, see van Steenberghen, *Maître Siger,* 218; Palemon Glorieux, *La Faculté des arts et ses maîtres aux XIIIᵉ siècle,* Études de Philosophie Médiévale, 59 (Paris: Vrin, 1971), 353.

10. Boethius of Dacia, *Opuscula: De aeternitate mundi, De summo bono, De somniis,* ed. Nicolaus Georgius Green-Pedersen, Corpus Philosophorum Danicorum Medii Aevi, 6.2 (Copenhagen: Gad, 1976). For a discussion, see John F. Wippel, introduction to *Boethius of Dacia: On the Supreme Good, On the Eternity of the World, On Dreams,* trans. John F. Wippel (Toronto: Pontifical Institute of Medieval Studies, 1987), 5–9; René Antonin Gauthier, "Notes sur Siger de Brabant," part 2, "Siger en 1272–1275, Aubry

de Reims et la scission des Normands," *Revue de sciences philosophiques et théologiques* 68 (1984): 20.

11. "Utrum aliquis posset magis amare alium quam seipsum." Siger, *QM,* q. 5 (PM 14, 103).

12. Siger, *QM* 5 (PM 14, 103–104). Cf. Aristotle, *Eth. Nic.* 9.8.1168b27–1169a18.

13. "Cui enim est homo magis unitus quam sibi? Amor autem quaedam unio esse videtur. Ex amicabilibus enim quae ad seipsum proferunt amicabilia quae ad alium." Siger, *QM* 5 (PM 14, 104). Cf. Aristotle, *Ethic. Nic.* 9.8.1168b6–10.

14. Thomas Aquinas*, Summa Theologia,* II–II, q. 25, arts. 5, 7.

15. Thomas, *S.T.,* II–II, q. 26, arts. 4, 5. A possible example to the contrary is *Sententie magistri Petri Abelardi (Sententie Hermanni)*, ed. Sandro Buzzetti (Florence: La Nuova Italia Editrice, 1983), 142–143. Perhaps Abelard's emphasis on freedom and the disinterestedness of love led to Hermann the German's belief that someone can and should love another more than himself. It is not clear to me what exactly is meant by love in this passage.

16. Siger, *QM* 5 (PM 14, 104–105). Cf. Aristotle, *Ethic. Nic.* 3.5.1115a32–35.

17. René Antonin Gauthier, "Trois commentaires 'Averroistes' sur l'Éthique à Nicomaque," *Archives d'histoire doctrinale et littéraire du moyen âge* 22–23 (1947–48): 294–297.

18. For the emphasis of Aubry and Boethius on philosophy, see Gauthier, "Siger en 1272–1275," 17–20. For the relevant passages from Aubry's *Philosophia,* see 29–40. In "Trois commentaires," 288–293, Gauthier also mentions that there are passages in Averroistic commentaries on Aristotle that exalt the contemplative life while at the same time they take into account the importance of political affairs.

19. Godfrey's relevant notes are printed in Boethius of Dacia, *Opuscula,* 443–447.

20. Boethius, *De somniis,* 381.

21. Boethius, *De summo bono,* 369–377.

22. "Et quia quilibet delectatur in illo quod amat et maxime delectatur in illo quod maxime amat, et philosophus maximum amorem habet primi principii . . . sequitur quod philosophus in primo principio maxime delectatur et in contemplatione bonitatis suae . . . Primum autem principium, de quo sermo factus est, est deus gloriosus et sublimis, qui est benedictus in saecula saeculorum." Boethius, *De summo bono,* 377.

23. For a description of Henry Bate's Christian version of intellectual aristocratism, see Guy Guldentops, "Henry Bate's Aristocratic Eudaimonism," in *Nach der Verurteilung von 1277,* ed. Jan A. Aertsen, Miscellanea Mediaevalia, vol. 28 (Berlin: de Gruyter, 2001), 670–681.

24. For the Arts Faculty and the condemnation, see Wieland, "Happiness," 680–683.

25. Thomas Aquinas, 3 Sent. d. 35, q. 1, a. 2, sol. 1 (Vivès, vol. 9, 582). Cf. sol. 3 (Vivès, vol. 9, 583). See Gauthier, "Trois commentaires," 268–269; G. Mansini, *"Similitudo, Communicatio,* and the Friendship of Charity in Aquinas," in *Thomistica, Recherches de théologie ancienne et médiévale,* Supplementa, 1 (Leuven: Peeters, 1995), 11.

26. Kimon Giocarnis, "An Unpublished Late Thirteenth-Century Commentary on the Nicomachean Ethics of Aristotle," *Traditio* 15 (1959): 304.

27. L-B. Gillon, "Le sacrifice," 243–244.

28. For the characteristics of Henry's philosophy, see Jean Paulus, *Henri de Gand: Essai sur les tendances de sa métaphysique,* Études de Philosophie Médiévale, 25 (Paris: Vrin, 1938), 382–383; Fernand van Steenberghen, *La Philosophie au XIIIe siècle,* 437–439; Steven P. Marrone, *Truth and Scientific Knowledge in the Thought of Henry of Ghent,* Speculum Anniversary Monographs, 11 (Cambridge, Mass.: The Medieval Academy of America, 1985), 7–9; Kempshall, *Common Good,* 157, citing Maurice de Wulf.

29. Matthias Laarman, "God as *Primum Cognitum.* Some Remarks on the Theory of Initial Knowledge of *Esse* and God according to Thomas Aquinas and Henry of Ghent," in *Henry of Ghent: Proceedings of the International Colloquium on the Occasion of the 700th Anniversary of His Death (1293),* ed. W. Vanhamel, Ancient and Medieval Philosophy, Series 1, 15 (Leuven: Leuven University Press, 1996), 171–191; Steven P. Marrone, "Henry of Ghent and Duns Scotus on the Knowledge of Being," *Speculum* 63 (1988): 22–57; Camille Bérubé, *De l'homme à Dieu selon Duns Scot, Henri de Gand et Olivi,* Bibliotheca Seraphico-Cappuccina, 27 (Rome: Istituto Storico dei Cappucini, 1983), 191–193; Raymond Macken, "Lebensziel und Lebensglück in der Philosophie des Heinrich von Ghent," *Franziskanische Studien* 61 (1979): 107–123; idem, "God as 'primum cognitum' in the Philosophy of Henry of Ghent," *Franziskanische Studien* 66 (1984): 309–315; idem, "God as Natural Object of the Human Will, according to the Philosophy of Henry of Ghent," in idem, *Essays on Henry of Ghent* (Leuven: Editions Philosophers of the Former Low Countries, 1995), vol. 2, 45–53.

30. Henry of Ghent, *Quodl.* 15, q. 9, in *Quodlibeta magistri Henrici Goethels a Gandavo doctoris solemnis* (Paris: Badius, 1518; repr. Louvain: Bibliothèque S.J., 1961), vol. 3, fol. 581r–v. See also Henry, *Summae Quaestionum Ordinariarum,* a. 4, q. 3, ad 2, Franciscan Institute Publications, 5 (Paris: Badius, 1520; repr. St. Bonaventure, N.Y.: Franciscan Institute, 1953), vol. 1, fol. 32r. The *Quodlibeta* will be abbreviated (Badius 3, fol. 581r), whereas the *Summa* will be abbreviated (Badius, vol. 1, fol. 32r).

31. "Utrum primum et per se obiectum voluntatis sit bonum sub ratione boni simpliciter an sub ratione convenientis." Henry, *Quodl.* 13, q. 9, in *Opera Omnia,* 18, ed. J. DeCorte (Leuven: Leuven University Press, 1985), 56. For an analysis of this question, see Macken, "God as Natural Object." For the date, see Macken, introduction to Henry, *Opera,* vol. 5, xvii.

32. Henry, *Quodl.* 13, q. 9 (*Opera,* vol. 18, 58).

33. Henry, *Quodl.* 13, q. 9 (*Opera,* vol. 18, 58–61).

34. "Et hoc est bonum simpliciter quod per se et primum est obiectum voluntatis, quia hoc est bonum quod non secundum aliud a voluntate iudicatur bonum, sed potius secundum hoc iudicatur bonum quodcumque aliud bonum . . ." Henry, *Quodl.* 13, q. 9 (*Opera,* vol. 18, 62).

35. Henry, *Quodl.* 13, q. 9 (*Opera,* vol. 18, 62). See Arist., *De An.* 3.10.433a27. Aristotle seems to be included under this criticism of the philosophers. See Macken, "God as Natural Object," 51–52.

36. Henry, *Quodl.* 13, q. 9 (*Opera*, vol. 18, 63). See Macken, "God as Natural Object," 52–53; Eustratius, *In Ethicam Nicomacheam* 1.7, in *The Greek Commentaries on the Nicomachean Ethics in the Latin Translation of Robert Grosseteste, Bishop of Lincoln*, vol. 1, ed. H. P. F. Mercken, Corpus Latinum Commentariorum in Aristotelem Graecorum, 6.1 (Leiden: Brill, 1973), 76–77: "Sed si quidem esset secundum intellectum Platonis de bono oppositiones faciens, non oporteret aliquid dicere ad ipsum nos, reverentes virum et necessitatem non habentes pro platonica opinione stare . . . Plato quidem enim unum et ineffabile et bonum communem causam entium omnium dixit, et super entia omnia unum ordinavit, causam quidem omnium illud dicens, nihil autem omnium . . . Omnia igitur secunda bona referri ad illud velut commune bonum et ab omnibus bonis participatum. Unumquodque enim quod post illud bonum, aliud quid ens, bonum est secundum participationem illius sicut illo participare unumquodque potest."

37. "Utrum bonum proprium magis sit procurandum quam commune." *Quodlibet* 9, q. 19, in *Opera Omnia*, 13, ed. R. Macken (Leuven: Leuven University Press, 1983), 293. For the date see Raymond Macken, introduction to Henry, *Opera*, vol. 5, xvii. For a discussion of this question, see de Lagarde, "*La philosophie, sociale,*" 86–89; Kempshall, *Common Good*, 165–170; Macken, "Henry of Ghent as Defender of the Personal Rights of Man," *Franziskanische Studien* 73 (1991): 172–176.

38. Henry, *Quodl.* 9, q. 19 (*Opera*, vol. 13, 293).

39. "Si vero utrumque bonum sit spirituale, tunc proprium magis est procurandum, quia modicum boni gratiae aut gloriae propter aeternam eius perseverantiam magis debet quilibet velle sibi quam maximum proximo, quemadmodum potius debet velle solus salvari et omnes alios damnari, quod econverso." Henry, *Quodl.* 9, q. 19 (*Opera*, vol. 13, 294).

40. "Contra. Ordinata caritas est prius et magis diligere se quam proximum. Bonum autem proprium procuratur ex amore sui, bonum commune ex amore proximi. Ergo, etc." Henry, *Quodl.* 9, q. 19 (*Opera*, vol. 13, 293). ". . . Henry's attitude to the common good of the political community represents a synthesis of Aristotelian self-love and an Augustinian *ordo caritatis*. Henry does not express a principle of the love for the common good which goes beyond the categories of love of self, love of neighbor, and love of God." Kempshall, *Common Good*, 178. See also Macken, "Henry as Defender," 176–179.

41. For discussions, see de Lagarde, *La naissance*, 181–183; Kempshall, *Common Good*, 158–160; Macken, "The Moral Duty of a Man Who Does Not Hope for a Future Life, to Offer in a Case of Necessity his Life for His Country in the Philosophy of Henry of Ghent," in idem, *Essays, on Henry of Ghent*, vol. 1, 85–101.

42. "Quorum primum et unicum erat pertinens ad infideles . . ." Henry, *Quodl.* 12, q. 13 (*Opera*, vol. 16, 67).

43. Henry, *Quodl.* 12, q. 13 (*Opera*, vol. 16, 69–71).

44. "Propter hoc igitur mori pro re publica non solum est simpliciter melius quia pluribus, sed etiam melius est sibi . . ." Henry, *Quodl.* 12, q. 13 (*Opera*, vol. 16, 71).

45. Henry, *Quodl.* 12, q. 13 (*Opera,* vol. 16, 72–73).

46. "Dico ergo quod ad hoc uterque eorum, scilicet tam felix politicus quam speculativus, tenetur de iure naturae, et quod peccaret, si illud non eligeret, et quod turpiter viveret. Melius est autem mori quam turpiter vivere." Henry, *Quodl.* 12, q. 13 (*Opera,* vol. 16, 73). For a discussion of a modern aspect of Henry's concept of natural right, see Brian Tierney, *The Idea of Natural Rights: Studies on Natural Rights, Natural Law, and Church Law,* Emory Studies in Law and Religion, 5 (Atlanta: Scholars Press, 1997), 78–89.

47. Henry, *Quodl.* 12, q. 13 (*Opera,* vol. 16, 68). 1 Cor 12:12–30.

48. Henry, *Quodl.* 12, q. 13 (*Opera,* vol. 16, 75–76).

49. ". . . licet bonum suum privatum aliquod positivum non includitur in illo bono publico, includitur tamen in illo bonum suum privatum quasi negativum, scilicet evasio turpitudinis et mali culpae, ut dictum est." Henry, *Quodl.* 12, q. 13 (*Opera,* vol. 16, 76–77).

50. Henry, *Quodl.* 12, q. 13 (*Opera,* vol. 16, 77–78).

51. Henry of Ghent, *Quodlibet* 10, q. 12, in *Opera Omnia,* vol. 14, ed. Raymond Macken (Leuven: Leuven University Press; Leiden: Brill, 1981), 277. Kempshall, *Common Good,* 176–177; James McEvoy, "The Sources and Significance of Henry of Ghent's Disputed Question, 'Is Friendship a Virtue?'" in Van hamel et al., *Henry of Ghent: 700th Anniversary,* 121–138; Raymond Macken, "Human Friendship in the Thought of Henry of Ghent," *Franziskanische Studien* 70 (1988): 176–184. For an older treatment, see Egenter, *Gottesfreundschaft* 117–121.

52. "Unde de perfecto amore caritatis dicit Ricardus, De Trinitate, capitulo 3°: 'Nullus privato et proprio sui ipsius amore dicitur proprie caritatem habere. Oportet igitur ut amor ad alterum tendat ut caritas esse queat.'" Henry, *Quodl.* 10, q. 12 (*Opera,* vol. 14, 277). Richard of St. Victor, *De trinitate* 3.2, 136.

53. "Circa secundum arguitur: quod deus non possit diligi super omnia dilectione naturali, quia dicit Philosophus in octavo Ethicorum, 'Amicabilia ad alterum procedunt ex eis quae sunt amicabilia ad seipsum. Sed origo amicitiae semper magis diligitur. Ergo dilectio semper maior est cuiuscumque ad seipsum quam ad alterum: et sic plus quam seipsum nullus potest diligere deum. Contra. Bonum per se naturaliter est diligibile. Ergo magis bonum magis et maxime siue summe bonum, maxime siue summe est diligibile naturaliter. Deus est bonum huiusmodi, et naturali dilectione diligitur bonum secundum quod naturaliter diligibile." Henry, *Quodlibet* 4, q. 11 (Badius 1, fol. 101v). For the date see Henry, *Opera* 5, xvii. For a discussion see Gillon, "L'argument," 207–210; Egenter, *Gottesfreundschaft,* 110–117; Kempshall, *Common Good,* 160–161.

54. Henry, *Quodl.* 4, q. 11 (Badius 1, fol. 101v).

55. "Circa primum sciendum quod amor seu dilectio est inclinatio vel motus in bonum." Henry, *Quodl.* 4, q. 11 (Badius 1, fol. 101v).

56. Henry, *Summa,* a. 61, q. 6, ad 1 (Badius, vol. 2, fol. 178r). Cf. a. 50, q. 1, ad 1 (Badius, vol. 2, fol. 48r).

57. Henry, *Quodl.* 4, q. 11 (Badius 1, fol. 101v). See Averroes, *In Libros Physicorum,* Book I, in *Aristotelis Opera cum Averrois Commentariis,* vol. 4 (Venice: Junctas, 1562; Frankfurt am Main: Minerva, 1962), fol. 46r.

58. "Et ideo Augustinus naturalem dilectionem comparat ponderi, cum dicit libro Confessionum: 'Amor meus pondus meum: eo feror quocumque feror.' Motus autem dilectionis liberalis est quasi pes, voluntarie se extendends ad processum et ad prosequendum bonum conveniens. Et ideo Augustinus liberalem dilectionem comparat pedi, secundum quod dicit Augustinus super illud psalmi noni: 'Comprehensus est pes eorum.' Pes animae recte intelligitur amor. Ex eo patet quod dilectio naturalis et deliberativa differunt sicut impetuosum et liberum ad motum." Henry, *Quodl.* 4, q. 11 (Badius 1, fol. 101v–102r). Augustine, *Conf.* 13.9(10) (CCL 27, 246); *Ennarratio in Psalmum IX,* 16 (CCL 38, 66–67).

59. For the will's self-motion, see Roland J. Teske, "Henry of Ghent's Rejection of the Principle: '*Omne quo movetur ab alio movetur,*'" in Vanhamel et al., *Henry of Ghent: 700th Anniversary,* 211–254.

60. Henry, *Quodl.* 4, q. 11 (Badius 1, fol. 102r).

61. "Et est in homine amor naturalis radix et origo amoris liberalis et omnium habituum virtuosorum . . ." Henry, *Summa,* a. 46, q. 4, sol., in *Opera Omnia,* vol. 29, ed. L. Hödl (Leuven: Leuven University Press, 1998), 154. Cf. a. 50, q. 1, ad 1 (Badius, vol. 2, fol. 48r).

62. Henry, *Quodl.* 4, q. 11 (Badius 1, fol. 102r). For the different types of love, see *Summa,* a. 46, q. 4, sol. (*Opera,* vol. 29, 152–153).

63. For the *voluntas ut natura,* see Macken, "Lebensziel," 145–146; cf. 154–158.

64. "Sed quia tali dilectione voluntatis, scilicet naturalis, ut natura est, nihil potest diligi nisi cognitum, dicente Augustino octavo de Trinitate capitulo quinto: Quis diligit quod ignoratur: sciri enim aliquid et non diligi potest?" Henry, *Quodl.* 4, q. 11 (Badius 1, fol. 102r). Augustine, *De trinitate* 8.4(6) (CCL 50, 275).

65. Henry, *Quodl.* 4, q. 11 (Badius 1, fol. 102r).

66. For Henry's understanding of the natural and philosophical knowledge of God, see Jean Paulus, "Henri de Gand et l'argument ontologique," *Archives d'histoire doctrinale et littéraire du moyen âge* 10–11 (1935–1936): 265–323; idem, *Henri de Gand,* 21–66; Anton C. Pegis, "Towards a New Way to God: Henry of Ghent," *Mediaeval Studies* 30 (1968): 226–247; 31 (1969): 93–116; 33 (1971): 158–197; Raymond Macken, "The Metaphysical Proof for the Existence of God in the Philosophy of Henry of Ghent," *Franziskanische Studien* 68 (1986): 247–260; Steven P. Marrone, "Henry of Ghent and Duns Scotus on the Knowledge of Being," *Speculum* 63 (1988): 22–57; Stephen Dumont, "The quaestio si est and the Metaphysical Proof for the Existence of God according to Henry of Ghent and John Duns Scotus," *Franziskanische Studien* 66 (1984): 335–367.

67. Paulus, "L'argument ontologique," 281–284, 300–301; Pegis, "New Way to God," 233; Marrone, "Henry and Scotus," 32; Dumont, "The quaestio si est," 347.

68. ". . . homo naturaliter ordinatur ad duplicem cognitionem intellectualem, quarum una est ad quam ex puris naturalibus studio et investigatione potest attingere: et talis cognitio procedit de deo et de creaturis, quantum philosophia se potest exten-

dere. Alia vero est, ad quam non potest attingere nisi dono luminis alicuius super-naturalis gratia vel gloria adiuta, et utraque via potest fieri homini notum deum esse . . ." Henry, *Summa,* a. 22, q. 5, sol. (Badius, vol. 1, fol. 134r). For this knowledge and its limits, see a. 22, qq. 2–5 (Badius, vol. 1, fol. 130r–135v); *Quodl.* 4, q. 9 (Badius 1, fol. 99r–v).

69. Henry, *Summa,* a. 24, q. 7, sol. (Badius, vol. 1, fol. 144r).

70. Henry, *Summa,* a. 22, q. 2, sol. (Badius, vol. 1, fol. 130v).

71. Henry, *Summa,* a. 22, q. 2, sol. (Badius, vol. 1, fol. 130v). Arist., *An. Post.* 1.17.71a17–26. See also Henry, *Summa,* a. 30, q. 3, sol. (Badius, vol. 1, fol. 179v–180v).

72. Henry, *Summa,* a. 24, q. 6, resp. (Badius, vol. 1, fol. 143r). Augustine, *De doctrina christiana* 1.7(7) (CCL 23, 10).

73. Gordon A. Wilson, introduction to Henry of Ghent, *Summa,* art. 35–40, *Opera Omnia,* vol. 28, ed. Gordon A. Wilson (Leuven: Leuven University Press, 1994), xxvii–xxviii.

74. "Si ergo quaestio de dilectione beneplacentiae: cum huiusmodi dilectione diligatur bonum simpliciter quia bonum, et nullum bonum participatum diligitur nisi quia in ipso est participata aliqua ratio boni simpliciter, quae perfecte habet esse in solo primo bono quod deus est, gratia cuius illud bonum participatum diligitur tanquam gratia eius quod est in se per se et primo dilectum, et cuius cognitione bonum participatum cognoscitur esse bonum, tanquam illo quod in se est per se et primum cognitum . . . Vera est autem illa regula generalis. Si simpliciter ad simpliciter, etc. Et similiter illa: propter quod unumquodque tale, et illud magis. Idcirco igitur absolute dicendum est: quod dilectione naturali beneplacentiae, deus diligitur a quacunque voluntate intellectualis creaturae naturaliter super omnia alia inquantum scilicet est bonus simpliciter, et quia bonus est et ratio diligendi omnis alterius boni, et bonum universale, cuiuscunque aliud bonum est quasi pars . . . ." Henry, *Quodl.* 4, q. 11 (Badius 1, fol. 102r). Arist., *An. Post.* 1.2.72a29–30.

75. Gillon, "L'argument," 209, maintains that the arguments differ because Thomas understands participation in terms of efficient causality whereas Henry understands it in terms of the perfect and imperfect. In the previous chapter it has been shown that Thomas's notion of participation embraces both aspects. The important difference is Henry's understanding of God as the first object of the intellect and will. For Henry's understanding of participation, see José Gómez Caffarena, *Ser participado y ser subsistente en la metafísica de Enrique de Gante,* Analecta Gregoriana, 93 (Rome: Gregorian University, 1958).

76. Henry, *Quodl.* 4, q. 11 (Badius 1, fol. 102v). Aristotle, *Eth. Nic.* 9.4.1166b14–15; *Pol.* 3.6.1278b28–30.

77. Henry, *Quodl.* 4, q. 11 (Badius 1, fol. 102v). Augustine, *De trinitate* 8.3(4) (CCL 50, 274).

78. Henry, *Quodl.* 4, q. 11 (Badius 1, fol. 102v).

79. Henry, *Quodl.* 4, q. 11 (Badius 1, fol. 102v). Aristotle, *Eth. Nic.* 8.7.

80. "Sicut enim dilectione amicitiae diligit primo et per se seipsum et extendit ex se huiusmodi dilectionem ad alium, sicut dictum est, diligendo primo bonum quod

ipse est in natura et essentia sua, et deinde bonum quod est alius, sic dilectione benivolentiae primo vult sibi bonum quod non est ipse, deinde alteri." Henry, *Quodl.* 4, q. 11
(Badius 1, fol. 102v).

81. Henry, *Quodl.* 4, q. 11 (Badius 1, fol. 102v-103r).

82. Henry, *Quodl.* 4, q. 11 (Badius 1, fol. 103r).

83. Henry, *Quodl.* 4, q. 11 (Badius 1, fol. 103r).

84. "Propter quod dixit Tullius in libro primo De Officiis in persona philosophorum: 'Propositum nostrum est secundum naturam vivere.' Quod re vera bonum erat,
et ad gratiam charitatis ordinans. Sed propositum perfectissimum est secundum charitatem vivere, quod est bonorum christianorum. Cum vero depravata per vitium naturae non congruit, tunc illo vel illis fruitur quae sunt obiecta sui peccati. Et ideo
dilectione deliberativa pro tali statu deum super omnia diligere non potest." Henry,
Quodl. 4, q. 11 (Badius 1, fol. 103r). Although the text refers to Cicero, Henry seems to
be quoting Seneca. See Seneca, *Ad Lucilium epistolae morales* 5.4, Loeb Classical Library
(Cambridge, Mass.: Cambridge University Press, 1934), 22.

85. See my "Augustinianism of Thomas Aquinas's Moral Theory."

86. Henry, *Quodl.* 13, q. 10 (*Opera,* vol. 18, 73–74).

87. See Henry, *Summa,* a. 3, q. 5 (Badius, vol.1, fol. 29v–30r). For the natural
desire to know and its supernatural fulfillment, see a. 4 (Badius, vol. 1, fol. 30v–35v).
Berubé, *De l'homme à Dieu,* 191–195; Macken, "Lebensziel," 116–123; Laurence Renault,
"Félicité humaine et conception de la philosophie chez Henri de Gand, Duns Scot et
Guillaume d'Ockham," in *Was ist Philosophie im Mittelalter?,* ed. Jan A. Aertsen and
Andreas Speer, Miscellanea Mediaevalia, 26 (Berlin: de Gruyter, 1998), 970–971.

88. Henry, *Quodlibet* 6, q. 11, *Opera Omnia,* vol. 10, ed. G. Wilson (Leuven: Leuven University Press, 1987), 135. For Henry's strong notion of original sin, see Richard
Cross, *John Duns Scotus* (Oxford: Oxford University Press, 1999), 96–97; A. Gaudel,
"Péché originel," *Dictionnaire de théologie catholique,* vol. 12.1, 491–492. For a good account
of the issues involved, see Cyril O. Vollert, *The Doctrine of Hervaeus Natalis on Primitive
Justice and Original Sin: As Developed in the Controversy on Original Sin during the Early Decades
of the Fourteenth Century,* Analecta Gregoriana, 42 (Rome: Gregorian University, 1947).

89. For Godfrey's relationship to Thomism, see Robert J. Arway, "A Half Century of Research on Godfrey of Fontaines," *New Scholasticism* 36 (1962): 202–203. Gillon remarks on Godfrey's *Quodl.* 4, q. 14: "Ce long exposé constitue le commentaire le
plus précis et le plus profond qui existe de la pensée de saint Thomas. Nous sommes
ici dans un des cas, où l'on peut sans aucune hésitation, parler du 'Thomisme' du
Godefroid." Gillon, "L'argument," 214; for Giles, see 211–212. Gillon thinks that only
Giles's first argument is Thomistic and that Giles's position is heavily influenced by
Henry. The greatest similarity between Giles and Henry is in their emphasis on participation. However, the important role that participation plays in Thomas's argument
was shown in chapter 3 above, so Giles's use of participation need not by itself indicate a great difference between his position and that of Thomas.

90. For the debate with Siger, see de Lagarde, "Philosophie," 101–103; Bernhard
Neumann, *Der Mensch und die himmlische Seligkeit nach der Lehre Gottfrieds von Fontaines*
(Limburg: Lahn, 1958), 34. Kempshall briefly mentions Siger (*Common Good,* 214).

91. For Godfrey's education, see Wippel, *Godfrey of Fontaines,* xvi–xix.

92. For Godfrey's belief in the identity of essence and existence, see Wippel, *Godfrey of Fontaines,* 39–99. For some Neoplatonic aspects of Godfrey's thought which involve the order of the universe, see 145–152

93. On the primacy of the common good, see especially Kempshall, *Common Good,* 204–234; de Lagarde, *La Naissance,* 170–174.

94. Godfrey of Fontaines, *Quodlibet* 14, q. 1, in *Les quodlibets treize et quatorze,* ed. Jean Hoffmans, Les Philosophes Belges, 5.3–4 (Louvain: Institut Supérieur de Philosophie, 1935), 304. See Aristotle, *Pol.* 1.2.1253a1–2.

95. Godfrey of Fontaines, *Quaestiones ordinariae,* q. 3, in *Le quodlibet XV et trois questions ordinaires,* ed. Odon Lottin, Les Philosophes Belges, 14 (Louvain: Institut Supérieur de Philosophie, 1937), 132.

96. Godfrey, *QO* 1 (PB 14, 89). For the patristic and classical description of the political community as an organic body and its medieval development, see Tilman Struve, *Die Entwicklung der organologischen Staatsauffassung im Mittelalter* (Stuttgart: Hiersemann, 1978).

97. Godfrey, *Quodl.* 14, q. 1 (PB 5.4, 306). See Kempshall, *Common Good,* 222–223.

98. "bonum quasi commune": Godfrey, *Quodl.* 10, q. 6 (PB 4.3, 318). For texts and the connection between the common good and charity, see Paul Tihon, *Foi et théologie selon Godefroid de Fontaines,* Mueseum Lessianum section théologique, 61 (Paris: Desclée, 1961), 183, note 1. For a discussion of the following issues, see Neumann, *Gottfrieds von Fontaines,* 29–39.

99. Godfrey, *Quodlibet* 5, q. 12, in *Les quodlibets cinq, six, et sept,* ed. Maurice de Wulf and Jean Hoffmans, Les Philosophes Belges, 3 (Louvain: Institut Supérieur de Philosophie, 1914), 55. For *bonum in communi,* see Kempshall, *Common Good,* 232.

100. *Quodl.* 5, q. 12 (PB 3, 59).

101. Godfrey, *Quaestio disputata* 19, in Odon Lottin, "Les vertus morales acquises sont elles de vraies vertus? La réponse des théologiens de saint Thomas à Pierre Auriol," *Recherches de théologie ancienne et médiévale* 21 (1954): 120. For Godfrey's *Quaestiones disputatae,* I follow the Borghese numbering. For a list of these questions, see Wippel, *Godfrey of Fontaines,* xxxi–xxxii.

102. For a discussion, see Bonnie Kent, "Justice, Passion, and Another's Good: Aristotle among the Theologians," in *Nach der Verurteilung von 1277,* ed. Jan A. Aersten, Miscellanea Mediaevalia, vol. 28 (Berlin: de Gruyter, 2001), 713–718.

103. Godfrey, *Quodl.* 14, q. 2 (PB 5.4, 331).

104. Kempshall, *Common Good,* 228, note 65. For an interesting approach to this problem, see Tihon, *Foi et théologie,* 217.

105. Godfrey, *Quodlibet* 10, q. 15 (PB 4.3, 386–387). See Neumann, *Gottfrieds von Fontaines,* 79–80.

106. "Non oportet etiam quod peccatum originale includat aliquam incurvationem moralem nisi in potentia et in habitu. Talis autem non repugnat naturae secundum se, ut dictum est." Godfrey, *Quodlibet* 10, q. 15 (PB 4.3, 387).

107. Godfrey, *QD* 19 (RTAM 21, 117). Cf. *Quodl.* 10, q. 5 (PB 4.3, 386); *Quaestio disputata* 11, in Odon Lottin, *Psychologie et morale aux XIIᵉ et XIIIᵉ siècles,* vol. 3.2 (Louvain: Abbaye du Mont César; Gembloux: Ducolot, 1949), 498. See Neumann, *Gottfrieds von Fontaines,* 70–92.

108. "Homo autem secundum potentias suas, scilicet intellectum et voluntatem, ordinatur ad duplicem perfectam vitam sive ad duplicem felicitatem; naturalem scilicet secundum civilitatem humanam, et supernaturalem secundum civitatem celestem." Godfrey, *Quaestio disputata* 15 (Neumann, 160).

109. Godfrey, *Quaestio disputata* 1 (Neumann, 156).

110. For the argument, see Gillon, "Le sacrifice," 246–248; idem, "L'argument," 212–214; Neumann, *Gottfrieds von Fontaines,* 32–39; Kempshall, *Common Good,* 207–214.

111. Godfrey, *Quodl.* 10, q. 6 (PB 4.3, 318). See Egenter, *Gottesfreundschaft,* 121–132.

112. Godfrey, *Quodl.* 10, q. 6 (PB 4.3, 318–319). For the part/whole argument in Godfrey, see Neumann, *Gottfrieds von Fontaines,* 37.

113. ". . . alioquin gratia et caritas destruerent et non perficerent naturam sive naturalem inclinationem." Godfrey, *Quodl.* 10, q. 6 (PB 4.3, 319).

114. Godfrey, *Quodl.* 10, q. 6 (PB 4.3, 19). Modern scholarship also suggests a link between this passage from John's Gospel and ancient theories of friendship.

115. Godfrey, *QD* 1 (Neumann, 155).

116. "Respondeo dicendum quod cum, prout dicit Philosophus, omnia bonum appetant quia unumquodque naturaliter inclinatur in suam perfectionem quae est bonum eius, oportet ponere quod intellectus cum non est in actu intelligendi appetat suam perfectionem quae est intelligere aliquod intelligibile sive suus actus intelligendi." Godfrey, *Quodl.* 6, q. 8 (PB 3, 173).

117. Godfrey, *Quodl.* 5, q. 12 (PB 3, 48).

118. Godfrey, *QD* 15 (Neumann, 160).

119. Godfrey, *Quodl.* 10, q. 6 (PB 4.3, 319–320).

120. ". . . dicendum quod, cum actus habeat formam et perfectionem ex obiecto et obiectum per se et principaliter quo Deus diligitur est bonum divinum; et ipsum bonum divinum est maxime simpliciter, obiectum autem dilectionis qua quis diligit se diligentem Deum et perfectum virtutibus est minus bonum, patet quod illa dilectio maior est et perfectior simpliciter et absolute; et sic videtur quod magis diligo Deum se perfectum quam me huiusmodi dilectione et aliis virtutibus perfectum." Godfrey, *Quodl.* 10, q. 6 (PB 4.3, 320).

121. Kempshall (*Common Good,* 210) thinks that Godfrey is here referring to Aquinas's distinction between the intrinsic and extrinsic goods of the universe. On the contrary, it is clear that Godfrey is referring to Siger's interpretation of Aristotle, which states that the good human can desire a greater extrinsic good more for another than for himself, but that he must love most of all his own intrinsic good of virtue.

122. Godfrey, *Quodl.* 10, q. 6 (PB 4.3, 320–321).

123. "Si ergo posset breviter dici quod alia est ratio dilectionis qua diligo bonum divinum ut finem et bonum extrinsecum, et bonum virtutis ut finem et bonum intrin-

secum; et ideo non sunt proprie ad invicem comparabilia." Godfrey, *Quodl.* 10, q. 6 (PB 4.3, 321).

124. "Sed adhuc non quietatur intellectus, quia licet talia sint diversarum rationum nec sint proprie ad invicem comparabilia . . . aliquo modo ad invicem se habent et sunt comparabila aliquo modo; et ideo remanet adhuc quaestio praedicta . . ." Godfrey, *Quodl.* 10, q. 6 (PB 4.3, 321).

125. Godfrey, *Quodl.* 14, q. 1 (PB 5.4, 312–313). See Kempshall, *Common Good,* 241.

126. Godfrey, *QO* 3 (PB 14, 133).

127. Godfrey, *Quodl.* 10, q. 6 (PB 4.3, 321–322.)

128. ". . . studiosum quantumcumque diligat se et suum bonum proprium et intrinsecum, magis tamen eligit bene et virtuose mori et non esse quam bonum commune perire." Godfrey, *Quodl.* 10, q. 6 (PB 4.3, 322). Aristotle, *Eth. Nic.* 9.8.1169a8–12.

129. "Sed quia illud bonum intrinsecum habet suam bonitatem ex bonitate obiecti dilecti principaliter, ideo sic magis volo maximum bonum mihi possibile, non tamen volo illud primo et principaliter et maxime quia nec illud est obiectum primum et per se voluntatis, sed illud ex quo habet huiusmodi actus qui est bonus mihi suam bonitatem." Godfrey, *Quodl.* 10, q. 6 (PB 4.3, 322).

130. ". . . quasi ex consequenti et implicite." Godfrey, *Quodl.* 9, q. 6 (PB 4.3, 323).

131. Godfrey, *Quodl.* 6, q. 12 (PB 3, 230); idem, *QD* 8 (Neumann, 166); idem, *QD* 10 (RTAM 21, 119).

132. Godfrey, *Quodl.* 6, q. 12 (PB 3, 229).

133. Godfrey, *Quodl.* 6, q. 10 (PB 3, 201); idem, *Quodl.* 6, q. 8 (PB 3, 177); *QD* 7 (Neumann, 162–164). See Neumann, *Gottfrieds von Fontaines,* 38–39, 135.

134. In contrast, Kempshall (*Common Good,* 208) thinks that Godfrey's argument for the natural love is based on his theory of transforming union through love. Godfrey does not discuss this unitive power in this context, but instead in a passage where it is shown how the friend can become another self: "Nam cum sic amantes se sint quodam modo unum, in quantum amor, secundum Dyonisium et Augustinum, est vis unitiva et transformativa amantis in amatum; et secundum Philosophum: amicus est alter ipse volens alicui bonum, tali amicitia vult hoc in quantum sunt quodam modo unum et in quantum bonum quod illi vult est bonum quod etiam sibi principaliter vult; quia amicabilia quae ad amicos videntur ex his quae ad se ipsum venisse, ut dicitur nono Ethicorum; illud quidem vult ipsi ut est quodammodo ipse; et sic talis actus volendi non est bonum et perfectio principalis ipsius volentis, sed obiectum talis actus quod est quiddam aliud quod est bonum et perfectio amici in se ipso, et ipsius amantis ut est unum cum illo." Godfrey, *Quodl.* 6, q. 10 (PB 3, 191). See Neumann, *Gottfrieds von Fontaines,* 135–136.

135. Godfrey, *Quodl.* 10, q. 6 (PB 4.3, 325). For the date, see Wippel, *Godfrey of Fontaines,* xxvii. Aristotle, *Top.* 3.2.118a10–11.

136. Godfrey, *Quodl.* 11, q. 6 (PB 5.1, 36–37).

137. Thomas Aquinas, *S.T.,* I–II, q. 66, art. 3.

138. For an interesting approach to this problem, see Tihon, *Foi et Théologie*, 217.

139. "... dicendum quod Philosophus loquitur de amicitia proprie dicta quae est inter aequales vel quasi aequales et in qua amici communicant quasi aequaliter in bono secundum quod in eis amicitia invenitur ... non autem de amicitia quae habetur ad alterum in quo invenitur bonum quod est amicitiae obiectum, secundum rationem eminentiae et cuiusdam totius quasi omne bonum includentis. Et secundum hoc patet quod male assignatur differentia inter Aristotelem et peripateticum et quemcumque doctorem theologicum ... Immo in his quae ad veram amicitiam pertinent concordat doctrina Aristotelis et peripatetici cum doctrina intelligentis theologi." Godfrey, *Quodl.* 10, q. 6 (PB 4.3, 325). It is worth asking, "Where would Godfrey put Siger?"

140. "Secundum hunc ergo modum exponendi praedictum verbum Philosophi patet quod non discordat a perfectissimo theologo christiano; immo quod dicit Aristoteles: amicabilia quae ad alterum, et cetera, nihil aliud videtur quam quod dicit Christus: diliges proximum tuum sicut te ipsum; et cetera." Godfrey, *Quodl.* 10, q. 6 (PB 4.3, 325). For a similar passage in Thomas Aquinas, see *S.T.,* I–II, q. 99, a. 1, ad 3. For a discussion of Thomas, see R. Mary Hayden, "The Paradox of Aquinas's Altruism: From Self-Love to Love of Others," *Proceedings of the American Catholic Philosophical Association* 63 (1989): 73–83.

141. Godfrey, *QO* 3 (PB 14, 133–134).

142. "Utrum homo magis debeat diligere Deum, quam seipsum?" Giles, *Quodl.* 4, q. 14, 235. For the argument, see Gillon, "L'argument," 210–212; de Lagarde, "La Philosophie," 96–98. See also my article, "James of Viterbo's Rejection of Giles of Rome's Arguments for the Natural Love of God over Self," *Augustiniana* 49 (1999): 235–249. Most of the discussion of Giles here is taken from this article.

143. Giles of Rome, *Quodlibet* 4, q. 13, in *Quodlibeta* (Louvain: 1646; repr. Frankfurt am Main: Minerva, 1966), 234–237. For the date of *Quodlibet* 4 as 1289, see Silvia Donati, "Studi per una cronologia delle opere di Egidio Romano I: Le opere prima del 1285. Il commenti aristotelici; parte II," *Documenti e Studi sulla Tradizione Filosofica Medievale,* 2, n. 1 (1991): 74. For a discussion of dates, see Francesco del Punta, Donati, and C. Luna, "Egidio Romano," in *Dizionario biografico degli italiani,* vol. 42 (Rome: Istituto della Enciclopedia Italiana, 1993), 321, 331; Glorieux, *Répertoire,* vol. 2, 300. For a recent discussion of Giles and bibliography, see Francesco del Punta and Cecilia Trifolgi, "Giles of Rome," in *The Routledge Encyclopedia of Philosophy* (London: Routledge, 1998), vol. 4, 72–78.

144. "... dicimus enim quod Deus sit magis intimus cuilibet rei, quam res ipsa sibi ..." Giles, *Quodl.* 4, q. 14, 235.

145. Giles, *Quodl.* 4, q. 14, 235–236. For Giles's understanding of *vestigium,* see Giles of Rome, *In primum librum sententiarum* (Venice: 1521; repr. Frankfurt am Main: Minerva, 1968), d. 3, q. 2, fol. 22v–23v.

146. "... Deus sit bonum totale habens in se quodcumque bonum." Giles, *Quodl.* 4, q. 14, 236.

147. "Intelligenda sunt de amore partis ad partem, nam amicabilia unius partis ad aliam surrexerunt ex amicabilibus, quae sunt ad seipsum. Non autem intelligenda

sunt esi [etsi?] de amore partis ad totum: quasi pars magis debeat diligere totum, quam seipsum." Giles, *Quodl.* 4, q. 14, 236.

148. Giles, *Quodl.* 4, q. 14, 236. Aristotle, *An. Post.* 1.2.72a29–30.

149. Giles, *Quodl.* 4, q. 14, 235.

150. Giles, *Quodl.* 4, q. 14, 236–237.

151. Giles, *Quodl.* 4, q. 14, 235. Cf. Rom 8:17.

152. Giles, *In secundum librum sententiarum* (Venice: Zilettus, 1581; Frankfurt am main: Minerva, 1968), d. 28, q. 1, art. 4 (vol. 2, 368, 370).

153. Thomas Aquinas, 2 Sent. d. 28, q. 1, art. 3 (Mandonnet, 724–726); *De Veritate,* q. 24, art. 14 (Leonine 22, 722–724). This position was common. Cf. Bonaventure, 2 Sent. d. 28, q. 1, art. 4 (vol. 2, 679–681).

154. James of Viterbo, *Quodlibet* 2, q. 20, in *Disputatio secunda de quolibet,* ed. Eelcko Ypma, Cassiciacum Suplementband, 2 (Würzburg: Augustin-Verlag, 1969), 202–214. For the date, see Eelcko Ypma, "Recherches sur la productivité littéraire de Jacques de Viterbe jusqu'à 1300," *Augustiniana* 25 (1975): 273–274; idem, introduction to James of Viterbo, *Disputatio prima de quolibet,* Cassiciacum Supplementband, 1 (Würzburg: Augustin-Verlag, 1968), vi; idem, introduction to *Disputatio secunda,* vi; Glorieux, *Répertoires des maîtres en théologie de Paris au XIIIᵉ siècle,* Études de Philosophie Médiévale, 17–18 (Paris: Vrin, 1933–1934), vol. 2, 310. For a recent discussion of James and bibliography, see Edward P. Mahoney, "James of Viterbo," in *The Routledge Encyclopedia of Philosophy,* 5:58–60. For a discussion of the argument, see Gillon, "Le sacrifice," 244–246; idem, "L'argument," 214–218; Neumann, *Gottfrieds von Fontaines,* 34–35; Osborne, "Natural Love," passim; Kempshall, *Common Good,* 214–217.

155. James, *Quodl.* 2, q. 20 (CS 2, 202).

156. Gillon, "L'argument," 214.

157. "Sed iste modus dicendi aliis non placet." James, *Quodl.* 2, q. 20 (CS 2, 203).

158. James, *Quodl.* 2, q. 20 (CS 2, 204).

159. Giles adopts a position nearer to the earlier position of Thomas, namely that such love is possible with respect to the substance of the act, but not according to the intention of the lawgiver. See Giles, 2 Sent., d. 28, q. 1, a. 4 (vol. 2, 367–370).

160. James, *Quodl.* 2, q. 20 (CS 2, 203).

161. For the connection to Godfrey, see Neumann, *Gottfrieds von Fontaines,* 34; Kempshall, *Common Good,* 214–217. Both contrast the general position of James with that of Godfrey, and neither of them recognizes that James is also attacking Giles. Neumann and Kempshall identify Godfrey's position with the third objection's three arguments about the different ways in which God is good. Although Godfrey and Giles use similiar arguments, in my article I showed that Giles is the source for these three arguments. In contrast, the first two objections should be identified with Godfrey, based on the similarity with Godfrey's language and argumentation.

162. James, *Quodl.* 2, q. 20 (CS 2, 204).

163. James, *Quodl.* 2, q. 20 (CS 2, 204–205).

164. James, *Quodl.* 2, q. 20 (CS 2, 205).

165. James, *Quodl.* 2, q. 20 (CS 2, 205–206).

166. James, *Quodl.* 2, q. 20 (CS 2, 206).

167. "Unde, sicut aliquis amat et se et alium, sic per amorem dicitur esse unum sibi et alii." James, *Quodl.* 2, q. 20 (CS 2, 206).

168. James, *Quodl.* 2, q. 20 (CS 2, 206–207).

169. James, *Quodlibet* 1, q. 7 (CS 1, 122; cf. 123, 126). For the dating, the most important source is John F. Wippel, "The Dating of James of Viterbo's Quodlibet I and Godfrey of Fontaine's Quodlibet VIII," *Augustiniana* 24 (1974): 348–386. But see also Ypma, introduction to *Prima,* vi; idem, "Recherches," 274; Glorieux, *Répertoire,* vol. 2, 210.

170. James, *Quodl.* 2, q. 20 (CS 2, 207–208). Cf. James, *Quodlibet* 3, q. 20, in *Disputatio tertia de quolibet,* ed. Eelcko Ypma, Cassiciacum Supplementband, 3 (Würzburg: Augustinus Verlag, 1973), 251.

171. "Et ita dicendum, quod in dilectione naturali et gratuita est ordo conversus." James, *Quodl.* 2, q. 20 (CS 2, 208).

172. "Dilectio enim naturalis prius et magis tendit in se quam in Deum. Unde, quantum ad hanc dilectionem, verum est quod ait Philosophus, scilicet quod amicabilia quae sunt ad alterum, venerunt ex amicabilibus quae sunt ad se ipsum. Dilectio vero gratuita, quae est caritas, econverso se habet; quia prius et magis tendit in Deum quam in proximum et in se, ita quod secundum hanc dilectionem amicabilia, quae sunt ad se vel ad proximum, veniunt ex amicabilibus quae sunt ad Deum." James, *Quodl.* 2, q. 20 (CS 2, 208).

173. James, *Quodl.* 2, q. 20 (CS 2, 208–209). For Bernard, see chapter 1.

174. James, *Quodl.* 2, q. 20 (CS 2, 209–211; cf. 208).

175. James, *Quodl.* 2, q. 20 (CS 2, 211).

176. James, *Quodl.* 2, q. 20 (CS 2, 211).

177. James, *Quodl.* 2, q. 20 (CS 2, 212).

178. James, *Quodl.* 2, q. 20 (CS 2, 212).

179. James, *Quodl.* 2, q. 20 (CS 2, 212–213).

180. ". . . dicendum est quod non semper magis diligimus meliores, sed nobis coniunctiores. Licet ergo Deus sit maxime bonus, naturaliter tamen quilibet est sibi ipsi maxime unus, et ideo naturali dilectione magis diligit homo se quam Deum. Arguit ergo ratio ista quod Deus sit maxime diligibilis, ex eo quod est maxime bonus, non tamen quod a nobis maxime diligatur naturali dilectione, sicut ex eo quod est maxime verum, arguitur quod sit maxime cognoscibilis; non tamen quod a nobis maxime cognoscatur." James, *Quodl.* 2, q. 20 (CS 2, 213). For Aristotle's phrase, see ibid., 203.

181. James, *Quodl.* 2, q. 20 (CS 2, 213–214).

182. "Utrum scientia theologiae sit scientia speculativa." Godfrey, *Quodl.* 13, q. 1 (PB 5.3, 169). For the dating, see Wippel, *Godfrey of Fontaines,* xxviii.

183. "Utrum scientia sacrae Scripturae sit dicenda simpliciter speculativa vel simpliciter practica." James, *Quodl.* 3, q. 1 (CS 3, 7). For the date, see Ypma, introduction to the *Prima,* vi; idem, "Recherches," 274; Glorieux, *Répertoire,* vol. 2, 210. It is

clear to me that James's *Quodlibet* 3 must be earlier than Godfrey's *Quodlibet* 13. For James as the target of Godfrey, see Jean Hoffmans, "Le table des divergences et innovations doctrinales de Godefroid de Fontaines," *Revue néoscolastique de philosophie* 36 (1934): 435–436. Kempshall, *Common Good,* 217, thinks that Godfrey is replying to James's *Quodlibet* 2.

184. Tihon (*Foi et théologie,* 222–228) gives an account of this position and Godfrey's rejection of it. For Giles, see *In secundum librum sententiarum,* d. 21, q. 1, a. 1, dub. 2 (Venice: Zilettus, 1581; repr. Frankfurt am Main: Minerva, 1968), vol. 2.2, 172–173. Cf. Tihon, *Foi et théologie,* 222, note 5; Hoffmans, 435. For James's approach to theology, see David Gutiérrez, *De B. Iacobi Viterbiensis O.E.S.A.: Vita, operibus et doctrina theologica* (Rome: Analecta Augustiniana, 1939), 73–78. For the issue in general, see Stephen Brown, "Sources for Ockham's Prologue to the Sentences—Part II," *Franciscan Studies* 5 (1967): 39–107.

185. For this point, see "Utrum beatitudo principalius consistat in actu intellectus quam in actu voluntatis." James, *Quodl.* 1, q. 8 (CS 1, 112–127).

186. James, *Quodl.* 3, q. 1 (CS 3, 18–19). Aristotle, *Eth. Nic.* 10.7–8.

187. James, *Quodl.* 3, q. 1 (CS 3, 20). Cf. Thomas, *In XII libros metaphysicorum Aristotelis expositio,* proemium (Marietti, 1–2).

188. James, *Quodl.* 3, q. 1 (CS 3, 20). Cf. Giles of Rome, 2 Sent., d. 21, q. 1, a. 1, dub. 2 (Venice 2.2, 172): "Non ergo finis Theologiae est scire Deum propter se, sed propter diligere Deum . . ."

189. "Iustitia enim illa, quae dicitur legalis, est forma huiusmodi virtutum, quia, cum finis eius sit commune bonum, movet alias virtutes et ordinat actus earum ad hunc finem." James, *Quodl.* 3, q. 21 (CS 3, 257–258). For a discussion, see Kent, "Justice, Passion and Another's Good," 710–713.

190. "Quanto igitur virtus infusa perfectior est quam acquisita, tanto perfectius ordinatur ad amorem theologia quam moralis." James, *Quodl.* 3, q. 1 (CS 3, 20).

191. James, *Quodl.* 3, q. 1 (CS 3, 20–21).

192. Godfrey, *Quodl.* 13, q. 1 (PB 5.3, 180).

193. Godfrey, *Quodl.* 13, q. 1 (PB 5.3, 180–181).

194. Godfrey, *Quodl.* 13, q. 1 (PB 5.3, 181–182).

195. "Nam sicut sumus nati diligere Deum supernaturaliter per caritatem et naturaliter, ita etiam nati sumus ipsum cognoscere per fidem supernaturaliter et per rationem naturalem, tamen non stant ista simul quod circa Deum cognoscam ipsum esse trinum supernaturaliter et per fidem et quod cognoscam ipsum non esse trinum per naturalem rationem; nec cognitio naturalis et supernaturalis repugnant." Godfrey, *Quodl.* 13, q. 1 (PB 5.3, 182).

196. Godfrey, *Quodl.* 13, q. 1 (PB 5.3, 183).

197. Godfrey, *Quodl.* 13, q. 1 (PB 5.3, 183).

198. "Quia ergo unio quae ad amicitiam per se requiritur non est unio quae solum consistit in coniunctione principiorum naturae alicuius entis ut est aliquid singulare secundum se existens, sed ut est pars quaedam alicuius totius, propter hoc etiam inclinatio naturalis hoc includit quod bonum partis ad bonum totius ordinetur

et quod unusquisque sic diligat se ipsum ut est aliquid unum ens singulare secundum naturam, sicut expedit in ordine ad bonum communitatis quod est principale bonum et principale obiectum voluntatis ordinatae, ita quod in hoc includitur quod pars magis diligit bonum commune quam privatum in quantum etiam bonum privatum ordinat ad bonum commune, non autem e converso . . ." Godfrey, *Quodl.* 13, q. 1 (PB 5.3, 183–184).

199. "Non enim exponit se morti pro communitate propter ipsum bonum communitatis propter bonum suum quod primo et principaliter in hoc attendat, sed propter ipsum bonum communitatis propter se quod est per se et primo obiectum sic agentis . . . non bonum totius ad se per se et principaliter referendo, licet etiam in hoc, ut dictum est, suum bonum optimum consequatur." Godfrey, *Quodl.* 13, q. 1 (PB 5.3, 184).

CHAPTER 5
John Duns Scotus

1. *Quaestiones super libros metaphysicorum Aristotelis,* 9, q. 15, in John Duns Scotus, *Opera Philosophica* (St. Bonaventure, N.Y.: Franciscan Institute, 1997), vol. 4, 675–699. This text can also be found in Allan B. Wolter, ed. and trans., *Duns Scotus on the Will and Morality* (Washington, D.C.: The Catholic University of America Press, 1986), 144–173. The condition of Scotus's texts is problematic. For this reason my interpretation of Scotus uses some texts which have not been critically edited. Although it would be preferable to use only edited texts, I think that my interpretation gives a viable reading of Scotus which is consistent with his thought in general. A critical edition of the philosophical works is being prepared under the guidance of Timothy Noone at the Catholic University of America. The theological works are being edited by the Scotistic Commission in *Opera Omnia* (Vatican City: Typis Polyglottis Vaticanis, 1950–). Since this edition is not near completion, it is often necessary to use *Opera Omnia,* 12 vols., ed. Luke Wadding (Lyons: Laurentius Durandus, 1639; repr. Hildesheim: Georg Olms, 1968). The main published works of Scotus are three commentaries on the *Sentences of Peter Lombard.* The major work is his *Ordinatio,* which the Wadding edition describes as the *Opus Oxoniense.* The *Lectura* are notes for the *Ordinatio.* The Vatican edition includes both works for the entire first book, and part of the second. Wadding's *Reportata Parisiensia* are students' notes, and Wadding's edition is useful but in many parts unreliable. To ensure the reliability of the texts cited, I most often follow Charles Balić, *Les commentaires de Jean Duns Scot sur les quatres livres de Sentences* (Louvain: Bureaux de la Revue d'histoire ecclésiastique, 1927). A survey of more recent scholarship can be found in Allan B. Wolter, "Reflections of the Life and Works of Scotus," *American Catholic Philosophical Quarterly* 57 (1993): 1–36. Balić thought that the *Ordinatio* for Book III did not continue beyond dist. 14. This issue is important because much of Scotus's ethics is contained in the later distinctions. Odon Lottin, "L'*Ordinatio* de Jean Duns Scot sur le livre III des Sentences," *Recherches de Théologie*

ancienne et médiévale 20 (1953): 102–119, argued that the final revision of Book 3 probably extends at least to dist. 36. Wolter, introduction to *Will and Morality,* 75, suggests that these distinctions could be described as "supplements" to Book 3. To avoid confusion, I will refer to any part of the *Ordinatio* not published in the Vatican edition, including those passages which Wolter describes calls "supplements," as *Opus Oxoniense.* I use Wolter's revised texts when possible. The following abbreviations will be used: "ABW" for *Duns Scotus on the Will and Morality,* "VC" for the Vatican edition, "WDG" for the Wadding edition, and "OP" for the *Opera Philosophica.*

2. Allan B. Wolter, "Native Freedom of the Will as a Key to the Ethics of Scotus," in *Deus et Homo ad mentem I. Duns Scoti, Acta tertii Congressus Scotistici Internationalis Vindebonae 28 Sept.–Oct. 1970,* Studia scholastico-Scotistica, 5 (Rome: Societas Internationalis Scotistica, 1972), 359–370; repr. in Wolter, *Philosophical Theology of John Duns Scotus,* ed. Marilyn McCord Adams (Ithaca: Cornell University Press, 1990), 148–162.

3. Allan B. Wolter, "Duns Scotus on the Will as Rational Potency," in Wolter, *Philosophical Theology of John Duns Scotus,* 163–180.

4. For a brief discussion, see Wolter, introduction, ABW 39–41.

5. Marilyn McCord Adams, "Duns Scotus on the Will as Rational Power," in *Via Scoti: Methodologica ad mentem Joannis Duns Scoti 1993, Atti del Congresso Scotistico Internazionale Roma 9–11 Marzo 1993,* ed. Leonardo Sileo, Studia scholastico-Scotistica, 5 (Rome: Edizioni Antonianum, 1995), 849; John Boler, "The Moral Psychology of Duns Scotus: Some Preliminary Questions," *Franciscan Studies* 28 (1990): 35–38; idem, "Transcending the Natural: Duns Scotus on the Two Affections of the Will," *American Catholic Philosophical Quarterly* 67 (1993): 110; Thomas Williams, "How Scotus Separates Morality from Happiness," *American Catholic Philosophical Quarterly* 69 (1995): 426–427, 435.

6. Boler, "Moral Psychology," 35. Rude A. te Velde uses a similar claim to contrast Scotus with Aquinas: "It seems to me that Aquinas would not accept the opposition between the *bonum in se* (as the correlate of the *affectio iustitiae*) and the *bonum sibi* (as the correlate of the *affectio commodi*), at least insofar as this opposition is based upon a distinction in the motivating forces behind different acts of will." "*Natura in se ipsa recurva est:* Duns Scotus and Aquinas on the Relationship between Nature and Will," in *John Duns Scotus: Renewal of Philosophy,* Acts of the Third Symposium Organized by the Dutch Society for Medieval Philosophy Medium Aevum, May 23–24, 1996, ed. E. P. Bos, Elementa, Schriften zur Philosophie und Ihrer Problemgeschichte, 72 (Amsterdam: Rodopi, 1998), 162. For Aquinas's acceptance of this distinction, see for example, chapter 3. For an extreme contrast between Scotus and Aristotle which reads Aristotle as a full-blown egoist, see Gérard Sondag, "Aristote et Duns Scot: sur le problème du sacrifice de soi: pour quelles raisons le citoyen courageux expose-t-il sa vie quand la cité est en danger," *Philosophie* 61 (1999): 75–88.

7. Mary Elizabeth Ingham, "Duns Scotus, Morality, and Happiness: A Reply to Thomas Williams," *American Catholic Philosophical Quarterly* 74 (2000): 173–195; cf. Eadem, "*Ea Quae Sunt ad Finem:* Reflections on Virtue as Means to Moral Excellence in Scotist Thought," *Franciscan Studies* 28 (1990): 179–181.

8. For the history of the discussion, see Wolter, introduction, ABW, 3–5. For a classic presentation of the issue, see Bernardine M. Bonansea, "Duns Scotus's Voluntarism," in *John Duns Scotus, 1265–1965,* ed. Bernardine M. Bonansea and John K. Ryan, Studies in Philosophy and the History of Philosophy, vol. 3 (Washington, D.C.: The Catholic University of America Press, 1965), 83–121. For a description of Scotus as a voluntarist with regard to secondary moral precepts, see Robert Prentice, "The Contingent Element Governing the Natural Law on the Last Seven Precepts of the Decalogue, according to Duns Scotus," *Antonianum* 42 (1967): 259–292; C. P. Ragland, "Scotus on the Decalogue: What Sort of Voluntarism?," *Vivarium* 36 (1998): 67–81.

9. Wolter, introduction, ABW, 3–29; Mary Elizabeth Ingham, "Scotus and the Moral Order," *American Catholic Philosophical Quarterly* 67 (1993): 127–150. For Ingham's general view, see *The Harmony of Goodness: Mutuality and Moral Living according to John Duns Scotus* (Quincy, Ill.: Franciscan Press, 1996).

10. Thomas Williams, "Reason, Morality, and Voluntarism in Duns Scotus: A Pseudo-Problem Dissolved," *The Modern Schoolman* 74 (1997): 73–75.

11. Williams, "Reason, Morality," 84–91. The strongest presentation of Scotus's voluntarism has been set forth in Williams's two most recent articles: "The Unmitigated Scotus," *Archiv für Geschichte der Philosophie* 80 (1998): 162–181; "A Most Methodical Lover? On Scotus's Arbitrary Creator," *Journal of the History of Philosophy* 38 (2000): 169–202.

12. te Velde, "*Natura,*" 156. For similar but more nuanced accounts, see Rohmer, *La Finalité morale,* 251–259; Berthold Wald, "Der Bestimmung der *ratio legis* bei Thomas von Aquin und Duns Scotus," in *Mensch und Natur im Mittelalter,* Miscellanea Mediaevalia, 21.2 (Berlin: de Gruyter, 1992), 662–681; Ludger Honnefelder, "Naturrecht und Normwandel bei Thomas von Aquin und Johannes Duns Scotus," in *Sozialer Wandel im Mittelalter: Wahrnehmungsformen, Erklärungsmuster, Regelungsmechanismen,* ed. Jürgen Miethke and Klaus Schreiner (Sigmaringen: Thorbecke, 1994), 197–211; Hannes Möhle, *Ethik als scientia practica nach Johannes Duns Scotus: Eine philosophische Grundlegung,* Beiträge zur Geschichte der Philosophie und Theologie des Mittelalters, n.f. 44 (Münster: Aschendorff, 1995); idem, "Wille und Moral zur Voraussetzung der Ethik des Johannes Duns Scotus und ihre Bedeutung für die Ethik Immanuel Kants," in *John Duns Scotus: Metaphysics and Ethics,* ed. Mechtild Dreyer, Ludger Honnenfelder, and Rega Wood, Studien und Texte zur Geistesgeschichte des Mittelalters, 53 (Leiden: Brill, 1996).

13. "Utrum sit aliqua virtus theologica inclinans ad diligendum Deum super omnia?" *Ox.* 3, d. 27, q. un. (WDG 7.2, 644–657). Most of this question is corrected and reproduced in ABW, 422–446. "Utrum ponenda sit charitas infusa?" *R.P.* 3, d. 27, q. un. (WDG 11.1, 531–534).

14. *Ord.* 2, d. 7, q. un., n. 22 (VC 8, 107).

15. "Angelus ex puris naturalibus potest diligere Deum super omnia . . . Igitur naturalis inclinatio potest Angelum ad hoc inclinare, ut diligat Deum ultra omnia, quia nullum accidens adueniens naturae potest magis inclinare naturam ad aliud, quam totum pondus naturae ad illud, ad quod natura inclinat: igitur si obstinatio in

Angelis tantum est per hoc quod permanet in actu malo habitualiter, potest in aliis Angelus habere actum bonum complete moraliter." *R.P.* 2, d. 7, q. 3, n. 29 (WDG 11.1, 297).

16. *Ord.* 2, d. 7, q. un, n. 24 (VC 8, 110–111); *R.P.* 2, d. 7, q. 3 nn. 29–30 (WDG 11.1, 297). For a discussion of this issue, see Möhle, *Ethik als scientia practica,* 281–286, 307–312.

17. ". . . si Doctor recte intelligatur, nulla apparebit contradictio." Francis Lychetus, *Commentarius* 2, d. 7, q. un. (WDG 6.2, 576).

18. *Ox.* 3, d. 17, q. un., n. 3 (ABW 182; WDG 7.1, 380). For an informative but dated collection and discussion of Scotus's texts on the will, see Parthenius Minges, *Ioannes Duns Scoti: Doctrina Philosophica et Theologica,* vol. 1 (Ad Claras Aquas: Collegium S. Bonaventurae, 1930), 272–387. For the will and natural inclination, see especially 324–326.

19. *Quodlibet,* q. 17, n. 2, in John Duns Scotus, *Cuestiones Cuodlibetales,* ed. and trans. Felix Alluntis (Madrid: Biblioteca de Auctores Cristianos, 1968), 612 (WDG 12, 459). The abbreviation "ed. Alluntis" will be used for this edition. For the English translation, see John Duns Scotus, *God and Creatures: The Quodlibetal Questions,* ed. and trans. Felix Alluntis and Allan B. Wolter (Princeton, N.J.: Princeton University Press, 1975).

20. *Ox.* 3, d. 15, q. un., n. 23 (WDG 7.1, 347).

21. *Ox.* 3 d. 18, q. un., n. 20 (WDG 7.1, 407).

22. *Ox.* 3, d. 17, q. un., n. 3 (ABW, 180; WDG 7.1, 379).

23. *Ord.* 2, d. 7, q. un., n. 26 (VC 8, 115).

24. *Super libros metaphysicorum* 9, 15, n. 22 (OP 4, 680; ABW, 150). Aristotle, *Metaph.* 9.2.1046b1–4. Cf. *R.P.* 3, d. 33, n. 21 (WDG 11.1, 548). For a detailed discussion of Scotus on the will, see especially Walter Hoeres, *Der Wille als Reine Vollkommenheit nach Duns Scotus,* Salzburger Studien zur Philosophie, 1 (Munich: Pustet, 1962). I have also consulted the Italian translation, *La volontà come perfezione pura in Duns Scoto,* trans. Alfredo Bizzoto and Antonio Poppi (Padua: Liviana, 1976). For a discussion of the will as rational potency, see Adams, "Scotus on the Will," 839–854; Etienne Gilson, *Jean Duns Scot,* Études de Philosophie Médiévale, 42 (Paris: Vrin, 1952), 574–593; Möhle, *Ethik als scientia practica,* 161–173; Wolter, "Will as Rational Potency," 163–180.

25. *Quodlibet,* q. 18, n. 9 (ed. Alluntis, 642–643; WDG 12, 481–482). *Metaph.* 9.5.1048a5–15. Cf. *Ox.* 3, d. 15, q. un., nn. 13–14 (WDG 7.1, 335).

26. *Ox.* 4, d. 49, q. 10, n. 2 (WDG 10, 505).

27. *Ord.* 2, d. 39, qq. 1–2, n. 5 (VC 8, 464; ABW, 202).

28. *Ox.* 4, d. 49, q. 10, n. 2 (WDG 10, 506). 2 Cor 5:4–5. See Rohmer, "La Finalité morale," 254–255.

29. Scotus does not think that it is possible through natural reason to be sure about the immortality of the soul. See *Ox.* 4, d. 43, q. 2, in *Duns Scotus: Philosophical Writings,* ed. and trans. Allan B. Wolter (Indianapolis: Hackett, 1987), 134–162 (WDG 10, 21–40). Although Scotus thinks that we cannot know God will punish in the afterlife, the universe might still be morally consistent: "Et esto quod sic diceretur

quod unicuique in bono actu suo sit retributio sufficiens . . ." Ibid., n. 28 (Wolter, ed., 157; WDG, 35). Another problem with understanding Scotus's view of the good citizen is that his political philosophy is poorly developed. See Anthony Soto, "The Structure of Society according to Duns Scotus," *Franciscan Studies* 11 (1951): 194–212; 12 (1952): 71–90; Maurice de Gandillac, "Loi naturelle et fondements de l'ordre social selon les principes du bienheureux Duns Scot," in *De doctrina Ioannis Duns Scoti, Acta Congressus Scotistici Internationalis,* by the Societas Internationalis Scotistica, vol. 3, Studia scholastico-Scotistica, 3 (Rome: Societas International Scotistica, 1968), 683–734; Jeannine Quillet, "De la nature humaine à l'ordre politique selon Jean Duns Scot," in *Via Scoti: Methodologica ad mentem Joannis Duns Scoti* 1993. *Atti del Congresso Scotistico Internazionale Roma, 9–11 Marzo 1993,* ed. Leonardo Sileo, Studia scholastico-Scotistica, 5 (Rome: Edizioni Antonianum, 1995), vol. 2, 261–273.

30. *Ord.* 2, d. 6, q. 2, nn. 10–12 (VC 8, 53–55; ABW, 472–474).

31. *Ord.* 2, d. 6, q. 2, nn. 8–9 (VC 8, 48–51; ABW, 468–470). See Anselm of Canterbury, *Opera Omnia,* vol. 1, 240–242. Cf. *Ox.* 4, d. 49, q. 10, n. 12 (WDG 10, 539).

32. For the contrast between Scotus and Anselm, see Douglas Langston, "Did Scotus Embrace Anselm's Notion of Freedom?" *Medieval Philosophy and Theology* 5 (1996): 145–159. Part of this article replies to William A. Frank, "Duns Scotus's Concept of Willing Freely: What Divine Freedom Beyond Choice Teaches Us," *Franciscan Studies* 42 (1982): 68–89. See also Tobias Hoffman, "The Distinction between Nature and Will in Duns Scotus," *Archives d'histoire doctrinale et littéraire du moyen âge* 66 (1999): 209–213.

33. *Ox.* 3, d. 18, q. un., n. 19 (WDG 7.1, 407).

34. For a detailed description of the different ways in which Scotus uses these terms, see Lychetus, *Comm.* 3, d. 18, q. un., nn. 3–4 (WDG 7.1, 388).

35. ". . . sed appetitus liber non est rectus ex hoc, quod conformatur alicui inferiori recto, sed ex hoc, quod vult illud, quod vult Deus eum velle. Unde illae duae affectiones commodi, et iusti regulantur per regulam superiorem, quae est voluntas divina . . ." *R.P.* 2, d. 6, q. 2, n. 10 (WDG 11.1, 289).

36. *Ord.* 2, d. 6, q. 2, n. 8 (VC 8, 48; ABW, 468).

37. *Ox.* 4, d. 46, q. 1, n. 7 (ABW, 246; WDG 10, 252).

38. *Ox.* 3, d. 26, q. un., n. 17 (ABW, 178; WDG 7.2, 635).

39. Adams ("Duns Scotus," 844–845) and Boler ("Transcending the Natural," 115–116) both argue that the two *affectiones* are not necessary conditions of freedom. Boler argues further that they are not sufficient conditions. Their views have been adequately addressed by Sukjae Lee, "Scotus on the Will: The Rational Power and the Dual Affections," *Vivarium* 36 (1998): 40–54. Cf. Thomas Williams, "The Libertarian Foundations of Scotus's Moral Philosophy," *The Thomist* 62 (1998): 198–199; Langston, "Anselm's Notion," 156–158.

40. *Ord.* 2, d. 39, q. 2, n. 5 (VC 8, 463; ABW, 202). For the distinction between rational and natural appetite, and its connection to Thomas's understanding of the will as a rational appetite, see Boler, "Transcending the Natural," 116; Williams, "How

Scotus," 426–427; idem, "Libertarian Foundations," 197–200 . One problem with the tendency to identify the *affectio commodi* with the will as described by Thomas is that Thomas thinks that the will is able to will the *bonum in se* as well as the *bonum sibi*.

41. For example, see Wolter, "Native Freedom," 152–153;

42. Williams, "How Scotus," 430–437.

43. *Ord.* 2, d. 6, q. 2, n. 12 (VC 8, 56; ABW, 476). For the distinction between the *bonum sibi* and the *bonum in se*, see Boler, "Moral Psychology," 35–38; Lee, "Scotus on the Will," 43–44.

44. *Ox.* 4, d. 49, q. 10, n. 12 (WDG 10, 539).

45. *R.P.* 2, d. 6, q. 2, n. 6 (WDG 11.1, 288).

46. *R.P.* 4, d. 39, q. 4, n. 2 (WDG 11.2, 900). For a discussion and relevant texts, see Minges, *Ioannes Duns Scoti,* vol. 1, 361–366.

47. *Ord.* 2, d. 6, q. 2, n. 3 (VC 8, 39–40; ABW, 462). See also *R.P.* 2, d. 6, q. 2, n. 4 (WDG 11.1, 288); *R.P.* 4, d. 39, q. 4, n. 2 (WDG 11.2, 900).

48. *Ord.* 2, d. 6, q. 2, n. 4 (VC 8, 41–42; ABW, 462–464). Cf. *R.P.* 3, d. 7, q. 3, n. 24 (WDG 11.1, 295–296).

49. *R.P.* 2, d. 22, q. un., n. 2 (WDG 11.1, 361). For the connection between this passage and Scotus's mild conception of original sin, see Norman Powell Williams, *The Ideas of the Fall and of Original Sin: A Historical and Critical Study* (London: Longmans, Green, 1938), 410.

50. "Nec est verisimile quod aliquod aliud a se nimis intense dilexerit actu amicitiae: tum quia inclinatio naturalis magis inclinavit ad se quam ad aliquid aliud creatum sic amandum,—tum quia non videtur quod aliquid aliud a se 'creatum' sic intellexerit sicut se, tum quia amicitia fundatur super unitatem, et etiam 'amicabilia ad alterum' procedunt ex amicabilibus ad se ipsum . . . Et hoc est quod dicit Augustinus, XIV *De civitate dei,* cap. ultimo: 'Duo amores fecerunt duas civitates: civitatem Dei amor Dei usque ad contemptum sui, et civitatem diaboli amor sui usque ad contemptum Dei.'" *Ord.* 2, d. 6, q. 2, n. 4 (VC 8, 41–42; ABW, 464). Cf. Aristotle, *Eth. Nic.* 8.4.1056b33–35; 9.41166b30–31; Augustine, *De civ. dei* 14.28 (CCL 40.2, 56).

51. ". . . quia pensatis rationibus bonitatis et unitatis, quae sunt rationes dilectionis et primo bonum infinitum in quo est perfectissimi ratio bonitatis, occurit in seipso alia ratio maxima, scilicet unitas, quae est perfecta identitas. Quilibet enim naturaliter inclinatur ad dilectionem sui post bonum infinitum. Inclinatio naturalis est semper recta . . ." *Ox.* 3, d. 29, q. un., n. 3 (ABW, 456; WDG 7.2, 667).

52. ". . . inclinatio naturalis duplex est: una ad commodum, alia ad iustum, quarum utraque est perfectio voluntatis liberae: tamen una inclinatio magis dicitur naturalis, quam alia: quia immediatius consequitur naturam, ut distinguitur contra libertatem, et illa est inclinatio ad commodum, quin sufficiat ad nolle oppositum, et ad tristitiam de opposito: potest tamen esse inclinatio naturalis, et ad iustum, quae non sufficit ad nolle liberum, sive ad tristitiam de opposito." *Ox.* 3, d. 15, q. un., nn. 15, 22, 24 (WDG 7.1, 339–346). For the tension between this passage and Scotus's thought as a whole, see Lychetus *Comm.,* loc. cit., n. 2 (WDG 7.2, 347).

53. "... peccatum est contra naturam, hoc est contra illum actum, qui natus est elici concorditer, et conformiter inclinationi naturali ..." *Ord.* 2, d. 7, q. un., n. 26 (VC 8, 115). Richard Cross writes: "Scotus's account of sin is wholly legal or forensic. Human sinfulness, according to Scotus, is not some kind of real quality inhering in the sinner" (*John Duns Scotus,* 95). As we shall see, Scotus is clear that sin is a lack of perfection; although a lack is not a real quality, neither is it just a relation between the agent and God.

54. "... accipiendo *naturalem inclinationem* pro dictamine naturali: et sic omnis peccans elicit actum contra rectum dictamen naturale rationis. Vel si volumus dicere quod sit contra inclinationem naturalem, potest dici sic, quod natura magis inclinatur ad actum perfectum, quam imperfectum; actus autem perfecte circunstantionatus est perfectior actu carente debitis circunstantiis. Vel tertio dici potest, quod ideo peccatum est contra naturam quia dicit tantum carentiam et priuationem: natura autem inclinatur ad bonum absolute, et ad actum, quo attingit illud bonum." Lychetus *Comm.* 2, d. 7, q. un., n. 8 (WDG 6.2, 581).

55. My interpretation most closely corresponds to that of Walter Hoeres, "Naturtendenz und Freiheit nach Duns Scotus," *Salzburger Jahrbuch für Philosophie und Psychologie* 2 (1958): 95–134. Nevertheless, Hoeres emphasizes too closely the connection between the good as convertible with being and the good as the end. Scotus himself distinguishes between these two uses of the word "good." Cf. *Lect.* 1, d. 1, p. 1, q. 2 (VC 16, 81–82).

56. There is an excellent treatment in Fernand Guimet, "Conformité à la droite raison et possibilité surnaturelle de la charité," in *De doctrina Ioannis Duns Scoti: Acta Congressus Scotistici Internationalis,* Studia scholastica-Scotistica, 3 (Rome: Societas Internationalis Scotistica, 1968), 549–557. See also Gilson, *Dun Scot,* 593–602, Hoeres, "Naturtendenz und Freiheit nach Duns Scotus," 119; Möhle, *Ethik als scientia practica,* 386.

57. *Ord.* 1, d. 3, p. 1, q. 3 (VC 3, 68–123); *Lect.* 1, d. 3, p. 1, q. 2, nn. 88–104 (VC 16, 258–264); Quod 14, art. 2, nn. 11–13 (ed. Alluntis, 510–516).

58. Renault, "Felicité humaine," 971–974.

59. *R.P.* 3, d. 27, q. un. (WDG 11.1, 531).

60. *Ord.* 1, d. 1, p. 1, q. 2, n. 60 (VC. 2, 44).

61. "... inter volibilia aliquid est propter se volendum; quia si quodlibet propter aliud, erit processus in infinitum: nullum etiam erit supremum, quia propter aliud volendum, minus est volendum, quam aliud propter quod est volendum, ex *primo Poster.*" *Ox.*, d. 49, q. 2, n. 20 (WDG 10, 345). Aristotle, *An. Post.* 1.2.72a29–30.

62. *Ord.* 1, d. 1, p. 1, q. 2, n. 31 (VC 2, 21). For the *uti/frui* distinction see Ingham, "Scotus and the Moral Order," 137.

63. *Ox.* d. 49, q. 2, n. 22 (WDG 10, 349).

64. The word "*volibile*" appears in only one authentic work of Thomas, the *In epistolam I ad Timotheum* cap. 2, lect. 1, n. 62, in *Super Epistolas S. Pauli Lectura,* ed. Raphael Cai, 8th ed., 2 vols. (Turin: Marietti, 1953), vol. 2, 225: "Sic in Deo salus omnium hominum secundum se considerata habet rationem ut sit volibilis ..." The

word is used twice in a work attributed to Thomas, the *De dilectione dei et proximi*, 2.3: "Verum inter utilia ordo est: nam quaedam secundum se magis, quaedam minus ad finem dirigent, et ideo secundum se quaedam magis, quaedam minus utilia et volibilia sunt. Unde sicut in scibilibus, secundum Aristotelem, plurima propter se nolumus quidam scire, propter aliud autem volumus, ut per haec aliquid aliud cognosceamus: ita et in volibilibus aliqua non propter se sed propter aliud volumus." (Parma 17, 269). This use of the term *"volibilia"* resembles closely Scotus's use of the term in the passage quoted above in note 61. This treatise is known to have been written by Helvicus Teutonicus, but it is not clear whether this Helvicus wrote in the thirteenth or the fourteenth century. See Thomas Kaeppeli, *Scriptores Ordinis Praedicatorum Medii Aevi,* (Rome: Istituto Storico Domenicano, 1975), vol. 2, 179–180.

65. For the commonly accepted connection between the *appetibile* and the will, see F. Ruello, "Les fondements de la liberté humaine selon Jacques de Viterbe O.E.S.A. Disputatio Prima de Quolibet, q. VII (1293)," *Augustiniana* 24 (1974): 289. The influential passage of Aristotle is *De anima* 3.433b10–15. For the connection between *appetibile* and *volibile*, see Hoeres, "Naturtendenz und Freiheit," 96. Cf. Thomas Aquinas, *Sentencia libri de anima,* loc. cit.: "Dicit ergo primo quod, si movencia considerantur formaliter et secundum speciem, *unum erit movens,* scilicet *appetibile* uel *appetitiuum,* quia inter omnia *primum* mouens est *appetibile. . ."* (Leonine 45.1, 247).

66. For a discussion of this issue as it relates to translating Anselm, see Hopkins, *Companion to Anselm,* 141–142.

67. *Ox.* 4, d. 49, q. 2, n. 24 (WDG 10, 350).

68. For the connection between *frui* and the *bonum infinitum,* see *Lect.* 1, d. 1, p. 1, q. 2, n. 34 (VC 16, 71): ". . . ubi est bonum infinitum, ibi est obiectum fruibile . . . " Cf. *Lect.* 2, d. 2, p. 1, q. 1, n. 10 (VC 16, 65).

69. *Ox.* 49, q. 8, n. 4 (WDG 10, 498). For Scotus's frequent use of *quiescere,* see Guimet, "Conformité," 571–572. For the theme of color and sight, see Guimet, "Conformité," 551–552, note 21.

70. ". . . quilibet enim naturaliter diligit plus esse suum quam esse alterius cuius non est pars vel effectus; autem nihil est ipsius *b* nec ut pars nec ut effectus; ergo plus diligit *a* se naturaliter quam ipsum *b*." *Ord.* 2, d. 2, p. 1, q. 3, n. 169 (VC 2, 228–229).

71. *Ord.* 1, d. 2, p. 1, q. 3, n. 171 (VC 2, 230).

72. "Perfectum etiam excludit defectum, qui est carentia eius, quod natum est inesse." *Ox.* d. 49, q. 2, n. 26 (WDG 10, 354). Cf. n. 32 (WDG 10, 357): ". . . citra quam ipsum est imperfectum priuative, quia natum est recipere ulteriorem, sed ultima sui habita, si non est simpliciter ultima, remaneat imperfectum negative, quia carens perfectione, licet non nata recipi in ipso."

73. *Ord.* 1, d. 1, p. 3, q. 5, n. 179 (VC 2, 117–118). Cf. *Lect.* 1, d. 1, p. 3, q. 5 (VC 16, 107). Augustine, *De civ. dei* 14.28 (CCL 40.2, 56); *De Gen. ad litt.* 11.15.20 (CCL 28.2, 347–348).

74. Cf. Thomas Aquinas, *S.T.,* I–II, q. 94, a. 2.

75. *Ox.* 3, d. 37, q. un., n. 5 (ABW, 276; WDG 7.2, 898); *R.P.* 4, d. 17, q. un., n. 3–4 (WDG 11.2, 742–743). See Gilson, *Duns Scot,* 609–624; Minges, *Ioannes Duns*

Scoti, vol. 1, 403–417; Möhle, *Ethik als scientia practica,* 330–367; Prentice: 261–264; Wald, 672–674; Wolter, ABW introduction, 57–64.

76. *Ox.* 4, d. 46, q. 1, n. 10 (ABW, 250; WDG 10, 253). See also *Ox.* 3, d. 27, q. un., n. 2 (ABW, 424; WDG 7.2, 645); *R.P.* 3, d. 27, q. un., n. 3 (WDG 11.1, 531).

77. *Ox.* 4, d. 46, q. 1, n. 269 (ABW, 240; WDG 10, 238). See also *Ord.* prol., p. 5, qq. 1–2, n. 269 (VC 1, 182).

78. Anthony Hickey, *Commentaria* 4, d. 46, q. 1, n. 6 (WDG 10, 240).

79. *R.P.* 2, d. 7, q. 3, n. 34 (WDG 11.1, 298).

80. *Ord.* 2, d. 7, n. 27 (VC 8, 116). See also *Ox.* 3, d. 36, q. un., n. 12 (WDG 7.2, 800–801).

81. Cf. Lychetus, *Commentaria* 3, d. 27, q. un., n. 1 (WDG 7.2, 645).

82. *Ox.* 3, d. 27, q. un., n. 10 (ABW, 282; WDG 7.2, 907).

83. *Ox.* 4, d. 50, q. 2, n. 11 (WDG 10, 633).

84. *Ord.* prol. p. 2, q. un., n. 108 (VC 1, 70). Matt 22:37–39; Mark 12:30–31; Deut 6:5; Rom 2:15.

85. Adams, "Scotus on the Will," 849, n. 38.

86. *Ox.* 4, d. 26, q. un., n. 3 (WDG 9, 575); *Ord.* prol., p. 5, qq. 1–2, n. 362 (VC 1, 234–235). Ragland, "Scotus on the Decalogue," 76, states that there are other commands, like the command to seek health or peace, which are strictly part of the natural law. Ragland supports his view with two texts: *Quodlibet,* q. 18, n. 3 (ed. Alluntis, 633; ABW, 210; WDG 12, 475) and *Ox.* 4, d. 15, q. 2, nn. 3–4 (WDG 9, 151). The first mentions health as suitable for humans, and the second mentions peace as suitable for the community. Neither of these passages implies the position that health and peace must always be sought. For the view that only loving God is strictly speaking part of the natural law, see Prentice, "Contingent Element," 262.

87. *R.P.* 4, d. 28, q. un., n. 6 (WDG 11.2, 787).

88. Thomas Aquinas, *S.T.,* I–II, q. 100, a. 8. For the contrast between Scotus and Thomas, see Klaus Hedwig, "Das Isaak-Opfer: Über den Status des Naturgesetzes bei Thomas von Aquin, Duns Scotus und Ockham," in *Mensch und Natur im Mittelalter,* ed. Andreas Speer and Albert Zimmerman, Miscellanea Mediaevalia, 21.2 (Berlin: de Gruyter, 1992), vol. 2, 645–661; Honnefelder, "Naturrecht," passim; Möhle, *Ethik als scientia practica,* 418–423; Prentice, "Contingent Element," 278–284; Wald, "Die Bestimmung der *ratio legis,*" passim.

89. *Ox.* 3, d. 37, q. un., nn. 6–7 (ABW, 276–278; WDG 7.2, 898).

90. *Ord.* prol., p. 5, q. 2, n. 269 (VC 1, 182–183).

91. "Non enim est necessaria bonitatis in his [praeceptis] quae ibi praecipiuntur ad bonitatem finis ultimi; nec in his quae prohibentur malitia necessario avertens a fine ultimo. Quin si istud bonum non esse praeceptum, posset finis ultimi attingi et amari. Et si illud malum non esset prohibitum, staret cum illo acquisito finis ultimi." *Ox.* 3, d. 37, q. un., n. 5 (ABW, 276; WDG 7.2, 898).

92. For Scotus's rejection of the Augustinian version of original sin that was held by Henry and Thomas, see N. P. Williams, *Original Sin,* 408–419; Cross, *John Duns Scotus,* 96–100.

93. *Ord.* 2, d. 29, q. un., nn. 1, 6 (VC 8, 306, 316).

94. *R.P.* 2, d. 28, q. un., n. 3 (WDG 11.1, 376). This passage presents a challenge because Scotus is developing Henry's complicated opinion about how it is possible for free choice to avoid sin without grace. Nevertheless, Scotus expresses agreement with the principle that "ought" implies "can," except insofar as it would imply that the damned angels have the ability to act meritoriously. This brings us back to the question of whether the evil agents can will good, which is discussed in *R.P.* 2, d. 7, q. 3 (WDG 11.1, 291–298). For another statement of the principle, see *Ord.* 2, d. 28, q. un., n. 3 (VC 8, 294–295). As we have seen, Scotus distinguishes between merit and goodness, and he argues that although the damned are able to act otherwise, they in fact obstinately choose evil. The qualification of the "'ought' implies 'can'" principle is intended to explain the obstinacy of the damned, and not the influence of concupiscence on the will. In another context, Scotus uses it to argue for the natural ability to love God over self.

95. *R.P.* 2, d. 28, q. un., n. 7 (WDG 11.1, 376–377).

96. *R.P.* 2, d. 28, q. un., n. 2. (WDG 11.1, 376).

97. *Ord.* 2, d. 28, q. un., n. 8 (VC 8, 302).

98. ". . . .talis dilectio sit dispositio ad gratiam ex determinatione divinae voluntatis . . . stante isto casu, quod aliqua voluntas diligit Deum super omnia ex puris naturalibus, quod est ei praeceptum, tunc Deus offert sibi gratiam, si non acceptat, peccat mortaliter, quia tenetur eam acceptare . . . Si vero acceptat, illud peccatum vitat, quod esset non acceptando. Non potest ergo vitare hoc peccatum quod esset non acceptare gratiam, nisi illam acceptet; ergo hoc peccatum actuale non potest vitare sine gratia." Lychetus, *Comm.* 2, d. 28, q. un., n. 5 (WDG 6.2, 916). Léon Veuthey, *Jean Duns Scot: Pensée théologique* (Paris: Éditions Franciscaines, 1967), 144, seems to argue that Scotus restricts the possibility of a purely natural love of God over self to the state of nature. Veuthey argues for his position by noting that at one point Scotus argues that such love is possible *saltem ex statu naturae institutae,* in *Ox.* 3, d. 27, q. un., n. 20 (ABW, 444; WDG 7.2, 656). I would make three points. First, this phrase does not entail that there is no purely natural love of God over self in the fallen state. Second, even if there were no such natural love, the reason might simply be that God chooses to accompany love of himself with grace and not that the will is hindered by original sin. Lychetus suggests this latter possibility. Third, there are no explicit statements of Scotus's which support Veuthey's interpretation, which also seems unlikely in the context of Scotus's wider thought.

99. *R.P.* 2, d. 28, q. un., n. 10 (WDG 11.1, 377). See Gilson, *Duns Scot,* 609.

100. *Ox.* 3, d. 27, q. un., n. 14 (ABW, 436; WDG 7.2, 652). For the assumption that no one can know whether they have charity, see *Ord.* 1, d. 17, p. 1, qq. 1–2, nn. 126–127 (VC 5, 200–201).

101. For an earlier version of this argument, see Giles of Rome, 2 Sent., d. 28, q. 1, a. 4 (Venice 2, 367).

102. *Ox.* 3 , d. 27, q. un., n. 2 (ABW, 424; WDG 7.2, 644). Cf. *R.P.* d. 27, q. un., n. 3 (WDG 11.1, 531). Wolter's text does not contain a good portion of the discussion

about the formal object of the will. This omission is strange, since Wolter does include replies to arguments which are found in the omitted text. The two replies on ABW, 444–446, respond to the objections on WDG 7.2, 646, n. 4.

103. *Ox.* 3, d. 27, q. un., n. 1 (ABW, 422; WDG 7.2, 644).

104. *Ox.* 3, d. 27, q. un., n. 21 (ABW, 444; WDG 7.2, 656).

105. *Ord.* 1, d. 1, q. 17, p. 1, qq. 1–2 (VC 5, 139–231). For a discussion, see Ingham, "*Ea Quae Sunt ad Finem,*" 186–191; Möhle, *Ethik als scientia practica,* 213–222.

106. *Ord.* 1, d. 17, p. 1, qq. 1–2, n. 32 (VC 5, 152).

107. *Ord.* 1, d. 17, p. 1, qq. 1–2, n. 46 (VC 5, 156–157).

108. *Ord.,* 1, d. 17, p. 1, qq. 1–2, n. 69 (VC 5, 171).

109. *Lect.* 1, d. 17, p. 1, q. un., nn. 76–87 (VC 17, 205–209).

110. *Ord.* 1, d. 17, p. 1, qq. 1–2, n. 81 (VC 5, 225). The following passage is a discussion of the influence of charity on the will according to the third way a habit can be involved in an act, which is as a partial cause: ". . . sicut enim voluntas inferior ad suam caritatem, sic et superior voluntas ad caritatem quam nata est recipere secundum proportionem geometricam, et extrema istius proportionis sunt inaequalia." *Lect.* 1, d. 17, p. 1, q. un., n. 80 (VC 17, 207). Cf. *Ox.* 3, d. 27, q. un., n. 19 (ABW, 442; WDG 7.2, 655).

111. My example is influenced by Wolter, introduction, ABW, 93–94.

112. *Ox.* 3, d. 23, q. un., n. 14 (WDG 7.1, 469; cf. 473, n. 19).

113. *Ox.* 3, d. 27, q. un., n. 1 (ABW, 424; WDG 7.2, 644).

114. *Ox.,* 3, d. 27, q. un., n. 21 (ABW, 444; WDG 7.2, 656).

115. *R.P.* 3, d. 27, q. un., n. 18–19 (WDG 11.1, 534). I assume that although God is the *bonum privatum sibi,* he is still loved as the *bonum in se.* This passage could be clearer.

116. *Quodlibet,* q. 17, n. 8 (ed. Alluntis, 621; WDG 12, 465). Scotus is reluctant to admit that there is a specific difference between the two acts. For Scotus's understanding of merit, see Cross, *John Duns Scotus,* 103–107.

117. *Ord.* 1, d. 17, p. 1, qq. 1–2 (VC 5, 217), n. 164. See also *R.P.* d. 17, q. 2, n. 6 (WDG 11.1, 97). For Scotus's use of the distinction between the absolute and ordained powers of God, see especially Mary Anne Pernoud, "The Theory of the *Potentia Dei* according to Aquinas, Scotus, and Ockham," *Antonianum* 47 (1972): 69–95. See also Möhle, *Ethik als scientia practica,* 424–425.

118. *Lect.* 1, d. 17, p. 1, q. un., n. 89 (VC 17, 209). Cf. *Quodlibet,* q. 17, n. 3 (ed. Alluntis, 613–614; WDG 12, 461); cf. *Ord.* 1, d. 17, p. 1, qq. 1–2, n. 142 (VC 5, 207–208).

119. For Scotus's opposition to Thomas's way of distinguishing between charity and natural love, see Guimet, "Conformité," 572–575.

120. *Ox.* 3, d. 27, q. un., n. 3 (WDG 7.2, 645–646). This passage is not included in ABW.

121. *R.P.* 3, d. 27, q. un., nn. 4, 6 (WDG 11.1, 531, 532).

122. *Ox.* 3, d. 27, q. un., n. 5 (WDG 7.2, 646).

123. *R.P.* 3, d. 27, q. un., n. 4 (WDG 11.1, 531).

124. *Ox.* 3, d. 26, q. un., n. 18 (ABW, 178–180; WDG 7.2, 635).

125. *Ox.* 3, d. 27, q. un., n. 6 (WDG 7.2, 646). Scotus may have in mind *Metaph.* 12.8. His commentary on the work finishes before this passage.

126. ". . . dico quod ratio obiectiva actus caritatis vel habitus potest intelligi tripliciter: vel prima, quae secundum se accepta nata est esse ratio terminandi per se; vel secunda, quae est aliqua ratio praecedens aliquem actum propter quam natus est actus elici circa obiectum; vel tertia, quae comitat ipsum actum, immo quasi consequitur ipsum actum elicitum." *Ox.* 3, d. 27, q. un., n. 7. (ABW, 426; WDG, 7.2, 647).

127. *Ox.* 3., d. 27, q. un., n. 7 (ABW, 426; WDG 7.2, 648).

128. "Et in isto secundo gradu amibilitatis potest poni omne illud in quo ratio amibilitatis potest demonstrare se, sive creando sive reparando sive disponendo ad beatificandum, ita quod inter haec non sit distinctio, nec caritas magis respiciat ultimam, nec secundum rationem magis quam primam, sed coniciuntur omnes sicut rationes quasdam, non solum boni honesti sed boni communicativi et amantis, et quia amantis, ideo digni redamari, iuxta illud de Ioanne, 'Diligamus Deum quoniam ille prior dilexit nos.'" *Ox.* 3., d. 27, q. un., n. 8 (ABW, 428; WDG, 648). See 1 Jn 4:19.

129. *Ox.* 3, d. 27, q. un., n. 9 (ABW, 428; WDG 7.2, 648).

130. *Ox.* 3, d. 27, q. un., n. 10 (ABW, 430; WDG 7.2, 650).

131. *R.P.* 3, d. 27, q. un., n. 11 (WDG 11.1, 533).

132. Godfrey is mentioned by the editors in the *scholium* on WDG 7.2, 649, and in the margin on WDG 7.2, 650.

133. *Ox.* 3, d. 27, q. un., n. 11 (ABW, 432; WDG 7.2, 650). Augustine, *De trinitate* 13.6(9) (CCL 50A, 393).

134. *Ox.* 3, d. 27, q. un., n. 11 (ABW, 430–432; WDG 7.2, 650).

135. "Impossibile enim est aquam [ABW: aqua] movere se ad sursum propter quodcumque bonum universi, quia ex quo habet formam naturalem, quae determinatur est ad actionem unam . . . Ipsa ergo aqua non se movet sursum, sed tantum movetur sic sursum ab aliquo extrinseco movente . . . Pars ergo ista non amat bonum totius, nec ex amore salvat totum, sed totum sive virtus regitiva in toto . . . movet quamlibet partem universi, sicut congruit bene esse totius." *Ox.* 3, d. 27, q. un., n. 12 (ABW, 432; WDG 7.2, 651).

136. Cf. Thomas Aquinas, *S.T.,* I, q. 105, a. 6, ad 1.

137. Thomas Aquinas, *S.T.,* I, 19, a. 9.

138. Thomas Aquinas, *S.T.,* I, q. 23, aa. 4, 6. For the connection between physical and moral corruptibility, see Jean-Hervé Nicolas, "La permission du péché," *Revue Thomiste* 60 (1960): 5–37; 185–206; 509–546.

139. ". . . scilicet ratio quaecumque arguit quod Deus magis diligit bonum esse universi, vel etiam bene esse eius, quam bene esse unius partis; et magis diligit bene esse partis principalis quam bene esse partis minus principalis . . . considerata secundum inclinationem suam propriam, numquam exponit se ad non esse pro alio." *Ox.* 3, d. 27, q. un., n. 12 (ABW, 432–434; WDG 7.2, 651).

140. *Ox.* 3, d. 27, q. un., nn. 11–12 (ABW, 432–434; WDG 7.2, 650–651).

141. Scotus generally assumes that love is deliberative: "... sed bruta non habent amorem, quia nec voluntatem, nec inhaerunt alicui rei propter se, sed propter bonum eorum ..." *Ord.* 1, d. 1, p. 3, q. 4, n. 167 (VC 2, 112).

142. For Scotus's conception of the hierarchy of being and essential order, see R. Prentice, *The Basic Quidditive Metaphysics of Duns Scotus as Seen in His "De Primo Principio,"* Spicilegium Pontificii Athenaei Antoniani, 16 (Rome: Ed. Antonianum, 1970), passim, but especially 66–114; Edward P. Mahoney, "Metaphysical Foundations of the Hierarchy of Being according to Some Late Medieval and Renaissance Philosophers," in *Philosophies of Existence: Ancient and Medieval,* ed. Parviz Morewedge (New York: Fordham Unversity Press, 1982), 179–182; Allan B. Wolter, *The Transcendentals and Their Function in the Metaphysics of Duns Scotus,* The Catholic University of America Philosophical Series, 96 (Washington, D.C.: The Catholic University of America Press, 1946), 140–161, 170–173; Gilson, *Duns Scot,* 181–183. For the historical background, see Mahoney, "Duns Scotus and Medieval Discussions of Metaphysical Hierarchy: The Background of Scotus's 'Essential Order' in Henry of Ghent, Godfrey of Fontaines, and James of Viterbo," in *Via Scoti: Methodologica ad mentem Joannis Duns Scoti 1993. Atti del Congresso Scotistico Internazionale Roma, 9–11 Marzo 1993,* ed. Leonardo Sileo, Studia scholastico-Scotistica, 5 (Rome: Edizioni Antonianum, 1995), vol. 1, 359–374.

143. *Ox.* 3, d. 27, q. un., n. 13 (ABW, 434; WDG 7.2, 652). The word "*habitus*" does not appear in Wadding's text.

144. "... ordo naturae, siue essentialis, necessario includit imperfectionem in altero extremorum, scilicet in posteriori ..." *Quodlibet,* q. 4, n. 3 (ed. Alluntis, 126–127; WDG 12, 89). See Alluntis and Wolter, *God and Creatures,* 85, note 5, and their glossary entry for "essential order" on 503.

145. Prentice, *Quidditative Metaphysics,* 100–102, 109–110.

146. *Tractatus de primo principio,* 2nd ed., ed. and trans. Allan B. Wolter (Chicago: Franciscan Herald Press, 1966), cap. 2, 14–39. For the structure of the argument and its connection to essential order, see Wolter's commentary, 173–223.

147. *TPP* 2.48 (ed. Wolter, 35). For the four causes and essential order, see especially Prentice, *Quidditive Metaphysics,* 110–114.

148. *TPP* 2.49–50 (ed. Wolter, p. 35). Aristotle, *Ph.* 2.2.194a21–b9. .

149. *Ox.* 4, d. 49, q. 4, n. 5 (WDG 10, 382); *Ord.* 1, d. 1, p. 1, q. 2, n. 27 (VC 2, 19).

150. *R.P.* 3, d. 27, q. un., n. 12. (WDG 11.1, 533).

151. *R.P.* 3, d. 27, q. un., n. 3 (WDG 11.1, 531).

152. *Ox.* 3, d. 27, q. un., n. 13 (ABW, 436; WDG 7.2, 652). Cf. *Ox.* 4, d. 50, q. 2, n. 11 (WDG 10, 633).

153. *R.P.* 4, d. 17, q. un., n. 7 (WDG 11.2, 743).

154. See supra, n. 29.

155. *Ox.* 3, d. 27, q. un., n. 14 (ABW, 436; WDG 7.2, 652).

156. *Ox.* 4, d. 50, q. 2, n. 11 (WDG 10, 633).

157. *Ox.* 3, d. 27, q. un., n. 1 (ABW, 422; WDG 7.2, 624). Aristotle, *Eth. Nic.* 8.7.159a4–8.

158. ". . . nulla virtus movet ad actum impossibilem habiti; sed impossibile est nos amare Deum super omnia. Quod probatur dupliciter: quia ex IX *Ethicorum,* c. 9, amicabilia ad alterum mensurantur ex his, quae sunt ad seipsum; mensuratum autem non excedit mensuram in mensuris acceptis cum perfectione; ergo amicitia quae est ad seipsum excedit illam quae est ad alterum. Secundo, quia amicitia fundatur super unitatem; impossibile est aliquid esse amanti aeque unum sibi." *Ox.* 3, d. 27, q. un., n. 1 (ABW, 422; WDG 7.2, 624). Arist., *Nic. Ethic.* 9.4.1166a1–25; 9.8.1168b29–1169b1; 9.10.1170b6–99.

159. *Ox.* 3, d. 27, q. un., nn. 19–20 (ABW, 442–444; WDG 7.2, 656).

160. *Ox.* 3, d. 27, q. un., n. 20 (ABW, 444; WDG 7.2, 656).

161. *Ox.* 4, d. 50, q. 6, n. 8 (WDG 10, 646).

162. ". . . dilectio fundatur in unitate." *Ox.* 4, d. 50, q. 6, n. 9 (WDG 10, 646).

163. *Ox.* 3, d. 27, q. un., n. 4 (WDG 7.2, 646).

164. *R.P.* 3, d. 27, q. un., n. 6 (WDG 11.1, 532).

165. *Ox.* 3, d. 27, q. un., n. 22 (ABW, 446; WDG 7.2, 657).

166. *Ox.* 3, d. 27, q. un. n. 9 (WDG 11.1, 532).

167. For a description of this tendency, see MacIntyre, *Dependent Rational Animals,* 1–9.

168. "Nominalism stirred up a veritable revolution in the moral world and its ideological structures. Nothing would ever be the same again." Servais Pinckaers, *The Sources of Christian Ethics,* trans. Mary Thomas Noble (Washington, D.C.: The Catholic University of America Press, 1995), 253. For a discussion of Nominalism and its influence, see 240–253; 327–353. For Ockham's views on the connection between ethics and human happiness, see also my "William of Ockham as a Divine Command Theorist," *Religious Studies* 41 (2005): 1–22.

169. William of Ockham, *Quaestiones Variae,* q. 8, art. 2, in William of Ockham, *Opera Theologica,* 10 vols. (St. Bonaventure, N.Y.: Franciscan Institute, 1967–88), vol. 8, 442–446.

170. Ockham, *Reportata* 4, q. 16 (OT 7, 351).

Conclusion

1. For an explanation of why most angels and natural things achieve their last end, whereas humans do not, see Thomas Aquinas, *S.T.,* I, q. 63, a. 9, ad 1; I, q. 23, a. 7, ad 3.

2. An argument for this position can be found in Kevin L. Flannery, *Acts Amid Precepts: The Aristotelian Logical Structure of Thomas Aquinas's Moral Theory* (Washington, D.C.: The Catholic University of America Press, 2001), 111–143.

3. For an argument that Thomas does not subscribe to this understanding of volition, see Anthony Kenny, *Aquinas on Mind* (London: Routledge, 1993), 75–88.

4. B. Williams, *Ethics,* 53

5. Cf. B. Williams, *Ethics,* 44.

6. Nagel, *Possibility of Altruism,* passim.

7. For this reason, Vernon J. Bourke denies that Aristotle and Thomas are eudaimonists strictly speaking. See his *Ethics: A Textbook in Moral Philosophy* (New York: Macmillan, 1966), 36.

8. Richard Kraut, "Egoism and Altruism," in *The Routledge Encyclopedia of Philosophy,* 10 vols, ed. Edward Craig (New York: Routledge, 1998), vol. 3, 246–248.

9. Kraut, *Human Good,* 86, n. 14.

10. This language is taken from John M. Rist, *Real Ethics: Reconsidering the Foundations of Morality* (Cambridge: Cambridge University Press, 2002), 140–177. For similar problems with contemporary "Thomistic" natural law theory, see Ernest L. Fortin, "The New Rights Theory and Natural Law," *Review of Politics* 44 (1982): 590–612; Ralph McInerny, *Aquinas on Human Action: A Theory of Practice* (Washington, D.C.: The Catholic University of America Press, 1992), 184–206; Russell Hittinger, *A Critique of the New Natural Law Theory* (Notre Dame, Ind.: University of Notre Dame Press, 1987).

11. MacIntyre, *Dependent Rational Animals,* 129–146.

12. De Koninck, "In Defence," 73–78.

13. De Koninck, "In Defence," 92–97.

Bibliography

Primary Works

Albert the Great. *Opera Omnia.* Edited by Bernhard Geyer and Wilheim Kubel. Monasterium Westfalorum: Aschendorff, 1951–.

———. *Opera Omnia.* Edited by Auguste Borgnet. 38 vols. Paris: Vivès, 1890–1899.

Alexander of Hales. *Summa Theologica.* 3 vols. Quaracchi: Collegium S. Bonaventurae, 1924–1948.

Anselm of Canterbury. *Opera Omnia.* Edited by Francis Sales Schmitt. 6 vols. Seckau and Edinburgh: 1938–1961.

Aristotle. *Ethica Nicomachea.* Translated by Robert Grosseteste. Edited by René Antonin Gauthier. *Aristoteles Latinus,* vol. 26, fasc. 1–3. Corpus philosophorum Medii Aevi. Leiden: Brill; Brusssels: Desclée, 1972–1974.

———. *Ethica Nicomachea.* Translated by Hermmanicus Germanicus. In *Aristotelis opera cum Averrois comentariis.* Vol. 3. Venice: Junctas, 1562; repr. Frankfurt am Main: Minerva, 1962.

———. *Nicomachean Ethics.* Loeb Classical Library. Cambridge, Mass.: Harvard University Press, 1926.

———. *Nicomachean Ethics.* Translated by Terence Irwin. Indianapolis, Ind.: Hackett, 1985.

———. *Eudemian Ethics.* 2nd edition. Translated by Michael Woods with a commentary. Oxford: Clarendon Press, 1992.

———. *Metaphysics.* Translated by W. D. Ross. *The Basic Works of Aristotle.* New York: Random House, 1941.

Aubry of Reims. *Philosophia.* Edited by René Antonin Gauthier. In "Notes sur Siger de Brabant: II. Siger en 1272–1275, Aubry de Reims et la Scission des Normands." *Revue de sciences philosophiques et théologiques* 68 (1984): 29–48.

Augustine of Hippo. *De civitate dei.* Edited by Bernard Dombart and Alphonsus Kalb. Corpus Christianorum. Series Latina, vols. 47–48. Turnhout: Brepols, 1955.

———. *Confessiones.* Edited by Lucas Verheijen. Corpus Christianorum. Series Latina, vol. 27. Turnhout: Brepols, 1983.

———. *De doctrina Christiana.* Edited by Joseph Martin. Corpus Christianorum. Series Latina, vol. 32 Turnhout: Brepols, 1962.

———. *Enarrationes in Psalmos.* Edited by Eligius D. Dekker and Joannes Fraipont. Corpus Christianorum. Series Latina, vols. 38–40. Turnhout: Brepols, 1956.

———. *De gratia et libero arbitrio liber unus.* Edited by Jacques-Paul Migne. Patrologia Latina, vol. 44.

———. *De libero arbitrio.* Edited by W. M. Green. Corpus Christianorum. Series Latina, vol. 29. Turnhout: Brepols, 1970.

———. *De moribus ecclesiae catholicae.* Edited by Johannes B. Bauer. Corpus Scriptorum Ecclesiasticorum Latinorum, 90. Vienna: Hoelder-Pichler-Tempsky, 1992.

———. *De peccatorum meritis et remissione.* Edited by Karl F. Urba and Joseph Zycha. Corpus Scriptorum Ecclesiasticorum Latinorum, 60. Vienna: Tempsky; Leipzig: Freytag, 1913.

———. *De perfectione justitiae hominis.* Edited by Karl F. Urba and Joseph Zycha. Corpus Scriptorum Ecclesiasticorum Latinorum, 42. Vienna: Tempsky, 1902.

———. *Sermones de tempore.* Edited by Jacques-Paul Migne. Patrologia Latina, 38.

———. *Sermones de vetere testamento.* Edited by Cyril Lambot. Corpus Christianorum. Series Latina, vol. 41. Turnhout: Brepols, 1961.

———. *De trinitate.* Edited by W. J. Mountain. Corpus Christianorum. Series Latina, vols. 50/50A. Turnhout: Brepols, 1983.

Averroes. *Aristotelis opera cum Averrois commentariis.* 9 vols. Venice: Junctas, 1562–1574; repr. Frankfurt am Main: Minerva, 1962.

Bañez, Domingo. *Comentarios inéditos a la prima secundae de Santo Tomàs.* 3 vols. Edited by Vincente Beltrán de Heredia. Madrid: 1942–1948.

Bernard of Clairvaux. *Sancti Bernardi Opera Omnia.* 8 vols. Edited by Jean Leclerq, Charles H. Talbot and H. M. Rochais. Rome: Editiones Cistercienses, 1957–1980.

Boethius of Dacia. *Opuscula: De aeternitate mundi, De summo bono, De somniis.* Edited by Nicolaus Georgius Green-Pedersen. Corpus Philosophorum Danicorum Medii Aevi, 6.2. Copenhagen: Gad, 1976.

Bonaventure of Bagnorea. *Opera Omnia.* 10 vols. Quarachi: Collegium S. Bonaventurae, 1882–1902.

Capreolus, Johannes. *Defensiones theologiae divi Thomae Aquinatis.* Edited by Ceslaus Paban and Thomas Pègues. Tours: Alfred Cattier, 1900–1907; repr. Frankfurt am Main: Minerva, 1967.

Cicero. *Laelius de amicitia.* Edited by Robert Combès. Paris: Société d'Édition 'Les Belles Lettres', 1971.

Pseudo-Dionysius the Areopagite. *De divinis nominibus.* Edited by Beate Regina Suchla. *Corpus Dionysiacum,* 1. Patristische Texte und Studien, 33. Berlin: de Gruyter, 1990.

———. *Dionysiaca.* 2 vols. Edited by Philippe Chevalier. Paris: Desclée, 1937.

Durandus of Saint-Pourçain. *In Petri Lombardi Sententias Theologicas Commentariorum libri IIII.* 2 vols. Venice: Typographica Guerrae, 1571; repr. Ridgewood, N.J.: Gregg Press, 1964.

Eustratius. *In Ethicam Nicomacheam.* In *The Greek Commentaries on the Nicomachean Ethics in the Latin Translation of Robert Grosseteste, Bishop of Lincoln.* Edited by H. P. F. Mercken. Corpus Latinum Commentariorum in Aristotelem Graecorum, 6.1. Leiden: Brill, 1973.

Giles of Rome. *Quodlibeta*. Louvain, 1642; repr. Frankfurt am Main: Minerva, 1966.

———. *In primum librum sententiarum*. Venice, 1521: repr. Frankfurt am Main: Minerva, 1968.

———. *In secundum librum sententiarum*. Venice: Zilettus, 1581; repr. Frankfurt am Main: Minerva, 1968.

Godfrey of Fontaines. *Les quatre premiers quodlibets*. Edited by Maurice de Wulf and Alfred Pelzer. Les Philosophes Belges, 2. Louvain: Institut Supérieur de Philosophie, 1904.

———. *Les quodlibets cinq, six, et sept*. Edited by Maurice de Wulf and Jean Hoffmans. Les Philosophes Belges, 3. Louvain: Institut Supérieur de Philosophie, 1914.

———. *Le huitième quodlibet*. Edited by Jean Hoffmans. Les Philosophes Belges, 4.1 Louvain: Institut Supérieur de Philosophie, 1924.

———. *Le neuvième quodlibet*. Edited by Jean Hoffmans. Les Philosophes Belges, 4.2. Louvain: Institut Supérieur de Philosophie, 1928.

———. *Le dixième quodlibet*. Edited by Jean Hoffmans. Les Philosophes Belges, 4.3. Louvain: Institut Supérieur de Philosophie, 1931.

———. *Les quodlibets onze-douze*. Edited by Jean Hoffmans. Les Philosophes Belges, 5.1–2. Louvain: Institut Supérieur de Philosophie, 1932.

———. *Les quodlibets treize et quatorze*. Edited by Jean Hoffmans. Les Philosophes Belges, 5.3–4. Louvain: Institut Supérieur de Philosophie, 1935.

———. *Le quodlibet XV et trois questions ordinaires*. Edited by Odon Lottin. Les Philosophes Belges, 14. Louvain: Institut Supérieur de Philosophie, 1937.

———. *Quaestiones disputatae 1, 7, 8, 13, 15*. Edited by Bernhard Neumann. In idem, *Der Mensch und die himmlische Seligkeit nach der Lehre Gottfrieds von Fontaines*, 152–156. Limburg: Lahn, 1958.

———. *Quaestiones disputatae 4, 5*. Edited by Odon Lottin. In idem, *Psychologie et morale au XIIe and XIIIe siècles*. Vol. 4, 581–588; 591–597. Louvain: Abbaye du Mont César; Gembloux: Duculot, 1954.

———. *Quaestio disputata 11*. Edited by Odon Lottin. In idem, *Psychologie et morale au XIIe and XIIIe siècles*. Vol. 3.2, 497–507. Louvain: Abbaye du Mont César; Gembloux: Duculot, 1949.

———. *Quaestio disputata 15*. Edited by Joseph Koch. In *Durandi de S. Porciano O.P. Tractatus de habitibus*, 59–69. Münster: Aschendorff, 1930.

———. *Quaestio disputata 17*. Edited by Johannes Gründel. In idem, *Die Lehre von dem Umständen der Menschlingen Handlung im Mittelalter*. 655–660. Beiträge zur Geschichte der Philosophie und Theologie des Mittelalters, Bd. 39, Hft. 5. Münster: Aschendorff, 1963.

———. *Quaestio disputata 19*. Edited by Odon Lottin. In idem, "Les vertus morales acquises sont-elles de vraies vertus? La réponse de théologiens de saint Thomas à Pierre Auriol." *Recherches de Théologie ancienne et médiévale* 21 (1954): 114–122.

———. *Sermon*. Edited by P. Tihon. "Le sermon de Godefroid de Fontaines pour le deuxième dimanche après l'Épiphanie." *Recherches de Théologie ancienne et médiévale* 43 (1965): 42–53.

Grosseteste, Robert. "Cur Deus Homo." Edited by Servais Gieben. *Collectanea Franciscana* 37 (1967): 101–141.

———. *The Greek Commentaries on the Nicomachean Ethics of Aristotle in the Latin Translation of Robert Grosseteste, Bishop of Lincoln.* Edited by H. P. F. Mercken, Corpus Latinum Commentariorum in Aristotelem Graecorum, 6.1, 3. Leiden: Brill, 1973, 1991.

———. *Aristoteles over der vriendschap: Boeken VIII en IX van de Nicomachische Ethiek met de commentaren van Aspasius en Michaël in de Latijnse vertaling van Grosseteste.* Edited by Wilfred Stinissen. Verhandelingen van de Koninklijke Vlaamse Academie voor Wetenschappen, Letteren en Schone Kunsten van België, Klasse de Letteren, jg. 26, nr. 45. Brussels: Paleius der Academiën, 1963.

Henry of Ghent. *Opera Omnia.* Edited by Raymond Macken et al. Leuven: University Press, 1979–.

———. *Quodlibeta magistri Henrici Goethals a Gandavo doctoris solemnis.* 4 vols. Paris: Badius, 1518; repr. Louvain: Bibiliothèque S.J., 1961.

———. *Quodlibetal Questions on Free Will.* Translated by Roland Teske. Milwaukee: Marquette University Press, 1993.

———. *Summae Quaestionum Ordinariarum.* 2 vols. Franciscan Institute Publications, 5. Paris: Badius. 1520; repr. St. Bonaventure, N.Y.: Franciscan Institute, 1953.

Hugh of St. Victor. *De sacramentis christianae fidei.* Edited by Jacques-Paul Migne. Patrologia Latina, 176.

James of Viterbo. *Disputatio prima de quolibet.* Edited by Eelcko Ypma. Cassiciacum, Supplementband, 1. Würzburg: Augustinus-Verlag, 1968.

———. *Disputatio secunda de quolibet.* Edited by Eelcko Ypma. Cassiciacum, Supplementband, 2. Würzburg: Augustinus-Verlag, 1969.

———. *Disputatio tertia de quolibet.* Edited by Eelcko Ypma. Cassiciacum, Supplementband, 3. Würzburg: Augustinus-Verlag, 1973.

———. *Disputatio quarta de quolibet.* Edited by Eelcko Ypma. Cassiciacum, Supplementband, 5. Würzburg: Augustinus-Verlag, 1975.

John Damascene. *De fide orthodoxa*: Versions of Burgundio and Cerbanus. Edited by Eligius M. Buytaert. Franciscan Institute Publications, 8. St. Bonaventure, N.Y.: Franciscan Institute, 1955.

John Duns Scotus. *Cuestiones Cuodlibetales.* Edited and translated by Felix Alluntis. Madrid: Biblioteca de Autores Cristianos, 1968.

———. *Duns Scotus: Philosophical Writings.* Edited and translated by Allan B. Wolter. Indianapolis: Hackett, 1987.

———. *Duns Scotus on the Will and Morality.* Edited and translated by Allan B. Wolter. Washington, D.C.: The Catholic University of America Press, 1986.

———. *God and Creatures: The Quodlibetal Questions.* Edited and translated by Felix Alluntis and Allan B. Wolter. Princeton, N.J.: Princeton University Press, 1975.

———. *Opera Omnia.* Edited by Luke Wadding. Lyons: Laurentius Durandus, 1639; repr. Hildesheim: Georg Olms, 1968.

————. *Opera Omnia*. Edited by Scotistic Commission. Vatican City: Typis Polyglottis Vaticanis, 1950–.

————. *Quaestiones super libros metaphysicorum Aristotelis*. In *Opera Philosophica,* vols. 3–4. St. Bonaventure, N.Y.: Franciscan Institute, 1997.

————. *Tractatus de primo principio*. Edited and translated by Allan B. Wolter. Chicago: Franciscan Herald Press, 1966.

John of Rupella. *Summa de anima*. Edited by Jacques Guy Bougerol. Textes Philosophiques de Moyen Age, 19. Paris: Vrin, 1995.

————. *Tractatus de diversione multiplici potentiarum animae*. Edited by Pierre Michaud-Quantin. Textes Philosophiques du Moyen Age, 11. Paris: Vrin, 1964.

Maximus the Confessor. *Opusculum I ad Marinum*. Edited by Jacques-Paul Migne. Patrologia Graeca, 91.

Peter Abelard. *Commentaria in epistolam Pauli ad romanos*. In *Opera Theologica,* vol. 1. Corpus Christianorum. Series Latina, Continuatio Mediaeualis, 11. Edited by Eligius Buytaert. Turnhout: Brepols, 1969.

————. *Sententie magistri Petri Abelard (Sententie Hermanni)*. Edited by Sandro Buzzetti. Florence: La Nuova Italia Editrice, 1983.

Peter Lombard. *Sententiae in IV libris distinctae*. Spicilegium Bonaventurianum, 4–5. Rome: Collegium S. Bonaventurae, 1971, 1981.

Philip the Chancellor. *Summa de bono*. 2 vols. Edited by Nikolaus Wicki. Corpus philosophorum Medii Aevi Opera philosophica Mediae Aetatis selecta, 2. Bern: Francke, 1985.

Richard Kilwardby. *Quaestiones in librum secundum sententiarum*. Edited by Gerhard Leibold. Bayerische Akademie der Wissenschaften, Veröffentlichungen der Kommission für die Herausgabe ungedruckter Texte aus der mittelalterlichen Geisteswelt, 16. Munich: Bayerische Akademie der Wissenschaften, 1992.

Richard of St. Victor. *Les quatres degrés de la violente charité*. Edited by Gervais Dumeige. Textes Philosophiques du Mòyen Age, 3. Paris: Vrin, 1955.

Seneca. *Ad Lucilium epistolae morales*. Loeb Classical Library. Cambridge, Mass.: Harvard University Press, 1934.

Siger of Brabant. *Siger de Brabant, Écrits de logique, de morale, et de physique*. Edited by Bernardo Bazán. Philosophes Médiévaux, 14. Louvain: Publications Universitaires; Paris: Béatrice-Nauwelaerts, 1974.

Thomas Aquinas. *In librum beati Dionysii de divinis nominibus expositio*. Edited by Ceslaus Pera. Turin: Marietti, 1950.

————. *In metaphysicam Aristotelis commentaria*. 2nd edition. Edited by M-R. Cathala and Raymond M. Spiazzi. Turin: Marietti, 1971.

————. *Opera Omnia*. 34 vols. Paris: Vivès, 1871–1872.

————. *Opera Omnia*. 25 vols. Parma: Petrus Fiaccadori, 1852–73; repr. New York: Misurgia, 1948–1950.

————. *Opera Omnia*. Rome: Commissio Leonina, 1884–.

————. *Scriptum super libros sententiarum*. Edited by Pierre Mandonnet and M. F. Moos. 4 vols. Paris: Lethielleux, 1929–1947.

———. *De spiritualibus creaturis.* Edited by Leo W. Keeler. Pontifica Universitas Gregoriana, Textus et Documenta, Series Philosophica, 13. Rome: Gregorian University, 1946.

———. *Summa Theologiae.* 3 vols. Turin: Marietti, 1952–63.

———. *Super Epistolas S. Pauli Lectura.* 2 vols. Edited by Raphael Cai. 8th ed. Turin: Marietti, 1953.

William of Auvergne. *Opera omnia.* 2 vols. Paris: Pralard, 1674; repr. Frankfurt am Main: Minerva, 1963.

William of Auxerre. *Summa aurea.* 5 vols. Edited by Jean Ribaillier. Spicilegium Bonaventurianum, 16–20. Paris: Éditions du Centre National de la Recherche Scientifique; Rome: Collegium Bonaventurae, 1980–.

William of Ockham. *Guillelmi de Ockham opera philosophica et theologica.* Edited by Gedeon Gál et al. St. Bonaventure, N.Y.: Franciscan Institute. *Opera philosophica,* 7 vols. (1974–1986). *Opera theologica,* 10 vols. (1967–1986).

Secondary Works

Adams, Marilyn McCord. "Duns Scotus on the Will as Rational Power." In *Via Scoti: Methodologica ad mentem Joannis Duns Scoti. Atti del Congresso Scotistico Internazionale Roma 9–11 Marzo 1993,* edited by Leonardo Sileo, 839–854. Studia scholastico-Scotistica, 5. Rome: Edizioni Antonianum, 1995.

———. "Scotus and Ockham on the Connection of the Virtues." In *John Duns Scotus: Metaphysics and Ethics,* edited by Mechtild Dreyer, Ludger Honnenfelder, and Rega Wood, 499–522. Studien und Texte zur Geistesgeschichte des Mittelalters, 53. Leiden: Brill, 1996.

Aertsen, Jan A. "'Eros' und 'Agape,' Dionysius Areopagita und Thomas von Aquin über die Doppelgestalt der Liebe." In *Die Dionysius Rezeption im Mittelalter: Internationales Kolloquium in Sofia vom 8. bis 11. April 1999 unter der Schirmherrschaft der Société Internationale pour l'Étude de la Philosophie Médiévale,* edited by Tzotcho Boaiadjiev, Georgi Kapriev, and Andreas Speer, 372–391. Recontres de Philosophie Médiévale, 9. Turnhout: Brepols, 2000.

Alszeghy, Z. *Grundformen der Liebe: Die Theorie der Gottesliebe bei dem Hl. Bonaventura.* Analecta Gregoriana, 38. Rome: Gregorian University, 1946.

———. "La teologia dell'ordine soprannaturale nella scolastica antica." *Gregorianum* 31 (1950): 414–450.

Amann, É. "Occam." *Dictionnaire de théologie catholique.* Vol. 11a, cols. 864–904. Paris: Letouzey et Ané, 1931.

Annas, Julia. *The Morality of Happiness.* Oxford: Oxford University Press, 1993.

Arway, Robert J. "A Half Century of Research on Godfrey of Fontaines." *New Scholasticism* 36 (1962): 192–218.

Asidieu, F. B. A. "The Wise Man and the Limits of Virtue in the *De beata vita*: Stoic Self-Sufficiency or Augustinian Irony?" *Augustiniana* 49 (1999): 215–234.

Baker, Richard Russell. *The Thomistic Theory of the Passions and Their Influence upon the Will.* Notre Dame, Ind.: University of Notre Dame Press, 1941.

Balić, Charles. *Les commentaires de Jean Duns Scot sur les quatres livres des Sentences.* Louvain: Bureaux de la Revue d'histoire ecclesiastique, 1927.

Baron, Roger. *Science et Sagesse chez Hugues de Saint-Victor.* Paris: Lethielleux, 1957.

Bérubé, Camille. "Amour de Dieu chez Duns Scot, Porete, Eckhart." In *Via Scoti: Methodologica ad mentem Joannis Duns Scoti. Atti del Congresso Scotistico Internazionale Roma 9–11 Marzo 1993,* edited by Leonardo Sileo, 51–75. Studia scholastico-Scotistica, 5. Rome: Edizioni Antonianum, 1995.

———. *De l'homme à Dieu selon Duns Scot, Henri de Gand et Olivi.* Bibliotheca Seraphico-Capuccina, 27. Rome: Istituto Storico Dei Cappuccini, 1983.

Blanchette, Oliva. *The Perfection of the Universe according to St. Thomas Aquinas: A Teleological Cosmology.* University Park: Pennsylvania State University Press, 1992.

Boler, John. "An Image for the Unity of the Will in John Duns Scotus." *Journal of the History of Philosophy* 32 (1994): 23–44.

———. "The Moral Psychology of Duns Scotus: Some Preliminary Questions." *Franciscan Studies* 28 (1990): 31–56.

———. "Transcending the Natural: Duns Scotus on the Two Affections of the Will." *American Catholic Philosophical Quarterly* 67 (1993): 109–126.

Bonansea, Bernadine M. "Duns Scotus' Voluntarism." In *John Duns Scotus, 1265–1965,* edited by Bernardine M. Bonansea and John K. Ryan, 83–121. Studies in Philosophy and the History of Philosophy, 3. Washington, D.C.: The Catholic University of America Press, 1965.

Bonke, E. "Doctrina nominalistica de fundamento ordinis moralis apud Gulielmum de Ockham et Gabrielem Biel." *Collectanea franciscana* 14 (1944): 57–83.

Bostock, David. *Aristotle's Ethics.* Oxford: Oxford University Press, 2000.

Bouillard, Henri. *Conversion et grâce chez S. Thomas d'Aquin.* Études publiées sous la direction de la Faculté de Théologie S.J. de Lyon-Fourvière, 1. Aubier: Montaigne, 1944.

Bourke, Vernon J. *Ethics: A Textbook in Moral Philosophy.* New York: Macmillan, 1966.

———. "Human Tendencies, Will, and Freedom." In *L'homme et son destin d' après les penseurs du moyen âge, Actes du premier congrès international de philosophie médiéval Louvain-Bruxelles, 28 Août–4 Septembre 1958,* 71–84. Louvain: Éditions Nauwelaerts; Paris: Béatrice-Nauwelaerts, 1960.

———. *Will in Western Thought: A Historico-Critical Survey.* New York: Sheed and Ward, 1964.

Bradley, Denis J. M. *Aquinas on the Twofold Human Good: Reason and Human Happiness in Aquinas's Moral Science.* Washington, D.C.: The Catholic University of America Press, 1997.

Brink, David O. "Self-Love and Altruism." In *Self-Interest,* 123–157. Cambridge: Cambridge University Press, 1997.

Brock, Stephen L. *Action and Conduct: Thomas Aquinas and the Theory of Action.* Edinburgh: T & T Clark, 1998.

Brown, Stephen. "Sources for Ockham's Prologue to the Sentences—Part II." *Franciscan Studies* 5 (1967): 39–107.

Bujo, Bénézet. *Die Begründung des Sittlichen: Zur Frage des Eudämonismus bei Thomas von
Aquin.* Paderborn: Schöningh, 1984.

Bullet, Gabriel. *Vertus morales infuses et vertus morales acquises selon saint Thomas d'Aquin.*
Studia Friburgensia, 23. Fribourg: Éditions Universitaires, 1958.

Burnaby, John. *Amor Dei: A Study of the Religion of St. Augustine.* London: Hodder and
Stoughton, 1938.

———. "Amor in St. Augustine." In *The Philosophy and Theology of Anders Nygren,* edited
by Charles W. Kegley, 174–186. Carbondale: Southern Illinois University Press,
1970.

Caffarena, José Gómez. *Ser participado y ser subsistente en la metafísica de Enrique de Gante.*
Analecta Gregoriana, 93. Rome: Gregorian University, 1958.

Canning, Raymond. *The Unity of Love for God and Neighbour in St. Augustine.* Leuven:
Augustinian Historical Institute, 1993.

Celano, Anthony J. "The Concept of Worldly Beatitude in the Writings of Thomas
Aquinas." *Journal of the History of Philosophy* 25 (1987): 215–226.

Châtillon, Jean. "L'Influence de S. Bernard sur la pensée scolastique au XIIᵉ et au
XIIIᵉ siècle." In *Saint Bernard Théologien: Actes du Congrés de Dijon, 15–19 Septembre
1953. Analecta Sacri Ordinis Cisterciensis* 9 (1953): 268–288.

Choquette, Imelda. "Voluntas, Affectio and Potestas in the Liber De Voluntate of St.
Anselm." *Mediaeval Studies* 4 (1942): 61–81.

Clark, David W. "Voluntarism and Rationalism in the Ethics of Ockham." *Franciscan
Studies* 31 (1971): 73–87.

———. "William of Ockham on Right Reason." *Speculum* 48 (1973): 13–36.

Coerver, Robert Florent. *The Quality of Facility in the Moral Virtues.* Washington, D.C.:
The Catholic University of America Press, 1946.

Colish, Marcia L. *Peter Lombard.* 2 vols. Brill's Studies in Intellectual History, 41.
Leiden: E. J. Brill, 1994.

Copleston, Frederick. *A History of Philosophy.* Vol. 2, *Medieval Philosophy: From Augustine
to Duns Scotus.* New York: Doubleday, 1962.

———. *A History of Philosophy.* Vol. 3, *Late Medieval and Renaissance Philosophy: Ockham,
Bacon, and the Beginning of the Modern World.* New York: Doubleday, 1963.

Cottingham, John. "The Ethical Credentials of Partiality." *Proceedings of the Aristotelian
Society* (1998): 1–21.

———. "The Ethics of Self-Concern." *Ethics* 101 (1991): 798–817.

———. "Partiality and the Virtues," in *How Should One Live?: Essays on the Virtues,* edited by Roger Crisp, 57–76. Oxford: Clarendon Press, 1996.

Cross, Richard. *John Duns Scotus.* New York: Oxford University Press, 1999.

Crowe, Michael Bertram. "St. Thomas and Ulpian's Natural Law." In *St. Thomas Aquinas, 1274–1974: Commemorative Studies,* vol. 1, edited by Armand Maurer et al.,
261–282. Toronto: Pontifical Institute of Mediaeval Studies, 1974.

Delfgaauw, Pacifique. "La nature et les degrés de l'amour selon S. Bernard." In *Saint Bernard Théologien: Actes du Congrés de Dijon, 15–19 septembre 1953. Analecta Sacri Ordinis Cisterciensis* 9 (1953): 234–252.

Delhaye, Phillippe. "Quelques aspects de la morale de saint Anselme." *Spicilegium Beccense,* vol. 1, 401–422. Le Bec-Hellouin: Abbaye Notre-Dame du Bec; Paris: Vrin, 1959.

Dewan, Lawrence. "St. Thomas, John Finnis and the Political Good." *The Thomist* 64 (2000): 227–374.

Diggs, Bernard James. *Love and Being: An Investigation into the Metaphysics of Thomas Aquinas.* New York: Vanni, 1947.

Dod, Bernard G. "Aristoteles Latinus." In *The Cambridge History of Later Medieval Philosophy: From the Rediscovery of Aristotle to the Disintegration of Scholasticism: 1100–1600,* edited by Norman Kretzmann, Anthony Kenny, and Jan Pinborg, 45–79. Cambridge: Cambridge University Press, 1982.

Donati, Silvia. "Studi per una cronologia delle opere di Egidio Romano I: Le opere prima del 1285. Il commenti aristotelici; parte II." *Documenti e Studi sulla Tradizione Filosofica Medievale* 2, no. 1 (1991): 1–111.

Doucet, Victor. "The History of the Problem of the Authenticity of the Summa." *Franciscan Studies* 7 (1947): 26–41; 274–312.

Dumeige, Gervais. *Richard de Saint-Victor et l'idée chrétienne de l'amour.* Paris: Presses Universitaires de France, 1952.

Dumont, Stephen. "The Necessary Connection of Moral Virtue to Prudence according to John Duns Scotus—Revisited." *Recherches de théologie ancienne et médiévale* 55 (1988): 184–206.

———. "The quaestio si est and the Metaphysical Proof for the Existence of God according to Henry of Ghent and John Duns Scotus." *Franziskanische Studien* 66 (1984): 335–367.

Edwards, M. J. "Porphyry and the Intelligible Triad." *Journal of Hellenic Studies* 110 (1990): 14–25.

Effler, Roy R. *John Duns Scotus and the Principle "Omne quod movetur ab alio movetur."* Franciscan Institute Publications, Philosophy Series, 14. St. Bonaventure, N.Y.: Franciscan Institute, 1962.

Egenter, Richard. *Gottesfreundschaft: Die Lehre von der Gottesfreundschaft in der Scholastik und Mystik des 12. und 13. Jahrhunderts.* Augsburg: Filser, 1928.

Elders, Léon. *Autour de saint Thomas d'Aquin: recueil d'études sur sa pensée philosophique et théologique,* 2 vols. Paris: FAC-éditions; Bruges: Uitgeverij Tabor, 1987.

Eschmann, I. Th. "A Thomistic Glossary on the Principle of the Preeminence of a Common Good." *Mediaeval Studies* 5 (1943): 123–165.

———. "In Defense of Jacques Maritain." *The Modern Schoolman* 22 (1945): 183–208.

Evans, G. R. *The Mind of St. Bernard of Clairvaux.* Oxford: Clarendon Press, 1983.

Fabro, Cornelio. *Participation et causalité selon S. Thomas d'Aquin.* Louvain: Publications Universitaires de Louvain; Paris: Éditions Béatrice-Nauwelaerts, 1961.

Fairweather, Eugene R. "Truth, Justice, and Moral Responsibility in the Thought of St. Anselm." In *L'homme et son destin d' après les penseurs du moyen âge, Actes du premier congrès international de philosophie médiéval Louvain-Bruxelles, 28 Août–4 Septembre 1958,* 385–391. Louvain: Éditions Nauwelaerts; Paris: Béatrice-Nauwelaerts, 1960.

Farges, Jacques, and Marcel Viller. "Charité." *Dictionnaire de spiritualité.* Vol. 2, cols. 523–569. Paris: Beauchesne, 1953.

Farthing, John. *Thomas Aquinas and Gabriel Biel: Interpretations of St. Thomas Aquinas in German Nominalism on the Eve of the Reformation.* Duke Monographs in Medieval and Renaisance Studies, 9. Durham, N.C.: Duke University Press, 1988.

Filthaut, Ephrem. *Rolan von Cremona O.P. und die Anfänge der Scholastik im Predigerorden: Ein Beitrag zur Geistesgeschichte der älteren Dominikaner.* Vechta: Albertus Magnus, 1936.

Finnis, John. *Aquinas: Moral, Political, and Legal Theory.* Oxford: Oxford University Press, 1998.

Flanagan, Owen. *The Science of the Mind,* 2nd ed. Cambridge, Mass.: MIT Press, 1984.

Flasch, Kurt. "Der philosophische Ansatz des Anselm von Canterbury in Monologion und sein Verhältnis zum Augustinischen Neuplatonismus." *Analecta Anselmiana* 2 (1970): 1–43.

Flannery, Kevin L. *Acts Amid Precepts: The Aristotelian Logical Structure of Thomas Aquinas's Moral Theory.* Washington, D.C.: The Catholic University of America Press, 2001.

Foot, Philippa. *Natural Goodness.* Oxford: Clarendon Press, 2001.

Fortin, Ernest L. " The New Rights Theory and Natural Law." *Review of Politics* 44 (1982): 590–612.

Frank, William A. "Duns Scotus on Autonomous Freedom and Divine Co-Causality." *Medieval Philosophy and Theology* 2 (1992): 142–164.

———. "Duns Scotus' Concept of Willing Freely: What Divine Freedom Beyond Choice Teaches Us." *Franciscan Studies* 20 (1982): 68–89.

Frede, Michael. "John of Damascus on Human Action, the Will, and Human Freedom." In *Byzantine Philosophy and its Ancient Sources,* edited by Katerina Ierodiakonou, 63–95. Oxford: Clarendon Press, 2002.

Freppert, Lucan. *The Basis of Morality according to William of Ockham.* Chicago: Franciscan Herald Press, 1988.

Froelich, Gregory. "The Equivocal Status of the *Bonum Commune.*" *The New Scholasticism* 63 (1989): 38–57.

Gagnebet, M-R. "L'amour naturel de Dieu chez Saint Thomas et ses contemporains." *Revue Thomiste* 48 (1948): 294–446; 49 (1949): 31–102.

Gallagher, David M. "Desire for Beatitude and Love of Friendship in Thomas Aquinas." *Mediaeval Studies* 58 (1996): 1–47.

———. "Person and Ethics in Thomas Aquinas." *Acta Philosophica* 4 (1995): 51–71.

———. "The Role of God in the Philosophical Ethics of Thomas Aquinas." In *Was ist Philosophie im Mitterlalter?,* edited by Jan A. Aertsen and Andreas Speer, 1024–1033. Miscellanea Mediaevalia, 26. Berlin: de Gruyter, 1998.

————. "Thomas Aquinas on the Will as Rational Appetite." *Journal of the History of Philosophy* 29 (1991): 559–584.

de Gandillac, Maurice. "Loi naturelle et fondements de l'ordre social selon les principes du bienheureux Duns Scot." In *De doctrina Ioannis Duns Scoti: Acta Congressus Scotistici Internationalis.* Vol. 3, 683–734. Studia scholastico-Scotistica, 3. Rome: Societas Internationalis Scotistica, 1968.

Garrigou-Lagrange, Reginald. "Le Problème de l'amour pur et la solution de Saint Thomas." *Angelicum* (1929): 83–124.

Gaudel, A. "Péché originel." *Dictionnaire de théologie catholique,* vol. 12.1, 491–492.

Gauthier, René Antonin. "Notes sur Siger de Brabant." *Revue de sciences philosophiques et théologiques.* Part 1, "Siger en 1265," 67 (1983): 201–232; Part 2, "Siger en 1272–1275, Aubry de Reims et la Scission des Normands," 68 (1984): 3–49.

————. "Trois commentaires 'Averroïstes' sur l'Éthique à Nicomaque." *Archives d'histoire doctrinale et littéraire du moyen âge* 22–23 (1947–1948): 187–346.

Geiger, Louis-B. *La participation dans la philosophie de S. Thomas d'Aquin.* Bibliothèque Thomiste, 23. Paris: Vrin, 1953.

————. *Le problème de l'amour chez Saint Thomas d'Aquin.* Conférence Albert le Grand, 1952. Montréal: Institut D'Études Médiévales; Paris; Vrin, 1952.

Gillon, L-B. "L'argument du tout et de la partie après saint Thomas d'Aquin." *Angelicum* 28 (1951): 205–223; 346–362.

————. "Aux origines de la 'Puissance Obédientielle.'" *Revue Thomiste* 47 (1947): 304–310.

————. "Genèse de la théorie Thomiste de l'amour." *Revue Thomiste* 46 (1946): 322–329.

————. "Primacia del apetito universal de Dios según Santo Tomás." *Ciencia Tomista* 63 (1942): 328–342.

————. "Le sacrifice pour la patrie et la primauté du bien commun." *Revue Thomiste* 49 (1949): 242–253.

Gilson, Étienne. *History of Christian Philosophy in the Middle Ages.* New York: Random House, 1955.

————. *Introduction a l'étude de Saint Augustin.* Études de Philosophie Médiévale, 11. Paris: Vrin, 1929.

————. *Jean Duns Scot.* Études de Philosophie Médiévale, 42. Paris: Vrin, 1952.

————. *The Spirit of Medieval Philosophy.* Gifford Lectures 1931–1932. Translated by A. H. C. Downes. Notre Dame, Ind.: University of Notre Dame Press, 1991.

————. *La Théologie mystique de Saint Bernard.* Études de Philosophie Médiévale, 20. Paris: Vrin, 1934.

Giocarnis, Kimon. "An Unpublished Late Thirteenth-Century Commentary on the Nicomachean Ethics of Aristotle." *Traditio* 15 (1959): 299–326.

Glorieux, Palemon. *La Faculté des arts et ses maîtres aux XIIIe siècle.* Études de Philosophie Médiévale, 59. Paris: Vrin, 1971.

————. "La littérature des correctoires." *Revue Thomiste* 33 (1928): 69–96.

————. *La littérature quodlibétique,* vol. 2. Bibliothèque Thomiste, 21. Paris: Vrin, 1935.

———. *Répertoire des maîtres en théologie de Paris au XIIIe siècle.* 2 vols. Études de Philosophie Médiévale, 17–18. Paris: Vrin, 1933–1934.

Goebel, Bernd. *Rectitudo, Wahrheit und Freiheit von Anselm von Canterbury: Eine philosophische Untersuchung seines Denkansatzes.* Beiträge zue Geschichte der Philosophie und Theologie des Mittelalters, nf. 56. Münster: Aschendorff, 2001.

Graf, Thomas Aquinas. *De subiecto psychico gratiae et virtutum secundum doctrinam scholasticorum usque ad medium saeculum XIV.* Rome: Herder, 1935.

Gründel, Johannes. *Die Lehre von den Umständen der menschlichen Handlung im Mittelalter.* Beiträge zur Geschichte der Philosophie und Theologie des Mittelalters, Bd. 39, Hft. 5. Münster: Aschendorff, 1963.

Guevin, Benedict. "Aquinas's Use of Ulpian and the Question of Physicalism Reexamined." *The Thomist* 63 (1999): 613–628.

Guimet, Fernand. "Conformité à la droite raison et possibilité surnaturelle de charité." In *De doctrina Ioannis Duns Scoti: Acta Congressus Scotistici Internationalis.* Vol. 3, 539–597. Studia scholastico-Scotistica, 1–4. Rome: Societas Internationalis Scotistica, 1968.

Gula, Richard M. *Reason Informed by Faith: Foundations of Catholic Morality.* New York: Paulist Press, 1989.

Guldentops, Guy. "Les amours d'Albert le Grand." In *Les Passions dans la philosophie médiévale,* edited by G. Jeanmart, forthcoming.

———. "Henry of Bate's Aristocratic Eudaimonism." In *Nach der Verurteilung von 1277,* edited by Jan A. Aertsen, 657–681. Miscellanea Mediaevalia, vol. 28. Berlin: de Gruyter, 2001.

Gutiérrez, David. *De B. Iacobi Viterbiensis O.E.S.A.: Vita, operibus et doctrina theologica.* Rome: Analecta Augustiniana, 1939.

Gustafson, Gustaf J.. *The Theory of Natural Appetency in the Philosophy of St. Thomas.* The Catholic University of America Philosophical Series, 84. Washington, D.C.: The Catholic University of America Press, 1944.

Haydn, R. Mary. "The Paradox of Aquinas's Altruism: From Self-Love to the Love of Others." *Proceedings of the American Catholic Philosophical Association* 63 (1989): 72–83.

Hedwig, Klaus. "Alter Ipse: Über die Rezeption eines Aristotelischen Begriffes bei Thomas von Aquin." *Archiv für Geschichte der Philosophie* 72 (1990): 253–274.

———. "Das Isaak-Opfer: Über den Status des Naturgesetzes bei Thomas von Aquin, Duns Scotus und Ockham." In *Mensch und Natur im Mittelalter,* vol. 2, edited by Andreas Speer and Albert Zimmerman, 645–661. Miscellanea Mediaevalia, 21.2. Berlin: de Gruyter, 1992.

Hissette, Roland. "La date de quelques commentaires à l'Ethique." *Bulletin de philosophie médiévale* 18 (1976): 79–83.

Hittinger, Russell. *A Critique of the New Natural Law Theory.* Notre Dame, Ind.: University of Notre Dame Press, 1987.

Hoeres, Walter. "Naturtendenz und Freiheit nach Duns Scotus." *Salzburger Jahrbuch für Philosophie und Psychologie* 2 (1958): 95–134.

———. *La volontà come perfezione pura in Duns Scoto.* Translated by Alfredo Bizotto and Antonino Poppi. Padua: Liviana, 1976.

———. *Der Wille als Reine Vollkommenheit nach Duns Scotus.* Salzburger Studien zur Philosophie, 1. Munich: Pustet, 1962.

Hoffman, Tobias. "The Distinction between Nature and Will in Duns Scotus." *Archives d'histoire doctrinale et littéraire du moyen âge* 66 (1999): 189–224.

Hoffmans, Jeans. "Le table de divergences et innovations doctrinales de Godefroid de Fontaines," *Revue néoscolastique de philosophie* 36 (1934): 412–436.

Honnefelder, Ludger. "Naturrecht und Normwandel bei Thomas von Aquin und Johannes Duns Scotus." In *Sozialer Wandel im Mettelalter: Wahrnehmungsformen, Erklärungsmuster, Regelungsmechanismen,* edited by Jürgen Miethke and Klaus Schreiner, 197–211. Sigmaringen: Thorbecke, 1994.

Hopkins, Jasper. *A Companion to the Study of St. Anselm.* Minneapolis: University of Minnesota Press, 1972.

Ilien, Albert. *Wesen und Funktion der Liebe bei Thomas von Aquin.* Freiburger theologische Studien, 98. Freiburg: Herder, 1975.

Incandela, Joseph M. "Duns Scotus and the Experience of Human Freedom." *The Thomist* 56 (1992): 148–180.

Ingham, Mary Elizabeth. "Duns Scotus, Morality, and Happiness: A Reply to Thomas Williams." *American Catholic Philosophical Quarterly* 74 (2000): 173–195.

———. *"Ea Quae Sunt ad Finem:* Reflections on Virtue as Means to Moral Excellence in Scotist Thought." *Franciscan Studies* 28 (1990): 177–195.

———. *Ethics and Freedom. An Historical-Critical Investigation of Scotist Ethical Thought.* Lanham, Md.: University of America Press, 1989.

———. *The Harmony of Goodness: Mutuality and Moral Living according to John Duns Scotus.* Quincy, Ill.: Franciscan Press, 1996.

———. "Practical Wisdom: Scotus's Presentation of Prudence." In *John Duns Scotus: Metaphysics and Ethics,* edited by Mechtild Dreyer, Ludger Honnefelder, and Regina Wood, 551–571. Studien und Texte zur Geistesgeschichte des Mittelalters, 53. Leiden: Brill, 1996.

———. "Scotus and the Moral Order." *American Catholic Philosophical Quarterly* 67 (1993): 127–150.

Irwin, Terence H. "Aristotle's Conception of Morality." In *Proceedings of the Boston Area Colloquium in Ancient Philosophy,* vol. 1, edited by John J. Cleary, 115–143. Lanham, Md.: University Press of America, 1985.

———. *Aristotle's First Principles.* Oxford: Clarendon Press, 1988.

Johanneson, Rudolf. "Caritas in Augustine and Medieval Theology." In *The Philosophy and Theology of Anders Nygren,* edited by Charles W. Kegley, 187–202. Carbondale: Southern Illinois University Press, 1970.

Jones, L. Gregory. "The Theological Transformation of Aristotelian Friendship in the Thought of St. Thomas Aquinas." *New Scholasticism* 61 (1987): 373–99.

Kaepelli, Thomas, and Emilio Panella. *Scriptores Ordinis Praedicatorum Medii Aevi.* 4 vols. Rome: Istituto Storico Domenicano, 1975–1993.

Kane, G. Stanley. *Anselm's Doctrine of Freedom and the Will.* Texts and Studies in Religion, vol. 10. New York: Mellen Press, 1981.

Kantorowicz, Ernst H. *"Pro Patria Mori* in Medieval Political Thought." *American Historical Review* 56 (1951): 472–492.

Keaty, Anthony W. "Thomas's Authority for Identifying Charity as Friendship: Aristotle or John 15?" *The Thomist* 62 (1998): 581–601.

Kempshall, M. S. *The Common Good in Late Medieval Political Thought.* Oxford: Clarendon Press, 1999.

Kenny, Anthony. *Aquinas on Mind.* London: Routledge, 1993.

Kent, Bonnie. "The Good Will according to Gerald Odonis, Duns Scotus, and William of Ockham." *Franciscan Studies* 46 (1986): 119–39.

———. "Justice, Passion and Another's Good: Aristotle among the Theologians." In *Nach der Verurteilung von 1277,* edited by Jan A. Aertsen, 704–718. Miscellanea Mediaevalia, vol. 28. Berlin: de Gruyter, 2001.

———. *Virtues of the Will: The Transformation of Ethics in the Late Thirteenth Century.* Washington, D.C.: The Catholic University of America Press, 1995.

Kerr, Fergus. "Charity as Friendship." In *Language, Meaning and God: Essays in Honor of Herbert McCabe OP.* Edited by Brian Davies. London: Geoffrey Chapman, 1987.

Knasas, John F. X. *Being and Some Twentieth-Century Thomists.* New York: Fordham University Press, 2003.

de Koninck, Charles. *De la primauté du bien commun contre les personalistes.* Québec: Éditions de l'Université Laval; Montréal: Éditions Fides, 1943.

———. "In Defence of Saint Thomas: A Reply to Father Eschmann's Attack on the Primacy of the Common Good." *Laval théologique et philosophique* 1.2 (1945): 9–109.

Korolec, J. B. "Free Will and Free Choice." In *The Cambridge History of Later Medieval Philosophy: From the Rediscovery of Aristotle to the Disintegration of Scholasticism: 1100–1600,* edited by Norman Kretzmann, Anthony Kenny, and Jan Pinborg, 629–641. Cambridge: Cambridge University Press, 1982.

Kraut, Richard. *Aristotle on the Human Good.* Princeton, N.J.: Princeton University Press, 1989.

———. "Egoism and Altruism." In *The Routledge Encyclopedia of Philosophy,* edited by Edward Craig, vol. 2, 246–248. New York: Routledge, 1998.

Laarman, Matthias. "God as *Primum Cognitum.* Some Remarks on the Theory of Initial Knowledge of *Esse* and God according to Thomas Aquinas and Henry of Ghent." In *Henry of Ghent: Proceedings of the International Colloquium on the Occasion of the 700th Anniversary of His Death (1293),* edited by W. Vanhamel, 171–191. Ancient and Medieval Philosophy, Series 1, 15. Leuven: Leuven University Press, 1996.

de Lagarde, Georges. *La naissance de l'esprit laïque au déclin du moyen âge.* 3rd ed. 5 vols. Louvain: Nauwelaerts, 1956–1970.

———. "La philosophie sociale d'Henri de Gand et Godefroid de Fontaines." *Archives d'histoire doctrinale et littéraire du moyen âge* 14 (1945): 73–152.

Landgraf, Artur Michael. "Charité." *Dictionnaire de spiritualité*. Vol. 2, cols. 572–579. Paris: Beauchesne, 1953.

———. *Dogmengeschichte der Frühscholastik*. 4 vols. Regensburg: Friedrich Pustet, 1952.

———. "Studien zur Erkenntis des Übernatürlichen in der Frühscholastik." *Scholastik* 4 (1929): 1–37; 189–220; 352–389.

Langston, Douglas. *Conscience and Other Virtues: From Bonaventure to MacIntyre*. University Park: Pennsylvania State University Press, 2001.

———. "Did Scotus Embrace Anselm's Notion of Freedom?" *Medieval Philosophy and Theology* 5 (1996): 145–159.

Laporta, Jorge. *La destinée de la nature humaine selon Thomas d'Aquin*. Études de la Philosophie Médiévale, 55. Paris: Vrin, 1965.

Lee, Sukjae. "Scotus on the Will: The Rational Power and the Dual Affections." *Vivarium* 36 (1998): 40–54.

Lohr, C. H. "The Medieval Interpretation of Aristotle." In *The Cambridge History of Later Medieval Philosophy: From the Rediscovery of Aristotle to the Disintegration of Scholasticism: 1100–1600,* edited by Norman Kretzmann, Anthony Kenny, and Jan Pinborg, 80–98. Cambridge: Cambridge University Press, 1982.

Lonergan, Bernard J. F. *Grace and Freedom: Operative Grace in the Thought of St. Thomas Aquinas*. Edited by J. Patout Burns. London: Darton, Longman, and Todd; New York: Herder and Herder, 1971.

Long, Steven A. "On the Possibility of a Purely Natural End for Man." *The Thomist* 64 (2000): 211–237.

———. "St. Thomas Aquinas through The Analytic Looking-Glass." *The Thomist* 65 (2001): 291–299.

Lottin, Odon. "La connexion des vertus morales acquises au dernier quart du XIIIᵉ siècle." *Recherches de théologie ancienne et médiévale* 15 (1948): 107–151.

———. *"L'Ordinatio* de Jean Duns Scot sur le livre III des Sentences." *Recherches de théologie ancienne et médiévale* 20 (1953): 102–119.

———. "Problèmes concernant la 'Summa de creaturis' et le Commentaire des Sentences de saint Albert le Grand." *Recherches de théologie ancienne et médiévale* 17 (1950): 319–328.

———. *Psychologie et morale au XIIᵉ and XIIIᵉ siècles*. 2nd ed. 6 vols. Louvain: Abbaye du Mont César; Gembloux: Duculot, 1942–1960.

———. "Les vertus morales acquises sont-elles de vraies vertus? La réponse des théologiens de Pierre Abélard à saint Thomas d'Aquin." *Recherches de Théologie ancienne et médiévale* 20 (1953): 13–39.

———. "Les vertus morales acquises sont elles de vraies vertus? La réponse de théologiens de saint Thomas à Pierre Auriol." *Recherches de Théologie ancienne et médiévale* 21 (1954): 100–129.

de Lubac, Henri. *The Mystery of the Supernatural*. Translated by Rosemary Sheed. New York: Herder and Herder, 1967.

———. *Surnaturel; études historiques*. Études publiées sous la direction de la Faculté de Théologie S.J. de Lyon-Fourvière, 8. Aubier: Éditions Montaigne, 1946.

Luscombe, D. E. *The School of Peter Abelard: The Influence of Abelard's Thought in the Early Scholastic Period.* Cambridge: Cambridge University Press, 1969.

MacDonald, Scott. "Egoistic Rationalism: Aquinas's Basis for Christian Morality." In *Christian Theism and the Problem of Philosophy,* edited by Michael D. Beaty, 327–354. Library of Religious Philosophy, 5. Notre Dame, Ind.: University of Notre Dame Press, 1990.

———. "Ultimate Ends in Practical Reasoning: Aquinas's Aristotelian Moral Psychology and Anscombe's Fallacy." *Philosophical Review* 100 (1991): 31–65.

MacIntyre, Alasdair. *After Virtue.* 2nd ed. Notre Dame, Ind.: University of Notre Dame Press, 1984.

———. *Dependent Rational Animals.* The Paul Carus Lectures, 20. Chicago: Open Court, 1999.

———. "Egoism and Altruism." In *The Encyclopedia of Philosophy,* edited by Paul Edwards, vol. 2, 462–466. New York: Macmillan, 1967.

———. "Politics, Philosophy, and the Common Good." In *The MacIntyre Reader,* edited by Kelvin Knight, 235–252. Notre Dame, Ind.: University of Notre Dame Press, 1998.

———. "The Relationship of Philosophy to Its Past." In *Philosophy in History: Essays on the Historiography of Philosophy,* edited by Richard Rorty, J. B. Schneewind, and Quentin Skinner, 31–48. Cambridge: Cambridge University Press, 1984.

———. *Three Rival Versions of Moral Inquiry: Enyclopaedia, Genealogy, and Tradition.* Notre Dame, Ind.: University of Notre Dame Press, 1990.

———. *Whose Justice? Which Rationality?* Notre Dame, Ind.: University of Notre Dame Press, 1988.

Macken, Raymond. "God as Natural Object of the Human Will, according to the Philosophy of Henry of Ghent." In *Essays on Henry of Ghent,* by Raymond Macken, vol. 2, 45–53. Leuven: Editions Medieval Philosophers of the Former Low Countries, 1995.

———. "God as 'primum cognitum' in the Philosophy of Henry of Ghent." *Franziskanische Studien* 66 (1984): 309–315.

———. "Heinrich von Gent im Gespräch mit seinen Zeitgenossen über die menschliche Freiheit." *Franziskanische Studien* 59 (1977): 125–182.

———. "Henry of Ghent as Defender of the Personal Rights of Man." *Franziskanische Studien* 73 (1991): 170–181.

———. "Human Friendship in the Thought of Henry of Ghent." *Franziskanische Studien* 70 (1988): 176–184.

———. "L'interpénétration de l'intelligence et de la volonté dans la philosophie de l'Henri de Gand." In *L'homme et son univers au moyen âge, Actes du Septième Congrès International de Philosophie Médiévale, 30 août–4 septembre, 1982,* edited by Christian Wenin, 808–814. Louvain-la-Neuve: Éditions de l'Institut Supérieur de la Philosophie, 1986.

———. "Lebensziel und Lebensglück in der Philosophie des Heinrich von Gent." *Franziskanische Studien* 61 (1979): 107–123.

———. "The Metaphysical Proof for the Existence of God in the Philosophy of Henry of Ghent." *Franziskanische Studien* 68 (1986): 247–260.

———. "The Moral Duty of a Man Who Does Not Hope for a Future Life, to Offer in a Case of Necessity His Life for His Country in the Philosophy of Henry of Ghent." In *Essays on Henry of Ghent,* by Raymond Macken, vol. 1, 85–101. Leuven: Editions Medieval Philosophers of the Former Low Countries, 1995.

———. "La volonté humaine, faculté plus elevée que l'intelligence selon Henri de Gand." *Recherches de théologie ancienne et médiévale* 42 (1975): 5–51.

Madigan, Arthur. "*Ethic. Nic.* 9.8: Beyond Egoism and Altruism?" In *Essays in Ancient Greek Philosophy IV: Aristotle's Ethics,* edited by John P. Anton and Anthony Preus, 73–94. Albany: SUNY Press, 1991.

Mahoney, Edward P. "Duns Scotus and Medieval Discussions of Metaphysical Hierarchy: The Background of Scotus's 'Essential Order' in Henry of Ghent, Godfrey of Fontaines, and James of Viterbo." In *Via Scoti: Methodologica ad mentem Joannis Duns Scoti. Atti del Congresso Scotistico Internazionale Roma 9–11 Marzo 1993,* edited by Leonardo Sileo, 359–374. Studia scholastico-Scotistica, 5. Rome: Edizioni Antonianum, 1995.

———. "James of Viterbo." In *The Routledge Encyclopedia of Philosophy,* edited by Edward Craig, vol. 5, 58–60. London: Routledge, 1998.

———. "Metaphysical Foundations of the Hierarchy of Being according to Some Late Medieval and Renaissance Philosophers." In *Philosophies of Existence: Ancient and Medieval,* edited by Parviz Morewedge, 165–257. New York: Fordham University Press, 1982.

Mandonnet, Pierre Felix. *Siger de Brabant et l'averroisme latine au XIIIe siècle.* 2nd ed. 2 vols. Les Philosophes Belges, 6–7. Louvain: Institut Supérieur de Philosophie de l'Université, 1908, 1911.

Mansini, G. "*Similitudo, Communicatio,* and the Friendship of Charity in Aquinas." *Thomistica, Recherches de théologie ancienne et médiévale,* Supplementa, 1, 1–26. Leuven: Peeters, 1995.

Marenbon, John. *The Philosophy of Peter Abelard.* Cambridge: Cambridge University Press, 1997.

Maritain, Jacques. *The Person and the Common Good.* Translated by John J. Fitzgerald. Notre Dame, Ind.: University of Notre Dame Press, 1966.

Marrone, Steven P. "Henry of Ghent and Duns Scotus on the Knowledge of Being." *Speculum* 63 (1988): 22–57.

———. *Truth and Scientific Knowledge in the Thought of Henry of Ghent.* Speculum Anniversary Monographs, 11. Cambridge, Mass.: The Medieval Academy of America, 1985.

Maurer, Armand. *The Philosophy of William of Ockham in the Light of Its Principles.* Studies and Texts, 133. Toronto: Pontifical Institute of Mediaeval Studies, 1999.

McCluskey, Colleen. "Worthy Constraints in Albertus Magnus' Theory of Action." *Journal of the History of Philosophy* 39 (2001): 491–533.

McEvoy, James. "Amitié, attirance et amour chez S. Thomas d'Aquin." *Revue philosophique de Louvain* 91 (1993): 383–408.

———. *"Anima una et cor unum*: Friendship and Spiritual Unity in Augustine.*" Recherches de théologie ancienne et médiévale* 53 (1986): 40–92.

———. "The Sources and the Significance of Henry of Ghent's Disputed Question, 'Is Friendship a Virtue?'" In *Henry of Ghent: Proceedings of the International Colloquium on the Occasion of the 700th Anniversary of His Death (1293),* edited by W. Vanhamel, 121–138. Ancient and Medieval Philosophy, Series 1, 15. Leuven: Leuven University Press, 1996.

McGrade, Arthur Stephen, John Kilcullen, and Matthew Kempshall, eds. *The Cambridge Translations of Medieval Philosophical Texts, Vol. 2: Ethics and Political Philosophy.* Cambridge: Cambridge University Press, 2000.

McGrath, Alister E. *The Intellectual Origins of the European Reformation.* Oxford: Blackwell, 1987.

———. *Iustitia Dei: A History of the Christian Doctrine of Justification.* 2nd ed. Cambridge: Cambridge University Press, 1998.

McGuiness, Raymond Ruthford. *The Wisdom of Love.* Rome: Catholic Book Agency, 1951.

McInerny, Ralph. *Aquinas on Human Action: A Theory of Practice.* Washington, D.C.: The Catholic University of America Press, 1992.

McKerlie, Dennis. "Aristotle and Egoism." *Southern Journal of Philosophy* 36 (1998): 531–555.

Meersseman, G. G. "Pourqui le Lombard n'a-t-il conçu la charité comme amitié?" In *Miscellanea Lombardiana,* 165–174. Turin: Pontificio Ateneo Salesiano, 1957.

Minges, Parthenius. *Ioannes Duns Scoti: Doctrina Philosophica et Theologica,* 2 vols. Ad Claras Aquas: Collegium S. Bonaventurae, 1930.

Miron, Cyril Harry. *The Problem of Altruism in the Philosophy of St. Thomas.* The Catholic University of America Philosophical Studies, 41. Washington, D.C.: The Catholic University of America Press, 1939.

Modde, André. "Le Bien Commun dans la philosophie de saint Thomas." *Revue philosophique de Louvain* 47 (1949): 221–247.

Möhle, Hannes. *Ethik als scientia practica nach Johannes Duns Scotus: Eine philosophische Grundlegung.* Beiträge zur Geschichte der Philosophie des Mittelalters, n.f. 44. Münster: Aschendorff, 1995.

———. "Wille und Moral zur Voraussetzung der Ethik des Johannes Duns Scotus und ihre Bedeutung für die Ethik Immanuel Kants." In *John Duns Scotus: Metaphysics and Ethics,* edited by Mechtild Dreyer, Ludger Honnefelder, and Rega Wood, 573–594. Studien und Texte zur Geistesgeschichte des Mittelalters, 53. Leiden: Brill, 1996.

Nagel, Thomas. *The Possibility of Altruism.* Oxford: Clarendon Press, 1970.

Neumann, Bernhard. *Der Mensch und die himmlische Seligkeit nach der Lehre Gottfrieds von Fontaines.* Limburg: Lahn, 1958.

Newman, John Henry. *An Essay on the Development of Christian Doctrine.* 6th ed. Notre Dame, Ind.: University of Notre Dame Press, 1989.

Nicolas, Jean-Hervé. "Amour de soi, amour de Dieu, amour des autres." *Revue Thomiste* 56 (1956): 5–42.

———. "La permission du péché." *Revue Thomiste* 60 (1960): 5–37; 185–206; 509–546.

———. *Les profondeurs de la grace.* Paris: Beauchesne, 1969.

———. "L'univers ordonné par Dieu vers Dieu." *Revue Thomiste* 91 (1991): 357–376.

Nygren, Anders. *Agape and Eros.* Translated by Philip F. Watson. Philadelphia: Westminister Press, 1953.

O'Connor, William R. *The Eternal Quest.* New York: Longmans, Green, 1947.

O'Donovan, Oliver. *The Problem of Self-Love in St. Augustine.* New Haven: Yale University Press, 1980.

O'Mahoney, James E. *The Desire of God in the Philosophy of St. Thomas Aquinas.* Cork: Cork University Press; New York: Longmans, Green, 1929.

O'Rourke, Fran. *Pseudo-Dionysius and the Metaphysics of Aquinas.* Studien und Texte zur Geistesgeschichte des Mittelalters, 32. Leiden: Brill, 1992.

Osborne, Thomas M. "The Augustinianism of Thomas Aquinas's Moral Theory." *The Thomist* 67 (2003): 297–305.

———. "James of Viterbo's Rejection of Giles of Rome's Arguments for the Natural Love of God over Self." *Augustiniana* 49 (1999): 235–249.

———. "William of Ockham as a Divine Command Theorist." *Religious Studies* 41 (2005): 1–22.

Pagan-Aguiar, Peter A. "St. Thomas Aquinas and Human Finality: Paradox or *Mysterium Fidei?*" *The Thomist* 64 (2000): 374–399.

Paulus, Jean. "Henri de Gand et l'argument ontologique." *Archives d'histoire doctrinale et littéraire du Moyen Âge* 10–11 (1935–1936): 265–323.

———. *Henri de Gand: Essai sur les tendances de sa métaphysique.* Études de Philosophie Médiévale, 25. Paris: Vrin, 1938.

Peccorini, Francisco L. "Henry of Ghent and the Categorical Imperative: His Ethics' Ultimate Reality and Meaning." *Franziskanische Studien* 70 (1988): 196–213.

Pegis, Anton C. "Towards a New Way to God: Henry of Ghent." *Mediaeval Studies* 30 (1968): 226–247; 31 (1969): 93–116; 33 (1971): 158–179.

Pernoud, Mary Anne. "The Theory of the *Potentia Dei* according to Aquinas, Scotus, and Ockham." *Antonianum* 47 (1972): 69–95.

Pétré, Hélène. *Caritas: Étude sur le vocabulaire latin de la charité chrétienne.* Spicilegium Sacrum Lovaniense, 22. Louvain: Spicilegium Sacrum Lovaniense, 1948.

Philips, G. "La doctrine de la charité dans les commentaires des sentences de saint Albert, de saint Bonaventure, et de saint Thomas." *Ephemerides theologicae Lovanienses* 24 (1948): 59–97.

Pieper, Josef. *Faith, Hope, Love.* Translated by Mary Frances McCarthy and Richard and Clara Winston. 7th ed. San Francisco: Ignatius Press, 1997.

———. *The Four Cardinal Virtues.* Translated by Daniel F. Coogan, Lawrence E. Lynch, and Richard and Clara Winston. Notre Dame, Ind.: University of Notre Dame Press, 1966.

Pinckaers, Servais. *The Sources of Christian Ethics.* Translated by Mary Thomas Noble. Washington, D.C.: The Catholic University of America Press, 1995.

Pope, Stephen J. *The Evolution of Altruism and the Ordering of Love.* Washington, D.C.: Georgetown University Press, 1994.

Potts, Timothy C. "Conscience." In *The Cambridge History of Later Medieval Philosophy: From the Rediscovery of Aristotle to the Disintegration of Scholasticism: 1100–1600,* edited by Norman Kretzmann, Anthony Kenny, and Jan Pinborg, 687–704. Cambridge: Cambridge University Press, 1982.

Pouchet, Robert. *La rectitudo chez saint Anselm: Un itinéraire Augustinien de l'ame à Dieu.* Paris: Études Augustiniennes, 1964.

Prat, Ferdinand. "Charité." *Dictionnaire de spiritualité.* Vol. 2. Paris: Beauchesne, 1953. cols. 508–523.

Prentice, R. *The Basic Quidditative Metaphysics of Duns Scotus as Seen in His "De Primo Principio."* Spicilegium Pontificii Athenaei Antoniani, 16. Rome: Ed. Antonianum, 1970.

———. "The Contingent Element Governing the Natural Law on the Last Seven Precepts of the Decalogue, according to Duns Scotus." *Antonianum* 42 (1967): 259–292.

———. "The Degree and Mode of Liberty in the Beatitude of the Blessed." In *Deus et Homo ad mentem I. Duns Scoti. Acta tertii Congressus Scotistici internationalis Vindebonae 28 sept.–2 oct. 1970,* 327–342. Studia scholastico-Scotistica, 5. Rome: Societas internationalis Scotistica, 1972.

Prince, Betsey B. "Henry of Ghent and the Tensions of Economics." In *Henry of Ghent: Proceedings of the International Colloquium on the Occasion of the 700th Anniversary of His Death (1293),* edited by W. Vanhamel, 255–277. Ancient and Medieval Philosophy, Series 1, 15. Leuven: Leuven University Press, 1996.

del Punta, Francesco, Silvia Donati, and C. Luna. "Egidio Romano." *Dizionario biografico degli italiani,* vol. 42, 319–341. Rome: Istituto della Enciclopedia Italiana, 1993.

del Punta, Francesco, and Cecilia Trifolgi. "Giles of Rome." In *The Routledge Encyclopedia of Philosophy,* edited by Edward Craig, vol. 4, 72–78. London: Routledge, 1998.

Quell, Gottfried. "ἀγαπάω." *Theologisches Wörterbuch zum Neuen Testament,* vol. 1, edited by Gerhard Kittel, 20–34. Stuttgart: Kohlhammer, 1933. Translated by Geoffrey W. Bromiley, in *Theological Dictionary of the New Testament,* vol. 1, 20–34. Grand Rapids, Mich.: Eerdmans, 1974.

Quillet, Jeannine. "De la nature humaine à l'ordre politique selon Jean Duns Scot." In *Via Scoti: Methodologica ad mentem Joannis Duns Scoti. Atti del Congresso Scotistico Internazionale Roma. 9–11 Marzo 1993,* edited by Leonardo Sileo, vol. 2, 261–273. Studia scholastico-Scotistica, 5. Rome: Edizioni Antonianum, 1995.

Quinn, John F. "St. Bonaventure's Fundamental Conception of Natural Law." In *S. Bonaventura: 1274–1974,* edited by Jacques Guy Bougerol, vol. 3, 571–598. Grottaferrata: Collegio S. Bonaventura, 1973.

Ragland, C. P. "Scotus on the Decalogue: What Sort of Voluntarism?" *Vivarium* 36 (1998): 67–81.

Reilly, Geoffrey C. *The Psychology of Saint Albert the Great Compared with that of Saint Thomas.* Washington, D.C.: The Catholic University of America Press, 1934.

Renault, Laurence. "Félicité humaine et conception de la philosophie chez Henri de Gand, Duns Scot et Guillaume d'Ockham." In *Was ist Philosophie im Mitterlalter?,* edited by Jan A. Aertsen and Andreas Speer, 970–971. Miscellanea Mediaevalia, 26. Berlin: de Gruyter, 1998.

Ries, Joseph. *Das geistliche Leben in seinen Entwicklungsstufen nach der Lehre des Hl. Bernard.* Freiburg im Breisgau: Herder, 1906.

Rist, John M. *Augustine: Ancient Thought Baptized.* Cambridge: Cambridge University Press, 1994.

———. *Eros and Psyche: Studies in Plato, Plotinus, and Origen.* Phoenix Supplementary Volumes, 6. Toronto: University of Toronto Press, 1964.

———. "A Note on Eros and Agape in Pseudo-Dionysius." *Vigiliae Christianae* 20 (1996): 235–243.

———. *On Innoculating Moral Philosophy Against God.* Aquinas Lecture, 64. Milwaukee: Marquette University Press, 2000.

———. *Real Ethics: Reconsidering the Foundations of Morality.* Cambridge: Cambridge University Press, 2002.

———. "Some Interpretations of Agape and Eros." In *The Philosophy and Theology of Anders Nygren,* edited by Charles W. Kegley, 156–173. Carbondale: Southern Illinois University Press, 1970.

Rohmer, Jean. *La Finalité morale chez les théologiens de Saint Augustin à Duns Scot.* Paris: Vrin, 1939.

Rousselot, Pierre. *Pour l'histoire du problème de l'amour au moyen âge.* Beiträge zur Geschichte der Philosophie und Theologie des Mittelalters, Bd. 6, Hft. 6. Münster: Aschendorff, 1908.

Ruello, F. "Les fondements de la liberté humaine selon Jacques de Viterbe O.E.S.A. Disputatio Prima de Quolibet, q. VII (1293)." *Augustiniana* 24 (1974): 283–347; 25 (1975): 114–142.

Ryan, Christopher J. "Man's Free Will in the Works of Siger of Brabant." *Mediaeval Studies* 45 (1983): 155–199.

Saarinen, Risto. *Weakness of Will in Medieval Thought: From Augustine to Buridan.* Studien und Texte zur Geistesgeschichte des Mittelalters, 44. Leiden: Brill, 1994.

Schlabach, Gerald W. *For the Joy Set Before Us: Augustine and Self-Denying Love.* Notre Dame, Ind.: University of Notre Dame Press, 2002.

Schmidtz, David. "Self-Interest: What's In It for Me?" In *Self-Interest,* 107–121. Cambridge: Cambridge University Press, 1997.

Schmitt, Francis Sales. "Anselm und der (Neu-)Platonismus." *Analecta Anselmiana* 1 (1969): 39–71.

Schneewind, J. B. "The Divine Corporation and the History of Ethics." In *Philosophy in History: Essays on the Historiography of Philosophy,* edited by Richard Rorty, J. B. Schneewind, and Quentin Skinner, 173–191. Cambridge: Cambridge University Press, 1984.

Schollmeier, Paul. *Other Selves: Aristotle on Personal and Political Friendship.* Albany: SUNY Press, 1994.

Shannon, Thomas. *The Ethical Theory of John Duns Scotus.* Quincy, Ill.: Franciscan Press, 1995.

Sharp, D. E. *Franciscan Philosophy at Oxford in the Thirteenth Century.* British Society of Franciscan Studies, vol. 16. London: Oxford University Press, 1930; repr. Westmead: Gregg, 1966.

Sheets, John R. "Justice in the Moral Thought of St. Anselm." *The Modern Schoolman* 25 (1948): 132–139.

Sherwin, Michael. "'The Friend of the Bridegroom Stands and Listens': An Analysis of the Term *Amicus Sponsi* in Augustine's Account of Divine Friendship and the Ministry of Bishops." *Gregorianum* 38 (1998): 197–214.

Sherwin, Nancy. "Commentary on Irwin." In *Proceedings of the Boston Area Colloquium in Ancient Philosophy,* 1, edited by John J. Cleary, 144–150. Lanham, Md.: University Press of America, 1985.

Siedler, Dionys. *Intellektuelismus und Voluntarismus bei Albertus Magnus.* Beiträge zur Geschichte der Philosophie und Theologie des Mittelalters, Bd. 36, Hft. 2. Münster: Aschendorff, 1941.

Simon, Yves. *A Critique of Moral Knowledge.* Translated by Ralph McInerny. New York: Fordham University Press, 2002.

Simonin, H-D. "Autour de la solution Thomiste du problème de l'amour." *Archives d'histoire doctrinale et littéraire du moyen âge* 6 (1931): 174–274.

———. "La doctrine de l'amour naturel de Dieu d'après le Bienheureux Albert le Grand." *Revue Thomiste* 36 (1931): 361–370.

Smith, Michael. *The Moral Problem.* Oxford: Blackwell, 1994.

Sober, Eliot, and David Sloan Wilson. *Unto Others: The Evolution and Psychology of Unselfish Behavior.* Cambridge, Mass.: Harvard University Press, 1998.

Solmsen, Friedrich. *Aristotle's System of the Physical World: A Comparison with His Predecessors.* Cornell Studies in Classical Philology, 33. Ithaca, N.Y.: Cornell University Press, 1960.

Sondag, Gérard, "Aristote et Duns Scot: sur le problème du sacrifice de soi: pour quelles raisons le citoyen courageux expose-t-il sa vie quand la cité est en danger." *Philosophie* 61 (1999): 75–88.

Soto, Anthony. "The Structure of Society according to Duns Scotus." *Franciscan Studies* 11 (1951): 194–212; 12 (1952): 71–90.

Southern, R. W. *Saint Anselm: A Portrait in a Landscape.* Cambridge: Cambridge University Press, 1990.

Spruyt, Joke. "Duns Scotus's Criticism of Henry of Ghent's Notion of Free Will." In *John Duns Scotus: Renewal of Philosophy,* edited by E. P. Bos, 139–154. Acts of the Third Symposium Organized by the Dutch Society for Medieval Philosphy Medium Aevum, May 23 and 24, 1996. Elementa, Schriften zur Philosophie und ihrer Problemgeschichte, 72. Amsterdam: Rodopi, 1998.

Stadter, Ernst. *Psychologie und Metaphysik der menschlichen Freiheit: Die ideengeschichtliche Entwicklung zwischen Bonaventura und Duns Scotus.* Veröffentlichungen des Grabmann-Institutes zur Erforschung der Mittelalterlichen Theologie und Philosophie, 12. Munich: Schöningh, 1971.

Stählin, Gustav. "φιλέω." *Theologisches Wörterbuch zum Neuen Testament,* vol. 9, edited by Gerhard Friedrich, 113–169. Stuttgart: Kohlhammer, 1973. Translated by Geoffrey W. Bromiley, *Theological Dictionary of the New Testament,* vol. 9, 114–171. Grand Rapids, Mich.: Eerdmans, 1974.

Stauffer, Ethelbert. "ἀγαπάω." *Theologisches Wörterbuch zum Neuen Testament,* vol. 1, edited by Gerhard Kittel, 35–55. Stuttgart: Kohlhammer, 1933. Translated by Geoffrey W. Bromiley, *Theological Dictionary of the New Testament,* vol. 1, 35–55. Grand Rapids, Mich.: Eerdmans, 1974.

van Steenberghen, Ferdinand. *Maître Siger de Brabant.* Philosophes Médiévaux, 21. Louvain: Publications Universitaires; Paris: Vander-Oyez, 1977.

———. *La Philosophie au XIIIᵉ siècle.* 2nd ed. Louvain-La-Neuve: Éditions de l'Institut Supérieur de Philosophie; Louvain: Éditions Peeters, 1991.

———. *Siger de Brabant d'après ses oeuvres inédites.* Vol. 2, *Siger dans l'histoire de l'aristotelianisme.* Les Philosophes Belges, 13. Louvain: Éditions de l'Institut Supérieur de Philosophie, 1942.

Stevens, Gregory. "The Disinterested Love of God according to St. Thomas and Some of His Modern Interpreters." *The Thomist* 16 (1953): 307–333, 497–541.

Struve, Tilman. *Die Entwicklung der organologischen Staatsauffassung im Mittelalter.* Stuttgart: Hiersemann, 1978.

Suk, Othmar. "The Connection of Virtues according to Ockham." *Franciscan Studies* 10 (1950): 9–32; 91–113.

Teske, Roland J. "Henry of Ghent's Rejection of the Principle: '*Omne quo movetur ab alio movetur.*'" In *Henry of Ghent: Proceedings of the International Colloquium on the Occasion of the 700th Anniversary of His Death (1293),* edited by W. Vanhamel, 211–254. Ancient and Medieval Philosophy, Series 1, 15. Leuven: Leuven University Press, 1996.

Tierney, Brian. *The Idea of Natural Rights: Studies on Natural Rights, Natural Law, and Church Law.* Emory Studies in Law and Religion, 5. Atlanta: Scholars Press, 1997.

Tihon, Paul. *Foi et théologie selon Godefroid de Fontaines.* Museum Lessianum section théologique, 61. Paris: Desclée, 1966.

Torrell, Jean-Pierre. *Saint Thomas Aquinas.* Vol. 1, *The Person and His Work.* Translated by Robert Royal. Washington, D.C.: The Catholic University of America Press, 1996.

te Velde, Rude A. "*Natura in se ipsa recurva est*: Duns Scotus and Aquinas on the Relationship between Nature and Will." In *John Duns Scotus: Renewal of Philosophy,* edited by E. P. Bos, 155–169. Acts of the Third Symposium Organized by the Dutch Society for Medieval Philosophy Medium Aevum, May 23 and 24, 1996. Elementa, Schriften zur Philosophie und ihrer Problemgeschichte, 72. Amsterdam: Rodopi, 1998.

———. *Participation and Substantiality in Thomas Aquinas,* Studien und Texte zur Geistesgeschichte des Mittelalters, 46. Leiden: Brill, 1995.

Veuthey, Léon. *Jean Duns Scot: Pensée théologique.* Paris: Éditions Franciscaines, 1967.

Vignaux, Paul. *Justification et prédestination au XIVe siècle.* Bibliothèque de l'École des Hautes Études. Sciences religieuses, 48. Paris: Leroux, 1934.

———. "Nominalisme." *Dictionnaire de théologie catholique.* Vol. 11a, cols. 717–784. Paris: Letouzey et Ané, 1931.

Vollert, Cyril O. *The Doctrine of Hervaeus Natalis on Primitive Justice and Original Sin: As Developed in the Controversy on Original Sin during the Early Decades of the Fourteenth Century.* Analecta Gregoriana, 42. Rome: Gregorian University, 1947.

De Vooght, Paul. "La méthode théologique d'après Henri de Gand et Gérard de Bologne." *Recherches de Théologie ancienne et médiévale* 23 (1956): 61–87.

Wald, Berthold. "Die Bestimmung der *ratio legis* bei Thomas von Aquin und Duns Scotus." In *Mensch und Natur im Mittelalter,* vol. 2, edited by Andreas Speer and Albert Zimmerman, 662–681. Miscellanea Mediaevalia, 21.2. Berlin: de Gruyter, 1992.

Warnach, Victor. "Agape in the New Testament." In *The Philosophy and Theology of Anders Nygren,* edited by Charles W. Kegley, 143–155. Carbondale: Southern Illinois University Press, 1970.

Weaver, Darlene Fozard. *Self-Love and Christian Ethics.* Cambridge: Cambridge University Press, 2000.

Weingart, Richard E. *The Logic of Divine Love: A Critical Analysis of the Soteriology of Peter Abailard.* Oxford: Clarendon Press, 1970.

Weisheipl, James A. "The Life and Works of Albert the Great." In *Albertus Magnus and the Sciences: Commemorative Essays,* 13–51. Toronto: Pontifical Institute for Mediaeval Studies, 1980.

Wieland, Georg. "The Reception and Interpretation of Aristotle's *Ethics.*" In *The Cambridge History of Later Medieval Philosophy: From the Rediscovery of Aristotle to the Disintegration of Scholasticism: 1100–1600,* edited by Norman Kretzmann, Anthony Kenny, and Jan Pinborg, 657–672. Cambridge: Cambridge University Press, 1982.

———. "Happiness: The Perfection of Man." In *The Cambridge History of Later Medieval Philosophy: From the Rediscovery of Aristotle to the Disintegration of Scholasticism: 1100–1600,* edited by Norman Kretzmann, Antony Kenny, and Jean Pinborg, 673–686. Cambridge: Cambridge University Press, 1982.

Williams, Bernard. *Ethics and the Limits of Philosophy.* Cambridge, Mass.: Harvard University Press, 1985.

Williams, Norman Powell. *The Ideas of the Fall and of Original Sin: A Historical and Critical Study.* Being Eight Lectures Delivered before the University of Oxford in the Year 1924, on the Foundation of the Rev. John Bampton, Canon of Salisbury. London: Longmans, Green, 1938.

Williams, Thomas. "How Scotus Separates Morality from Happiness." *American Catholic Philosophical Quarterly* 69 (1995): 425–446.

———. "The Libertarian Foundations of Scotus's Moral Philosophy." *The Thomist* 62 (1998): 193–215.

————. "A Most Methodical Lover? On Scotus's Arbitrary Creator." *Journal of the History of Philosophy* 38 (2000): 169–202.

————. "Reason, Morality, and Voluntarism in Duns Scotus: A Pseudo-Problem Dissolved." *The Modern Schoolman* 74 (1997): 73–91.

————. "The Unmitigated Scotus." *Archiv für Geschichte der Philosophie* 80 (1998): 162–181.

Wilms, Hieronymus. *Albert the Great: Saint and Doctor of the Church.* Translated by A. English and P. Hereford. London: Burns, Oates & Washbourne, 1933.

Wippel, John F. Introduction to *Boethius of Dacia: On the Supreme Good, On the Eternity of the World, On Dreams.* Translated by John F. Wippel. Toronto: Pontifical Institute of Medieval Studies, 1987.

————. "The Dating of James of Viterbo's Quodlibet I and Godfrey of Fontaine's Quodlibet VIII." *Augustiniana* 24 (1974): 348–386.

————. *The Metaphysical Thought of Godfrey of Fontaines.* Washington, D.C.: The Catholic University of America Press, 1981.

————. *The Metaphysical Thought of Thomas Aquinas: From Finite Being to Uncreated Being.* Monographs of the Society for Medieval and Renaissance Philosophy, 1. Washington, D.C.: The Catholic University of America Press, 2000.

Wohlman, Avital. "Amour du bien propre et amour de soi dans la doctrine Thomiste de l'amour." *Revue Thomiste* 81 (1981): 204–234.

Wolter, Allan B. "Duns Scotus on the Will as Rational Potency." In idem, *Philosophical Theology of John Duns Scotus,* 163–180.

————. "Native Freedom of the Will as a Key to the Ethics of Scotus." In *Deus et Homo ad mentem I. Duns Scoti. Acta tertii Congressus Scotistici internationalis Vindebonae 28 sept.–2 oct. 1970,* 359–370. Studia scholastico-Scotistica, 5. Rome: Societas internationalis Scotistica, 1972; repr. in idem, *Philosophical Theology of John Duns Scotus,* 148–162.

————. *The Philosophical Theology of John Duns Scotus.* Edited by Marilyn McCord Adams. Ithaca, N.Y.: Cornell University Press, 1990.

————. "Reflections on the Life and Works of Scotus." *American Catholic Philosophical Quarterly* 57 (1993): 1–36.

————. *The Transcendentals and Their Function in the Metaphysics of Duns Scotus.* The Catholic University of America Philosophical Series, 96. Washington, D.C.: The Catholic University of America Press, 1946.

Ypma, Eelcko. *La formation des professeurs chez Les Ermites de Saint-Augustin de 1256 à 1353: Un nouvel ordre à ses débuts théologiques.* Paris: Centre d'Études des Augustins, 1956.

————. "Recherches sur la productivité littéraire de Jacques de Viterbe jusqu'à 1300." *Augustiniana* 25 (1975): 223–282.

Index

THOMAS M. OSBORNE, JR.,

*is an assistant professor at the Center for Thomistic Studies,
University of St. Thomas, Houston, Texas.*

Milton Keynes UK
Ingram Content Group UK Ltd.
UKHW011813280723
425933UK00014B/204

9 780268 037222